BLACK RODEO

A HISTORY OF THE
AFRICAN AMERICAN
WESTERN

MIA MASK

**UNIVERSITY OF
ILLINOIS PRESS**
Urbana, Chicago, and Springfield

Much of chapter 2 was previously published in
*Poitier Revisited: Reconsidering a Black Icon in the
Obama Age*, eds. Ian Gregory Strachan and Mia Mask
(New York: Bloomsbury Academic, 2015).

Library of Congress Cataloging-in-Publication Data
Names: Mask, Mia, author.
Title: Black rodeo : a history of the African American
    western / Mia Mask.
Description: Urbana : University of Illinois Press, [2023]
    | Includes bibliographical references, filmography, and
    index.
Identifiers: LCCN 2022030917 (print) | LCCN 2022030918
    (ebook) | ISBN 9780252044878 (cloth) | ISBN
    9780252086977 (paperback) | ISBN 9780252054020
    (ebook)
Subjects: LCSH: African Americans in motion pictures. |
    Western films—United States—History and criticism. |
    African American cowboys in motion pictures. | African
    Americans in the motion picture industry. | African
    American cowboys. | Race in motion pictures. | BISAC:
    PERFORMING ARTS / Film / Genres / Westerns | SOCIAL
    SCIENCE / Ethnic Studies / American / African American
    & Black Studies
Classification: LCC PN1995.9.B585 M37 2023 (print) |
    LCC PN1995.9.B585 (ebook) | DDC 791.43089/96073—
    dc23/20220811
LC record available at https://lccn.loc.gov/2022030917
LC ebook record available at https://lccn.loc.gov/2022030918

They rode with white Texans, Mexicans, and Indians. All the real cowboys—black, brown, red and white—shared the same jobs and dangers. They ate the same food and slept on the same ground; but when the long drives ended and the great plains were tamed and fenced, the trails ended too. The cattle were fenced in, the Negroes fenced out. Years later, when history became myth and legend, when the cowboys became folk heroes, the Negroes were again fenced out. They had ridden through the real West, but they found no place in the West of fiction. That was peopled by tall, lean, tanned—though lily-white under the shirt—heroes who rode through the purple sage made dangerous by dirty villains, red Indians and swarthy "greasers," only occasionally being helped by "good Indians" and "proud Spanish-Americans." Even the Chinese survived in fiction, if only as pigtailed caricatures who spoke a "no tickee, no washee" pidgin as they shuffled about the ranch houses. Although the stereotypes were sometimes grotesque, all but one of the races and nationalities of the real West appeared in fiction.

All but the Negro cowboy, who had vanished.

—Philip Durham and Everett L. Jones, *The Negro Cowboys*

Contents

Preface and Acknowledgments

I have loved horses since I was eight years old. Well, that's not entirely true. There were days when I was afraid of them given their size and unfamiliarity. But for the most part, I really adored them. I started horseback riding the summer my parents sent me to Camp Auxilium in Newton, New Jersey. The camp was a Roman Catholic sleep-away summer retreat for girls, managed and run by a cadre of strict, caring nuns and a few itinerant priests who would visit to officiate mass. The nuns who ran the camp back then took us for pony rides one Wednesday afternoon. And just like that, I was hooked.

When the summer ended and I returned home, I begged my parents to take me to riding lessons. I also obsessed endlessly over horses. The time I'd spent on horseback (or pony-back) had proven more transcendent than daily rosary recitations (particularly for a non-Catholic like me). I was fascinated by the way horses looked, how their coats felt, and the rhythms with which they moved at different gaits. Horses have a way of making you feel vibrantly alive and yet remarkably calm at any age. They give you a feeling of mastery and movement but with the mutually understood, yet unspoken, caveat that without them you're just a two-legged human.

I desperately wanted to continue riding. But growing up in Brooklyn meant there were few, if any, places to see horses, much less go riding. Miraculously, my mother and father scouted far and wide. Whether it was by searching in the yellow pages or hearing by word of mouth, they finally found a stable where I could take riding lessons. They had located Clove Lake Stables in Brighton on Staten Island, and I took my first lessons not far from the North Shore of Staten Island in the New Brighton neighborhood.

Clove Lake had changed hands over the years. Back in the late nineteenth century, from 1897 through the 1920s, the stables housed ice truck horses for the Richmond Ice Company, which had its headquarters on Clove Road. The company was incorporated in 1881 and was a shipper to points in the Carolinas, the Virginias, Georgia, and Tennessee. E. D. Haley, a resident of Maine, was the company's president and an ice dealer in New England and New York.[1]

By the early to mid-twentieth century, the property had become home to Clove Lake Stables, a riding academy that in the 1950s was owned by the Franzreb family. Founders John and Adele Franzreb passed the business to their grandsons Jeffrey and Jarad Franzreb.[2] When I started taking lessons, the outfit was a modest hunter-jumper barn still run by Franzreb family members. Sisters Merri and Grace offered English riding lessons, Western pleasure riding, hayrides, and horse shows, and occasionally fox hunted on weekends. Merri and Grace even took me to watch the National Horse Show at Madison Square Garden, which, for me, was more magical than a three-ring circus.

As impressionable as I was, and as formative as those days were, my father and I found the trek to Staten Island long and arduous. It was especially tiring for my dad because my lessons were available on his one weekday off from work, since he usually worked Saturdays and some Sundays. Staten Island was far from our Brooklyn residence. So we eventually looked for alternatives closer to home. But I never forgot Merri, Grace, Clove Lake Stables, or the horses we rode there. Merri had been a tough and exacting instructor who instilled discipline, confidence, and horsemanship. She was one of the many instructors who helped me develop a lifelong love of, and respect for, these truly majestic yet surprisingly forgiving animals.

As my parents and I searched for new places to ride, more and more venues were closing. Author Diana Shaman had documented the trend years several earlier in her October 2, 1977, *New York Times* article.[3] Shaman wrote about the bleak fate of urban stables. Most of the hundreds of stables that once existed in metropolitan areas had either been torn down or were being converted to other uses—and understandably so. Cities are not a natural or particularly hospitable habitat for horses. Nowhere is this more evident than in the recent film *Concrete Cowboy* (Ricky Staub, 2020), which addressed the struggles of the Fletcher Street Urban Riding Club in Philadelphia, Pennsylvania. Director Ricky Staub aptly demonstrated how challenging it can be to maintain horses in urban centers and that such locations are usually not amenable to quality horse care regardless of how passionately caretakers are devoted to horsemanship and animal husbandry. While there are exceptions to the rule (such as the Compton Cowboys in

Los Angeles and the Compton Jr. Posse), cities are typically ill-disposed to horses and horse care. Urban centers generally lack the open, green-space environments where horses naturally roam, dwell, and normally thrive.

For millions of urban-dwelling Americans, particularly many people of color, access to horses is linked to land access. More specifically, it is linked to land ownership. Gradually, I began to understand why so few African Americans that I knew rode horses—Western or English. It was not because horseback riding was a "bougie," "haughty," or "white sport," as so many people jeeringly insisted or sarcastically taunted. Nor was it because people of color didn't like or understand the value of horses or the traditions of competitive equestrian sports (i.e., cutting, barrel racing, calf roping, dressage, hunter-jumpers, vaulting, driving, three-day eventing). It was an issue of access (to farms, to equipment, to jobs, to sports). Horses taught a city girl like me about the importance of access to open land and led me to question the history of access to opportunities (economic, social, and cultural) that came with land ownership.

Why, then, did so few people of color, particularly African Americans, own farms and barns where they could maintain livestock and horses?

The answer to my question had, of course, been well documented by scholars like Pete Daniel in his book *Dispossession: Discrimination against African American Farmers in the Age of Civil Rights* and in journal scholarship like "The Inheritance of Inequality" by Sam Bowles and Herbert Gintis.[4] Even the mainstream press carried articles such as Leah Douglas's critique in *The Nation* and Dillon Hayes's video blog on Black cowboys in the *New York Times*.[5] Legal scholars, journalists, and pundits were presenting the same case about African American dispossession and disenfranchisement.

According to Douglas, for instance, in the forty-five years following the Civil War, freed slaves and their descendants accumulated roughly 15 million acres of land across the United States, most of it in the Southern states. Land ownership meant stability and opportunity for Black families. It also meant a shot at upward mobility and economic security for future generations. This was precisely the aspirational dream depicted in revisionist westerns such as Sidney Poitier's *Buck and the Preacher* (1972), John Singleton's *Rosewood* (1997), and Larry Clark's *Cutting Horse* (2002). This history even made its way into the television series *Queen Sugar* produced by Ava DuVernay and Oprah Winfrey. Hard-won property was generally used for farming, the primary occupation of most Southern Blacks in the early twentieth century. By 1920 there were 925,000 Black-owned farms, representing approximately 14 percent of all farms in the United States. Over the course of the twentieth century, however, that number dropped precipitously. Between 1940 and 1974 the number of African American farmers fell from

681,790 to approximately 45,594—a drop of 93 percent. Millions of farmers of all races lost their land in the early part of the century, including around 600,000 Black farmers. By 1975 just 45,000 Black-owned farms remained.[6] But Black agricultural land ownership, having peaked at the turn of the twentieth century, underwent a sharper decline from 1910 to 1997.[7]

In the national data on racial and ethnic dimensions of agricultural land ownership in the United States, whites accounted for 96 percent of the owners, 97 percent of the value, and 98 percent of the acres of all private U.S. agricultural land in 1999. According to Jess Gilbert in 2002, four minority groups (Blacks, American Indians, Asians, and Hispanics) owned approximately 25 million acres of agricultural land, with a total value of over $44 billion. The acreage has significant social, economic, cultural, and political consequences for minority communities in rural America.[8] However, more recent research, such as Dania Francis's study "Black Land Loss: 1920–1997," asserts that African American land ownership peaked at 16 million acres. Francis and her colleagues claim that these sixteen million acres were the most land that Blacks would ever own in the United States:

> Black Farmers acquired land against a backdrop of extreme racial violence sometimes directed at landowners. Planters conspired to restrict land sales to African Americans. Because many banks refused to lend to African Americans, they had limited credit resources when the Great Depression hit.
>
> Even though the federal government enacted massive spending programs to halt the farm crisis of the Depression era, the insistence by Southern Democrats that these programs be administered at the local level effectively blocked Black farmers from receiving relief.
>
> In addition to controlling government benefits, White Southern elites found other ways to take Black farmers' land. . . . A common tactic was for a federal agent to delay a loan in order to cause a farmer to plant late, reap a smaller harvest, and end up in debt. All available evidence suggests schemes like these were widespread.
>
> Black farmers made a direct attack on this system in the 1960s, when they worked with civil rights organizations to run election campaigns to integrate USDA county committees. White elites, however, used threats of job loss to repel voters and even resorted to blatant fraud with no consequences.[9]

The land loss that Francis and her colleagues describe is both a major contributor to the racial wealth gap in the United States and an issue that has marred the relationship between the U.S. Department of Agriculture (USDA) and minority farmers. Equally remarkable is the fact that the disenfranchisement of African American farmers parallels the disenfranchisement of African American homeowners in cities across America. Scholars and activists have documented how the U.S. government segregated America. They have shown the racist machinations of bank discrimination, "redlining," subprime loan management, and government policies that were employed in the mid-twentieth century to enforce residential racial segregation (or de jure segregation) in metropolitan areas nationwide. As Richard Rothstein points out, racial segregation in housing was not merely a project of Southerners in the former slaveholding Confederacy. It was a nationwide project of the federal government in the twentieth century designed and implemented by liberal leaders.[10] The convergence and cumulative impact of these colluding forces and intersecting schemes resulted in the financial underdevelopment of Black America.[11] Eventually, I realized that the answer to the question of where all the Black riders had gone could be found in the same place as the answer to the question of where all the Black farmers and Black homeowners had gone.

The community-based work of Mayisha Akbar is a testament to my thesis. In 1988, Ms. Akbar became aware of the ten-block zone in the Los Angeles basin that is the largest urban agriculturally zoned enclave in LA. It is an area known as Richland Farms. It was in Richland Farms that her dream of owning horses and other farm animals came true. "Shortly after moving there, she purchased a horse for herself and one for each of her three children. Upon realizing that the neighborhood kids had a positive connection with her horses, she launched an after-school equestrian leadership program for at-risk youth. That was how the Compton Jr. Posse (CJP) was born."[12]

Many years later, as an adult, I grasped that the history of African American dispossession and disenfranchisement dovetailed with the history of our marginalization in, and near erasure from, western cinema. More specifically, it paralleled the erasure of African Americans from the history and mythology of the western frontier after the Great Migration brought millions to the western territories. Not only had African American history been obscured and its transliteration as cinematic myth been ignored, but the history was also unknown in academic film circles. Documentaries like Jeff Kanew's *Black Rodeo* (1972) and Poitier's *Buck and the Preacher* were either unfamiliar or rarely discussed in cinema studies. I set out to research some of these Black western films and to make a contribution to the scholarly discourse. It is my hope that my close readings of westerns will facilitate more discussion of these movies and how they revised the genre in light of nascent Black nationalism peaking at the Black National Convention in 1972.

• • •

I am thankful for the existence of peer titles by scholars Michael K. Johnson and Blake Allmendinger. Johnson's book, *Hoodoo Cowboys and Bronze Buckaroos: Conceptions of the African American West* (2014), and Allmendinger's tome, *Imagining the African American West* (2005), demonstrated that others were working in related fields. Traditional historians Quintard Taylor, Sara Massey, Art Burton, John Nankivell, Tricia Martineau Wagner, and Frank Schubert were among the pioneering scholars to develop Black western studies or what some refer to as Race and Ethnicity in American Western Studies. I am also indebted to their scholarship because although their work is not about visual culture, they offer confirmation of African American lived experience in the West. They gave me the backdrop against which to rethink certain moments in American cinema.

My first foray into Black westerns resulted in a published chapter for *Poitier Revisited: Reconsidering a Black Icon in the Obama Age* (2014), an anthology coedited with Ian Strachan. While researching Poitier's directorial debut, I discovered there were many other western movies that starred, or at least featured, African American actors. They were similarly neglected. Their low budgets, newcomer performers, and modest quality were not the only reasons these movies were overlooked. Volumes had been dedicated to various kinds of exploitation movies.[13] These Black westerns also seemed like a perfectly reasonable subject for cinema studies. Thus, the idea for *Black Rodeo: A History of the African American Western* was born. It derived from my work on Poitier's westerns. This project also enabled me to link my own academic background and personal passions with an inquiry into the history of Black disenfranchisement.

I would like to thank my editor, Daniel Nasset, for believing in and supporting this book project from the outset. From the first time I pitched the manuscript of *Black Rodeo* to him, he was supportive and encouraging. I don't mind saying, he has excellent taste. It does not surprise me that in the intervening years, Danny has risen to become the editor-in-chief at the University of Illinois Press. He assembled a wonderful editorial team (including Tad Ringo, Jill Hughes, Jennifer Fisher, Michael Roux, and Mariah Mendes Schaefer, among others) to assist with the editing, design, and promotion of the book. A huge debt of gratitude is owed to my student research assistants who assisted with this project over the last five years. A heartfelt thank you goes out to Anna Iovine, Patrick Higgins, Tatiana Santiago, Alexandria Shaw, Danielle Ncube, and Mareme Fall. Each one of these lovely young undergraduates played an integral role in helping me find articles; visit archives; select films; weed out titles; locate missing books; identify fanzines; collect articles, reviews, art, photographs; and even identify musical artists whose work related to *Black Rodeo*.

I would be remiss if I didn't acknowledge my grad school "besties" who graciously supported me. Thank you to Mabel Wilson, Donette Francis, and Jerry Philogene for reading early chapter drafts, offering substantive feedback, and suggesting related scholarship for my edification. I send love and hugs to my husband, Mark, for his forbearance, emotional support, and childcare for our son, George. Without the aforementioned, this book would not have been possible.

The Schomburg Center for Research in Black Culture is an invaluable archive. The Schomburg Center has been a wellspring of resources and information throughout my career. The Moving Image and Recorded Sound Division as well as the Manuscripts, Archives, and Rare Books Division provided essential material that cannot be located elsewhere. It is my sincere hope that this essential archive—crucial for the study of the African diaspora—continues to be supported financially by the New York Public Library system. My visits to the Schomburg were aided by my friend and curator-filmmaker Shola Lynch. She helped me obtain the materials from the collection that I needed most. I hope that this book proves as enjoyable for readers as it has been for me as the writer. And I hope that it raises awareness about the need for historical, cinematic, and economic reparations.

BLACK RODEO

Introduction

> What *Cheyenne Autumn* is to Native Americans, and *Sergeant Rutledge* is to African Americans, *7 Women* is to women. It's an apology. More than that, better than that, it's a narrative that challenges and ultimately recalibrates the bullshit narrative tropes and clichés that are and have been so casually appended to female characters throughout all of cinema's history. At the time of the film's release, Ford's name was already well-associated with the Western genre, and so we think of *7 Women* as a Western even if there may be an argument as to whether the title fits. But though the film takes place in China, far away from the frontiers that are so emblematic of the Western's identity, and though its characters are not cowboys and bandits but Christian missionaries and hard-drinking doctors, it still tackles ideas that are near to the genre's center.
>
> —Andy Crump, "The 100 Best Western Movies of All Time"

The western film genre has its origins in early silent "raid-and-rescue" pictures such as *The Great Train Robbery* (1903), *The Lonedale Operator* (1911), and *The Hazards of Helen* (1914). Even today these early one-reel motion pictures are used to teach the basic vocabulary of moviemaking to aspiring filmmakers. The first African American westerns similarly have their beginnings in early rodeo actualities such as *The Bull Dogger* (1922) and *The Crimson Skull* (1922), featuring stunt rider Bill Pickett as the star of the Miller Brothers' 101 Ranch Wild West Shows.[1] Originally a local attraction, the Millers' Wild West Show went on the road in 1907.

In the summer of 1921, the Millers employed roughly one hundred cowboys on their ranch, ten of whom were African American. The most renowned among them was Bill Pickett, a legendary rodeo and trick rider with a wide fan following. Pickett was born in 1870 in Williamson County, Texas. His family was of African American and Cherokee ancestry. The second of thirteen children, he dropped out of school in the fifth grade and worked as a ranch hand, ultimately becoming a talented rider. As an adult he joined the Miller Brothers shows, performing nationwide and in Canada, South America, and even Great Britain.[2] "Silent filmmaker Richard Edward Norman (1891–1960)—best remembered for the popular Black-cast, black-oriented feature films he produced between 1919 and 1928—attended one of Pickett's performances."[3] Norman signed Pickett for a salary of fifty dollars per week, with assurance of an extra twenty-five dollars for each week Pickett spent on the road promoting the films after they were completed. He cast Pickett in at least two films that historians have documented: *The Bull Dogger* and *The Crimson Skull*. With this film debut, Pickett made history as the first known African American cowboy film star. He would eventually be recognized as the greatest cowboy of his day. He died in 1932 at the age of sixty-two after being kicked in the head by a horse. He is buried near a stone monument to Ponca tribal chief White Eagle, a testament to his relationship with the tribe. Pickett left a legacy that inspires entertainers, rodeo competitors, and stunt performers to this day.[4]

In 1970, nearly fifty years after the debut of the earliest one-reel shorts and actualities, Hollywood was still producing what had become one of the most popular movie genres: westerns. By this time, the tropes and conventions, plots, and devices of the mainstream western were well known and well worn. *Revisionist* westerns had emerged in every variety, from noir westerns, to musicals, to social problem pictures (e.g., *Stars in My Crown*, 1950; *Seven Brides for Seven Brothers*, 1954; *Johnny Guitar*, 1954; *Flaming Star*, 1960; *Sergeant Rutledge*, 1960; *Cheyenne Autumn*, 1964). Shortly thereafter, even the concept of "revisionism," as used by erudite critics, clever reviewers, and theory-bound academics, was gradually being replaced by postmodernist frameworks such as the "*post*-western." Both the genre and the ever-evolving discourse have undergone constant reconfiguration as critics and scholars attempt to explain the western's ongoing oxymoronic permanence and obsolescence, its imperialism and postcoloniality.

As the epigraph at the beginning of this chapter suggests, *Sergeant Rutledge* was among a cohort of pictures produced to revive the genre's social relevance during the civil rights era. The civil rights movement contributed to the nation's collective awareness of this country's misaligned moral compass. Motion pictures generated popular discourse about race, nation, class, gender, and sexuality. *Black Rodeo: A History of the African American Western* addresses the social and political relationship of western films from this period to Black Power and African American liberation. This political connection between the western and social movements has precedent in other contexts. As Sarina Pearson has noted, the western's tendency to reaffirm the dominance of white masculinity at the expense of indigenous people suggests that the western ought to attract contempt, particularly in colonial settings like Samoa and New Zealand, for example.

As Pearson points out, however, the opposite has been true: westerns and cowboys were not only admired in Oceania but even imitated in these contexts.[5] Similarly, in *The Western in the Global South*, Mary Ellen Higgins, Rita Keresztesi, and Dayna Oscherwitz examine the ways different national cinemas "interact, overlap, and inter-relate with the classic western and as a result appropriate, reimagine, and subvert its tropes for new political and aesthetic purposes."[6] Cynthia Miller and A. Bowdoin Van Riper make an analogous argument in their book *International Westerns: Relocating the Frontier*. For Miller and Van Riper, there are other kinds of meanings— particularly national and ethnic meanings—that appropriate, adapt, and reinvent the western outside of the geographic and cultural confines of North America. Diverse national and cinematic contexts such as Brazil, England, Hungary, Kurdistan, Japan, and Bangladesh demonstrate that the power of western themes, tropes, and characters knows no borders or boundaries.[7] This analytical consensus among many scholars (e.g., Pearson, Higgins, Keresztesi, Oscherwitz, Miller, and Van Riper) relates to how Black westerns have functioned. African American–themed westerns appropriate, adapt, and reinvent the themes, tropes, and characters for a Black national-ist, Black abolitionist, pro–civil rights, discursive agenda.

Classic Hollywood westerns, or traditional westerns, produced between 1930 and 1955 adhered to a standard format. Traditional westerns empha-sized the establishment of law and order and presented an essential, ritu-alistic conflict between civilization and savagery, with plot elements that were constructed into various Manichean oppositions—East versus West, light versus dark, social order versus anarchy, community versus individual, town versus wilderness, cowboy versus Indian, schoolmarm versus dancehall girl—and were manifested externally in the landscape and internally in the community.[8] A physically strong, yet weathered, white male protagonist/ hero defended the territorial, expansionary interests (i.e., migratory, mon-etary, entrepreneurial, and religious) of so-called civilized people (white settler/colonialists) against the putatively "uncivilized" (usually indigenous) people obstructing their path. This classic Hollywood cinematic paradigm, carved out in the 1910s and '20s, presented simple Manichean dichotomies in which "good guys," usually depicted as Anglo-Saxon men, were set against the "bad guys," often depicted as swarthy criminals or Native Americans, who were rarely—if ever—depicted as three-dimensional human beings. With few exceptions, white female characters in these movies—even when portrayed by major stars—were marginalized in the diegesis or narrative world. Women were symbolic or ornamental objects of domesticity, dependency, femininity, and fragility (e.g., Jean Arthur as a homesteader's wife in *Shane* [1953] or Shirley Temple as a cavalry officer's daughter in *She Wore a Yellow Ribbon* [1949]). They were props, or part of the mise-en-scène of westerns, in narrative worlds where women had such low social status as to be comparable to livestock. Manhood was usually demonstrated in a homosocial environment for other men's approval.[9] When they weren't homebound ornaments or a form of currency, women were portrayed as versions of the jilted girlfriend or "fallen woman" (e.g., Claire Trevor as Dallas in *Stagecoach* [1939] or Julie Christie as Mrs. Miller in *McCabe & Mrs. Miller* [1971]).

Revisionist films flouted generic conventions, upended narrative expectations, and allowed outlaws, criminals, women, blacks, Mexicans, and Native Americans to be featured—and sometimes heroic—protagonists. Some revisions went so far as to incorporate the undead into the narrative. Movies featuring the undead first began to menace the West in the late 1950s with Edward Dein's *Curse of the Undead* (1959) and would later include pictures like *Billy the Kid vs. Dracula* (William Beaudine, 1966).[10] In most revisionist films, someone's "outlaw" status was typically itself a reflection of an unjust justice system or systemic corruption that denied their inalienable rights. Revisionist motion pictures presented morally ambiguous story lines without clear heroes or with *anti*heroes. Such antiheroes first emerged in French cinema in the fifties. The ethos of existentialism in French New Wave and European art cinema popularized Nouvelle Vague films with youth audiences worldwide. They were enormously profitable. American studio executives were eager to exploit this box office opportunity and began following suit by tailoring genre pictures in kind.

The concept of right and wrong was now blurred. Characters could no longer be judged "good" or "bad" because their worlds were untenable, unjust. Revisionist movies inverted the logic, politics, and poetics of traditional westerns (and often the ideology of manifest destiny undergirding them). The films enabled spectators to reorient themselves and identify with oppressed people of color, women, and outsiders (e.g., Native Americans, African Americans, or Mexican Americans), or at least view these people as new heroes and vindicated sufferers. Some revisionist films featured antiheroes or sympathetic villains in a manner thought impossible before the global impact of Italian *neorealism*, the Nouvelle Vague, and Brazilian Cinema Novo. Such antiestablishment cinematic identification would have been unthinkable and deemed unacceptable under Hays Production Code regulations.

Some of the earliest revisionist westerns emerged in the 1950s, when "social problem pictures" began to surface (e.g., *Pinky*, 1949; *Gentleman's Agreement*, 1949; *No Way Out,* 1950). Some of these pictures were an attempt to strike back against the HUAC (House on Un-American Activities Committee) blacklisting of artists in the film industry. The most notable were *High Noon* (1952), starring Gary Cooper, Grace Kelly, Katy Jurado, and Lee Van Cleef, and *Stars in My Crown*, featuring Joel McCrea and Juano Hernández. As adherence to the Hays Production Code relaxed (and was later abolished), directors of the New Hollywood generation, like Sam Peckinpah, George Roy Hill, and Robert Altman, produced revisionist westerns. Notable examples include Peckinpah's *The Wild Bunch* (1969), Hill's *Butch Cassidy and the Sundance Kid* (1969), and Altman's *McCabe & Mrs. Miller*. Meanwhile, in Europe, directors including Sergio Leone and Sergio Corbucci had been directing westerns unencumbered by the American Hays Code control. Their Italian-style films, later dubbed "spaghetti westerns," provided a new aesthetic perspective on the genre.[11]

Black westerns were—and still are—a subset of those aesthetically significant revisionist motion pictures that altered, appropriated, reimagined, and subverted the western's tropes for new political and aesthetic purposes. These films altered the cultural landscape because they depicted African American stories (albeit mythologized) on screen. Spaghetti westerns and Black westerns shared unique qualities. This might be why they blended so easily in Black westploitation pictures (e.g., in the *Nigger Charley* trilogy [*The Legend of Nigger Charley*, 1972; *The Soul of Nigger Charley*, 1973; and *Boss Nigger*, 1975]; *Take a Hard Ride*, 1975; *Joshua*, 1976; and *Django Unchained*, 2012).[12] For example, both spaghetti westerns and Black westerns featured protagonists who lived outside of society not because they were gunslingers but because society was corrupt, rapacious, and brutally violent. And both genres placed unique emphasis on the actors to create atmosphere. Writing about his work in Italian westerns, actor Franco Nero observed as much, saying:

> The Western all'Italiana is one of those few kinds of films where often the actors count as much as the directors themselves in characterizing the film and ensuring its importance and success. Although this may also be true of American westerns, we cannot forget the way the Italian western creates its own stylized and picaresque characters, so often surrounded by that all-consuming mythical almost mystical quality which makes them so different from the more realistic characters to be found in the traditional western. What is more, the various Djangos, Sartanas, Sabatas, Keomas and Ringos with their unusual and well-worn outfits (ponchos, black capes,

and three-quarter dust coats) replaced the Hercules and Samsons of the mythological films, often finding themselves in the same schematic and absurd situations, suspended between epic and irony, between fairy tale and reality. . . .

Here we also find role confusion. The heroes are never completely "good," their dialogues have grotesque tones and are often punctuated with black humor. Another characteristic typical of the Italian western is that extreme and shocking violence tending towards a "grand-guignol" sadism, a kind of violence later used by directors in other kinds of films (Quentin Tarantino is perhaps the more classic example) of modern-day American cinema.[13]

Nero makes compelling points about the centrality of the actor in Italian-style westerns. He captures the dark humor and sardonic tone these actors brought to the screen. His description could be extended to Black westerns because they also depended on actors (e.g., Woody Strode, Jim Brown, Fred Williamson, Sidney Poitier, Ving Rhames, Jamie Foxx, and Idris Elba) to create atmosphere and set tone. The *Charley* films and *Joshua* hinged on a perverse use of language and an embrace of the "N-word." Soul food westerns, like spaghetti westerns, similarly placed their leading male character between fairy-tale myth and reality. And they depicted the extreme racially motivated violence that African Americans faced during the antebellum and Reconstruction eras. Finally, Black westploitation pictures (the *Nigger Charley* trilogy, *Joshua*, *Take a Hard Ride*) relied on dark parody.

Some of these pictures were in intertextual dialogue with their more mainstream counterparts: the celebrated New Hollywood films. For instance, *Thomasine & Bushrod*, the 1974 blaxploitation western directed by Gordon Parks Jr., was often referred to as "the black *Bonnie and Clyde*" (1967) by critics and audiences. Significantly, some Black westerns used several of the same settings, stock characters, and conventions as mainstream films.

African American–themed films "flipped the script" in terms of African American representation and race relations in movies depicting the march toward modernity. Unlike their mainstream cinematic counterparts, these motion pictures applied African American historical perspectives to address the injustices of slavery, Jim Crow, poll taxes, Black Codes, and American apartheid. This perspective is their point of departure or narrative raison d'être. They overturned the "narration of nation" and shattered the mythic depiction of America as the land of the free and the home of the brave.[14] Some pictures addressed the tensions between African Americans and Native Indians by indicting African American participation in the American Indian Wars and colonial campaigns. But all were revisionist and reflected the shifting zeitgeist.

If the Black protagonist's actions (or even his personal moniker) were morally ambiguous (e.g., *100 Rifles*, 1969; *The Legend of Nigger Charley*; *Skin Game*, 1971; *Joshua, Posse*, 1993), it was because he lived in an unjust world predicated on white supremacy, racial injustice, and vulgarity. When the idea of manifest destiny was openly contravened or mocked (e.g., *The McMasters*, 1970; *Buck and the Preacher*, 1972; *Skin Game*; *Blazing Saddles*, 1974), it was largely because World War II and the civil rights movement had changed the conversation about who was entitled to the American dream. If the African American western heroes (and heroines) were *antiheroic*, it was because their survival depended on noncompliance. Survival forced them to abandon mainstream society's values upon which heroism was normally predicated (e.g., *Thomasine & Bushrod*; *Take a Hard Ride*; *Posse*; *Rosewood*, 1997; *The Harder They Fall*, 2021). Black people's survival required a discourse of abolitionism. Or survival necessitated that African American characters circumvent racist lawmen, defy white supremacy, and escape the capitalist exploitation that would dehumanize, disenfranchise, or deny their inalienable rights. Since most Black characters in major studio films rarely survived through the third reel, all of these survival trajectories within African American westerns were revisionist-abolitionist departures from conventional Hollywood aesthetics.

The protagonists of Black-empowerment westerns were subject to the typical injustices and to racial injustice. They faced dispossession and dislocation as a matter of course, setting them apart from the disaffected protagonists of Sam Peckinpah's, Robert Altman's, or George Roy Hill's revisionist art house "oaters" (slang for westerns, i.e., fodder for horses). Moreover, the 1960s and '70s were seminal years of Black empowerment, economic self-determination, and racial uplift against the climate of Jim Crow and white supremacist oppression. Filmmakers utilized and capitalized on these issues. *Black Rodeo: A History of the African American Western* offers close textual analysis of many of these Black revisionist-abolitionist films.

Due to their reliance on Black nationalist themes (e.g., economic self-empowerment, Black pride, Black community, racial separatism, cultural nationalism),[15] African American westerns presented men, and to a lesser extent women, as protagonists, heroes, and heroines of cinematic spectacles. Although Black nationalism and separatism had many proponents and iterations, several of the movement's public figureheads in the '60s and '70s were men (e.g., Elijah Muhammad, Malcolm X, Jesse Jackson, Stokely Carmichael, Bobby Seale, Fred Hampton, George Jackson, Harold Cruse, Bayard Rustin).[16] Consequently, the nationalist and Black Power movements reflected *masculinist* sensibilities and biases. Feminists Angela Davis, Toni Cade Bambara, Barbara Smith, Michele Wallace, and Wahneema Lubiano (among many others) have critiqued the masculinist predisposition and shortcomings of nationalism in Black Power circles. But the hegemony of masculinist political rhetoric and semiotics was already solidified and entrenched throughout arts movements, popular culture, and mainstream movies like westerns.

The hegemony of masculinist discursive practices is precisely what makes a blaxploitation western vehicle like *Thomasine & Bushrod* unusual; its female lead, the titular Thomasine, has more narrative agency, screen time, and political relevance than most women in New Hollywood cinema. Similarly, *The Harder They Fall* presents strong female characters. Due to their shared reliance on conventional modes of masculinity, both African American westerns and mainstream westerns provide a primer on how masculine ideals were, and perhaps still are, imagined heroically and how masculinity functions in society generally.

As sociologist Michael Kimmel asserts, men are under the constant scrutiny of other men. Because other men watch them and grant their acceptance into the realm of manhood, manhood is demonstrated for other men's approval. Men boast to one another of their accomplishments, from their latest sexual conquest to the size of the fish they caught. They parade the signifiers of manhood (i.e., wealth, power, status, sexy women) in front of other men, longing for their approval. Men prove their manhood in the eyes of other men, Kimmel argues, because "masculinity is a *homosocial* enactment."[17]

The mutual imbrication (and reinforcement) of masculinity and Black nationalism rendered western movies fertile ground for screenwriters who were eager to tap current events for filmmaking. The genre served as a kind of palimpsest upon which writers superimposed metaphors for emerging civil rights discourses: Black migration, empowerment, racial uplift, and critiques of white supremacy and settler colonialism. These sentiments were gaining traction, with political activism occurring in major cities nationwide such as Chicago, Sacramento, and Gary, Indiana.

Nineteen seventy-two was a year marked by major political *and* cinematic events for African Americans. Among them was the National Black Political Convention (aka the Gary Convention) held on March 10–12 in Indiana. Approximately ten thousand African Americans met to discuss, and advocate for, Black communities across the country that were experiencing economic and social crises. The convention's objectives were to (1) increase the number of Black politicians elected to office, (2) increase voter representation, and (3) lay out an agenda for fundamental societal change. The convention leaders published the "Gary Declaration,"[18] which stated that the American political system was failing its black citizens and that the only way to address this failure was to transition to independent black politics.

The National Black Political Convention of 1972 was documented, in cinema verité style, by renowned filmmaker and television producer William Greaves (b. 1926–d. 2014). It was narrated by international film stars and cultural icons Sidney Poitier and Harry Belafonte. The resulting product was titled *Nationtime* (1972) and marked the onset of the Black documentary film movement, which was then propelled by the work of practitioners including Carlton Moss (*The Negro Soldier*, 1944), Gordon Parks (*Diary of a Harlem Family*, 1968), St. Clair Bourne (*Something to Build On*, 1971; *Malcolm X Liberation University: Black Journal segment*, 1969), and Bill Greaves (*The First World Festival of Negro Arts*, 1966; *Still a Brother*, 1968; *Black Power in America: Myth or Reality?* 1988). The Black documentary movement also included white directors such as Agnes Varda (*The Black Panthers*, 1968), Arnold Perl and Marvin Worth (*Malcolm X: In His Own Words as It Really Happened*, 1971), Peter Watkins (*Punishment Park*, 1971), and Jeff Kanew (*Black Rodeo*, 1972).

Nationtime depicted a historic event that gathered Black voices from across the political spectrum, including Jesse Jackson, Dick Gregory, Coretta Scott King, Dr. Betty Shabazz, Richard Hatcher, Amiri Baraka, Charles Diggs, Isaac Hayes, Richard Roundtree, and H. Carl McCall. Considered too militant for television broadcast at the time, the documentary circulated only in an edited fifty-eight-minute version until its recent restoration, which returned the film to its original eighty-minute length and visual quality, according to distributor Kino Lorber.

The documentary included speeches by Gary mayor Hatcher and an introduction of Jesse Jackson by Malcolm X's widow, Betty Shabazz. As Jackson steps up to the podium microphone, we hear the voice-over by Sidney Poitier avowing, "The days of silence are over. For each and every murdered martyr, five hundred thousand strongmen and women take their place. . . . Here is one." In his rousing speech, Jackson asks, "Brothers and sisters, what time is it?" To which the audience fervently responds, "*Nation-time!*" The voice-over, images, and ambient audio captured the groundswell of dedicated political engagement from community representatives. Political commitment grew in the wake of the assassinations of Medgar Evers (June 1963), John F. Kennedy (November 1963), Malcolm X (February 1965), Martin Luther King Jr. (April 1968), and Robert Kennedy (June 1968).

Black political movement was signaled by other indicators as well. In 1972 politician/educator/author Shirley Chisholm announced her bid for the presidency. She became the first African American major-party candidate to run for president of the United States, making her the first woman ever to run for the Democratic Party's nomination. Just as 1972 marked important political events, it also marked notable cinematic events.

The spring of '72 witnessed the release of the two most groundbreaking Black westerns of the decade: Jeff Kanew's full-length documentary, *Black Rodeo*, and Sidney Poitier's directorial debut, *Buck and the Preacher*. Kanew's film captured real rodeo culture as practiced by everyday cowboys, bronco riders, and cattle rustlers. Poitier's picture was a period "actioner" (or action film), depicting the mass migration of Exodusters to the Western states in search of freedom from racial tyranny in Southern states.[19] Both Kanew's documentary and Poitier's narrative featured well-known actors.

Audiences may have been surprised to see Muhammad Ali and Woody Strode making unexpected appearances in a documentary about everyday rodeo folk. Poitier's movie had cast Harry Belafonte and Ruby Dee as his costars. Strikingly different in style and form, *Black Rodeo* and *Buck and the Preacher* exemplified contrasting aesthetic approaches toward the same significatory goal: capturing and reframing authentic African American frontier history, culture, and everyday practices.

For both Kanew and Poitier, these films were labors of love. Of all the films in which he appeared and directed, Poitier stated that *Buck and the Preacher* was his favorite. He favored it because the film marked both his directorial debut and an opportunity to authenticate his political solidarity with communities of color through Hollywood studio production. Poitier affirmed that *Buck* was his favorite film via a group conference call at the Sidney Poitier International Conference and Film Festival, held in Nassau, Bahamas, in February 2010. In a separate interview with Jeff Kanew (see appendix), Kanew acknowledged that *Black Rodeo* was the centerpiece of his short-lived directorial career.

Although neither *Buck and the Preacher* nor *Black Rodeo* became big box office moneymakers, they nonetheless "stand the test of time" for documenting underexplored and underrepresented history, culture, and lived traditions that are still being uncovered today in the archeological reconstruction of African American life. Because *Buck* and *Rodeo* captured the shifting political zeitgeist, and still endure the test of time as politically and aesthetically progressive cinematic texts, this book-length study is titled: *Black Rodeo: A History of the African American Western*.

Their profitability notwithstanding, Black westerns were in steady production for at least another two years. Studio executives still believed they could (1) capitalize on such films' audience appeal, (2) exploit the "celebrification" of black athletes,[20] and (3) explore the panoply of salaciously taboo historical subjects (e.g., miscegenation, Black masculinity, Black sexuality, and Black Power movements). The "celeb*rification*" of 1960s era Black athletes (e.g., Woody Strode, Jim Brown, Fred Williamson) comprised changes at the individual and societal levels, especially in the wake of Jackie Robinson's (and others') struggles with white supremacy. With the notable exception of Paul Robeson, Black athletes heretofore had not successfully transitioned from professional sports to film stardom. And Paul Robeson had proven his appeal and success on stage and in music before turning to film.

Something shifted with the 1960s' western movies. Black westerns expanded the process through which public figures or ordinary people were transformed into celebrities (e.g., film stars, "academostars," celebrity politicians, or socialites). Not only were individual athletes transformed into motion picture celebrities, but their transformation was also a result of "celebri*tization*": it involved the meta-process of societal and cultural changes implied by the democratization of celebrity. Strode's, Brown's, and Williamson's film careers exemplified another means of the embedding of celebrity in American culture through its democratization and diversification.[21]

Though this book derives its impetus from Kanew's *Black Rodeo* and Poitier's *Buck and the Preacher*, there were other, less well-known westerns released in proximity. *Skin Game*, starring James Garner and Louis Gossett, was released by Warner Bros. in 1971, a year before Poitier's and Kanew's movies. *The Red, White, and Black*, first released in 1970, was rereleased under the new title *Soul Soldier* (John Cardos, 1972). It was one of several blaxploitation westerns produced. Paramount Pictures also released Martin Goldman's *The Legend of Nigger Charley* (in March 1972), spawning the "Black westploitation" *Nigger Charley* trilogy starring football-icon-turned-movie-celebrity Fred Williamson.[22]

"Black westploitation" is a term used throughout this book to refer to African American–themed exploitation westerns. Blaxploitation is well known as a subgenre of exploitation films that emerged in the early 1970s. The films, while popular, suffered backlash for their disproportionate numbers of stereotypical characters depicting evil or questionable motives, including criminals, pimps, drug dealers, and prostitutes. However, the western films ranked among the first in which Black characters and communities were the heroes and subjects of film and television rather than sidekicks, villains, or victims of brutality.

Westploitation is a subgenre of westerns in much the way sexploitation and teen-exploitation are cultural by-products of women in prison pictures and teen cinema. All were cheaply made B westerns that were produced quickly by relying on recycled themes, characters, plot devices, and cinematic clichés. They often utilized deliberate camp aesthetics, with an emphasis on failed seriousness.

Black westploitation films fused westploitation and blaxploitation production practices. Despite being lowbrow and low cost—which often put them under the radar of many critics—the *Nigger Charley* trilogy pictures were culturally and politically significant in part because they set off a backlash against, and conversation about, the use of the N-word in cinema and popular culture. In this regard Quentin Tarantino is in debt to the *Nigger Charley* films. Tarantino has even acknowledged his debt to blaxploitation cinema in interviews such as the one he gives in the 2002 documentary *BaadAsssss Cinema*. They also reflected the changing zeitgeist with their empowerment themes and generic revisionism. They were created for audiences who were eager to see visceral representations of inverted race relations.

The resurgence of Black westerns in the 1960s and '70s is notable because African American westerns had not been produced (by major studios, minor-major studios, or the bargain-basement independent "Poverty Row" studios) for thirty years.[23] Many B film studios came and went between the 1920s and the early 1960s as they struggled to compete with larger and more lucrative corporations. In their heyday, Poverty Row outlets survived on western fare, producing mostly inexpensive westerns. Companies such as Tiffany Pictures, Mascot Pictures, Larry Darmour Productions, Monogram Pictures, Republic Pictures, Grand National Films Inc., and CBC Productions relied heavily on westerns for profits.[24]

During the Great Depression, however, and the transition to sound cinema, several small outlets failed to withstand the challenges associated with the new sound equipment required to compete with the major studios. Poverty Row companies as well as African American independent producers (e.g., Lincoln Motion Picture Company, Micheaux Film and Book Company, Million Dollar Productions, Hollywood Productions) were also hard hit by the financial downturn of the Depression. Consequently, only a handful of the "race movies" produced during this era—among them westerns—exist today.

Richard C. Kahn directed three all-Black-cast oaters starring singing cowboy Herbert Jeffries. *Two Gun Man from Harlem* (1938), *Bronze Buckaroo* (1939), and *Harlem Rides the Range* (1939) were immensely popular with Black audiences, especially young Black boys.[25] They are three of the only pre–World War II African American westerns available today. With improving technology and continuing archival exploration, it is possible that additional titles will resurface. These prewar motion pictures are not the focus of this book. Instead, *Black Rodeo: A History of the African American Western* is a postwar study that begins in the 1960s with *Sergeant Rutledge*. However, director Jacques Tourneur's *Stars in My Crown* is a key precursor that sits on the border between social problem pictures and western genre movies.

Gordon Parks's *The Learning Tree* (1969) is another important film that— despite being a postwar movie situated within New Hollywood—is not central to this book, because it is not a typical western in the manner most moviegoers and cinephiles imagine (i.e., narrative structure, generic elements, or formal devices). Nor is it a revisionist western. *The Learning Tree* is a "coming of age" story set among Exodusters living in Fort Scott, Kansas, at the turn of the twentieth century. That said, *The Learning Tree* does perform in many of the ways revisionist Black westerns do. First, it sits in intertextual dialogue with New Hollywood films about adolescence such as *Billy Liar* (John Schlesinger, 1963); *The Heart Is a Lonely Hunter* (Robert Ellis Miller, 1968); *Kes* (Ken Loach, 1969); *The Sterile Cuckoo* (Alan J. Pakula, 1969); *Sounder* (Martin Ritt, 1972); *Badlands* (Terrence Malick, 1973); *Cornbread, Earl and Me* (Joseph Manduke, 1975); and *A Hero Ain't Nothing but a Sandwich* (Ralph Nelson, 1978). Second, it presents a world in which the concept of right and wrong is blurred, complicated, and unclear for the protagonist and his teenage friends. *The Learning Tree* dispenses with the notion of manifest destiny and European settler entitlement by presenting African Americans as part of the settler movement. Moreover, it creates a diegesis in which spectators identify with oppressed people of color by rendering their suffering visible and relatable.

The Learning Tree is not the only "odd man out" missing from this book. The made-for-TV movie *Buffalo Soldiers* (Charles Haid, 1997) starring Danny Glover is mentioned herein but not discussed in detail. A worthwhile film with fine performances, it tells the story of the all-Black U.S. Cavalry troop that protected the Western territories in post–Civil War times. The story focuses on Troop H's attempts to capture an Apache warrior named Vittorio in New Mexico. But when they come face-to-face with a poor, diminutive man struggling to keep a small tribe of women and children alive, Vittorio makes them confront the ugly truth that they've been duped by army propaganda into fighting for a nation that respects neither Blacks nor Native Americans. *Buffalo Soldiers* is one part western and one part historical war picture in the tradition of *Glory* (Edward Zwick, 1989), which is why it was excluded. However, it does have antecedents in early Black western experiments such as the low-budget movie *Soul Soldier*.[26]

The concurrent release of several revisionist, countercultural, Black empowerment westerns in the early to mid-1970s suggests that earlier African American westerns like *Rio Conchos* (1964), *100 Rifles*, and *El Condor* (1970) performed well enough with audiences to convince studios of their commercial viability. In recent years, Phillip J. Skerry has claimed that the 1963 assassination of President John F. Kennedy engendered the loss of American "innocence" and with it the death or disappearance of the western genre.[27] However, the emergence of several Black westerns between 1960 and 1975 suggests otherwise. In 2013 several film scholars proclaimed that the genre was already "dead" in the 1960s; however, not only was it very much alive, but several other scholars moved to explain the western's subsequent reinvention and longevity (e.g., Vera Dika, Clark Mitchell, Jim Kitses, Greg Rickman, Neil Campbell).

Skerry's claim regarding the death of the genre raises two unsettling issues: first, it is disappointing that some researchers failed to view Black westerns as constitutive of this always already evolving genre such that they proclaimed its death during the heyday of Black western production. Although, African American westerns offered a pro–Black Power, postcolonial reimagining of the mythic West, these pictures were uncomfortably constitutive of the hegemonic sign system they sought to critique. The western had not yet died by 1963. It was still evolving. Second, Skerry was naïve to assert that America as a nation was ever "innocent." It was not innocent of genocide, settler colonialism, or the white supremacy upon which its imperialistic campaigns were waged. Therefore, Black westerns make obvious the tensions and contradictions embedded in African American participation in colonial projects whether as cavalry officers, Exoduster homesteaders, or lonesome cowboys. The complexities of African American participation in these colonial campaigns are an under-researched subject. Thankfully, there is a legacy of African American history upon which to build.

The 1965 seminal book by Philip Durham and Everett Leroy Jones (a.k.a. Amiri Baraka), *The Negro Cowboys*, is also part of the inspiration for *Black Rodeo: A History of the African American Western*. It was their book that brought the figure of the Black cowboy back to American historical consciousness and informed the production of Poitier's *Buck and the Preacher*. Their book also inspired the creation of Lobo, the first African American comic book hero:

> Not only is *Lobo* the first series to be driven by a black lead character, but the issues also deal directly with themes of slavery and the Civil War. [Some felt these were] very peculiar topics to appear in a 1965 newsstand comic book. [According to Ethan Persoff and other comic book aficionados,] . . . it's said most copies of *Lobo* were rejected by store owners at first sight. While that isn't proven, the bold move to put a black cowboy hero, holding a gun, on the cover of his own comic in the mid-sixties (distributed all around to the country's small towns) is a provocative and rather wonderful thing to come from Dell Comics. Dell was nearing bankruptcy at this point, and it's one of the more culturally interesting things they ever did, even if it was only driven by a desperate interest in finding a title that would succeed. *Lobo* only lasted two issues.[28]

FIGURE 0.1 Lobo, the first Black comic book hero.

Durham and Jones clearly inspired many creators to take up the mantle and address repressed Black western history. To Poitier's credit, *Buck and the Preacher* refuted whitewashed generic conventions. It challenged the reductive homogenization of Native American people into faceless hordes, it subverted the normalization of white supremacy, and it disputed dominant historical narratives about the political economy of western settlement.

Because of the long history of cultural bias in the American educational system, the Afro-diasporic experience in the United States has been marginal or omitted from mainstream historical narratives until recently. David Zucchino's Pulitzer Prize–winning book, *Wilmington's Lie: The Murderous Coup of 1898 and the Rise of White Supremacy*, demonstrates the lengths to which white supremacists would go to disempower African Americans and suppress history. As Durham and Jones note in their introduction, colored folks were forgotten when it came to western history. "When history became myth and legend," writes Durham, "when the cowboys became folk heroes, the Negroes were again fenced out. They had ridden through the real West, but they found no place in the West of fiction."[29] The paucity of representation (in myth and popular culture) still holds true. Only a handful of actors broke the barriers to become screen cowboys in cinematic myth.

Additionally, we cannot forget that at times African Americans were complicit with the dominant colonizing enterprise. Quintard Taylor notes as much in his introduction to *Buffalo Soldier Regiment* when he writes, "Black Americans had long derived considerable pride from the soldiers' role as the 'sable arm' of the U.S. government. Some soldiers consciously embraced that role. Tenth Cavalry Pvt. Henry McCombs boasted, 'We made the West,' by which he meant that they had defeated hostile tribes of Indians and made the country safe to live in."[30] The complex, contradictory, and colonialist roles African Americans played on the frontier is nonetheless an important, albeit shameful, component of our shared past.

American cinema long preserved monolithic myths of the western United States. African Americans were virtually nonexistent. American Indians were represented as a people from another time. As Ward Churchill aptly notes, "Indigenous people were defined exclusively in terms of certain (conflict and demise) interactions with Euro-Americans. . . . There is no cinematic recognition whatsoever of a white-free and autonomous Native past. Similarly, no attention is paid to the many indigenous nations not directly involved in the final period of Anglo-Indian warfare.[31]

Since the publication of *The Negro Cowboys*, the discipline of western historical studies has grown considerably thanks to the scholarship of William Loren Katz, Sara Massey, Quintard Taylor, Frank Schubert, Tricia Martineau Wagner, Art Burton, Brian Shellum, John Nankivell, and Michael Johnson, among others. There is now a fuller, although still incomplete, understanding of the Black diasporic presence in the western United States. This knowledge derives primarily from military history because what is documented pertains principally to the Ninth and Tenth Cavalries and the Twenty-Fourth and Twenty-Fifth Infantries. "Along with black cowboys," writes Taylor, "these troops were the first African-American western historical figures to capture widespread public attention in the 1960s."[32] However, the only Hollywood western to address Black consciousness or racial themes before 1960 was Metro-Goldwyn-Mayer's *Stars in My Crown*.

Arguably more Southern than Western, *Stars in My Crown* is principally about the morality of a preacher and the community to which he ministers. It opens in a Western-style saloon as Civil War veteran Josiah Gray (Joel McCrea), arrives in nineteenth-century Walesburg and outdraws the first lost souls he meets for the right to preach a sermon to them. Here the gunslinger is more preacher than fighter. Juano Hernández portrays Uncle Famous Prill, a kindly old Black farmer who is terrorized by hooded vigilantes trying to intimidate him into selling his land. When he refuses, Klansmen (in cahoots with a mine owner who covets Prill's property) try to lynch him. The good preacher Josiah saves Prill from the hooded riders in the final reel by shaming them with Uncle Famous's purported intent to bequeath his meager possessions to them. Humbled by and ashamed of this new information, the vigilantes leave or ride away one by one, and Josiah's young son (the film's narrator) expresses surprise at his father's having faked the reading of a will from a blank sheet of paper. Joel McCrea's clergyman affirms that there is a will: the will of God. In many ways, the early civil rights era ethos and sentimentality of *Stars in My Crown* anticipates the tenor of Harper Lee's 1960 novel, *To Kill a Mockingbird*, which was adapted to the screen in 1962 and is similar in style, tone, and social problem picture design.

In his book *Showdown: Confronting Modern America in the Western Film*, John Lenihan expresses understandable skepticism about the false liberal sentimentality of *Stars in My Crown*. He notes that "the one western to deal explicitly with blacks was more a justification of the southern dream of harmonious segregation than a forceful indictment of social discrimination."[33] Lenihan anticipated what Brian Henderson (and other scholars) later detected in John Ford's *The Searchers* (1956). As productions about Black-white social problems declined in the '60s, Hollywood westerns offered more prolific and pointed commentary on issues of racial inequality through stories about frontier intolerance toward the Indian. Thus, white-Indian relations became metaphors for Black-white race relations. Except for *Stars in My Crown*, there were few, if any, studio films about African Americans on the frontier until the 1960s. That is also partially because during the classic Hollywood studio era, African Americans were typically cast in either stereotypical roles, supporting bit parts, or as singing and dancing entertainers in wartime musicals.

Black Rodeo: A History of the African American Western offers a close reading of some of the seminal post–World War II westerns. In doing so, the book seeks to pose questions regarding Black masculinity on the frontier. For example, the first chapter is titled "Football Heroes Invade Hollywood" and begins with the ascent of Woody Strode as a western film icon who was mentored by John Ford. It considers how Strode functioned as an early paradigm of Black western stardom and a harbinger of stars to come. His immediate successor was Jim Brown. The chapter addresses both the films and the extra-cinematic endeavors Brown pursued as he parlayed his athletic capital into cultural and political capital. Smaller, less impressive vehicles like *The McMasters*, featuring Brock Peters and Burl Ives were released in the early years of the decade as foreign directors tested their skills and experimented with western themes.

Chapter 2, "Black Masculinity on Horseback: From *Duel at Diablo* to *Buck and the Preacher*," offers a close reading of Sidney Poitier's two western vehicles: *Duel at Diablo* (1966) and *Buck and the Preacher*. This chapter places the films into the context of Poitier's other work. It also addresses his attempt to redeem himself after the *New York Times* takedown by Clifford Mason and criticisms of his assimilationist screen persona. *Buck* was a collaboration between Poitier and his close companion Harry Belafonte. It also marked Poitier's directorial debut, which was financially and professionally supported by his close friend. Notably, Poitier reciprocated in kind. Belafonte's wife, Julie Robinson, appears in the film portraying a Native American woman named Sinsie. Significantly, Robinson learned an authentic Native American language for the role. Columbia Pictures provided recordings for voice training during preproduction in an effort to heighten realism and historical accuracy. Ruby Dee delivers a stoic but nuanced performance as Ruth, Buck's faithful and cunning spouse. It was an interesting variation of her role as Ruth in *A Raisin in the Sun* (Daniel Petrie, 1961), also opposite Poitier. Both Ruth and Sinsie are atypically strong women who are prominent in the narrative. They mark another significant departure from western movie conventions.

Chapter 3, "Blaxploitation versus Black Liberation: The *Nigger Charley* Trilogy," examines the cinematic celebrity of Fred Williamson through a set of three blaxploitation films. This set of pictures was influenced by multiple sources: sauerkraut and spaghetti westerns, Black empowerment, and exploitation cinema. The *Nigger Charley* trilogy was also informed—whether knowingly or not—by Sergio Leone's internationally popular *Dollars* trilogy: *A Fistful of Dollars* (1964), *For a Few Dollars More* (1965), and *The Good, the Bad, and the Ugly* (1966). It is widely known that Leone's films completely upended generic conventions to establish their own uniquely irreverent yet baroque orthodoxy. Leone's films were more violent, raunchy, and rife with Christian symbolism than previous pictures. What is *not* widely known is that the East German or "sauerkraut" westerns were another source of unrecognized, unacknowledged inspiration. These movies were based on the nineteenth-century novels of Karl May (b. 1842–d. 1912). The character Winnetou is a fictional Native American hero of several best-selling novels written in German by May, who sold approximately 200 million copies worldwide, including the Winnetou trilogy.

Many people do not know that the early East German westerns *preceded* spaghetti westerns. More relevantly, East German westerns were the first to "flip the script"—that is, to depict Native Americans as the heroes and white settlers as villains. Winnetou became the chief of the tribe of the Mescalero Apaches after his father, Intschu-tschuna, and his sister, Nscho-tschi, were slain by the white bandit Santer. And there were several pictures in this tradition released *before* 1966. For example, *Der Schatz im Silbersee* (1962) was rereleased as *The Treasure of Silver Lake* in 1965; *Winnetou Teil* (1963) was rereleased as *Apache Gold* in 1965; *Old Shatterhand* (1964) was rereleased as *Apaches' Last Battle* in 1964; and *Winnetou 2* (1964) or *Last of the Renegades* and *Unter Geiern* (1964) or *Frontier Hellcat* all preceded Leone's spaghetti films. Black western trilogies like the *Charley* films took a page out of the East German playbook. This history—and inverted Native settler moral hierarchy—becomes relevant to current cinema when considering Quentin Tarantino's *Django Unchained*, which features Christoph Waltz portraying the politically progressive German character Dr. King Schultz and Kerry Washington portraying an enslaved (German-speaking) African woman named Broomhilda von Shaft. There are entire volumes dedicated to close, interpretive analysis of *Django Unchained* that fail to acknowledge the Karl May–inspired westerns.

Additionally, the Fred Williamson vehicles overturned linguistic conventions and jettisoned bourgeois sensibilities long before Quentin Tarantino by employing the N-word. While it is first used as a racial epithet within the diegesis, it becomes a moniker of strength and heroism. The *Nigger Charley* trilogy enabled Williamson's character to face down white supremacists and vigilantes in typical blaxploitation style. Chapter 3 concludes by examining the films that emerged alongside and shortly after the *Nigger Charley* trilogy. Williamson grew so confident in his marketability as a western hero that he began producing his own star vehicles, including *Joshua*, a rape-revenge story that Williamson wrote and co-produced with Lee Winkler and Cal Bartlett. And there was *Thomasine & Bushrod*, which is arguably a precursor to new millennial movies such as Melina Matsoukas's *Queen & Slim* (2019). Matsoukas's picture offers updated ruminations on racial injustice, mass incarceration, and the American judicial system. It also evokes earlier films with its homage to Perry Henzell's *The Harder They Come* (1972).

Chapter 4, "Harlem Rides the Range: Nobody Told You There Were Black Cowboys," is dedicated to a close reading of the documentary *Black Rodeo*. Researching and watching the film was initially challenging because it was a phantom orchid. There were no viewable prints, and it had not yet been transferred to DVD. I first discovered it at the Library of Congress, where I watched a 16mm print in the motion picture screening room while taking copious notes, not knowing where else I might find it for a second viewing. After leaving the library and returning to New York, I searched other archives, libraries, museums, and video stores for a copy to study more closely. I was unable to find it anywhere. As it turns out, the film was unavailable.

I later learned, from director Jeff Kanew, that the Library of Congress owns the only extant print of *Black Rodeo*, from which the current DVD version was rendered. *Black Rodeo* is a fascinating record of Western idioms and culture as practiced by African Americans in the 1970s. Not only does it document a traveling rodeo show, but it also captures a predominantly African American and urban audience, many of whom are witnessing a traveling Black rodeo for the first time.

The audience within the film, the direct camera address, the visible cameras, and the sound recorders facilitate meta-cinematic reflexivity. Kanew engages the rodeo's audience in the project of historical revision by inviting them to comment on the significance of the event for African Americans, particularly children. Consequently, *Black Rodeo* is interesting both for its western content and for its mixed cinema verité and expository documentary style. It captures Midwestern Black rodeo riders staging a cultural and historical intervention for their East Coast urban-based brothers and sisters. For the diegetic spectators at Randall's Island Stadium in Manhattan, the rodeo was an affirmation of suppressed history, a confirmation of Black presence on the frontier and participation in nation formation. Kanew's film stood in synecdochically for subjugated history and for experimental Black documentary.

Chapter 5, "Westerns and Westploitation: Brothas and Sistas at the O.K. Corral," offers a close reading of *Posse*, *Rosewood*, and *Django Unchained*. Not all of the films in this chapter are set in the West, but they are all recognizably westerns. For example, although *Rosewood* is set in the hamlet of Rosewood, Florida, it is arguably still a western. The film presents many of the narrative conventions of westerns (e.g., small family farmers, innocent schoolteachers in distress, fallen women, a heroic gunslinger). Chief among the conventions is the trope of the western cowboy hero. Ving Rhames gives a powerful and memorable performance as Mr. Mann, an honorable gun-carrying war veteran who rides into town on a beautiful black horse named Booker T. Even Mann's horse is an homage to, and metaphor for, the life and times of educator/author/orator Booker T. Washington. Narratively, Mr. Mann (whose name underscores his masculinity in comic book style) is a quintessential western hero and a composite of previous characters. He embodies the moral virtue of Poitier's Buck, the fearless strength of Williamson's Charley, and the sex appeal of Jim Brown's Sergeant Ben Franklyn.

Whether serious dramas and melodramas (e.g., *Sergeant Rutledge*, *Rio Conchos*, *Buck and the Preacher*), escapist exploitation (e.g., the *Nigger Charley* trilogy, *Skin Game*, *Joshua*, *Thomasine & Bushrod*), or documentaries (e.g., *Black Rodeo*), African American westerns engaged in political critique, even though that critique is incomplete and mired in history. As Neil Campbell asserts, far from dead, the western survived generic negotiations and constant reinvention. Campbell is correct in saying that various cinemas interact, overlap, and interrelate with the classic western and, as a result, appropriate, reimagine, and subvert its tropes for new political and aesthetic purposes.[34] The incorporation of African Americans into the mythical landscape of the genre, and the evolution of westerns, marks one manifestation of the genre's renegotiation and reimagining.

The box office success of some of these westerns is one indication that the films often resonated with minority and majority audiences. Their appeal—particularly to African American spectators—was a function of the narratives, containing themes of racial uplift, Black empowerment, self-determination, civil rights, economic enfranchisement, and countercultural themes contesting white supremacy. Black westerns structurally altered the politics *and* poetics (the ideology and the construction) of traditional westerns through a reinterpretation of the genre's myths, conventions, and conceits. They reconstructed a Black national imaginary or "imagined community" of Exodusters who persevered and triumphed against the odds when searching for a prosperous future.

Similarly, these westerns were responding metaphorically to the political tumult of their time rather than the colonial history from which they were more than a century removed. Nowhere was this more clearly expressed than in the reemergence of the genre during the civil rights era. And in the wake of the Black Lives Matter movement, which articulated the ongoing struggle for civil rights, it should come as no surprise that African Ameri-can–themed westerns still inspire filmmakers and attract audiences. The release of *Concrete Cowboy* (Ricky Staub, 2020), based on the novel *Ghetto Cowboy* by Greg Neri, and *The Harder They Fall* (Jeymes Samuel), starring Idris Elba, are two examples.

The fifth chapter is followed by a transcription of my conversation with director Jeff Kanew about the production of the documentary *Black Rodeo*. I was interested to learn how he and his brother secured Woody Strode's participation as an interview subject. I also wanted to know how Kanew had incentivized Muhammad Ali to appear in the films.

There were also production questions about cameras, equipment, fund-ing, and location. Was it difficult to edit? Where did it appear in theaters? These questions propelled the interview. Kanew was open and patient. He shared his narrative of the film's production history. Content to relay what he remembered, he was pleasantly surprised that anyone was so interested in his little-known film that they would seek him out and track him down. Among my many questions, I wanted to know what inspired this young Jewish man to travel uptown to Harlem and make a film about African Americans running an all-Black traveling rodeo. I suppose Kanew also reminded me of silent filmmaker Richard E. Norman, another white director who—fifty years prior to 1971—recorded a different black rodeo, the 101 Wild West Rodeo Shows featuring Bill Pickett.

1

Football Heroes
Invade Hollywood

Though the phenomenon of the black athlete-turned-actor has really just begun and the participants are most often something other than stars, some observers have been led by the fact that today's actor-athlete has increased dignity to conclude that the times are over when a black actor may be asked, as Woody Strode once was, to take the title role in a film like *Androcles and the Lion*, and find himself, as Strode did, playing the lion.
—"Football Heroes Become Movie Stars," *Ebony*, October 1969

In his essay "Cowboys, Cooks, and Comics: African American Characters in Westerns of the 1930s," Michael K. Johnson discusses the depiction of Black characters as objects of derisive humor in mainstream westerns. "The Hollywood Western," writes Johnson, "feminized or de-sexualized the African American male character by associating him with a domesticity that precluded him from participating in the masculine adventures of the white male characters. The character Pinky (Ernest Whitman) from *Jesse James* and *The Return of Frank James* is both farmhand and cook, but he appears primarily in domestic spaces, making and serving dinner, washing dishes and sometimes even wearing an apron."[1] The domestication of Black male characters in mainstream pictures was more commonplace than most historical accounts have acknowledged. It occurred in the cinematic representation of pre–World War II western pictures and mainstream films made before the civil rights movement. Donald Bogle has noted as much in his authoritative study of African American representation in motion pictures, *Toms, Coons, Mulattoes, Mammies, and Bucks: An Interpretive History of Blacks in American Films*.[2]

However, as the scholarship on blaxploitation cinema (e.g., Ed Guerrero, Yvonne Sims, Novotny Lawrence, Gerald Butters, Christian Metz) has demonstrated, a sea-change occurred in the 1960s and '70s.[3] By the early 1960s, when the national political climate began shifting, African Americans—particularly Black men—began appearing more prominently, authoritatively, and seriously in dramas and westerns. The shift to more authoritative and respected characters foreshadowed, and later coincided with, the shift to more authoritative Black masculinity in films generally. *Black Rodeo* offers a close reading of those westerns featuring African American characters and how some of these films handled the evolving trope of the African American western differently from mainstream motion pictures before the '70s.

In several instances, all-Black-cast westerns, and integrated westerns featuring Black leads or heroes, strove to redress historical inaccuracies, stereotypes, and misrepresentation by providing upstanding, morally respectable characters. The most popular westerns sought to present cowboys as moral heroes. According to Cynthia Miller, "The cinematic West of the 1930s was, in many ways, a place of certainty and reinforcement for mainstream American identity, and the western frontier."[4] Western heroes did far more than refrain from smoke, drink, and rough language; they were steadfast in the face of challenges presented by modernity. To paraphrase Miller, these characters withstood changes wrought by the economic hardships, increasing urbanization, industrialization, and the rapid cultural change that characterized America at the beginning of the twentieth century and into the 1930s. Singing cowboys—both African American and white—were a particular iteration of the upstanding hero.[5] They represented compassionate, respectable manhood or individuals who ascribed to, and defended, mainstream American values. The singing cowboy plots typically drew on a standard set of familiar conflicts that were ultimately resolved in a culturally agreeable fashion, thus calming fears and fulfilling mainstream fantasies.[6]

Many of the all-Black-cast films produced in the 1930s were commercially successful, particularly with African American audiences. World War II interrupted the steady production of western genre pictures as the film industry turned its sights toward new priorities determined by the Roosevelt administration and the Office of War Information. In their book *Hollywood Goes to War*, Clayton Koppes and Gregory Black discuss how regulatory agencies such as the Production Code Administration, studio executives, and the government began to coalesce in the defense effort:

> The war brought the most sustained and intimate involvement yet seen in America between the government and a medium of mass culture as the Roosevelt administration applied pressure on Hollywood to make feature

films that were propaganda vehicles. The conflict between the studios and the government, and the eventual cooperation between them, helped shape public opinion during and after the war. The relationship between government and propagandists and a medium of mass culture brought into sharp focus crucial questions about how the public is mobilized for war and the control of a popular but corporate entertainment medium.[7]

Koppes and Black establish that by 1940 Hollywood had crossed an important threshold: studios began making explicitly interventionist films. By July 1940, the Hays Office, which administered the regulatory production code, established the Motion Picture Committee Cooperation for Defense, dedicated to short, interventionist "Why We Fight" documentaries rather than isolationist pictures.[8]

Between 1941 and 1945, the production of World War II combat pictures proliferated at Hollywood studios. In the era of vertical integration,[9] the Production Code Administration, and the Office of War Information's Bureau of Motion Pictures, combat films dominated Hollywood production. As early as 1942, the Bureau of Motion Pictures strengthened its liaison with major studios and became even more involved in ensuring Hollywood's compliance with the war effort.[10] The change was engendered by the shifting tide in the international theater of war.

After the war was over, combat film motifs manifested in westerns, which in the postwar era relied more heavily on metaphors and incorporated conventions from other genres. In a thorough study of war pictures, Jeanine Basinger aptly states, "World War II gave birth to the isolation of a story pattern which came to be known and recognized as the *combat genre*, whether it is ultimately set in World War II, in the Korean War, in Vietnam, or inside some other genre such as the Western."[11] She makes a compelling case for the relationship between the western and the combat film, and she explicates the changing tone and tenor of combat films in the post–World War II era:

> After World War II, the combat film about the Civil War was frequently removed from the South and real battles and reset in the West as a Western. If we can believe our Hollywood films, the West was a hotbed of Civil War intrigue, with plots to take over California, spies under every cactus, attempts to steal payrolls and seize gold and silver mines. Presumably, the nature of the Civil War—the sense of family conflict, the threat to our very existence as a nation, and the sight of destruction of American property— was abhorrent to us. Shifting it West made it acceptable, and the Indians made an acceptable enemy. Instead of us against us, it was us against *them*, even if national shame should be connected to this conflict. Also, the West

is a traditional setting of fighting, conflict, death, killing, and destruction. It is the place where we accept it as a necessary event. There is a strong link between the Western and the combat film, part of which is natural to their common patrol-in-hostile-territory situation. Both also have actual historical roots, and both undergo the evolutionary process, reflecting changing ideology. (The Western evolves from a celebration of American colonialism to a criticism of it.) It is always interesting to compare the two. Westerns are based on myths, even though there was a real West. World War II films are based on reality, even though there is a myth. This has to do with the development of film. We never saw the real West of the 1870s captured on moving film for us, but we did have the real World War II on film. This changes a viewer's relationship to filmed narratives.[12]

Due to the proliferation of World War II combat pictures during the 1940s, and postwar malaise film noir in the late '40s, Exodusters and African American Westerners generally do not reemerge as cinematic subjects until 1960 when Hollywood films utilized Native-settler (red-white) race relations as metaphors for Black-white race relations during the civil rights movement. The rare exceptions include unusual "social problem pictures" like *Stars in My Crown*, which emerged a few years before *Brown v. Board of Education* and predated *The Searchers*.[13] Nevertheless, the western's evolution (from complicity to criticism of American colonialism and race relations) made it the perfect palimpsest upon which to rewrite new civil rights era iterations of western myths with reimagined heroes, dilemmas, and moral questions.

Woody Strode and *Sergeant Rutledge*

John Ford's *Sergeant Rutledge*, starring Woody Strode and Jeffrey Hunter in Technicolor widescreen, is one example of a western that featured a Black cavalry officer. The film is an example of the new focus in western movies after World War II. Like *The Searchers*, *Flaming Star*, and *The Unforgiven* (1960), Ford's *Sergeant Rutledge* capitalized on the slippage between Indian-settler racial wars and Black-white race relations during the civil rights era. Films set in the 1860s (addressing white-Indian conflict) were legible as overt metaphors for Black-white race relations at a time when sensational imagery was readily employed to entice American audiences to go to the theater rather than watch television at home.

Woodrow Wilson Woolwine Strode was no stranger to film, television, or the distasteful racial politics of Hollywood image production. He grew up in Southern California, and as a natural athlete, he wanted to wrestle and play football. Strode had no idea he would make a living at professional sport. No Blacks played in the National Football League (NFL) during his college days because the NFL had developed, and enforced, a strict color barrier until 1946. But then something unexpected happened: the Hollywood Bears showed up and offered to pay him eighteen hundred dollars for half a year of semi-pro football.[14] During World War II, Strode had played for an integrated service team in a segregated arena at March Field Air Force Base in Riverside, California. Clearly he was following his passion, because he thrived in professional sport. Strode would ultimately become a football star, a world-class decathlete, and an exhibition wrestler.[15] Like Paul Robeson before him, and Jim Brown and Fred Williamson immediately after, Woody Strode's superior athleticism was one element of his physical persona that filmmakers such as John Ford (and TV producers) sought to exploit. In his autobiography, titled *Goal Dust*, Strode recalls:

> Hollywood loved physical actors. When I first worked for John Ford, he said, "Can you ride a horse, shoot a gun? Can you fight?" "Yes, sir!" I developed a personal relationship with him because I was tough, and he respected toughness. I made four pictures for him because there was no other actor in Hollywood physical enough to play the roles. My first Ford picture was *Sergeant Rutledge*, a major role for a black actor at that time. That one gave me dignity. After the fourth picture I was on the world market. I didn't realize until later, when I moved to Italy and became a true star, what John Ford had done for me. I could step off a plane anywhere in the world and people would recognize me. John Ford made me a character actor because there wasn't any work for black stars. And, because of my mixed background, I could play anyone from the Third World. I played native in the old jungle pictures; I fought Tarzan to death. They stuck a pigtail on me for *Genghis Khan*, and slanted my eyes and made me Chinese in *Seven Women*, and I could play all the Indians. I never played myself, a Negro-Indian breed, until I did *The Professionals* with Lee Marvin and Burt Lancaster.[16]

One of Strode's first acting jobs was in the television show *Ramar of the Jungle*, a syndicated television series (1952–1954) starring Jon Hall as Dr. Tom Reynolds (the titular "Ramar," which is an African title for a white medicine man). The program emulated the then-popular *Jungle Jim* movies, with the first season set in Africa, the second in Asia, and the third back in Africa.

During the early days of his acting career, Strode couldn't make a living as an actor, so he oscillated between wrestling and acting jobs. His first major payday would come when he fought Johnny Weissmuller on the *Jungle Jim* show. His next role was to play the lion in an animal costume for RKO's *Androcles and the Lion* (1952), for which he received five hundred dollars a week. After performing in costume (and reportedly losing seven pounds of water per day sweating), he learned that the standard rate for actors performing these roles was twenty-five hundred dollars a week.

In 1958 he landed a part in *Tarzan's Fight for Life*, and that started him on the road to recognition as a legitimate actor. Between 1958 and 1959 he appeared in several recognizable pictures, including *Pork Chop Hill* (1959), with Gregory Peck; *Spartacus* (1960), with Kirk Douglas; *The Last Voyage* (1960), with Robert Stack and Dorothy Malone; and *Sergeant Rutledge*, with Jeffrey Hunter.[17]

Long before shooting began on *Rutledge*, John Ford met and had become acquainted with Strode's wife, Princess Luana, and her family while vacationing in Hawaii, where Luana had grown up. Ford had also mentored and "adopted" the young Wai brothers. Francis and Conkling Wai were sons of a prominent Hawaiian banker with whom Strode had played football at the University of California at Los Angeles. Because he knew Strode indirectly, Ford felt comfortable working with, mentoring, and guiding the otherwise inexperienced athlete-turned-actor.

According to Strode, Ford was interested in telling a story using the Ninth and Tenth Cavalries as the backbone for a drama set somewhere between 1866 and the 1880s.[18] The army was said to have trained African American men to think and act like Native Indians. After the African Americans were trained, the government set them loose on the Indians. An unsettling metaphor, it reveals much about the thinking of white officers during colonial times. Furthermore, this history is a complex and reprehensible element of African American heritage that deserves more scrutiny and discussion.

Allegedly, when Indians first saw these Black soldiers, it was the dead of winter. The soldiers hid in the snow under buffalo skins, so they became known to Indians as the "Buffalo Soldiers." Henceforth came the (now) famous Bob Marley and the Wailers reggae recording "Buffalo Soldiers." First recorded in 1978, it memorialized the title in an anthem that was beloved around the world. A protest song, it was written by Bob Marley and Noel "King Sporty" Williams. Marley and Williams had been both troubled and fascinated by how the United States government had coerced a cavalry out of former slaves by giving them no choice. Marley linked the willingness to fight as cavalry to a "fight for survival" and recast their status as a symbol of African American resistance. The sad irony of coerced African American participation in the Indian Wars is captured in Marley and Williams's haunting lyrics and forlorn lament.[19] Many of the last of the great Indian leaders, such as Geronimo and other Apache chiefs, were chased down by the Ninth and Tenth Cavalry.

There are at least two films titled *Buffalo Soldier*. First there is the 1970 movie *Soul Soldier* (produced under the working title "Men of the Tenth," originally released as *The Red, White, and Black*), later released on home video in the United States as *Buffalo Soldier*. There is also the 1997 made-for-TV movie *Buffalo Soldiers*, directed by Charles Haid and starring Danny Glover, Carl Lumbly, Clifton Powell, Matt Ross, Glynn Turman, Michael Warren, and Mykelti Williamson.

Despite John Ford's influence, the acclaimed director allegedly had a difficult time securing Woody Strode for the titular role in *Rutledge*. The studio brass at Warner Bros. wanted an established actor like Sidney Poitier or Harry Belafonte to play the title role, but Ford felt they were not tough enough. "He didn't care that I didn't have a lot of acting experience," quipped Strode. "He wanted somebody who could portray the image of a fighting man. . . . He didn't want an actor who needed a double." Given his power and influence, Ford prevailed, securing Strode for the role. Throughout production, the director worked closely with his apprentice to craft the performance he wanted from Strode.

In *Goal Dust*, Woody Strode recounts how bulldogged and tough Ford was:

> Sometimes I would be listening to him but I wouldn't be looking at him. Boy, that would really make him angry. He'd scream at me, "WHY AREN'T YOU WATCHING ME?" . . .
>
> In one scene he really upset me. I was supposed to be spying on the Indians. I was sneaking through the bushes, he hollered, "WOODY, YOU SON OF A BITCH, QUIT NIGGERING UP MY GOD-DAMNED SCENE!"
>
> I had been tiptoeing, like I was scared. He wanted me to move with intelligence and cunning. Sergeant Rutledge wasn't a tiptoer; he was proud and dignified.[20]

In this instance, and in the climactic courtroom scene, John Ford pushed and provoked Strode by testing his personal limits, at times reportedly bringing Strode to the brink of tears. The actor recalls the big courtroom scene as the most emotional moment of his entire acting career, calling it "the truest moment I ever had on the screen." Ford's use of racist epithets and racial intimidation elicited the performance of demoralization and mortification he wanted from the browbeaten Woody Strode. However, the director's methods also indicate that virulent racism and emotional abuse were not off limits to John Ford but merely another set of tools he deployed when he deemed necessary.

When they finished making the picture, Strode felt tremendously lucky to have connected with John Ford, saying that while he almost had a nervous breakdown making *Sergeant Rutledge*, the experience helped him to become an actor.[21] The backing of someone with Ford's industry clout and stature was certainly a boon to Strode's budding career. Strode undoubtedly surmised he was paying his dues. Nevertheless, he was assailed by the director's deploying the very racial mistreatment and prejudice that Ford supposedly sought to expose with the movie's themes. Baiting Strode with the N-word to belittle, disparage, and unnerve him, Ford successfully pushed Strode to (re)act by striking back in a manner that was uncharacteristic for this otherwise mild-mannered Cherokee African American man. These scenes—and Ford's general tactics—speak volumes about the circuitous and distasteful routes Hollywood directors sometimes used to tackle American race relations.

Brian Henderson's influential structural analysis of *The Searchers* addresses how myth operates by transposing the terms of the actual conflict into other sets of binary oppositions. *The Searchers*, Henderson argues, had to do with 1956, not with the 1868–1873 period in which it is set.[22] But by the time *Sergeant Rutledge* emerged four years later, in 1960, the need to transpose Native Indians for Black Americans was beginning to wane. Black-white race relations could be openly addressed, particularly as studios needed more salacious content to compete with competition from television. What's more, John Ford sought to distinguish *Sergeant Rutledge* from redface westerns like John Huston's *The Unforgiven* and Don Siegel's *Flaming Star*, in which white celebrities (e.g., Natalie Wood, Jeffrey Hunter, Audrey Hepburn, and Elvis Presley) portrayed Native Americans. Released the same year as *Rutledge*, both *The Unforgiven* and *Flaming Star* functioned as mythical tales about Native-settler racism on the frontier.

The social dramas addressing interracial desire, (e.g., *Island in the Sun* [Robert Rossen, 1957], *Band of Angels* [Raoul Walsh, 1957], *Tamango* [John Berry, 1958]) sought to capitalize on taboo race relations and conflicts in American society. Many mainstream American spectators longed to see what was considered forbidden and to peer inside these taboo relationships. Social problem pictures offered a brief peephole glimpse of sexual taboos in much the same way fin de siècle flipbooks and primitive motion pictures offered peep show images of scantily clad women for patrons of Thomas Edison's kinetoscope sixty years earlier.

According to Joseph McBride and Michael Wilmington, scenarist Willis Goldbeck presented Ford with a Frederic Remington painting of Black cavalrymen and suggested they write a script to present the story of the colored soldier and his contribution to the Western march of American empire. McBride and Wilmington claim, "Ford's goal was to turn this reactionary idea into a brutally frank examination of American social justice." The filmmakers considered this project progressive and provocative because it centered on an enduring *modern* fear of Blacks in 1960, not Indians in 1860. More significantly, it emerged when access to civil rights was a pressing national issue. The two authors claim that Ford's intention was to confront what he believed was the primary issue at the heart of racism: sex.[23] But even if McBride and Wilmington are correct about Ford's objectives, Ford's narrow framing of racial tensions is problematically reductive, wrought with simplistic misunderstandings. There are many complex issues at the heart of racism, including power, capital, and the social construction of "whiteness as property."[24]

In *Sergeant Rutledge* the eponymous African American soldier is a liberated slave who now identifies as First Sergeant Braxton Rutledge, C Troop, Ninth Unites States Cavalry. This is the highest rank a Black officer could have reached in the nineteenth century. When the story begins, Rutledge is caught at the scene of a crime and stands on trial before an all-white court-martial. He is prosecuted and defended by white officers for the rape and murder of a white woman at a U.S. Army fort in early 1881. The crimes of which Rutledge is accused are both symbolically and literally insurrectionary because he is also accused of killing the woman's father, who is his post commander and senior officer. A gold cross, torn from the young woman's neck and now missing, stands in as a metonym for the purity he has defiled.[25] Rutledge is defended by Lieutenant Tom Cantrell (Jeffrey Hunter), Rutledge's troop officer.

The story is told through a series of flashbacks, expanding the testimony of witnesses as they describe the events following the murder of Rutledge's commanding officer, Major Dabney, and the rape and murder of Dabney's daughter. The circumstantial evidence suggests Rutledge's guilt, especially since he was seen leaving the major's house at the time of the murders. Worse still, Rutledge deserts his post after the killings. Ultimately he is tracked down and arrested by Lieutenant Cantrell. At one point, Rutledge escapes from captivity during an Indian raid, but later he voluntarily returns to warn fellow cavalrymen that they are about to face an ambush, thus saving the troops. He is brought in to face the charges and prejudices of an all-white military court. Through a series of flashbacks reminiscent of Akira Kurosawa's *Rashomon* (1950), extradiegetic spectators watching the film learn of Rutledge's true heroism.

A chivalrous man and loyal soldier, he had actually saved Mary Beecher, another white woman, from Apaches and prevented his patrol from being ambushed. Daniel O'Brien notes that in one flashback, Rutledge interrogates Mary to extract vital information to save both of their lives when they are hiding from Apaches. He strips to the waist in front of her so that she can dress his wounds. Consequently, the sexual tension between them is mitigated by his injuries. Having lost much blood, he slumps into an unconscious state. As O'Brien notes, promotional material for *Sergeant Rutledge* included images of a bare-chested Strode, but the film carefully skirts the aggressive primitive sexuality it marketed.[26] It toys with the titillation of interracial sexual tension but complies with the Hays Production Code regulations.

The film concludes with attorney Cantrell exonerating Rutledge of rape and murder charges after a local white storekeeper breaks down under questioning and admits that *he* attacked the girl. As McBride and Wilmington note, Ford had previously used the courtroom drama "trial as theater" device in *Young Mr. Lincoln* (1939). In these films the trial was a metaphor for a society coming to terms with guilt by acquitting an ostracized defendant. The device proved successful in *Stars in My Crown*, but *Rutledge* failed, in many ways, to deliver an honest examination of American social injustice despite Ford's intentions.

Frank Manchel is one defender of the film and Ford's ideological stance. In his essay "Losing and Finding John Ford's *Sergeant Rutledge* (1960)," Manchel offers an explanation for why the film failed commercially. He challenges its "lackluster status," claiming it provides insight to John Ford, to Hollywood, and to challenges facing African Americans in the 1960s.[27] Manchel asserts that because Rutledge is Black, public opinion assumes he is guilty, particularly because the film is ensconced in the "miscegenation taboo" and the assumed desirability of white women to Black men.[28]

At one point, Rutledge himself laments the Victorian cult of white womanhood when he solemnly tells a fellow soldier, "I walked into something none of us can fight: *white woman* business." This melodramatic yet campy double entendre in Rutledge's statement needs little explanation. But it is unpacked in Richard Dyer's analysis of the construction of whiteness and the function of white *femininity* within the construction of whiteness. Dyer writes:

> The celebration of the Victorian virgin ideal in the cinema, in stars like Lillian Gish and Mary Pickford, was part of a bid for the respectability of the medium, a class issue but indissociable from ethnicity in the USA in the early years of the twentieth century, in the form of both mass immigration of non-Nordic groups to the USA and the internal migration of African Americans from the scattered rural South to the concentrated, urban North. The white woman as angel was in these contexts both the symbol of white virtuousness and the last word in the claim that what made Whites special as a race was their non-physical, spiritual, indeed ethereal qualities. . . .
>
> The ideal itself was unstable. . . . It accorded white women a position of moral superiority and required deference to their needs, yet it was also a trap of moral obligation and unreal moral demands. It provided white men

with an object of inspirational devotion, but one which might also provoke resentment of moral superiority and sexual unavailability.[29]

Therefore, when Rutledge says, he's stepped into "white woman business," the film is acknowledging the representational quagmire or semiotic trap of white womanhood for all involved. The angelic notion of womanhood established an unobtainable ideal requiring constant surveillance or protection from frontier threats of the 1860s and Black masculinity of the integrationist 1960s. Countless films of various genres contain plots that hinge on the defense of white femininity.

Sergeant Rutledge implies that Rutledge is ensnared in a scandal from which no lawyer—indeed, no man—can extricate him. The movie tacitly underscores the universal appeal or sexual desirability of white womanhood. Problematically, Manchel does not unpack these moments of ideological ambiguity or the way *Sargent Rutledge* leaves its commentary of American institutions (e.g., the legal system, the army, Victorian womanhood) open to interpretation.

In resurrecting *Sergeant Rutledge* from obscurity and its lackluster status, Manchel notes that "during the first sixty years of film history, premiere American directors, led by John Ford and Howard Hawks, depict a frontier

FIGURE 1.1 Woody Strode plays Sergeant Rutledge and Jeffrey Hunter is Lieutenant Cantrell.

society where African Americans play an almost non-existent role." He acknowledges that had it not been for companies like the Lincoln Motion Picture Company, depictions of African American westerners in film would have been completely nonexistent. "Knowing this," says Manchel, "helps focus our attention on why *Sergeant Rutledge* is a much more revolutionary film than generally realized."[30] O'Brien concurs, saying, "*Sergeant Rutledge* valorizes African American masculinity within the context of the western genre" because it depicts Rutledge leading his men back through Monument Valley with the rousing theme song "Captain Buffalo" at the film's closing.[31]

Holding up *Rutledge* as a revolutionary cinematic text, Manchel claims the movie is consistent with Ford's changing attitudes toward the military, his new focus on the military's "arrogance and racist heritage." Second, by calling attention to race, he finds that the film aligns with the civil rights movement, a position reminiscent of Brian Henderson's well-known essay on *The Searchers*.[32] Finally, for Manchel, reading Rutledge as a Supermasculine Menial "reveals the pervasive racism of its officers, their wives and [white] civilians."[33] It intentionally positions its eponymous Black character as an unrecognized valiant hero who is steadfastly loyal to the military and whose sullied reputation must be cleared. Clearing Rutledge's reputation is the only way the legal system—and, by extension, the collective white consciousness—can be absolved of guilt for institutional inequality and racial prejudice.

Although Manchel makes provocative observations about the dominant or intended reading of *Sergeant Rutledge*, it is unclear how much John Ford's attitude toward the military had changed. Ford's films had shifted in tone in the 1950s because they depicted individual characters who had gone rogue, who were blatantly racist (e.g., Ethan Edwards) in a more liberal landscape, or who were simply outlaws. But these positions rarely reflected changed attitudes about hallowed institutions (e.g., the military, the Catholic Church, domesticity, or discourses of white femininity). The institutions were still depicted as trustworthy, sacrosanct, and inviolable.

Moreover, the film stands as a missed opportunity for both John Ford and American cinema to render a more humane and empowered portrait of the African American soldier by giving him a strong speaking voice, or more agency with which to defend himself. Within the film's diegesis, Rutledge's choice to remain silent (rather than speak to defend himself) is rationalized and motivated by the character's saintly selflessness. He is a harbinger of the "Magical Negro" trope in cinema.[34] Rutledge refuses to deny charges against him because he knows that even the suspicion of involvement with white women is enough to hang him and to reflect negatively on the other Black soldiers. He chooses to "plead the fifth" to avoid any blowback that might befall the Ninth Cavalry's remaining African American soldiers. The extradiegetic audience is led to believe that Rutledge would allow incrimination—even death—to sacrifice himself for the greater good of the Ninth's unblemished record. The character is a perverse example of the "noble savage" or sacrificial Negro who gives of himself so that the white characters may thrive.

The noble savage plot device, which functions to render Rutledge silent, ultimately denies the character agency. As a consequence of the silent martyr plot maneuver, Sergeant Braxton Rutledge personifies the African American man whom white society instinctively fears and seeks to render impotent.[35] To paraphrase Manthia Diawara, he is "the reinscription of the image of the castrated Black male in contemporary Hollywood films."[36] But rather than render Rutledge completely castrated, Ford's film allows Jeffrey Hunter's white cavalry lieutenant, Tom Cantrell, to rescue Rutledge's manhood—literally and figuratively coming to his defense by proving his innocence. In some ways, Rutledge is simultaneously the symbolic Black brute of yesteryear/the Gus of *The Birth of a Nation*/the Willie Horton of his day (read: Black rapist and murderer), and the self-sacrificing noble savage or selfless Uncle Tom (read: silent soldier and Magical Negro), willing to die so that others might live.

The irreconcilability of these opposing racial tropes (and the absence of any nuanced realism) renders Rutledge an implausibly stoic puppet rather than a fully realized character or human being. He is as wooden and stiff as the campy kangaroo courtroom is corny, clichéd, and overdone in Technicolor. The absence of Rutledge's agency stands out as a cinematic flaw. After all, he was being portrayed by an actor *Ebony* magazine described as "the former football star with the most seniority in Hollywood" and as "movieland's beautifully muscled gladiator-witchdoctor-revolutionary."[37] But Strode's strength was carefully contained by narrative maneuvers. The containment stood out as particularly peculiar because even Sidney Poitier's 1950s screen characters (which were maligned by both critics and Black activists for their assimilation and integration) exhibited anger, frustration, and even indignation at systemic racism, prejudice, and entrapment in *No Way Out, Blackboard Jungle* (1955), and *The Defiant Ones* (1958).

If scenarist Goldbeck and director Ford were seeking to avoid the tepid whitewash approach of Poitier's star vehicles by confronting interracial sexuality head-on, as McBride claims, they inadvertently made other missteps. First, the film's flashbacks confuse consensual and nonconsensual interracial sex by suggesting that any proximity between white women and Black men results in assault. But consensual (interracial) sex is not the same as (interracial) rape; nor should the two be conflated. In the film, Rutledge is not accused of having consensual sex with Mary Beecher (Constance Towers), despite consensual intimacy between them. He is accused of raping a white girl, making his alleged crimes reminiscent of Gus's pursuit of Flora Cameron, or "Little Sister," in *The Birth of a Nation* (1915). That there was any slippage between consensual sex and rape speaks volumes about how Ford and Goldbeck (in conceptualizing Black masculinity, interracial sexuality, and consent) sought to critique race prejudice. They attempted to do it without revising the dominant images and stereotypes of Black men as potential rapists.

Second, the narrative world seems false because the extradiegetic film audience knew what would have happened to Rutledge in the "real" world. He would have been disciplined by the dominant discourses of white hetero-patriarchy. The silent soldier would have faced execution. As McBride and Wilmington note in their essay, "The end of the film, superficially, is a triumph but it is really only a triumph for white society which has been redeemed from an act of barbarism. Under ordinary circumstances, Rutledge would probably have been found guilty and condemned to hang or would perhaps have been lynched without a trial."[38]

Watching *Rutledge* today, it is nearly impossible for contemporary audiences to ignore these truisms about racial representation and the lack of realism in the courtroom scenes, which present the entire legal proceedings in naïve camp. *Sergeant Rutledge* fails to be believable in part because it neglects to give its eponymous character a voice with which to speak directly, rendering the story totally implausible.

Third, the director's attempt to belie prevailing societal fears of Black men is undermined by the film's focus on Jeffrey Hunter's heroics in his role as Lieutenant Cantrell. This is consistent with Heather Hicks's thesis that the supernatural forces ascribed to many Black male characters cannot be separated from certain contemporary crises surrounding white masculinity.[39] The antiracist message is drowned out by *Sergeant Rutledge*'s cliché white liberalism, making it no more cutting edge than *Blackboard Jungle*, with its similarly liberal-minded character Richard Dadier (Glenn Ford) and similarly stoic Black male character Gregory Miller (Sidney Poitier). Nevertheless, *Rutledge* is a film worth watching because it was one of the first mainstream Hollywood westerns to take the figure of the Buffalo Soldier (or Black cavalryman) seriously as part of frontier life. It was one of the first westerns—possibly the only western—released after *Stars in My Crown* to overtly condemn anti-Black racism.

Rutledge also deserves reconsideration because it's a constitutive part of a cohort of American movies relying on (and reifying) a specific brand of Black masculinity. The African American football-hero-turned-film-star epitomized the new virile Black masculine prowess that Hollywood film-makers branded and commodified. Moreover, this new brand of manhood was now in contestation with white masculinity. In America's complex and contradictory minefield of sexualized racial politics, Black and brown male bodies have been constructed by gender stereotypes that idealize and com-modify them as strong, muscular, and physical. But they have also been subordinated by racial stereotypes that deny Black men access to socially constructed notions of patriarchal authority.[40]

In popular cinema this minefield is navigated by actors portraying Black men in movies. We saw the first of many examples in the films of Paul Robeson, chiefly *Borderline* (1930), *The Emperor Jones* (1933), *Sanders of the River* (1935), *Show Boat* (1936), *Song of Freedom* (1936), and *Big Fella* (1937). The trope of the sexualized Black male athlete (who embodies supermascu-linity) reemerged in the career of Woody Strode. The images and signifiers associated with strong Black male athletes would be replicated throughout the 1960s and '70s with the cinematic careers of Jim Brown, Harold Bradley, Bernie Casey, Fred Williamson, and O. J. Simpson, among others.

By the early 1960s, this commodification of Black athletes was com-monplace and even fodder for mainstream magazines. *Ebony* magazine ran a cover story titled "Football Heroes Become Movie Stars." The article lightheartedly suggested that football heroes were "invading" Hollywood. Some have speculated that African American athletes came to the studios as commodities with preexisting fans. Even otherwise prejudiced specta-tors were more likely to overlook their bias for athletes who had proven themselves on the field. After all, these football stars were familiar figures on televisions in American living rooms.

Scholar Keith Harris discusses the transition of football players to film stars in his pivotal work on the ethics of Black masculinity in film and popular culture. Harris writes, "The [*Ebony*] article catalogues the then recent emergence of the black athlete as the black actor, commenting on Jim Brown, Fred Williamson, Rosie Grier, O. J. Simpson, and the earlier Paul Robeson and Woody Strode, among others."[41] To this list we should add actor Rafer Lewis Johnson, the former Olympic games decathlon champion. He portrayed the easygoing, rugged Private Armstrong in *Soul Soldier*, a drama based on the exploits of the U.S. Tenth Cavalry.[42]

According to Harris, Jim Brown's brand of masculinity is marked as both sexually aggressive and physically brutal. Symbolically, Brown represented the antithesis of Sidney Poitier, whose brand of masculinity, Harris notes, was contained by class, effeminacy, and passivity. But dichotomies between oppositional tropes or conventions of Black masculinity (e.g., tough-guy Jim Brown vs. sensitive man Sidney Poitier) leave little room for a liminal figure like Woody Strode, who stood at the interstice between the Super-masculine Menial (or hypersexual Black masculinity) and the Omnipotent Administrator (or passive, asexual, white middle-class man).

Viewing these actors through the prism of their performances in west-erns sheds light on how Strode, Poitier, Brown, Williamson, and others were iconic figures on a continuum of Black masculine superhero archetypes (or brands) deemed marketable as mainstream movie icons. Their emergence parallels the arrival of Black male comic book superheroes who possessed a similar duality or contradictory identity. As cultural historian Jeffrey Brown notes, nearly every comic book hero is a variation on the wimp-versus-warrior binary. The story of all superheroes has always been a wish-fulfilling fantasy for young men and boys.[43] Black comic book heroes had to balance conventional male attributes coded as desirable (e.g., toughness, muscularity, strength, power, mastery) with survivalist behaviors coded as undesirable but derived from challenges to their authority posed by racial inequality (e.g., circumspection, subordination, invisibility, submis-sion). A given western star's position on the masculinity continuum might change over time, particularly as Black Power emboldened later figures and impacted the sociopolitical tide of their marketability for mainstream consumption. But actors were always required to straddle these competing expectations of manhood.

Jim Brown: Rio Conchos, *100 Rifles*, and *El Condor*

James Nathaniel Brown was a fullback for the NFL's Cleveland Browns from 1957 through 1965. When his relationship with management began to deteriorate, Brown left football to star in nine films. The first three of these can be described as a western trilogy: *Rio Conchos, 100 Rifles*, and *El Condor*. A decade earlier, director John Ford had helped legitimize the western genre as arthouse fare with his Cavalry trilogy (*Fort Apache*, 1948; *She Wore a Yellow Ribbon*; and *Rio Grande*, 1950). Unpacking Brown's westerns reveals much about his brand of celebrity and commodifica-tion, about the shifting concepts of acceptable Black masculinity in 1960s America, and about the evolution of the western genre as it gradually transformed to maintain cultural relevance.[44] Examining these movies also puts the careers of multiple African American actors into dialogue. For example, whereas Sidney Poitier was a mainstream commodity and therefore allowed to portray a fuller range of characters and emotions in his film work, Jim Brown was generally limited to exemplifying and personifying stoic Black macho.

Today Brown is still considered to be among the greatest football players of all time. If there was one person who embodied mainstream America's fantasy of virile Black masculinity coupled with sexual prowess and progressive activism, it was Brown. He was able to assume this iconic status and challenge some social taboos upheld for others because he excelled in sports and exuded charisma and leadership qualities. His emergence as a marquee name in movies was a direct result of his status as a leader on the football field and as an enterprising businessman. As biographer Mike Freeman observed:

> No player in the long tenure of the NFL had risen to such a position of league-wide dominance as rapidly as Brown. . . . He was named Rookie of the Year in 1957. . . . By the late 1950s, Jim was not just influential, he was one of the most powerful men inside the [Cleveland] Browns organization, particularly among the black players. . . . Black players in those days were treated as second class citizens and Jim decided to do something that others had discussed but never enacted. Jim organized. . . . Brown's message was, "I'm a man. Don't disrespect me." Black players in the NFL were not saying that then. As Black players were signed by the Browns, their attitude changed overnight, they became more proud and defiant. That was Jim. He set the tone across the league for black players.[45]

But Brown had managed to invest in many businesses along the way, demonstrating successful entrepreneurship in radio, restaurants, and consumer products. He continued to be one of the most visible players in the early '60s when the NFL was growing from a niche league to a powerful national enterprise, and his leadership extended beyond the NFL. He represented the changing persona of professional athletes because he was more outspoken about civil rights and more dedicated to African American socioeconomic uplift than many other athletes at the time.

Forming the Black Economic Union was one example of his growing racial consciousness. Brown enabled African American football players to literally invest in civil rights activism by establishing the Negro Industrial Economic Union (NIEU), a Black financial organization chartered to build a financial infrastructure for Black and minority businesses.[46] From Frederick Douglass to Richard Wright, to Stokely Carmichael, to Rosa Parks and Maya Angelou, the term "Black Power" had various meanings. To some it meant Black nationalism, to others Black separatism, and to still others it said Black self-determination. The common denominator among various interpretations was the idea of Black *enfranchisement*. All of Brown's well-known biographers (Stan Isaacs, Mike Freeman, Steve Delsohn, and Dave Zirin) noted his resolute belief in the relationship between Black self-determination (or racial uplift) and economic empowerment. Zirin, for example, observes that for Brown, Black Power meant the "patriotic assertion of black capitalism: the idea that Black America needed to build up its own economic institutions and enrich itself as a path to liberation. Only that path, not the path of protest, could bring power in a society that valued wealth even more than maintaining white supremacy."[47]

By the early 1960s, Brown epitomized Black Power. He was a star athlete, an entrepreneur, a civil rights leader in the public eye, and a lothario known for some ill-fated womanizing. His successful antiracist activism led the Federal Bureau of Investigation (FBI) to investigate him, as it did many Black athletes and activists, to diminish the credibility and popularity of African American leaders. Ironically, while the FBI was spying on him, the Nixon administration was working with Brown's NIEU foundation (at one point contributing as much as a quarter of a million dollars).[48] Even Malcolm X and Muhammad Ali sought him out as a comrade and colleague. Their friendship was commemorated in Regina King's film *One Night in Miami* (2020), a fictionalized account of a February 1964 meeting between Malcolm X, Muhammad Ali, Jim Brown, and Sam Cooke in a room at the Hampton House to celebrate Ali's surprise title win over Sonny Liston.

In the 1960s Jim Brown signified more than rugged, handsome athlete. He epitomized Black financial empowerment, self-determination construed as militancy, and audacious sexual libertinism. These were considered threatening attributes for Black men to possess—particularly after the Sixteenth Street Baptist Church bombing in 1963, which was a turning point in the civil rights movement. But Brown appealed to competing constituencies. He appealed to Black Power activists, professional athletes, and struggling Hollywood studios that were trying to produce politically and culturally relevant movies for youth audiences. Many viewed him as the antidote to, or the antithesis of, Sidney Poitier's virtually sexless screen persona. Arguably, it is not enough to identify the semiotics of Brown's iconicity; it is also important to consider the intersecting forms of social, cultural, and athletic capital to understand the multivalence of his celebrity as a western movie icon.

Brown made three key western films early in his career: *Rio Conchos*, *100 Rifles*, and *El Condor*. He would also co-star with Fred Williamson and Jim Kelly in *Take a Hard Ride* and make other action pictures as well, but his first foray into filmmaking was in this hallowed American genre. In his autobiography, *Out of Bounds*, the athlete/actor disavowed the idea that his films—particularly the westerns—were blaxploitation pictures. He proclaimed, "Not only did I *not* make black exploitation films, but I was also playing roles that normally went only to white guys."[49] In point of fact, that much is true. In *Rio Conchos*, Brown's first film, his character exhibits conventional, conservative American values: frontier stoicism, a jingoistic patriotism, obedient soldiering, and anti–Native American bias. If there was ever any question that African Americans were committed to defending the Union and to westward expansion, Jim Brown's character Ben Franklyn was there to cinematically set the record straight. One is hard-pressed to find any critique of American colonialism or countercultural, antiestablishment political resonance in the picture.

What's more, such roles have not been taken seriously by most critics. Mike Freeman describes Brown's performance in comic book terms when he says, "In *Rio Conchos* Brown blasted his way onto the screen bare-chested and biceps bulging, getting into gunfights and saving damsels in distress. . . . He plays a sergeant from the United States Cavalry attempting to track down stolen weapons in a post–Civil War America. He was not a thespian, not a superb speaker of dialogue; he was all testosterone and guts. . . . In other words, he was like every other action star of the time, except he possesses a different skin color."[50] Even Brown admitted he resisted any formal dramatic training. In the press kits he remarks, "Fortunately, I had Gordon Douglas as director on my first picture, *Rio Conchos*. Otherwise, I might have quit. He was very sympathetic, very easy to work with. He told me not to try to act."[51]

Similarly, in *100 Rifles* Brown's character, Lyedecker, is a duty-bound police officer. There's little to distinguish him as a Black American. Finally, in *El Condor* he and Lee Van Cleef are unsavory fortune seekers in an interracial buddy western adventure that foreshadows the comedic antics of Richard Pryor and Gene Wilder two decades later. Once again there are only a few passing references to race relations. In summary, Freeman's comment is accurate. Brown *was* playing the Westerner like every other action star—with no overt political bite. From Brown's perspective, this is what made the films revolutionary. Perhaps filmmakers were also thinking the mere "fact of his blackness" at this time was itself enough to call attention to racial politics and complicate the genre's semiotics. Nevertheless, it is productive to look at *Rio Concho* alongside *100 Rifles* and *El Condor* to understand the coalescence between Brown's celebrity capital, the changing parameters for Black masculinity, and the evolution of the western genre.

Rio Conchos opens with a shocking scene of a white man shooting several Indians from a distance in cold blood. What makes the scene even more disturbing is the fact that the shooting takes place as the victims are burying their own dead. We soon learn that the shooter (a character who reads like a revival of John Wayne's Ethan Edwards from *The Searchers*) is Major Jim Lassiter (Richard Boone), an ex-Confederate officer who begins killing Apaches because his wife and child were tortured to death by Apache chief Bloodshirt's men. Lassiter is discovered and arrested by U.S. Army officer

Captain Haven (Stuart Whitman) when he's found drunk at his burned-down home and—importantly—in possession of an expensive rifle that was part of a cache of firearms stolen from the army.[52]

Haven is accompanied by Sergeant Ben Franklyn (Brown), whose status as a Buffalo Soldier evokes Lassiter's enmity. Lassiter's racial prejudice is revealed during their initial meeting. First, he brazenly boasts about being an Apache killer. And when he's commanded to saddle up to be taken to Fort Davis, he sneers in disgust before hurling his saddle in Franklyn's face. Without blinking or wincing, Franklyn stares back, unfazed by Lassiter's petty aggression. The opening encounter between Boone's roguish Lassiter and Brown's upstanding Franklyn established the latter's unflinching tough-guy screen persona and evoked the strength Brown was known for on the football field and in civil rights struggles. These traits typify his screen roles, particularly in this western trilogy.

Once apprehended, Lassiter is taken back to Fort Davis for questioning by Colonel Wagner (Warner Anderson). Lassiter withholds the location of the remaining two thousand stolen rifles and refuses to cooperate. But after he is imprisoned, he eventually admits to purchasing the firearms from a band of Southern renegades.

Lassiter agrees to a bargain to secure his freedom. He accepts Colonel Wagner's mission: to track Pardee and uncover where Pardee is staging a Confederate attack on the Union with an army of Apaches using the stolen rifles.

The character of Juan (played by Anthony Franciosa) is an over-the-top stereotype of Mestizo identity all too common in American westerns of this era. Referred to as a "half-breed" to signify his mixed Spanish and Indian heritage, he's portrayed as the epitome of a selfish, greedy, and duplicitous "greaser" caricature common in countless westerns. Franciosa plays the caricature with campy inflection.[53] When Lassiter appoints Juan, he rescues him from being hanged only to dispose of him later. Colonel Wagner accepts Lassiter's terms (agreeing to Juan's appointment) because he believes it's the only way that Lassiter will guide the search for Pardee.

Despite distrusting each other, the four men (Captain Haven, Sergeant Franklyn, Major Lassiter, and Juan Rodriguez) set out for Presidio, Texas, in search of Pardee at Colonel Wagner's command.[54] Their goal: retrieve the stolen arms by using a wagon full of gunpowder as bait for Pardee's stockpile. They successfully defeat the banditos and take along an Apache girl named Sally (Wende Wagner) as translator and guide. Whereas Lassiter tries first to kill her, Haven intervenes and safeguards Sally, showing her kindness with the goal of learning Pardee's whereabouts. She knows where Pardee plans to amass and equip the Apache marauders.

The unlikely confederation rides onward to Presidio to cross the Rio Grande. At a Presidio saloon, racial tensions erupt. A bartender refuses to serve Franklyn (despite the presence of Mexican senoritas cavorting with Texas Rangers). To create a diversion, Lassiter flips to defend Franklyn and toasts the Union instead (a change of political sides). He angers the men in the bar with his pro-Union slogans and a brawl breaks out. Lassiter and Franklyn use this commotion to divert attention while Rodriguez takes the wagon across the river. Once the group has crossed to the other side, they encounter more obstacles. They come across a burned-out homestead, where a ravaged woman and sick infant lay in bed. But the woman and child have been left as bait in a trap. Even worse, they are a brutal reminder of Lassiter's own deceased family. Initially, Jim Brown's Ben Franklyn comforts the crying child in a gesture that demonstrates sensitivity. Franklyn's gentle childcare is juxtaposed against Lassiter's "mercy killing" of the infant's mother, whom he shoots moments before, upon discovering her molested, near-dead body.

In these scenes and throughout the movie, *Rio Conchos* repeatedly juxtaposes Franklyn's (and Haven's) morality and tolerance with Lassiter's immorality and bigotry. The contrast is legible as a 1960s countercultural metaphor for the Northern civil rights activists (embodied by the interracial "union" of Union soldiers Franklyn and Haven with Sally) versus the Southern resistance to desegregation (as personified by the aging Confederate major Jim Lassiter). Here the Black soldier joins an ensemble of resisters against the tyranny of intolerance, which becomes more meaningful by the film's dénouement.

Lassiter tracks Colonel Pardee's encampment to Rio Conchos in the Mexican state of Chihuahua, where he pretends he's a gunpowder salesman. After an initial reunion, Lassiter realizes that Pardee's gun customer is none other than Chief Bloodshirt (Rodolfo Acosta). In a transition suggesting that some of the film's continuity was left on the cutting room floor, Pardee turns against Lassiter when Bloodshirt arrives. The colonel allows the Apaches to horse-drag and bull-whip Lassiter, Haven, and Franklyn together for their attempted subterfuge.

Ironically, it is Sally who, after witnessing their torture, takes pity on her bruised former captors and frees them. She realizes that Pardee's plan will only bring more war to her tribe and other Indians. Together Lassiter, Haven, Franklyn, and Sally set off a destructive chain reaction by setting fire to the paddocks and igniting the wagon of gunpowder. When it explodes, Colonel Pardee helplessly watches it, and his entire camp, go up in flames. The Confederate insurgency is thwarted in the end.

Throughout *Rio Concho*, Brown's cavalry officer is part of an ensemble of characters. Within the film's diegesis, his identity as an African American man takes a backseat to his status as a loyal, upstanding U.S. military man and cavalry officer. Brown's Ben Franklyn is not politically progressive or critical of U.S. policies toward Native Americans, which is what led film historian Donald Bogle to observe that Brown's characters rarely express overt political views in these films. In *Rio Concho* he is a steadfastly loyal cavalry soldier, dedicated to service.

However, the portrait of an African American man valiantly fighting to protect the Union from a rogue Confederate colonel was itself political. The commercial success of *Rio Conchos* and the understated (or nonthreatening) nature of Brown's character enabled filmmakers to hazard casting him in more risqué roles, like that of Lyedecker in *100 Rifles*. Immediately after the release of *Rio Conchos*, Brown starred in several other films, including *The Dirty Dozen* (Robert Aldrich, 1967); *Ice Station Zebra* (John Sturges, 1968); *The Split* (Gordon Flemying, 1969); *Riot* (Seymour Buzz Kulik, 1969); *100 Rifles*; *The Grasshopper* (Jerry Paris, 1970); *Kenner* (Steve Sekely, 1970); . . . *tick . . . tick . . . tick . . .* (Ralph Nelson, 1970); and *El Condor*. With the exception of *The Grasshopper*, all were either action films, westerns, or war pictures.

None of these films was as controversial as *100 Rifles*, which politicized Brown's screen persona. The film was even more contentious because of the interracial relationship (and sex scene) between Brown and Raquel Welch, who was playing an Apache rebel named Sarita. In making *100 Rifles*, Brown raised the volume on his sexual persona with their lovemaking scene, brief though it is, and, together with Welch, challenged American cinema's long-held miscegenation taboo. According to some historians, this choice was an ill-fated decision that led to the gradual demise of Brown's screen career by splitting his audience between those Southerners for whom interracial sexuality was offensive and those Northerners for whom the sex scene didn't live up to the film's sensational advertising.

There's yet another way of interpreting the mixed audience response to Brown's (and Welch's) work in *100 Rifles*. In the 1960s love scenes were somewhat uncharacteristic and atypical of the western genre—with or without the titillation of interracial coupling to spice things up. The classic western hero archetype was incompatible with domesticity, family, traditional relationships, or long-term intimacy because his chosen life as a wandering gunslinger precluded them. The mixed response to Brown's sex scenes might have been a result of spectator expectations being challenged by the overt, intimate relationship.

In earlier westerns and war pictures, romance and sexuality were rarely foregrounded mainly due to the self-regulatory censorship of the Hays Production Code. There were exceptions to the conventions, such as Howard Hughes's *The Outlaw* (1943), which featured buxom bombshell Jane Russell, and King Vidor's *Duel in the Sun* (1946), featuring Jennifer Jones, which came to be known as "lust in the dust." With some exceptions, the Hays Code (and concomitant generic conventions) precluded explicit romance. Until this point, the western was known for solidifying Hollywood's brand of rugged American masculinity—minus intimacy with women. Masculinity is fundamentally a homosocial enactment demonstrated in an all-male arena for other men's approval. Classic Hollywood westerns were known for their predominantly (white) male casts (add the lonesome prostitute or "hooker with a heart of gold"). Westerns were less appreciated for scenes of passionate lovemaking, and the genre's typical fans did not go to these movies seeking romance.

The film *100 Rifles*, and a handful of others like it, represented the beginning of a cultural shift in which American movies became more sexually explicit in part as a way of competing commercially with the European modernist art cinema featuring scantily clad French sex symbols like Mylène Demongeot and Brigitte Bardot, or Italian pinups Sophia Loren and Gina Lollobrigida, and Swedish beauties Anita Ekberg, Harriet Andersson, and Berit (Bibi) Elisabet Andersson.

In his article "Jim Brown: From Integration to Re-segregation," Joshua Gleich offers an excellent close reading of Brown's sexuality and career as an action hero, but he mistakenly marks *The Dirty Dozen* (1967) as the beginning of Brown's film career. Brown announced he was retiring from acting at age twenty-nine during the making of the film. Allegedly, the owner of the Cleveland Browns, Art Modell, demanded Brown choose between football and acting. Even with Brown's considerable accomplishments in the sport (he was already the NFL's all-time leading rusher, was well ahead statistically of the second-leading rusher, and his team had won the 1964 NFL Championship), he chose acting. The filming of *The Dirty Dozen* was held up until after *Rio Conchos* was released.

Brown began carving out his screen persona with 20th Century Fox's western *Rio Conchos*. Both *Rio Conchos* and *100 Rifles* were produced and distributed by Fox. And *El Condor* was distributed by National General Pictures, a division of National General Corporation, the successor of 20th Century Fox's theater division (a theater-chain holding company for film distribution and production that was considered one of the "instant majors" in operation from 1951 to 1973).[55] All three movies were Fox-affiliated productions, all three featured Jim Brown, and all three placed him as the only Black American in an otherwise western milieu of white settlers versus Native Americans.

The film *100 Rifles* is set in 1912 Sonora, Mexico. It begins when Lyedecker, an African American police officer (and bounty hunter) from Phoenix, rides into Sonora to find Yaqui Joe Herrera (Burt Reynolds), a half-Indian, half-white bank robber who has stolen six thousand dollars to buy the eponymous rifles for his people who are struggling under the Mexican government's yoke. After shamelessly mistreating a prostitute (Soledad Miranda) with whom he'd spent the previous night, Yaqui Joe's whereabouts are revealed to authorities when the prostitute screams out the window to broadcast his location. The despotic Mexican general Verdugo (Fernando Lamas)—scripted as a caricature of the proverbial corrupt South American military officer—apprehends Joe for creating the massive disruption. Verdugo is particularly perturbed at Joe because a group of Yaqui men Verdugo pressed into service nearly escapes during the disturbance. Just as the general tries to execute Joe, Lyedecker intervenes and informs the general that Joe is worth six thousand dollars.

Back at General Verdugo's quarters, Lyedecker learns that Yaqui Joe already purchased the one hundred rifles for the oppressed Yaqui Indian people. Unconcerned with their oppression, Lyedecker cares only about returning the money to a Phoenix bank within his jurisdiction so that he can earn a two-hundred-dollar reward and a permanent position as a policeman. Lyedecker and Joe escape Verdugo's wrath by fleeing into the mountains, where they are joined by Sarita, a beautiful Indian revolutionary who watched Verdugo's men hang her father.

With General Verdugo and his men in close pursuit, Joe picks up Sarita to secure her help obtaining rifles for the Indians. But Lyedecker intervenes, refusing to join them. Before they can convince Lyedecker of their cause, their meeting is interrupted by Verdugo's men, who take them prisoners. Back at Verdugo's compound, the general has already confiscated the rifles. Facing execution by Verdugo's firing squad, Joe and Lyedecker have their first real argument about race, class, and racial discrimination. Ironically, it is Yaqui Joe who lectures Lyedecker about the prejudice and racial profiling practiced by northern policemen. Seconds before the firing squad opens fire, Sarita and a group of armed Yaqui arrive and attack Verdugo's compound, liberating Lyedecker and Joe and retrieving the weapons. After the shootout, only Verdugo; the railroad manager, Steve Grimes (Daniel Peter O'Herlihy); and Lt. Franz Von Klemme (Eric Braeden) remain alive. Lyedecker pulls Joe onto his horse and they ride double out of the camp, following Sarita's lead.

In the mountains, Sarita tends to the wounded men while Joe and Lyedecker strategize their next steps. Despite being handcuffed together, Lyedecker still intends to transport Joe to Phoenix rather than assist in liberating the Yaqui Indian people. Cursed by Joe for this selfish individualism, Lyedecker responds, "Look, I spent fifteen years in the Ninth Cavalry, keeping the law and chasin' *bad* Indians. But *this* one ain't my business, it ain't my fight. And it ain't my job! Besides . . . I don't much like Indians, anyway."

Significantly, this is the narrative moment when Lyedecker's anti-Indian bigotry metaphorically represents the sentiments of mainstream society. This conflict in the film plays out in an exchange of racial epithets and eventually a brawl between the handcuffed fugitives. Their fight, which takes place on the edge of a cliff, plays like a scene from Stanley Kramer's *The Defiant Ones* (1958). Kramer's classic social problem picture (starring Sidney Poitier and Tony Curtis) was the first to involve the racial, class, and even homoerotic tensions inherent in having two escaped convicts (one Black, one white) handcuffed together and on the lam. The fight exhausts both Lyedecker and Joe, and they fight to a draw. Unable to force each other into submission, they agree to cooperate. When Lyedecker saves Joe from falling off the cliff, he spares both of their lives. No sooner do they cease fighting than they mount up to flee Verdugo and his men, who have emerged on the horizon.

In their quarrel we see the two diverging modes of masculinity commonly on display in the western genre. There is the age-old tension between two key points of attraction: the *symbolic figure* (who represents social integration, marriage, and respectability) and the nostalgic narcissism of the *social outsider* or gunslinger. In Jim Brown's Lyedecker we find the desire for social integration, the pursuit of regular employment, longing for stability, and respectability as a lawman.

FIGURE 1.2 Looking like the defiant ones, Burt Reynolds and Jim Brown in *100 Rifles*.

In Burt Reynold's Yaqui Joe we find the anachronistic social outsider who (though he delivered rifles to aid his people's cause) resists social integration, eschews responsibility, and maintains a lifestyle of wanderlust and drunken revelry.[56] The Yaqui Joe character is a reprisal of Burt Reynolds's similarly named Indian character in the film *Navajo Joe* (1966), an influential Italian western directed by Sergio Corbucci.[57] In *Navajo Joe*, Reynolds stars as the titular character who opposes a group of bandits responsible for killing his tribe. Thus, in both movies he portrays wild-eyed indigenous men battling anti-Native aggression (e.g., bandits, militia, American colonialism). These characters are "Hollywoodized" Indians, caricatures with no meaningful reference to actual Native American resisters.[58]

Sarita's choice of the African American Lyedecker over the Native American Yaqui Joe as a romantic interest and sexual partner suggests that she recognizes the difference between their competing brands of masculinity regardless of race. It also suggests that the filmmakers were more interested in exploiting the Black-white miscegenation taboo between Brown and Welch, which was much more threatening to the status quo.

In many ways, an African American athlete/actor like Jim Brown was an ideal figure to embody the symbolic in the narrative. After all, African American aspirations for equal opportunity, access to education, civil rights, and economic enfranchisement are constitutive of the symbolic order. The fact that Brown was a civil rights leader among world-class athletes strengthened his semiotic value as a signifier of masculine leadership. This is the extradiegetic context the film used to support its last chapter. After delivering the rifles to the Yaqui resistance, the Indians elect Lyedecker, rather than Joe, as their general, and he reluctantly accepts. The film clearly harnessed the the image of Brown as a respected political figure.

When Verdugo's men descend upon a Yaqui village and kidnap the children, it's the tipping point that convinces Lyedecker to join forces with Joe and Sarita in pursuit of the kidnapped children and apprehend Verdugo. After a successful raid on Verdugo's encampment, Lyedecker sits in the bedroom half-dressed, injured, and bleeding. Sarita gently tends to his wounds. While admiring his physique, she kisses him to express desirous appreciation. But what starts out as tender affection quickly turns aggressive. Lyedecker reciprocates roughly by grabbing Sarita, caveman-style, and she willingly submits. At this moment *100 Rifles* reanimates the stereotype of the brutal Black buck who manhandles, mistreats, or molests women (particularly white, Indian, or Mexican women). The stereotype has cinematic origins in *The Birth of a Nation* and many other cultural productions in which Black men are depicted as sexually threatening to white women. Historically, this trope stood in metonymically for civil society. The messaging to audiences was clear: Black men should be contained because they threaten the social order.

In the heat of the moment, Sarita belts out, "No! Please, not like this! Not with you." In a sudden reversal, Lyedecker responds caringly. He releases her, steps back, and approaches her a second time. This time he is gentle. He walks slowly toward the bedpost and carefully embraces her. They tumble backward onto the bed, and the camera slowly pans away to the exterior of the ranch, where Yaqui objectors feverishly raid Verdugo's ranch. This oddly schizophrenic love scene—set against the background of a raid—suggests that what lurks inside Lyedecker is the primitive, brute force that can be tamed.

Hereafter, there is no mention of Sarita and Lyedecker's physical relationship other than one momentary exchange. After cooking dinner for him the next day, Sarita tells Lyedecker, "You're my man," to which he responds, "You know, you have to be careful about a thing like that." The script and director Tom Gries leave it ambiguous as to whether Lyedecker is referring to attachments generally or their coupling particularly. The ambiguity works to the film's benefit because it serves the dual purpose of enabling the male character—and the viewing audience—to remain ambivalent about monogamous heterosexual commitment. Though *100 Rifles* depicts an interracial romantic intimacy that other films avoided, it ultimately shows the relationship to be ill-fated, thereby avoiding any endorsement of long-term interracial unions.

Outside of the film, the scene caused considerable controversy—at least according to the leading actors. But the reports are contradictory. In documentary interviews Jim Brown and Raquel Welch reported that the set of *100 Rifles* was riddled with tensions and beset by problems. Brown claims that Welch was uncomfortable rehearsing the nude scenes with him. Welch claims that Brown was disrespectful and insensitive to her as a female actor. She has also said that her husband was protective and uncomfortable with rumors about Brown and Welch's intimacy on set. And in other interviews, both actors contradicted these statements by saying they shared a perfectly professional and unproblematic working relationship.[59] They maintained that the rumors were more publicity than truth. The conflicting accounts make it impossible to know with certainty if Welch's husband believed improprieties had taken place. And it is difficult to know the true nature of the relationship between the two actors.

Within the film, Lyedecker is elected leader of the Yaqui people because he successfully spearheads the children's rescue and leads the team onward to capture Verdugo. He successfully derails the general's train in Nogales. In the culminating battle (complete with the rifles and explosives), Lyedecker rides into Nogales to defeat Verdugo and the remaining Mexican army. With their mission accomplished and their friendship solidified, Lyedecker renounces his plan to return Joe to Phoenix. Joe assumes leadership of the Yaqui tribe after Lyedecker's departure. With Sarita fallen in battle, Lyedecker rides out of Sonora alone as the credits roll.

In *100 Rifles* the two male leads begin as adversaries, on opposite sides of the law. But they gradually unite as comrades against a common enemy. They ride double together, fight side by side with guns blazing, and plot Verdugo's demise. Their crusade is carefully coded as ultra-macho in the tradition of the western, and yet they become trusted, caring allies. The excessive display of machismo functions to disavow homoerotic tension between the men, particularly in a milieu (westerns, war films, action pictures) with few, if any, women. For decades the Hays Production Code forbade any hint of same-sex desire and required displays of heteronormativity for a film to receive the code's seal of approval.

Oftentimes villains were coded as queer, as homosexual, as pedophiles, or simply as gender-nonconforming in order to expediently (and unambiguously) demonize them within the film's diegesis.[60] In *100 Rifles* General Verdugo (who kidnaps the Yaqui children) is portrayed as the deviant villain in part because actor Fernando Lamas plays him as an exaggerated campy character.[61] The obvious pomposity of his military wardrobe, the grandiosity of his gestures and speech, his exaggerated display of masculine authority, his indifference to women, and his sadistic treatment of prisoners all function to code Verdugo as the narcissistic queer monster.[62] However, it is not only Verdugo who is played up for cinematic excess.

The entire narrative world of *100 Rifles* evokes excess. The excess includes a flamboyant performance by Welch as the stereotypical "hot tamale" spitfire Sarita. It also includes the exaggerated he-man masculinity performed by Jim Brown as Lyedecker. It encompasses Burt Reynolds as Joe, a clichéd screaming Indian outfitted with sweaty bandanas and colorful sombreros. And it includes the predictably explosive gunplay and the expected—if not hackneyed—opening and dénouement. In fact, even the actors themselves seemed to be cognizant of the film's formulas and conventions.

Burt Reynolds admitted as much about his performance by saying, "I play a *half-breed* but . . . I send it up. I make it seem like the other 'half' of the guy is from Alabama. I play it nasty, dirty, funky. I look like a Christmas tree—wrist bands, arm bands. At the beginning I even wore these funky spurs. But every time I walked, I couldn't hear dialog."[63] The role is a combination of stereotypes ("the Greaser" and "the lazy Mexican") clearly outlined and critiqued in Susan Racho's 2002 documentary, *The Bronze Screen: A Hundred Years of the Latin Image in Hollywood*.[64] Reynolds was not alone in playing to excess. Verdugo's queer villain also calls attention to the conventional masculinity of leading characters (Joe/Reynolds and Lyedecker/Brown) who are united as buddies against Verdugo's despotic deviant, thereby undergirding their heteronormativity.

The centrality of friendship between Joe and Lyedecker distinguishes *100 Rifles* (alongside *Duel at Diablo* before it) as one of the first interracial buddy westerns. Heretofore white characters acted for or on behalf of their African American or Native Indian brethren. But *100 Rifles* possesses the components of interracial buddy films as outlined by Melvin Donalson in his instructive book *Masculinity in the Interracial Buddy Film*.[65] For example, the relationship between Joe and Lyedecker is situated as the story's centerpiece, providing narrative continuity from beginning to end. Despite the extradiegetic, real-world controversies over Jim Brown's taboo-breaking love scene with Raquel Welch, it is Lyedecker's lasting bond with Joe that endures after her character's death. Second, the emotional, personal, and professional lives of Joe and Lyedecker intertwine throughout the picture. Lyedecker's bounty hunting leads him to pursue Joe and binds them symbolically. Once handcuffed, they are bound literally, giving resonance to this western as a male bonding experience. Third, as noted earlier, both men are unequivocally heterosexual. Joe frequents prostitutes, and Lyedecker sleeps with Sarita. Their heterosexuality rules out romance between them. Finally, both men make sacrifices for each other in a gesture of "mutual vulnerability," another hallmark of buddy pictures.

The interracial buddy elements that emerged subtly in *100 Rifles* are fully developed in Jim Brown's next western, *El Condor*. A more generically self-conscious, somewhat formulaic film, *El Condor* is a deliberately campy and raunchy romp about two men and a band of Apaches who try to conquer an impregnable fortress containing a fortune in gold. In the film it is General Chavez (Patrick O'Neal), one of many powerful Mexican military leaders after the American Civil War, who hides Mexico's treasury gold in the fortress El Condor. Luke (Jim Brown), a chain gang prisoner in the post–Civil War West, is informed by a fellow inmate of the fortune hidden at El Condor. Immediately after escaping the chain gang, Luke sets out to find the fortress and steal its treasure. Along the way, he allies himself with Jaroo (Lee Van Cleef) a weather-worn con man who promises Luke one hundred Apaches in exchange for half of the gold.

Along the way, they get caught shoplifting. As punishment the men are tarred and feathered by authorities. But these two super-tough guys laugh off their painful and embarrassing misfortune like schoolboys. Their silly tongue-in-cheek antics foreshadow the commercial growth of interracial buddy capers that followed, including James Garner and Louis Gossett in

Skin Game (1971); Gene Wilder and Richard Pryor in *Silver Streak* (1976), *Stir Crazy* (1980), and *See No Evil, Hear No Evil* (1989); and Eddie Murphy in *48 Hours* (1982) with Nick Nolte, in *Trading Places* (1983) with Dan Aykroyd, and in *Beverly Hills Cop* (1984) with Judge Reinhold. That's not to mention Danny Glover and Mel Gibson in the *Lethal Weapon* franchise (1987–1998). Earlier interracial buddy pairings exist (e.g., *Home of the Brave*, 1949; *Broken Arrow*, 1950; *Blackboard Jungle*, 1955; *The Defiant Ones*), but in 1950s social problem pictures, racial inequality remained intact. Black characters were still struggling for respect. This differs considerably from *Duel at Diablo*, *100 Rifles*, and *El Condor*, in which camaraderie, equality, and respect between interracial partners exists and is assumed at the outset. Or in the case of *100 Rifles* and *El Condor*, Jim Brown's characters are constructed as more physically dominant, more sexually virile, and more intellectually competent than his white co-stars Burt Reynolds and Lee Van Cleef.

Eventually, the main characters, Luke and Jaroo, reach the fortress El Condor. Once there, they come face-to-face with General Chavez and his mistress, Claudine (Mariana Hill). Luke's flirtation with Claudine ignites the ire of Chavez, who banishes them to be scorched by the Mexican sun. Escaping this punishment, Luke and Jaroo steal uniforms from Chavez's abusive soldiers, who have abducted women from the local village. Disguised in army uniforms, Luke and Jaroo sneak into the fortress and blow up a water tower. Chavez is forced to seek a truce, which Jaroo negotiates. But Jaroo double-crosses Luke by accepting a wagon of gold bars, horses, and wagons for the Apaches. When Luke refuses Chavez's deal, the partners fist-fight but discover that Chavez has outsmarted them: the wagon contains only gold-coated bars made of lead.

Luke devises another plan to reenter the fortress by scaling the walls with spiked boots. He is aided by Claudine, who performs a striptease to distract the guards. She has decided to help Luke because she's in love with him. After Luke and Jaroo penetrate the fortress, they blow it up, forcing Chavez to flee. Luke, Claudine, and Jaroo find themselves in possession of the treasure but no means of transporting it. Chavez returns with more troops and Luke walks out to meet him alone. To prevent further bloodshed, Luke and Chavez agree to a duel. Chavez, commanding the troops, will retire if defeated. They fight and Luke kills Chavez. Luke is wounded but returns to El Condor knowing it's time for a final showdown with Jaroo, who is killed in the ensuing gunfight. A triumphant Luke has taken the fortress and captured Claudine's heart.

Taken together, the narrative themes of *Rio Conchos*, *100 Rifles*, and *El Condor* overlap much like a western trilogy. For example, the repeated use of Brown as a central western hero parallels the recurring use of Clint

Eastwood in Sergio Leone's unintentional *Dollars* trilogy (aka *Trilogia del dollaro*). Second, the presence of iconic western villain Lee Van Cleef—who starred in over two hundred films, including *High Noon*—in *El Condor* only a few years after his appearance in *For a Few Dollars More* (1965), invites comparison with classic spaghetti westerns (e.g., *A Fistful of Dollars*; *For a Few Dollars More*; *The Good, the Bad, and the Ugly*).

Third, two of the three films (*100 Rifles* and *El Condor*) were shot in Almeria, Spain. It was common for Italian westerns to be shot in Spain or Italy. Many of the so-called "spaghetti," "paella," and "sauerkraut" westerns were international co-productions involving funding from companies based in different countries. Sometimes these were joint ventures between companies based in various countries such as France, West Germany, Britain, Portugal, Greece, Israel, Yugoslavia, or the United States. The term "Euro-westerns" eventually emerged as a catchall to describe the over six hundred European western films made between 1960 and 1978.

Fourth, although different directors helmed each Jim Brown star vehicle (e.g., Gordon Douglas, Tom Gries, and John Guillermin), their shared status as 20th Century Fox–affiliated pictures suggests a collaborative intentionality at the level of executive production. The films resemble other cinematic trilogy filmmaking, with their reprisals of characters and themes. Whereas *Rio Conchos* is about a band of soldiers tracking stolen rifles to prevent U.S. versus Indian warfare, *100 Rifles* features Brown portraying the police officer who reclaims missing ammunition. Other characters and roles are repeated as well. In *100 Rifles* Burt Reynolds assumes the role of the outrageous mestizo (previously played by Anthony Franciosa in *Rio Conchos*).

Ostensibly white-passing actresses like Raquel Welch and Wende Wagner portrayed Native American women in these movies (e.g., buxom bombshell Welch was to *100 Rifles* what Wagner was to *Rio Conchos*—a white woman in "redface" playing Indian). They are reminiscent of Debra Paget in *White Feather* (1955), Donna Reed in *The Far Horizons* (1955), Natalie Wood in *The Searchers*, Audrey Hepburn in *The Unforgiven* (1960) and even Julie Robinson-Belafonte in *Buck and the Preacher* (1972). The portrayal of Indians by non-Native Americans is complicated by the fact that Native people were rarely (if ever) given opportunities to portray themselves in westerns. They were always played by whites in redface makeup, Latinos, or other mixed-race persons. Both Wagner and Welch portray sultry, sulky Indian women coded as desirably exotic. Finally, all three films were conventional "actioners," delivering explosive thrills,[66] the implication being that these women were tough enough and hot enough to handle the geographical and situational heat. The films thus tapped into, and mobilized, sexual stereotypes of Latin and Native women as hot tamales, saucy spitfires, and emotionally racy.

These cast reshufflings are akin to casting practices in Italian western trilogies. However, Brown's star vehicles never reached the level of art-house cinema like that achieved by the signature spaghetti westerns. Despite reasonable production values, his first movies were aesthetically conventional rather than innovative or modernist like European cinema. They relied on action and spectacle instead of ambiguity and formalism. This was typical of Hollywood westerns in the years before existentialism, European modernism, and Third Cinema (i.e., French New Wave, Italian Neorealism, Polish and Czech New Waves, and Brazilian Cinema Novo) started informing New Hollywood aesthetics.

The primary appreciable difference between the films is the on-screen relationship between Welch and Brown. While there are competing interpretations of the significance of Brown's screen persona, none of them address his westerns or this specific trio of movies. Even Donald Bogle, for instance, read Brown's persona primarily as another incarnation of the Black buck racial stereotype with little or no political resonance, because Brown was rarely antiestablishment in his films.[67]

By contrast, Joshua Gleich finds that Brown's 1960s films represent attempts to establish an uncompromised Black masculinity in mainstream cinema. For Gleich, "Brown served as the crucial transition figure between the desexualized sanctity of Sidney Poitier and the hypersexualized empowerment of Blaxploitation heroes."[68] Gleich echoes the insightful scholar Keith Harris, who viewed Brown as an integrationist icon whose athleticism enabled him to participate in a filmic masculinity alongside white men. But for Gleich, Harris fails to address the controversy generated by interracial sexuality in *100 Rifles*, which required disparate advertising campaigns in the North and South and faced outright censorship in Charlotte, North Carolina. The threatening depiction of Brown on screen in *100 Rifles* is what Gleich believes fragmented his audience and ultimately shortened his film career.[69]

Gleich offers an analysis of Brown and the attempt to render the miscegenation taboo less threatening. He incorrectly reads the disjointed sex scene (which starts out with rough manhandling sex and ends passionately with a joint embrace) as normative rather than as incoherent and out of place in the western genre. Another, better reading of this scene is to consider it within the context of genre. Explicit sexuality was rare in western films. While much attention was paid to Brown and Welch's lovemaking in *100 Rifles* at the time of its production and release, little scrutiny has been given to parameters of genre. The mythology of Black sexual prowess did not dovetail easily with the trope of the western hero, because sexuality itself rarely dovetailed with '60s westerns. Prostitutes hinted at frontier sexuality in the mise-en-scène, but intimacy was rarely the focus. And many prostitutes were tools or vehicles, damsels in distress to be made wholesome by domestication.

Even Brown himself believes there were other potential reasons (beyond the scene with Welch) why his film career suffered:

> I was also a casualty of timing, just as timing had been my ally when I broke in. In the 1960s Hollywood reacted to the liberal mood of the country, some of its own liberal leanings, the pressures exerted on it by the Civil Rights Movement, and gave blacks some decent roles. I played in scenes that were unprecedented: I made love to white women on the American screen. In America, in Hollywood, that is not small potatoes. When Hollywood returned to business as usual in the 1970s, it made sense that I would be the first guy they'd prefer to forget. I symbolized a screen image they wanted nothing but distance from, and have been avoiding to this day. . . .
>
> And it wasn't only white folks who were upset about my love scenes with Jackie Bisset and Stella Stevens and Raquel Welch. A lot of blacks didn't care for it either. . . . Returning to why I was blackballed, deep in my gut I think the primary factor was my activism. I was increasingly perceived as a militant. I had spent time with Malcolm X and Malcolm made many people nervous. Even after Malcolm was killed, many people believed I was a Muslim. . . . Regardless, when people want to bring things out of your past, pit them against you, they do, and my personal relationships did not endear me to Hollywood. Nor did my friendship with Louis Farrakhan. I also used my celebrity status as a platform to make statements about the oppression of blacks. Historically, Hollywood has felt more comfortable when one of its white liberals says: Yes, let's free the blacks. When a black man stands up there is an entirely different reaction.[70]

Brown's interpretation of Hollywood's blacklisting presents an alternative to Gleich's insistence that Brown's sexuality was his cinematic undoing. It is likely Brown was correct that his activism was more threatening—at least in the North. Independent and studio-based filmmakers continued to produce movies immediately after *100 Rifles* in which African American men were intimate with white and non-Black women. Among them were westerns like *The McMasters*, featuring Brock Peters in an interracial relationship with Chinese actress Nancy Kwan (playing a Native American woman). The tagline for the movie read, "In 1865 there was nothing more dangerous than a black man living with a red woman on white man's land." Alternatively, there were underground grindhouse movies like *Sweet Sweetback's Baadasssss Song* (Melvin Van Peebles, 1971) and studio pictures like *Shaft* (1971). Furthermore, Brown had interracial love scenes with Jacqueline Bisset in *The Grasshopper* (Jerry Paris, 1970) and Stella Stevens in *Slaughter* (1972).

Had interracial relations truly been what turned audiences away, subsequent filmmakers working with Brown would probably have avoided it.

The 1960s witnessed the emergence of a Black western hero with Woody Strode's *Sergeant Rutledge*. The figure of the Black cowboy or cavalry officer evolved over the decade. In the early westerns featuring Black characters and Black-white race relations like *Sergeant Rutledge*, African American characters were silent or stoic martyrs to be admired for their nobility and rescued from their fate at the hands of white racists. The emergence of Jim Brown in *Rio Conchos* represented the ascent of an authoritative, physically strong, and steadfastly loyal African American soldier. In subsequent iterations, the Black Westerner evolves again. He is no longer merely a member of an ensemble cast as in *Rio Conchos*. He is the central protagonist, the hero. In *100 Rifles* the Black Westerner is the brawn and the brains, the moral authority who separates right from wrong. By the time *El Condor* is released, Jim Brown's African American western hero has been liberated from his duty as a moral authority and functions as a partner in the interracial buddy antics of campy comedy. In Jim Brown vehicles and the films of Fred Williamson, we see the evolution of the Black Westerner.

Almost concurrently with Jim Brown, Sidney Poitier was starring in his own western films, *Duel at Diablo* and *Buck and the Preacher*. With the first film, *Duel*, Poitier sought to ennoble African American masculinity as chivalrous, valiant, and self-sacrificing. In the latter, he successfully infused the Black cavalry officer with a radical political consciousness never seen before in a western movie.

2

Black Masculinity on Horseback

From Duel at Diablo *to* Buck and the Preacher

In making *Buck and the Preacher*, Poitier achieved several important goals. He established himself as a competent director and cemented his links to the black community. Even normally hostile militants like Donald Bogle were swayed by this film. Bogle declared it [was] "one of the more pleasant surprises of the new decade," noting that: "Here the fine American actor attempts to redeem himself and re-establish his roots with the black community. His character not only questions the inhuman white system and his white oppressors, but also takes direct action against them." As a result, Bogle observes, Poitier regained the audience his recent films had been alienating, the young urban black audience. "Black audiences openly screamed out in joy, and *Buck and the Preacher* emerged as a solid hit with the community."

—Lester Keyser and André Ruszkowski, *The Cinema of Sidney Poitier*

Between 1966 and 1972, Sidney Poitier starred in ten films, two of which were western genre pictures: *Duel at Diablo* and *Buck and the Preacher*. These two motion pictures were not merely star vehicles for the actor, who in 1967 was the most successful Hollywood leading man thanks to three releases that year (*To Sir with Love*, *In the Heat of the Night*, and *Guess Who's Coming to Dinner*). The latter of the two westerns—*Buck and the Preacher*—was also Poitier's unplanned directorial debut. Significantly, Poitier was amenable to the notion of making his directing debut within this genre. For many years, the western genre was hallowed mythological terrain in America and personally important to Poitier. He had long been fascinated by the landscape, iconography, and folklore. Culturally, the

western has been central to notions of nation and narration, the lore surrounding American colonization, and to beliefs about territorial expansion-
ism. Westerns foreground ever-changing ideas of masculinity. Politically,
they have contributed to the enterprise of U.S. imperialism. Historically,
many westerns were predicated on the ideology of manifest destiny, which
led to their chronology supplanting actual history.

Historian Richard Slotkin has written critically and influentially about
the myth of the frontier and its relationship to theories of western development. "The Myth of the Frontier," for Slotkin, "is the American version
of the larger myth-ideological system generated by the social conflicts that
attended the modernization of the Western nations, the emergence of capitalist economies and nation-states."[1] To Slotkin's theory of development, I
would add specificities regarding nation as it pertains to racial and ethnic
demographics. The myth-ideological system to which he refers relied on a
range of historical erasures with respect to Native American sovereignty,
indigenous culture, and history, and it effaced African American participation in the appropriation of Western lands from indigenous peoples during the American Frontier Wars (1906–1924). The cultural dimensions of
myth are not unfamiliar to Slotkin. He does not specifically discuss Poitier's
career, but he writes eloquently, saying, "Myth performs its cultural function by generalizing particular and contingent experiences into the bases of
universal rules of understanding and conduct; and it does this by transforming secular history into a body of sacred and sanctifying legends."[2] These
sacred and sanctifying legends, their mythic landscapes and settings, as
well as the concomitant dreams of mastery that naturalized their ideology,
enamored the young, impressionable Sidney Poitier. He was struck by the
images of America and manhood therein depicted. Poitier longed to see
African American participation in the West depicted on film.

The western as a cinematic genre has historically portrayed an American
society based on codes of honor and personal (direct or private) justice
rather than rationalistic, abstract law. In these narratives people have no
social order more significant than their immediate peers, family, or even
themselves alone. Most westerns are narratives about European American
settlers and their conquest over nature or the removal of Native Americans. To many resistant spectators these motion pictures are ideologically
deceptive. They mythologize the extermination of American Indians as
a matter of Euro-American manifest destiny. These movies are precisely
what Ward Churchill describes in his book *Fantasies of the Master Race:
Literature, Cinema, and the Colonization of American Indians.*[3] Joanna Hearne
makes a similar argument in her essay addressing silent westerns. Beginning with the earliest silent films, westerns were, according to Hearne, "a

window on Euro-American popular culture representations of the encounter between tribal peoples and the United States military and educational establishments."[4]

This encounter between native and settler was usually mediated by the western hero. As tales of wagon train expeditions (*The Big Trail*, 1930; *Covered Wagon*, 1923), settler journeys through hostile territory (*The Battle at Elderbush Gulch*, 1913; *Stagecoach*, 1939; *Fort Apache*), cross-country cattle drives (*Red River*, 1948), cavalry pictures (*Fort Apache*; *She Wore a Yellow Ribbon*; *Rio Grande*), settler nostalgia (*Destry Rides Again*, 1939; *Shane*), lynching parables (*The Ox-Bow Incident*, 1943; *The Unforgiven*; *Rosewood*), codes of machismo (Budd Boetticher's *Seven Men from Now*, 1956; *The Tall T*, 1957; *Decision at Sundown*, 1957; *Buchanan Rides Alone*, 1958; *Ride Lonesome*, 1959; *Comanche Station*, 1960), frontier injustice (*Johnny Guitar*; *The Searchers*; *The Unforgiven*; *Flaming Star*; *Heaven's Gate*, 1980), most of the narratives revolved around the struggle of the lone, semi-nomadic wanderer. He was typically a gunfighter who valiantly defended the underdog or essentially powerless, aggrieved parties (e.g., the family farmer/homesteader or everyday family man and his progeny).[5] This formula of narrative conventions proved incredibly malleable and commercial.

Jeanine Basinger has written extensively about the pliability of the western in relationship to other cinematic genres. More specifically, she has discussed the relationship between combat films and westerns:

> A Western, after all, is a *Western*. But one does not have to dip too far into that most complicated of genres to know that it can be a musical (*Red Garters*), a *film noir* (*The Halliday Brand*, *The Furies*, *Pursued*), an epic (*Duel in the Sun*), a comedy (*Destry Rides Again*), a historical drama (*They Died with Their Boots On*), a biography (*Buffalo Bill*), a woman's film (*Cimarron*), and even a combat film (*Ulzana's Raid*). . . . Furthermore some Westerns have been remade directly "as is" from other genres (the *film noir House of Strangers* remade as the Western *Broken Lance*, and the gangster film *High Sierra* remade as the Western *Colorado Territory*). . . . Most film viewers know that some Westerns *are* combat films, just as they know some combat films are Westerns, and that some gangster films are Westerns and some Westerns are gangster films. . . . Many films are not genre films at all and many others are too hybrid a form to be classified as one thing or another.[6]

In his directorial work, Sidney Poitier attempted to expand and politicize our collective national conceptualization of frontier life, and this genre, by rendering it more multidimensional, multicultural, and historically accurate. His vision was in concert with Jeanine Basinger's more expansive understanding of the western as both more complex and pliable than some believe.

The malleability and versatility of the genre is an important part of
breaking down dominant conceptions of the West. The national semiotic
language and imagery has been occupied or "colonized." For instance, it is
difficult to imagine Black cowboys, Black infantry, and Black cavalrymen.
Most Americans—even many knowledgeable film historians—associate the
genre with white, heterosexual, masculine icons such as John Wayne, Gary
Cooper, Henry Fonda, Randolph Scott, Ward Bond, Ernest Borgnine, Clint
Eastwood, and Lee Van Cleef. Often spectators are unaware that counter-
cultural and reconstructive westerns (e.g., Sidney Poitier's *Duel at Diablo*
and *Buck and the Preacher*) exist. These films are an important part of film
history and are some of the formally innovative amalgamations produced
nationally and internationally.[7] While many of these films do not have anti-
colonialist or antiracist themes, some, like Poitier's *Buck and the Preacher*,
do. Unsurprisingly, some of the antiracist and anti-colonialist films were
produced outside U.S. borders.

For example, *The Treasure of Silver Lake* is a West German–Yugoslav co-
production from 1962, the first of the so-called sauerkraut westerns of
the 1960s. It was adapted from a Karl May novel of the same name. West
German westerns portrayed the struggle of the American Indians against
the advancing United States as inspirational but tragic examples of anti-
imperialist and anti-capitalist struggle. In keeping with their political ori-
entation, the films were not labeled "westerns" but rather *Indianerfilme*
("Indian movies").

Given the popular western's history as a component of colonial discourse, genocide, and imperial enterprise, spectators are often surprised
to discover that African American western history and movies about that
history exist. But for Sidney Poitier and Harry Belafonte, the Black West and
Black-themed westerns were constitutive of American culture. For those
two actors, westerns informed American myths and ideology, even though
they did not articulate the connection in precisely those terms. Nevertheless, Poitier and Belafonte did articulate the importance of depicting Native
Americans and African Americans as full human beings in an interview on
The Dick Cavett Show.

On May 5, 1972, *The Dick Cavett Show* aired an episode in which the host
interviewed Harry Belafonte and Sidney Poitier together about their work
on *Buck and the Preacher*. During the interview, Poitier spoke eloquently
about their efforts to depict Native Americans.

POITIER: You mentioned earlier that when people think of the West, they
   very rarely—if ever—think of Black people.
CAVETT: They think of red and white.

POITIER: Yes. Unfortunately, because the imagery we get of the West is one of an entire people (the Indian people, for instance) who have been brutalized in their imagery with the American public. For instance, in our film we try to treat the Indians as a *whole* people. I have never been accustomed to seeing Indians on film where they were human beings. I mean *a man* and *a woman*. I've seen them as stereotyped concepts of a kind of subhuman entity. They were never particularly intelligent. They were all too often extremely brutal and uncivilized. When we came to our film, I tried to present to the American public an image of an Indian man and Indian woman as whole, human beings, as people. You've not seen the film yet, have you?

CAVETT: No, I haven't seen it. I'm about to see a little bit of it now, aren't I?

POITIER: Well, we tried to do this for Indians. Others have tried to do it for Blacks. Some of the men that Harry spoke of. Even to this day, however, we have not yet—we nor the Indians—have been properly represented in films. Particularly in relationship to the West. But we'll get into that.[8]

To their credit, Poitier and Belafonte were purposeful on the *Dick Cavett Show*. They made certain to stress the parallels between the misrepresentation of African Americans and Native Americans in popular culture.

Almost all classic Hollywood westerns were associated with the hope, promise, and enterprising spirit signified by the Great Plains, Monument Valley, and the American landscape. Against the backdrop of this physical landscape, Poitier hoped his *Buck and the Preacher* could help transform secular history into legends about African American freedom, Native American humanity, racial uplift from slavery, and a reimagining of Reconstruction. Working in this genre gave Poitier an opportunity to address criticisms that he was politically compromised, a "sellout," an "Uncle Tom," or an over-assimilated actor who was disconnected from Black liberation struggles of the time. Harry Belafonte's work at the forefront of the civil rights movement protected him from such accusations. But Poitier's extensive film career left him more vulnerable to accusations of compromise with Hollywood's whitewashing.

Poitier knew there was more to the West, and to westward expansion, than narratives of American imperialism, masculine prowess, the taming of wilderness, and the settlement of territories through the subordination of nature and Native in the name of manifest destiny. He was interested in the lives of people of color. The dispossession of Native peoples, the confiscation of their land rights, and their gradual annihilation concerned him. Poitier understood that this treatment of Native peoples was considered collateral damage, justified by the strategies and rhetoric of empire.

Consequently, in his two western genre vehicles—but particularly in *Buck and the Preacher*—he sought to offer a different vision of the frontier, an alternative model of the cowboy hero.

Poitier's western star vehicles are interesting for three reasons. First, his attempt to broaden the genre demonstrates a commitment to depict Black experience as constitutive of national folklore. His participation was not naïve or uncritical of the myth-ideological system. He was aware of the politics and ideology embedded in motion pictures and their global dispersal. As biographers Lester Keyser and André Ruszkowski have noted, "Poitier wasn't fond of all the material in *Duel at Diablo* but he made it to restore an important piece of history and folklore to black people."[9] One of Poitier's primary aims was to amend and complicate the cinematic record.

Second, these movies are notable because they were personally significant for Poitier. They marked the beginning of his personal connection to cinema at key junctures. It was in Nassau, Bahamas, that a young Sidney was first exposed to the movies, becoming an avid fan. According to his biographer Carol Bergman, "He saw many westerns starring such cowboy film idols as Tom Mix, Bob Steele, Gene Autry and Roy Rogers. Mesmerized by these gunslingers who seemed so real to him on the screen, . . . he decided someday he would like to move to Hollywood, which he believed was the home of all cowboys. Caught up in the masculine performativity and mannerisms of westerns, he developed a swagger of his own, which he used to impress the local girls."[10] In some ways, the western was partially the impetus for, and the boyhood origin of, Sidney Poitier's movie career.

Third, this is the genre in which Poitier made his directorial debut. Joseph Sargent was *Buck and the Preacher*'s originally slated director. But it was Poitier who would bring the movie to fruition. The western marks Poitier's movement from performing actor to contemplative director, inaugurating another phase of his career.

Black Liberation

Duel at Diablo and *Buck and the Preacher* are fascinating because they reveal how deeply contradictory the genre is. In terms of classic Hollywood filmmaking, the western represents the best of times and the worst of times. From an industrial standpoint, the western was *the* most commercially successful genre. But from a postcolonial standpoint—from the perspective of viewers of color—the western represented the cinematic "imperial imaginary" (the tropes, metaphors, and allegorical motifs constitutive of white supremacy).[11] In their deconstruction of the western genre, numerous scholars, including Ward Churchill, Ella Shohat and Robert Stam, Jacqueline

Kilpatrick, and Angela Aleiss, have explained how it not only spectacularized anti-Native violence but also glorified and desensitized viewers to colonial domination while sustaining the film industry financially.[12] How, then, did Poitier negotiate these contradictions?

Poitier's appearance as a leading actor in these movies was always already contradictory; a Bakhtinian "disruptive speech act" or an oxymoronic utterance. On the one hand, an African American protagonist in these pictures was an intervention that problematized the dominant construction and representation of the West in history and in cinematic discourses. His presence requires that we recall the "real," albeit difficult, existence, sacrifice, and patriotism of Buffalo Soldiers, Black Rough Riders, and African American entrepreneurs in the West, who were *not* fictionalized as "reel" screen characters.[13]

This point is expressed in the scholarship of Christine Bold in her essay "Where Did the Black Rough Riders Go?" She opens by contrasting history with its cinematic depiction: "In 1898, for example, the African American Ninth and Tenth Cavalry rode into Cuba as part of what was widely trumpeted as the United States' first overseas war. Almost one hundred years later, they rode out as a band of vigilantes, intent on taking revenge for white racist violence, in Mario Van Peebles' film *Posse* (1993). What happened to them between these two moments—representationally and actually—reveals a central racial dynamic in the making of US mass culture."[14]

Similarly, the scholarship of Quintard Taylor calls to mind the erasure of Black history in the West. For Taylor, the saga of African American life in the West began in November 1528 with the experiences of an African slave who came ashore in Galveston, Texas, as one of the survivors of an ill-fated expedition of 260 men that began in Havana, Cuba, eight months earlier.[15] Taylor recounts the experiences of Black men who played crucial roles in Western history, some of whom moved to the Rocky Mountains and Pacific Northwest or settled in Montana, Santa Fe, and New Mexico during the antebellum years.

Another way of looking at the suppression of history within western films is to recognize that Poitier rendered visible the invisible naturalization of whiteness in popular film and cultural memory. The mise-en-scène of the frontier in mainstream movies is almost always a landscape populated by salt-of-the-earth Euro-American settlers, honor-bound gunslingers, and supposedly savage Indians. Native Americans are grossly misrepresented, and African Americans—in all their complicity with the U.S. government as cavalrymen and their complexity as doubly conscious subjects—are largely absent. That's not to mention Mexican or Asian Americans. Therefore, Poitier's casting and performance marks a progressive disruption of the otherwise regressively homogenous phantasm of masculinity and chivalry expressed through the trope of the white western hero. While his presence in *Duel at Diablo* could be read as a capitulation to the Hollywood status quo or the imperial imaginary, a close reading of *Duel at Diablo* and *Buck and the Preacher* includes acknowledgment and discussion of these films as *revisionist* westerns. We might even view them as anti-western westerns.

According to genre theorist John Cawelti, the revisionist western emerged partially as a response to classic westerns as the genre evolved. Revisionist genre pictures often assume an oppositional or negotiated approach to the dominant cinematic paradigms and their narrative conventions.[16] They offered an alternative episteme, a new way of looking at and understanding the subject, often incorporating previously taboo, repressed, or radically unconventional themes, ideas, and aesthetics. They tended to present more feminist sympathizing, racially sensitive, queer-friendly, class-conscious narratives. They are *not* uniformly progressive by contemporary standards, but they question the archetypes of old that preceded them. For example, revisionist genre films have jettisoned the stereotypes of Native Americans as savages—noble or otherwise. Revisionist westerns also revise the depiction of the western hero.

The term "anti-western" overlaps with the notion of revisionism. It refers to films released between the late 1960s and early 1970s. It earmarks movies that sought to question the ideals and style of the traditional genre pictures with a darker, more cynical tone, with a focus on the lawlessness of the period. The term encompasses films favoring realism over romanticism. For the purposes of this study, it refers to westerns in which antiheroes are common, as are stronger roles for women and more sympathetic portrayals of American Indians, Mexicans, and African Americans.[17] The presence of Buffalo Soldiers, Rough Riders, and Black entrepreneurs in western films like *Duel at Diablo*, *Buck and the Preacher*, *Posse*, or *Rosewood* illustrates why these movies are examples of generic revisionism. Furthermore, the inclusion of these underrepresented and countercultural subjects ironically renders revisionist pictures more historically accurate in some ways than their mainstream counterparts.

The Unforgiven and *Duel at Diablo*

Released in 1966, *Duel at Diablo* emerged at a moment when the western genre was already undergoing significant revision. Only six years earlier, United Artists had released John Huston's *The Unforgiven*, starring Burt Lancaster and Audrey Hepburn in an adaptation of Alan Le May's novel about an Indian foundling adopted by the Zacharys, a white settler family.

Some westerns after 1955 began to underscore the predicament of human nature and a sense of searching, as the films included more controversial themes such as racial prejudice, marital infidelity, rape, cowardly citizens, and graphic violence. Those elements had not been entirely absent from westerns prior to 1955, but after that year the implicit and covert became explicit and overt.[18] Westerns released in the late 1950s and 1960s had heroes, but they were different from traditional western heroes. *The Unforgiven*, like *The Searchers* before it, presented antiheroes. The classical western hero with superior moral qualities, like Will Kane of *High Noon* (dir. Fred Zinnemann), were, by now, long gone. The new protagonists and antiheroes were deeply flawed figures. Sometimes they were men of questionable moral character who were scorned or held in contempt by members of the community. There were a few exceptions to this new pattern. Director Bud Boetticher's *Ranown* series of the late 1950s, starring Randolph Scott as a taciturn and steadfast lawman, is one example.

Reflecting the tenor of the zeitgeist, a new pattern was discernible. *The Unforgiven*, for example, questions the morality of white homesteaders in a tale about a settler family and their adopted daughter, Rachel. When the story begins, the Zacharys are a thriving and respected family on the Texas frontier. Yet rumors of the young woman's Indian heritage begin spreading among white townsfolk and set off a series of events that culminate in a lynch mob.

Years earlier, Rachel's father, Will Zachary, was killed by Kiowa Indians, leaving his oldest son, Ben (Burt Lancaster), as the family patriarch. Ben's business partner is Zeb Rawlins (Charles Bickford). Zeb's shy son, Charlie Rawlins (Albert Salmi), wants to marry Rachel. Early in the film, local ranchers gather to prepare for a cattle drive to Wichita, Kansas. In front of the assembly, old man Abe Kelsey (Joseph Wiseman), believed to be crazy, comes forward claiming that Rachel Zachary is a Kiowa Indian. Her brothers, Ben and Cash, believe Kelsey's story to be a vengeful lie. They attempt to murder Kelsey in order to silence him. Suddenly, a small group of Kiowas appears one night offering to trade horses with Ben in return for Rachel because they believe Rachel is their long-lost Kiowa sister. Soon after their offer to trade is rebuked, marauding Kiowas launch an attack. The Kiowas randomly kill Charlie Rawlins upon his return home as payback for the theft of Rachel. In her grief, Charlie's mother, Hagar Rawlins (June Walker), accuses Rachel of being a "dirty Injun" whose presence is responsible for the Kiowas' raid.

In response to these accusations against Rachel, Ben leads the ranchers as they track down Abe Kelsey and bring him back to the Rawlinses' ranch to be hanged as a horse thief. Ben's true motive is vengeance for Kelsey's assertion that Rachel is Indian. With a noose around his neck, old man Kelsey tells the firelit lynch mob that during an avenging raid against the Kiowas led by himself and Will Zachary, Will found an infant and took the baby for his own. Kelsey's final confession—uttered with a noose around his neck—confirms the rumor circling Rachel and ignites white racist retaliation against the Zachary family.

Huston's *The Unforgiven* parallels John Ford's *The Searchers*. Like *The Unforgiven*, Ford's film was also adapted from a novel by Alan Le May (the books were published in 1954 and 1957, respectively). More specifically, both texts reveal the alignment of anti-Black and anti-Indian sentiments within the American mainstream more blatantly than previous westerns. Both depict anti-Black and anti-Indian sentiments as coterminous and as constitutive of white supremacy. As Richard Slotkin asserts, these themes always existed in the western but became more explicit and overtly expressed.[19]

In the climactic scene wherein Charlie's grieving mother, Hagar, denounces Rachel as an Indian in front of the homesteader community, she calls Rachel a "*red* nigger." Earlier westerns did not depict white racism explicitly. The hostile tone of the scene was further heightened—for mainstream audiences—by the fact that the object of vicious racism was a character being portrayed by an admired English actress. Rachel was portrayed by the strikingly aristocratic Audrey Hepburn. In her prime, the British Hepburn was one of Hollywood's most iconic female screen legends, having starred in *Roman Holiday* (1953), *Sabrina* (1954), *Funny Face* (1957), and *The Nun's Story* (1959) all before making *Breakfast at Tiffany's* (1961). The scene's shock value was one indication that '60s-era westerns were upping the political ante and intentionally reflecting the national conversation about race.

As Brian Henderson's seminal essay on *The Searchers* has established, Ford's film was evidently a metaphor for the racial politics of the 1950s (e.g., *Brown v. Board of Education*). *The Searchers*, like *The Unforgiven* after it, is only explicable, according to Henderson, if we substitute Black for red and read a film about red-white relations in 1898 as actually a film about Black-white relations in 1956.[20] Hence the portmanteau "red nigger," which makes more sense following Henderson's analysis. The point is that several westerns released after 1956 are films in which we see generic transformation, historical revisionism, metaphors for civil rights activism, and a shift in tone.[21] Sidney Poitier's *Duel at Diablo* and *Buck and the Preacher* manifest generic transformation and overt evocations of civil rights discourse just as *The Unforgiven* and *The Searchers* had years earlier.

Scholarly and biographical accounts of Poitier's films gloss over or omit the westerns, viewing them as less important than other work in his oeuvre. *Diablo* and *Buck* are not as well known as social problem pictures like *The Defiant*

Ones, for which Poitier became the first Black male actor to be nominated for an Academy Award. They are not as celebrated as *Lilies of the Field* (1963), with which he made history by becoming the first African American to win a Best Actor Oscar. They are not as groundbreaking as his performances in the first production of *A Raisin in the Sun* on Broadway (1959) and the film adaptation released in 1961. Nor are they as popular as the top three 1967 releases (*To Sir with Love, In the Heat of the Night*, and *Guess Who's Coming to Dinner*) that made him the number one box office film star—of any race—that year. Finally, they are not as controversial as the much-analyzed *Guess Who's Coming to Dinner*. However, *Duel at Diablo* and *Buck and the Preacher* are central to the scope and complexity of his star persona because they are part of how he broadened the depiction of Black masculinity in cinema. The generic shifts apparent in films like *The Searchers* and *The Unforgiven*, coupled with the emergence of Italian, Spanish, and East German westerns throughout Europe and the United States, demonstrated that the western could reflect African American characters, protagonists, and heroes.

Based on Marvin Albert's best-selling 1957 novel, *Apache Rising, Duel at Diablo* is set in 1880. *Diablo*'s credit sequence begins after lone Utah frontier scout Jess Remsberg (James Garner) is shown surveying a desolate valley. Through his binoculars, he spots the body of a white man still hanging upside down from an Indian tipi cross. Farther in the distance, he spots a lone mounted rider crossing the desert on an exhausted horse. When the rider's horse collapses, the man is pursued by two alleged Apaches who emerge from hiding. Jess guns down the assailants and rescues the exhausted rider, whom he discovers is a beautiful young woman named Ellen Grange (played by Ingmar Bergman's Swedish muse, Bibi Andersson). As they gallop across the plains to safety, celebrated composer Neal Hefti's orchestral score swells in the background to kick off the credit sequence.[22]

Addressing *Diablo*'s opening sequence and its musical tone, critic Deborah Allison writes, "Ralph Nelson's *Duel at Diablo* (1966), which tracks the course of a barely visible rider, makes particularly explicit the filmic attraction of the landscape itself: its stunning cinematography is coupled with a title announcing the shooting location. In the vastness of such terrains as these, the riders are shown to be both bold and vulnerable."[23] Like the sharp, deep-focus cinematography, the opening music is noteworthy. It was composed and conducted by Hefti, who had arranged for some of the biggest-name bands in the country before he went on to become one of the most prolific writers of modern music. At the time, his most recent hit was the Academy Award–nominated song "What's New Pussycat?" written by Burt Bacharach and Hal David. In *Diablo*'s press kit, the score and theme song are described as featuring "a new musical approach."

This new approach included introducing folk-rock as well as R&B-inspired motifs. Newer, trendier scores were designed to attract younger audiences, including members of the "beat generation," who were familiar with the Beatles and the British invasion, which began in earnest with the Beatles' U.S. arrival in 1964. Central elements of "beat" culture included rejection of conventions, innovations in style, experimentation with drugs, alternative sexualities, increased racial tolerance, interest in religious exploration, a rejection of materialism, and explicit portrayals of the human condition. The soundtrack for *Duel at Diablo* altered the film's tone and tenor in a way consistent with the youth-oriented zeitgeist and the film's liberal political themes (e.g., greater racial tolerance, accepting interracial relationships, recognition of mixed-race children, and more political open-mindedness). This political tone was linked, in one way or another, to Poitier's character in the film and to the revisionism already in motion.

Not everyone appreciated this new musical approach. Neal Hefti's use of guitars evokes the soundtracks of spaghetti westerns, which were newly emerging and quickly becoming immensely popular. In 1964 Italian director Sergio Leone hired and began collaborating with composer Ennio Morricone to create a distinctive score for his groundbreaking movie *A Fistful of Dollars*. With the score for that film, Morricone began his twenty-year collaboration with his childhood friend and composer Alessandro Alessandroni. Alessandroni was a talented musician in his own right, having founded I Cantori Moderni, an eight-member choir, in 1961. For Morricone, Alessandroni provided the whistling and the twanging guitar on film scores. Morricone's orchestration called for an unusual combination of instruments and voices. Alessandroni's twangy guitar riff was central to the main theme for *The Good, the Bad, and the Ugly*. And he can be heard as the whistler on the soundtracks for Sergio Leone's films *A Fistful of Dollars*, *For a Few Dollars More*, *Once Upon a Time in the West* (1968), and other films.

The first mainstream, crossover spaghetti western, *A Fistful of Dollars* was released in Italy in 1964 and in the United States in 1967. At least one reviewer noted how much *Duel at Diablo* as a movie resembled (and to a lesser extent sounded like) a spaghetti western, writing, "Though the Spaghetti Western had not yet fully penetrated the United States, it is clear in 1966 the genre was starting to have an influence on American directors." In fact, spaghetti westerns were beginning to have an impact on American directors. The impact of Italian films on the aesthetics and artistry of *Diablo* can also be seen before the opening credit/title sequence. When the United Artists logo first appears, it is suddenly cut and punctured in 3D illusion. The logo is seemingly sliced from behind the screen by a long scalping knife with fresh blood dripping from it. This particular use of 3D illusion is intended to evoke the threat (for thrill-seeking spectators) of being endangered by knife-wielding Indians. The knife stands in metonymically for the absent but impending menace of violent Indians that westerns have historically manufactured.

The use of 3D illusion in the opening was a revival of devices popularized a decade earlier. The golden era of 3D filmmaking had been from 1952 to 1954, during which it was used to heighten the appeal of movies and entice the newly enamored TV audience at home to return to the theaters. The first full-length 3D movie was *Bwana Devil* (1952). An adventure B movie written, directed, and produced by Arch Oboler, *Bwana Devil* was shot in Natural Vision.[24] One of *Bwana Devil's* early audiences was captured in J. R. Eyerman's iconic photograph of theater audience wearing 3D glasses while watching *Bwana Devil* in 3D at the Paramount Theater for *Life* magazine. The photograph was later used on the cover of Guy Debord's seminal tome *Society of the Spectacle*.[25] A variety of genres were given new life with 3D technology such as funhouse thriller *House of Wax* (1953); science fiction films *It Came from Outer Space* (1953) and *Robot Monster* (1953); and adventure pictures *The Mad Magician* (1954), *Dangerous Mission* (1954), and *Son of Sinbad* (1955).

Three-dimensional filmmaking enjoyed a revival in the 1960s. Although 3D films appeared sparsely during the early part of the decade, the true second wave of 3D cinema was set into motion by Oboler, the producer who had started the craze in the 1950s. Late '60s audiences saw the return of 3D, with Oboler's new system called Space-Vision. Using Space-Vision 3D, Oboler once again had the vision for the system that no one else would touch and put it to use on his film *The Bubble* (1966), which starred Michael Cole, Deborah Walley, and Johnny Desmond. Critics panned *The Bubble*, but audiences flocked to see it. The film became financially successful enough to prompt other studios, particularly independents, which did not have the money for expensive dual-strip prints of their productions, to try this new method of producing 3D movies. *Duel at Diablo's* credit sequence was a

FIGURE 2.1 3D special effects were used for the *Duel at Diablo* opening credits.

playful, self-reflexive use of 3D to incorporate graphic novel antics popular-ized by Italian westerns and comedies.

Duel at Diablo's generic self-reflexivity recalls earlier American western films with similarly reflexive title sequences. The 1965 western musical com-edy *Cat Ballou*, directed by Elliot Silverstein, opens with a playful animated cartoon version of the Columbia Pictures "Torch Lady" logo. At the beginning of *Cat Ballou*, the Torch Lady morphs into an animated version of herself, strips off her toga to reveal a cowgirl outfit, and then starts shooting like Annie Oakley. Twenty seconds into the titles, the filmmakers have already established the comedic and campy tone of the film. Films use their opening title sequence to prepare audiences for the viewing experience ahead. Accord-ing to Deborah Allison's research on title sequences, "Westerns, perhaps more than any other genre, have tended to use extremely evocative titles."[26] Allison makes a persuasive case that many such title sequences refer to objects or events that are totemic of life in the American West. In short, the main title sequence should indicate the nature of the movie, anticipate its main plea-sures, and help ensure that audiences respond correctly to the film's tone.

These kinds of playful credit sequences were characteristic of spaghetti westerns too. Leone's *Dollars* trilogy was known for its abstract, cartoon, and graphic novel title sequences. Trilogies were common in the genre fol-lowing the commercial and critical success of John Ford's Cavalry trilogy.

After the title credits, the story of *Duel at Diablo* unfolds at Fort Con-cho. Colonel Foster, played by director Ralph Nelson, commands the fort. Jess Remsberg returns runaway Ellen to her embittered husband, Willard Grange (Dennis Weaver, aka Chester of TV's *Gunsmoke*). Grange has grown resentful of his wife, whom he now considers "ruined" after her capture by Indians signal that she had been "taken" (code for raped or having engaged in interracial sex). The intermixing of white women with Native Indians was considered a violation of the miscegenation taboo in cinema and in society. Interracial relations were literally forbidden in film by the Hays Production Code and stigmatized in civil society. It was not until 1967 that the landmark decision in *Loving v. Virginia* struck down statutes against interracial mar-riage. Ellen's racial purity is further sullied in the narrative (within the logic of mainstream '60s racial politics) by the presence of her biracial offspring. Willard eventually learns that Ellen has given birth to a half-Indian child. The acceptance of Ellen's beautiful baby (affectionately embraced by Poitier's character, Sergeant Toller) becomes a major plot point later in the picture.

Back at Fort Concho, Colonel Foster requires Jess Remsberg to scout for an expedition led by Lt. Scotty McAllister (Bill Travers). Jess incidentally reports that he found McAllister's former scout, Tom Vance, hanged by Apaches. An Indian sympathizer who stands for greater racial tolerance,

Jess has married a Comanche woman. But he is reluctant to help Scotty on any military expedition, because he has recently learned that a white man killed his Indian wife during a raid on her mixed-race community. Herein lies the film's revision of western generic codes, as it positions white racial bigotry and retaliatory violence as equally unjust.

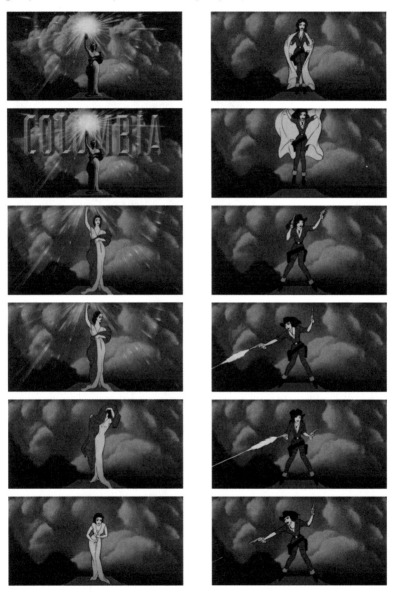

FIGURE 2.2 Cat Ballou's carnivalesque credit sequence foreshadows the playful tone of the film.

FIGURE 2.3 Poitier's
character Toller holds a
baby in *Duel at Diablo*.

Reluctantly, Jess Remsberg agrees to guide Lieutenant McAllister's expedition to move ammunition and water through hostile territory, hoping to save Ellen, who has since secretly fled from Fort Concho to find her baby. Former Buffalo Soldier and Tenth Cavalry veteran Sergeant Toller also reluctantly rides along.[27] Retired from military service, Toller is now a horse wrangler hired by the army to break, train, and deliver forty mounts for the U.S. Cavalry. Toller no longer wants any part of the military but joins the scouting party because it's the only way he can collect what he's owed for the horses he delivered. After reconciling a misunderstanding about Jess's murdered wife, Toller and Remsberg become allies (in what might be one of the first iterations of the interracial buddy film genre after *The Defiant Ones*[28]).

Meanwhile, Ellen returns to Indian chief Chata and his people, hoping to reunite with her infant son. But her return is met with hostility and the threat of vivisepulture (live burial). Chata's hostility toward Ellen, and his promise to bury her alive, marks a turning point of audience sympathy in this film. Whereas Jess functioned as the liminal figure (the trope of the white-man-gone-native), and Ellen's abuse at the fort is proof that whites could behave savagely, Chata's threat to bury Ellen alive trumps these other aggressions and subverts the film's initial suggestion of Indian civility.

As McAllister's expedition enters hostile Indian Territory, Poitier's Toller rides along. On the way, he's sent on a dangerous mission into a trap laid for the cavalry. The Apaches hide, allowing him to pass only to entrap the cavalry and their supply wagons once they follow behind. When the Apache fire ignites, Toller doubles back to fight and defend white interests, aiding the cavalry. Herein lies the complex and contradictory nature of African American participation in the Indian Wars as Buffalo Soldiers and U.S. citizens.

Both Poitier's Toller and Garner's Remsberg respect the Native Americans' collective quest for sovereignty. This is demonstrated when Ellen sorrowfully asks, "Do you think they'll stay on the reservation this time?" "Why *should* they?" Jess bitterly responds. The character's respect for indigenous people's dignity is further validated when Toller confronts Ellen's husband, Will, about his anti-Indian racism and mistreatment of her infant son. Jess and Toller are the voices of racial tolerance within the larger community and the film's diegesis. Toller even defends Ellen from Will, disarming him at one point. But Toller's kindly actions toward Ellen contradict his earlier interactions with townsmen. His very first line in *Duel at Diablo* is to ask, "How much for that scalp?" He unknowingly inquires about a trophy taken from Jess's murdered wife. But it's a moment that reminds audiences that, far from being united with other people of color, many African American cavalrymen and cowboys participated in the anti-Native colonial culture practiced on the frontier. Though *Duel at Diablo* portrays Toller as more tolerant than most of his white counterparts (barring Jess), the myth of Indian instigation overtakes the film's narrative. The movie has some pro-Native, anti-colonialist moments but still largely conforms to hegemonic discourses and anti-Native imperialism.

Eventually the U.S. Cavalry, Toller, and Ellen find themselves bunkered at a makeshift fort. Under continual enemy fire, the cavalrymen prove no match for the warring Apaches. One by one they are picked off. Lieutenant McAllister suffers a broken leg in the crossfire. During an extended two-day shoot-out, Toller guides the remaining men. But they are outnumbered. Will Grange is captured and tortured, and Lieutenant McAllister dies from his wounds. Even Toller is wounded when an arrow penetrates his arm. He and Ellen soon realize they are the sole survivors. Encircled by enemy arrows, Toller helps Ellen hide her baby in a safe place. Here *Duel at Diablo* reproduces the "imagery of encirclement" that Ella Shohat and Robert Stam discuss in their book *Unthinking Eurocentrism*, thereby employing a conventional visual trope of the western genre.[29] Wounded and low on ammunition, Ellen and Toller are finally rescued upon the arrival of additional U.S. cavalrymen, led by Jess Remsberg, who has finally returned from avenging his wife's murder.

FIGURE 2.4 Sidney Poitier's Toller and James Garner's Remsberg come to blows in *Duel at Diablo*.

At the time of its release, audiences responded to *Duel at Diablo* with some skepticism. Authors Lester Keyser and André Ruszkowski note that even with Poitier as a cavalry-trained gunfighter, director Ralph Nelson revealed in an interview that there was a good deal of audience backlash: "In *Duel at Diablo*, the audiences seemed to have been surprised and skeptical about the presence of a *Negro* cowboy."[30] But Nelson and Poitier, who had collaborated previously on the Academy Award–winning film *Lilies of the Field*, based Poitier's character Toller on a book titled *The Negro Cowboys*, a 1965 publication by University of California professors Philip Durham and Everett Leroy Jones, which was serialized by several newspapers around the time of *Duel at Diablo*'s release. The book was a powerful indictment of the omissions and oversights of historians.[31] And it would also inspire Poitier when he was making *Buck and the Preacher* a few years later.

Despite attempts at historical accuracy with *Duel at Diablo*'s inclusion of Black cowboys, some critics felt that Poitier failed to project the kind of virile masculinity associated with westerns. Costume choices may have thwarted his performance of traditional Western masculinity; one critic went so far as to say as much when he wrote that Poitier appeared "as a rather dandified Army veteran."[32] Such criticism questioned both his character's masculinity and Poitier's acting ability by implying an undisguisable effeminacy. Toller does remain remarkably well-dressed and unsullied until the final scenes of the film. The criticism dovetails with film historian Ed Guerrero's assertion that "the conventions of the war story and the Western isolate Poitier from romantic encounters."[33] Heterosexual rituals have long been the conventional means by which virility is visualized in American film (apart from combat). For Poitier to be without a romantic interest—even if nonsexual—was to render him less manly. Furthermore, to cast him opposite white women as love interests positioned him as a racial/political sellout in '60s-era America. Taking these criticisms of inefficacy one step further, African American playwright Clifford Mason wrote, "In *Duel at Diablo* (Poitier) did little more than hold Garner's hat, and this after he had won the Academy Award. What white romantic actor would take a part like that? He gets to kill a few Indians, but Garner gets the girl and does all the fighting. Poitier was simply dressed up in a fancy suit with a cigar stuck in his mouth and a new felt hat on his head."[34]

Throughout the 1960s, Mason was one of Poitier's most stringent critics. The playwright found Poitier lacking in political zeal, without charismatic appeal, and bereft of masculine prowess regardless of the role he played. However, it is possible to view Poitier's work in *Duel at Diablo*, and elsewhere, as a "hegemonic negotiation," to use Stuart Hall's analytical paradigm. Arguably, Poitier's character Toller exists in negotiation with white masculinity, with white supremacy, with manifest destiny, and with the sacred and sanctified legends upon which the western film genre was predicated. To address Mason's specific criticism of effeminacy, it is helpful to review a key scene that contradicts the claim that the actor appears weak and unmanly.

In a scene that demonstrates Toller's horsemanship, bravery, and endurance, he is shown riding and training unbroken, untamed, wild horses. Debatably, this scene functions to validate Poitier's Toller as a Westerner, as a cowboy, and as a physically virile specimen of a man. His abilities (to ride, tame, and break horses) stand in synecdochically for the lore, the landscape, and the lifestyle of the Western frontier. And while his work with these animals positions him as a "cow*boy*" rather than a cowhand or "cattle*man*," with all that this distinction implies,[35] it also reflects some of the real labor performed by exploited frontier workers (e.g., African Americans, Mexicans, and Native Indians). Nonetheless, the horsemanship adduces the character's masculinity; it's a literal and symbolic testament to Toller's ability to domesticate, cultivate, and tame the Wild West.

It is important to note that women and romantic entanglements have long been peripheral to the themes featured in the western genre. To know the western genre is to know that women and heterosexual romance— perhaps more than anything else—symbolized the domestication of virile masculinity rather than its liberation or actualization. Therefore, the absence of romance might not signify negatively on his masculinity. In his book *The Invention of the Western Film* Scott Simmon addresses this very point: "There is little denying that the woman in the A-western is so marginalized that the very ideas she embodies prove unworthy even of synthesis into the films' resolutions."[36] Elsewhere Simmon makes a related point more emphatically when he writes:

> But the definitional antagonism of men and women in Westerns is never used as dynamically as it is routinely in Hollywood's other genres to explore conflicting ideas. When the man and woman come together at the end of a Western, it's without the satisfying reconciliations that end, say, a Kather-ine Hepburn–Cary Grant screwball comedy or an Astaire-Rogers musical. "Cowboys don't get married—unless they stop being cowboys."[37]

Seeing Poitier—and his stunt double (the world-famous Black rodeo champion Roy Quirk[38])—subdue the bucking broncos evokes the memo-rable equestrian theatrics of John Ford's famous film *Rio Grande*, the third installment of Ford's Cavalry trilogy, in which young, able-bodied cavalry recruits ride Roman-style over fences. Suffice it to say, good horsemanship has always been a tenet of the genre and proof of masculinity. This scene in *Duel at Diablo* and the film in general make an intervention. They link the African American presence in the West (and Poitier's star persona) to the mythic mise-en-scène of western movie heroics.

Not insignificantly, Toller's disciplining of these horses is echoed in a later scene when Will Grange steps out of line. Toller is the only man on the expedition to strip Will's gun and make him stand down. It's a scene in which Toller "breaks" Will the way he broke the wild horses. In the process, Toller simultaneously defends the rights of women, mothers, children, and those marked as racially Other against the racism, sexism, and xenophobia exhibited by Grange. Thus, to openly disagree with Clifford Mason's critique, Toller's/Poitier's masculinity is not deficient within the logic of western cinematic convention.

What was confusing for 1960s civil rights–minded audiences was that Poitier's Toller joined forces with white men against Indians, something Poitier would revisit and overturn with his next foray into the genre, his directorial debut, *Buck and the Preacher*.

Buck and the Preacher

In 1970 Poitier was slated to star in *Buck and the Preacher*. In an interview for the documentary *Sidney Poitier: One Bright Light* (Lee Grant, 2000), the actor/director/producer admits that his longtime friend Harry Belafonte initially approached him with the idea for *Buck and the Preacher*. "There had never been a film about the relationship between Blacks and Indians," he tells the interviewer.[39] Based on the story written and researched by Black writer (and assistant director) Drake Walker, *Buck and the Preacher* addresses this void in American history and film. And it gave Poitier and Belafonte an opportunity to collaborate again.

Over the years, Poitier and Belafonte had grown up together in the American Negro Theater and Black theatrical world. Both had been mentored by actor/singer/dignitary Paul Robeson, who was an intellectual father figure to many young Black artists, including Lorraine Hansberry, James Baldwin, Poitier, Belafonte, and others. Despite shared experiences, their friendship had been through ups and downs over the years because of their divergent career choices. Belafonte thought Poitier compromised himself and accepted questionable roles. During preproduction for the film, television director Joseph Sargent was chosen by Columbia Pictures to direct the film, and Poitier and Belafonte agreed. But when the rushes for the early scenes came in, all were disappointed. One week after the crew arrived in Durango, Mexico (a town an hour by air northwest of Mexico City), Poitier threw Sargent a going-away party and let him leave.

According to various reliable accounts, Poitier had an "almost . . . maniacal devotion to the project and to the integrity of a black vision of the West." Sargent claims it was Poitier who "had lived and breathed with it since its conception. No one knew the material better than he did. He should be the man to put it on the screen. In no way would it work with another director. He had thought it all out beforehand, and whenever I wanted to change that concept, I [was] met with resistance. It's his film. It's as simple as that, and there was nothing racial about it whatever."[40]

While Sargent stated publicly that racial politics played no role in the decision-making, accounts confirm that Poitier did want to make an ideological intervention with this film. To do that, he needed someone with a particular political sensibility. Poitier realized that the movie required what we now call an "intersectional" understanding of race, class, and nation.[41] The actor assuredly wanted someone who understood how African Americans, Native peoples, and women of color felt about their displacement and disenfranchisement. He needed someone who could comprehend the terms on which marginalized groups could collaborate. Arguably, he wanted to rewrite the sacred and sanctified legends of early American history on film. He sought to depict the Black American journey and contribution to the Western United States on film, a medium to which he had devoted his life.

Look magazine journalist George Goodman told a different story. In his well-illustrated article, Goodman claimed that Sargent's dismissal from the picture was because he was shooting it like a television show.[42] Most of Sargent's work had been in television as an actor. In the mid-1950s he started directing. For the next fifteen years, his directing credits included episodes of the television series *Lassie* (1954–1974), *The Invaders* (1967–1968), *The Man from U.N.C.L.E.* (1964–1968), and *Star Trek* (1966–1969). Goodman reported Poitier flatly telling Belafonte, "We might as well face it; we needed a Black man for a sensitive job about *Black* people."[43] It would have made sense for Sargent to capitalize on the possibility of this film having televisual exposure, which would further his television career. But it was unlikely Sargent could fully understand how Poitier felt about the project.

It was on *The Dick Cavett Show* that Poitier and Belafonte dismissed as untrue the phony story that George Goodman told about their disagreements on set. Goodman brought his own agenda to the production and sought to sow seeds of dissension regarding Poitier's and Belafonte's relationship.

By this point in his career, Poitier had formed E & R Productions (using the initials of his his parents' first names: Evelyn and Reginald). He told the press that E & R Productions would "make films that show a truer picture of American Negroes to movie audiences."[44] A few years earlier, while working on the movie *Brother John* (1971), executive producer Joel Glickman and Poitier started an apprentice program to train film technicians. They recruited and hired novices, or trainees, paying them $150 a week plus living expenses.

The goal was to break down the barriers created by Hollywood's complex union system, which systematically excluded minority groups, particularly African Americans. In a March 1971 *Variety* magazine article addressing the rising costs of film production and union-related issues, Glickman was quoted as saying, "You can't do big period westerns in the States anymore. The costs are prohibitive. And the Hollywood unions have to realize they no longer have a majority on the technical expertise." The article went on to say that the "Mexican union regulations require a full Mexican crew, but as on all American productions there is a nucleus supervisory crew brought from Hollywood. The unique thing about *Buck and the Preacher*'s production is that half of that nucleus of production personnel, the stuntmen, and the cast, are black."[45]

Still, despite the apprentice program, barriers remained. "Even if the trainees get their cards," said Glickman, "they're still bucking the seniority list, which is an outdated, medieval system that has nothing to do with a man's creativity or skill. Every man with a union card in his pocket in Hollywood should have the right to be employed on an equal basis, regardless of race, creed or color."[46] Thus with a budget of $2.5 million, most of which

Belafonte and Poitier raised, Poitier, his actors, and a predominantly Mexican crew were able to realize a goal that had heretofore eluded Poitier.

In the film, Poitier portrays Buck, a former Union cavalryman who, after the Civil War, decides to put his talents as an army scout to work as a wagon master leading newly freed slaves (or Exodusters) from the Louisiana Territory to settle somewhere in the Northwest near Canada.[47] The Exodusters are being harassed and hunted by night riders (read: Klan members). These night riders are working for the Southern plantation owners who want their (exploited) laborers to return. Along the trail, Buck encounters a jackleg minister going by the moniker "Preacher." The self-styled "Reverend" introduces himself as an official of the High and Low Order of the Holiness Persuasion Church. A comical, itinerant evangelist with a penchant for bad rhymes and failed haikus, Preacher quickly becomes Buck's partner against the Confederate night riders.

Before joining the *Buck and the Preacher* cast, Harry Belafonte had amassed wealth and fame singing in swank supper clubs and on television. He had appeared in films like *The Bright Road* (1953), *Carmen Jones* (1954), and *Island in the Sun* (1957). He appeared in *Odds Against Tomorrow* (1959). But he turned away from filmmaking because he felt the roles were too stereotypical. With his honey-toned voice, he turned to singing instead and became a major recording artist—the first to sell a million LPs. It was on television that Belafonte produced a series of successful programs, winning

FIGURE 2.5 An Exoduster wagon train on the move in *Buck and the Preacher*.

Emmy awards for his musical entertainment. According to New York *Daily News* entertainment writer Wanda Hale, Belafonte preferred singing to film-making. He stated as much in his biography, *Harry Belafonte: My Song*, and in the documentaries *Sing Your Song: Harry Belafonte* (Susan Rostack, 2012) and *Sit-In: Harry Belafonte Hosts the Tonight Show* (Yoruba Richan, 2020). On many occasions he discussed disillusionment with Hollywood's reliance on racial stereotypes and his decision to walk away from filmmaking. Yet by all accounts the very idea for *Buck and the Preacher* was initially Belafonte's.

Belafonte and Poitier had fallen out a few years earlier in 1968 over Belafonte's desire to host an all-night vigil for Dr. Martin Luther King in the wake of his assassination. Consequently, they had not spoken in two years. In 1970 Belafonte reached out to Poitier to break the two-year silence with an idea for a black western film based on a script by Belafonte's intern Drake Walker. Walker was an intern on the film *The Angel Levine* (Ján Kadár, 1970), which Belafonte had just finished. Since the two men had discussed plans to produce a black western many years earlier, Poitier loved the idea. It proved the pathway for them to mend fences and let bygones be bygones. Together they decided to employ their respective production companies (E & R Productions and Belafonte Enterprises), as well as the production team Poitier had been working with on *Brother John* (James Goldstone, 1971). That is how executive producer Joel Glickman and screenwriter Ernest Kinoy became involved in the picture.

When Poitier asked Belafonte to play the Preacher and described the character he was to play, Belafonte was intrigued. "'The Preacher is something different, and I wanted to give it a try,' said Harry."[48] Belafonte's wife, Julie Robinson-Belafonte, was cast as Sinsie, an Indian woman and interpreter who speaks fluent English. In the film, Sinsie is the wife of an Apache Mescalero Indian chief, played by Mexican actor Enrique Lucero. While it's impressive that Mrs. Belafonte played the role with dignity and authority, it still stands out as a problematic example of a phenotypically white-passing actress in redface. Furthermore, it's reminiscent of the industry practice of casting white actors and actresses as people of color in social problem pictures. Examples include classical Hollywood films and more recent twenty-first-century pictures such as Jeanne Crain in *Pinky*; Natalie Wood in *The Searchers*; Susan Kohner in *Imitation of Life*, 1959; Audrey Hepburn in *The Unforgiven*; Elvis Presley in *Flaming Star*; and Sir Anthony Hopkins in *The Human Stain*, 2003. Such casting limits the already scarce job opportunities for actors of color, and it socializes audiences to sympathize with white-passing subjects rather than black and brown people.

Nevertheless, Mrs. Belafonte worked diligently to craft the character of Sinsie. According to Columbia Pictures, she obtained, through the studio, a taped recording of the voice of an Apache reading the lines delivered in an Apache dialect by her and Lucero in the script. Mrs. Belafonte spent several days in seclusion on the Venezuelan island of Aruba getting a deep tan and practicing Apache pronunciation. This was her first major film role and first significant show business appearance since her marriage to Belafonte fifteen years earlier. She had been a member of the famed Katherine Dunham dance troupe. The regal Ruby Dee, Poitier's co-star from *A Raisin in the Sun* (who had appeared in films with him as far back as *No Way Out* in 1950), stars as Ruth, Buck's loving and cunning wife. Dee gives an impressive performance as his dignified and clever companion, who saves her husband from falling into a trap.

While some scholars and critics have asserted that Poitier and Belafonte were too chauvinistic to fully develop Ruby Dee's character, it is important to remember the generic context. Dee's role in *Buck and the Preacher* was smaller than her role of Ruth Younger in *A Raisin in the Sun*, but it incorporated her as an important figure in the action. She rides on horseback, and she is a central figure in multiple action scenes. Moreover, in this genre few women were major characters. Finally, Poitier was already altering the genre's political content with the coalition between African Americans and Native Indians, a fact that few of Poitier's critics (or Belafonte promoters) have addressed.

The first title images in *Buck and the Preacher* are sepia-toned stills of Exodusters driving wagon trains set against a Western landscape. Young cinematographer Alex Phillips Jr. helped to craft the sepia-toned titles. This title sequence, like the reflexive title sequences in *Duel at Diablo, Cat Ballou*, the *Dollars* trilogy, and *Butch Cassidy and the Sundance Kid*, also reveals generic reflexivity and revisionism. Similar sepia credits had been used in *Butch Cassidy and the Sundance Kid* with great success. The opening credit sequence design helped *Buck and the Preacher* achieve a similar reflexive revisionism and historical sensibility as had been achieved in *Butch Cassidy*, starring Paul Newman and Robert Redford.

The opening credits roll to the folksy syncopated rhythms by legendary jazz composer Benny Carter. Notable blues musicians Sonny Terry and Brownie McGhee are among those who performed on Carter's soundtrack. Terry, a blind African American Piedmont blues musician, played the memorable harmonica for the soundtrack. He was widely known for his energetic blues harmonica style, which frequently included vocal whoops and hollers along with imitations of trains and foxhunts. The soundtrack included the Jew's harp, which created similar reverberated rhythms. Benny Carter's soulful soundtrack set a distinctive mood for *Buck and the Preacher*, much like Ennio Morricone's whistler had for Sergio Leone's *Dollars* trilogy. It not only gave *Buck and the Preacher* a distinctive bluesy tonal quality, but it also offered a twist on the conventional western score that hinted at history and memory but with a new sensibility.

Alex Phillips Jr., the director of photography, manages a transition between these sepia title images and the opening scene, which gradually fades from sepia to Technicolor. This transition from sepia to color had previously been used to great success in *Butch Cassidy and the Sundance Kid*. The sepia-toned titles were compared to the sepia images in *Bonnie and Clyde* and noted for the way they evoked nostalgia and a confrontation with history that the film would enliven and elaborate.[49]

The film's opening scenes depict small caravans of Exoduster wagon trains moving northwest. En route, a posse of white mercenaries led by the villainous Deshay (Cameron Mitchell) emerges in the distance. Deshay and his gang try to stop Buck and the wagon train because his employers want to keep these newly manumitted laborers working on the plantations they've left behind.

During one of many raids on the Black wagon train, the ruthless Confederate gang overturns family wagons; kills livestock; shoots men, women, and children; and burns grain to deter the newly freed slaves from seeking greener pastures. Deshay dutifully serves his employers: the landed Southern gentry anxious to maintain prewar master-slave relationships. These scenes are crucial to redressing the history of slavery and the history of Reconstruction on film. *Buck and the Preacher* seeks to set the cinematic record straight about the kinds of retaliatory vigilantism and Red Shirt and Ku Klux Klan violence that African Americans faced during Reconstruction. The attempt to make such a historical intervention is itself a reason to review a groundbreaking film like *Buck and the Preacher*.

Upon witnessing the impact of multiple attacks on these salt-of-the-earth settlers, the otherwise itinerant Preacher is motivated to join forces with Buck. Together, Buck and Preacher take out the no-account, lowbrow, womanizing posse that has been terrorizing the wagon trains. But they can succeed only if they join forces with local Native Indian tribes and warriors. Buck needs the help of Native tribes to gain safe passage through the territory. The scene in which a Native American and African American alliance is negotiated is the most powerful in the film. It is also a scene that depicts how Poitier attempted to revolutionize the genre by bringing these two communities together.

To recuperate the financial losses endured by the Exodusters, Buck and the Preacher decide to rob the town bank. But the conversation that engenders their decision is itself revealing of the characters' motives and indicative of generic transformation. While sitting on a hillside one morning, Preacher shares his sad life story of having been a slave. We learn that he inherited

FIGURE 2.6 Ruby Dee's Ruth defies Cameron Mitchell's Deshay in *Buck and the Preacher*.

his profession (uniform and Bible) from his former slave master, a man who was also a charlatan or religious con artist. Preacher's master was also an unscrupulous pastor, who owned Preacher when he was just a boy. One day the white minister sent the sixteen-year-old boy on an errand. When the youth returned home, he discovered that the old man had sold his mother off for two hundred dollars. That night, when his master asked to be put to bed, the young man drowned him, thus inheriting his possessions and trade.

After sharing this woeful tale of servitude, Preacher asks Buck how he plans to obtain the money needed for the remaining Exoduster families. Together they craft a plan to replace the livestock and grain that the Exodusters lost to Klan night riders. Buck and Preacher hold up a poker game in a brothel where the riders are bunking. Next they decide to rob a bank. Their decision to become bank robbers puts them on the wrong side of the law, but it parallels the banditry of other mythic western characters, chiefly the iconic eponymous figures of *Butch Cassidy and the Sundance Kid*. Buck and Preacher justify their banditry by citing white townsfolks' exploitation of colored folks and the injustices of slavery.

The extradiegetic viewing audience would have sympathized with these acts of retributive justice given the socioeconomic climate outside of movie theaters—namely, the climate of "Nixonomics."[50] The "Nixon Shock" had taken hold in 1971, a year before the film's release. The country had entered an era of stagflation characterized by slow economic growth and high unemployment, which hit African American workers particularly hard.

Whereas Butch and Sundance robbed banks out of iconoclastic self-interest, Buck and Preacher stole to achieve remuneration for slavery and Black disenfranchisement. This was a radical revision of the western genre. It evoked the tenets of self-determination, economic enfranchisement, and Black political power embedded in Black nationalist organizing occurring at the Black National Convention held in March 1972 in Gary, Indiana. Coincidentally, *Buck and the Preacher* was released on April 28, 1972. A few days later, *Black Rodeo* was released (on May 1, 1972), and *The Legend of Nigger Charley* was released on May 17, 1972. This is not to suggest that these films were made because of the Black National Convention. They were in development and production well beforehand. However, the timing of these films points out that their emergence coincided with landmark events and with evolving national politics. *Buck and the Preacher* therefore had diegetic and extradiegetic political resonance with Black nationalism.

In town, Buck, Preacher, and Ruth successfully pull off their bank heist. But a vicious posse of gunmen pursues them. Eventually they come to an open range with the posse close behind. Suddenly, out of nowhere, a Native American war party, defending the boundaries of their territory, rides up from the hills, allowing Buck, Preacher, and Ruth to pass by while creating a barrier for the sheriff and his posse. The message is clear: they have crossed the line into Indian Territory. This is the climax of the movie—not because it's a chase scene with stunt riding but because it marks the moment when the movie reveals the previously unknown alliance between Native Indians and Black Americas. It's an alliance that would have resonated with civil rights–era audiences, who were keenly aware of the necessity for interracial and cross-cultural coalitions of political protest.

Once they ride up into the mountains, Buck meets with an Indian chief and his translator wife, Sinsie. Buck requests the tribe's assistance in fighting the gang of white men. But the chief refuses, explaining he cannot spare his men or ammunition to fight the "Yellow Hair" (a general term given to white people). The chief also reminds Buck that they were once enemies when Buck fought for the white man's army against Indians. Buck leaves with his request denied. With this denial, the film instills its Native Indian characters with a sense of diplomacy atypical of most celluloid Indians. They are shown as people who are negotiating politics and the existential threats ahead. Shortly thereafter the posse tries again to attack the wagon trains. This time the Native Americans who initially said they would not fight Buck's battle send several warriors to help turn the tide in Buck's favor.

FIGURE 2.7 Buck and Ruth on horseback.

Together, this Black-Indian armed coalition thwarts the corrupt sheriff and his racist posse. This scene stands out as remarkable, if not an outright revolutionary moment in American film, because there are few, if any, films like it in the history of world cinema.

Buck and the Preacher is one of the only films to imagine strategic political community between African Americans and Native Americans. This moment coincided with a rise in civil rights activism among both African Americans and Native Americans. For example, in 1973, the following year, Native actress-model Marie Louise Cruz (also known as Sacheen Littlefeather), represented Marlon Brando at the 45th Academy Awards. At the awards program, she declined the Best Actor award that he won for his performance in *The Godfather*. Brando boycotted the ceremony as a protest against Hollywood's portrayal of Native Americans. Through his protest and her speech, Brando and Lightfeather sought to draw attention to the standoff at Wounded Knee.[51]

The closing scenes of *Buck and the Preacher* resonate on two levels. They resonate at the diegetic and non-diegetic registers. At the diegetic level, this ending provides a historic cinematic critique of white supremacy and its role in the colonization of the United States. It also offers a powerful account of the destruction of Indian civilizations, and it gives Poitier's Buck a chance to repent for his complicity with the U.S. Army as a Buffalo Soldier. Finally, it forges an alliance between subjugated communities of color.

FIGURE 2.8 Julie Robinson-Belafonte and Enrique Lucero in *Buck and the Preacher*.

At the extradiegetic level, these closing scenes enable Sidney Poitier to demonstrate his talent as a new, yet skilled director. Using this film as a vehicle, Poitier offers revision of the western genre. He molds the western into a myth and sacred legend for African American, Native American, and Mexican American civil rights–era audiences. He overturns the tropes and conventions of the genre by positioning and aligning spectators with African Americans and Indians rather than white cowboys, cattlemen, and settlers. Taken collectively, *Buck and the Preacher* is not only a creative product; it's also a liberating act of resistance, like much of Sidney Poitier's career. Out of recognition for Poitier's career-long efforts to challenge stereotypes and caricatures of Black masculinity, President Barack Obama awarded Poitier the Medal of Freedom.[52] In the larger context of what Poitier sought to achieve through his films, the presidential award for his landmark career makes sense.

It is worth mentioning that the reception of the film was intriguing. Generally, African American audiences enjoyed the picture. Biographers have documented as much; take, for example, the work of film historians Keyser and Ruszkowski. The African American press was also favorable. For example, *Black Stars* magazine described Buck as "Daniel Boone and John Shaft without the usual Hollywood glitter."[53] But in this celebratory review, the critic inadvertently champions the politically reprehensible notion of killing Indians when he writes, "John Wayne has been settling the West and murdering redskins singlehandedly for far too long. The meaning and dramatic role played by America's black population in the development of the West has lain dormant."[54] Ironically, *Buck and the Preacher* is antithetical to the kind of white supremacist cowboys-and-Indians role-playing this reviewer references. Critical commentary of this nature reflects that some reviewers failed to understand the nuanced politics of the picture. In a *New York Times* interview, Harry Belafonte was quoted as saying:

> Other critics complain that it's too violent. Well, we told it like it was. I don't know how one shows what took place in the West without showing the white as the villain. In fact, Sidney and I were most gracious in our efforts not to polarize. We did not show the real bestiality that took place. I guess you cannot expect whites to accept a picture of themselves as the oppressors. It might have been more acceptable if there had been a white character in the movie to lead us benevolently to the promised land. I'm sorry some white critics have found our movie offensive. I don't believe it is a great work of art. Sidney and I did not set out to make a great work of art. But we did make a movie that deals with social, political, and ideological realities. We made compromises; everyone compromises—that's the name of the game. But we are artists, and we made an honest film.[55]

Even when white critics were not overtly critical, they were clearly underwhelmed by the picture because they were unsure how to read the film's political commentary. Take Vincent Canby's *New York Times* review as a case in point. Canby described the film in lukewarm terms by saying, "Sidney Poitier's first film as director, as well as star, is a loose, amiable, post–Civil War Western with a firm though not especially severe Black Conscience."[56] It is telling that even white critics felt comfortable questioning Poitier's political commitment. Canby continues, saying:

> *Buck and the Preacher* is otherwise a perfectly ordinary example of the kind of Western that seeks to prove that the West was not lily-white. The movie West, of course, has never been completely lily-white. There have always been a certain number of Indians horsing around, scalping, drinking, shooting, getting shot, and being poorly dealt with by just about everybody, including the movie makers. For the most part, however, blacks showed up on the frontier only as servants or, occasionally, as outcasts and loners, most notably in Ford's "Sergeant Rutledge" and "The Man Who Shot Liberty Valance." If they do nothing else, these new Soul Westerns may serve to desegregate our myths, which have always been out of the jurisdiction of the Supreme Court.[57]

Belafonte and Poitier intended to make an intervention with this film, and they did not want the politics embedded in their celebrity to overshadow the picture or its reception. Yet Poitier, who had received so much more criticism than Belafonte, was aware of his status as Super Sidney, as a token or "model minority," and sensed the potential impact of his public persona on his filmmaking. For example, in his 1980 autobiography, *This Life*, he makes this concern evident by writing:

> I was somehow being pushed to save the world. I was somehow being pushed to raise my black brothers and sisters to the next level. I was being pushed to change the world as it related to me and mine. I was being pushed to do the impossible. I figured that black people just wouldn't survive without me saving them through dealing with the pressures on myself. I didn't think the *world* would survive if I didn't live and develop in a certain way. And my eye was fastened to the possibility that somewhere in those years my dream could materialize and I could shoot through a barrier into uncharted waters where no black actor had ever been before.[58]

Buck and the Preacher ultimately did push the boundaries of American film culture. It helped Poitier restore his reputation with Black communities. For example, according to Donald Bogle, Poitier regained the audience his recent films had been alienating: the young urban black audience. "Black audiences openly screamed out in joy, and *Buck and the Preacher* emerged as a solid hit with the community."[59] It demonstrated an alternative vision of filmmaking that included more African American production staff. It also offered generic revision by constructing a credible depiction of the frontier with people of color. It challenged the cinematic landscape by providing filmic representation of white supremacy defeated by Black-Indian solidarity long before similarly progressive television miniseries like *Roots* (on which screenwriter Ernest Kinoy would also work) or movies like *12 Years a Slave* (Steve McQueen, 2013). To some extent it provided an alternative to the assimilationist and integrationist movies for which Poitier was vehemently criticized during the civil rights movement (e.g., *Lilies of the Field*, *Guess Who's Coming to Dinner*, *A Patch of Blue*). Finally, *Buck and the Preacher* sought to redress the relationship between film and historical memory.

Sidney Poitier tried to pass on his commitment to radical social change to the next generation through his films and his family life. In an interview with entertainment journalist Wanda Hale, Poitier said, "I'm going to ask my daughters to promise me to be Women's Lib. Women have the right to be a man's equal and I want them to take advantage of it for progress."[60] Clearly, Poitier's two western vehicles, *Duel at Diablo* and *Buck and the Preacher*, are much like his life and career. They stand as remarkable examples of his attempts to negotiate the racial hegemony of American film culture while moving the discourse created therein to more fertile, complex, and progressive ground.

3

Blaxploitation versus Black Liberation

The Nigger Charley *Trilogy*

> Another reality is that the Western cowboy, as portrayed in film, is a distorted image held by both white and Black American males. The Hollywood Western cowboy exists as a loner to prove that unnatural self-reliance is a virtue and that rebellious behavior and non-conformist violence is the best part of injustice, and society's view of the matter be damned. Yesterday's cowboy has been replaced by today's detective, policeman, doctor and attorney on the television screens. In order to understand the Black reality and the portrayal of Black performers on screen, there must be an understanding of Hollywood Western film, a form that grew out of the popularity of the dime novel which glamorized and exaggerated a rapidly disappearing Western frontier.
>
> —Waliyy Gill, "The Western Film: Hollywood Myths and One Black Reality"

Only one month after *Buck and the Preacher* was released in April 1972, *The Legend of Nigger Charley*, starring newcomer Fred Williamson, debuted. The American motion picture industry found another Jim Brown in Williamson, a tall, handsome, brawny football star willing to parlay his athletic celebrity into motion picture stardom. He was another African American man who was able to personify the myth of "reel," irrepressible Black masculine power. This image was particularly meaningful in a political era when "real" Black male leadership outside of the cinema (e.g., Medgar Evers, Malcolm X, Martin Luther King Jr., Bobby Seale, Huey P. Newton, Fred Hampton, Bayard Rustin) was being profiled by a repressive state apparatus–sanctioned police, surveilled by FBI agents, attacked by police dogs, or targeted by white supremacist assassins. This climate necessitated films that addressed race relations more seriously than Paul Bogart's western satire of slavery, *Skin Game*, a film that made light of slavery at a time when civil rights activists were lobbying for reparations. Out of this tumultuous climate emerged a handful of Black actors who symbolized counter-cultural resistance and rebellion against a repressive state. Fred Williamson was one such performer. Although his western films were not sophisticated pictures, they were nonetheless part of the discursive link between Blackness, nationhood, and masculinity in mainstream American action cinema.[1]

Born on March 5, 1938, in Gary, Indiana, Williamson was the son of a welder and grew up in a tough Chicago neighborhood. He was frequently bullied. In one interview he jokingly reminisced about those years, saying, "Get beat up? I used to get my lunch money taken away so regularly that I finally just went down to the corner and said, 'Line up for the lunch money everybody.' Finally, I hit six feet tall and started getting a little lunch money back!"[2] In the mainstream press like the *New York Times*, Williamson recalled his youth similarly, saying, "When I was a kid, pimps, gambling, stealing and robbery surrounded me. That was in the fifties." But once he discovered that girls admired football players, his interest in gangs disappeared. He excelled in the scholastic sports of basketball, track, and football and was offered several athletic scholarships, settling for one with Northwestern University.[3]

At college he earned degrees in psychology and architecture. After college, Williamson was drafted by the Houston Oilers (of the now defunct American Football League). In 1960 he was signed by the San Francisco 49ers and then quickly traded to the Pittsburgh Steelers. In 1961 he played for the Oakland Raiders, and in 1965 he played as a member of the Kansas City Chiefs. Williamson played defensive back in Super Bowl I (1967), when the Chiefs played the Green Bay Packers. Throughout his professional football career, Williamson was nicknamed "The Hammer" by sports commentators, journalists, and fans because he had an aggressive style of playing. Long before modern safety rules, he often used his forearm to deliver karate-style blows to the heads of opposing players, especially wide receivers. After nearly ten years playing pro football, he had played for four teams, in ninety-three games, and intercepted dozens of passes.

He retired from pro football in 1968–1969. Reflecting on that period in an interview, he told journalist Chris Wyse, "I don't miss football. I got tired of it because I couldn't relate to it anymore, but while I was in it, I was one of the best and everybody knew it."[4] Williamson retired and moved to Montreal, Canada, to set up an architecture business. After only six months in Montreal, the retired athlete knew he'd had enough of that business and sought out a new life and career in Hollywood.[5]

Williamson moved to California and immediately began knocking on the doors of Hollywood producers, agents, and directors. He connected with producer Hal Kanter. Enamored with Kanter's television sitcom *Julia* (1968–1971), starring Diahann Carroll, Williamson decided he wanted the role of Julia's boyfriend, Steve Bruce. He succeeded in impressing the producer of the hit comedy series and was immediately cast as Bruce. Another opportunity arrived when he met agent Haines Palish, who got Williamson a stint on the rapid-fire sketch comedy show *Laugh-In* (1963–1973), the *Saturday Night Live* of its day. Having seen him on *Laugh-In*, Otto Preminger picked up Williamson for one of the leads in *Tell Me That You Love Me, Junie Moon* (1970), starring Liza Minnelli.

Soon afterward director Robert Altman recruited Williamson for the movie *M*A*S*H* (1972). He got his first opportunity to direct, albeit in a limited capacity, when he handled the choreography and directing of the movie's famed football sequence. The former Kansas City cornerback was one in a long line of African American men who in the 1960s and '70s turned their attention and careers from football to film. The list includes Cleveland Browns player Harold Bradley, L.A. Rams split end Bernie Casey, Philadelphia Eagles back Timmy Brown, and New York Giants tackle Rosie Grier (Pam Grier's brother), not to mention Richard Roundtree and San Francisco running back O. J. Simpson.

Not all of these men found success in the American film industry, however. Harold Bradley, for instance, made most of his films in Italy. Bradley's trajectory might have influenced Williamson's decision to set up foreign distributorship for his films, where American companies were selling Black-themed films inexpensively by 1978.[6] This development is significant, nevertheless. Several 1960s and '70s roles for Black actors were in western-themed pictures primarily because the genre was enjoying a counter-cultural renaissance based on the success of international Euro-westerns. These roles provided a canvas on which the history of American race relations and Black Power themes intersected.

As Louis Paul notes of Williamson's motion pictures, "Most of the early films, defiantly anti-establishment, fulfilled the suppressed fantasies of millions of American youths."[7] Though these motion pictures resisted the dominant culture and white supremacy, they were not necessarily progressive. They were often just as patriarchal, heterosexist, homophobic, and violent as most New Hollywood films, which were often politically regressive.

Whether these were understated rebellious men (as with Jim Brown's characters) or over-the-top, badass avengers (as in Fred Williamson's portrayals), these star vehicles provided—in mythic form—what was systematically denied to Black people: self-determination, economic opportunity, leadership, and the basic freedoms accompanying civil rights. It's no accident that Woody Strode, Jim Brown, Fred Williamson, and other Black actors emerged in rapid succession, with increasing degrees of intensity and authority ascribed to their screen personas.[8] As different as they were cinematically, Strode and Brown had one thing in common: both had eased their way into edgy, tough-guy roles. They began playing dutiful, almost sheepish, cavalry officers and Union soldiers who were deferential to their white superior officers. This racial deference paved the way for those characters and actors who followed them.

Fred Williamson, by contrast, rose to cinematic fame in the early 1970s, riding the tide of Black political activism. It was an era of change. Congressional redistricting, combined with other factors in the wake of the civil rights movement, resulted in the number of Black Congress members increasing from nine to thirteen.[9] Shirley Chisholm referred to the group as "unbought and unbossed." The Democratic Select Committee (DSC) was established in 1969 as a predecessor to the Congressional Black Caucus (a group of Black members of the House of Representatives including Shirley Chisholm of New York, Louis Stokes of Ohio, and William L. Clay of Missouri). Black representatives had begun to enter the House in increasing numbers during the 1960s, and they had a desire for a formal organization. The DSC was renamed the Congressional Black Caucus in February 1971 on the motion of Charles B. Rangel of New York.

In 1970 Chisholm published her autobiography, *Unbought and Unbossed*, in which she related her remarkable rise from a girlhood in Brooklyn to a political career as the first African American congresswoman.[10] In the same year, revolutionary Brazilian educator Paulo Freire published his Marxist class analysis, *Pedagogy of the Oppressed* (first published in 1968), in English. It would become a groundbreaking text worldwide.[11] A few months later, in July 1971, Congresswoman Chisholm began exploring her presidential candidacy.[12] Meanwhile, the Black Power movement had grown more militant in its approach to institutional racism, more revolutionary in philosophy, and advocated self-defense "by any means necessary."[13] These sea changes culminated in the Black National Convention held March 10–12, 1972. The political tide had changed. The cinematic culture was also changing.

Fred Williamson's screen persona was constructed to buck white authority in an appeal to audiences of color who had witnessed Chicago police and FBI agents systematically pursuing Black Panther Party members. Few historians dispute that the FBI murdered activist and revolutionary Panther Fred Hampton, a charismatic orator who was successfully building a

"Rainbow Coalition" across racial and class lines. The FBI had opened a file on Hampton in 1967, and his mother's phone was tapped in 1968. Nothing was more threatening to FBI chief J. Edgar Hoover than a so-called "Black savior." Hoover feared a leader like Hampton who could unite people with a revolutionary bipartisan platform and successfully connect disenfranchised Blacks, poor Appalachian-based whites, dissident college student Yippies, Vietnam protesters, NAACP organizers, and Bible Belt Black Christians against the U.S. government's agenda.[14] By 1971 director Howard Alk and producer Mike Gray had released their informative documentary *The Murder of Fred Hampton* (The Film Group, 1971).

Multiple developments undergirded Williamson's rise to action film stardom. Chief among them was a growing appetite for Black heroes who could stand in metonymically for slain leaders and function symbolically as the "return of the repressed/oppressed."[15] The truly repressed and oppressed Black Power militants (Bobby Seale, Fred Hampton, Huey P. Newton) laid the real-world foundation upon which Fred Williamson created a reel-world screen persona that was more pugnacious and confrontational than his cinematic predecessors.

More quickly than Strode or Brown, Williamson merged Black Power, Black masculinity, and counter-cultural anti-authoritarianism. The bold subjects and increasingly brazen movie titles of his star vehicles articulated a grittier, tougher sensibility than even the films of Jim Brown. They reflected the reality that major and minor Hollywood studios—in this case Paramount—were eager to exploit: the trope of the "bad (ass) nigger." And Williamson wanted to play characters who would not bend to the slave whip or kowtow to "whitey." He wanted to develop the role of the rebel who stuck around to kill slave masters and lived to tell the story.[16] In many ways he was aiming for an aesthetic amalgamation of spaghetti western tenacity and Black Power irrepressibility.

Jim Brown and Fred Williamson also benefited from other important developments in the zeitgeist. Both enjoyed a celebrity that coincided with the growing wave of African American representation in popular culture broadly. Comic book heroes—Black superheroes in particular—were a by-product and symbol of a counter-cultural groundswell (exemplified in the 1970s by blaxploitation). The "Silver Age of Comic Books," a period from 1956 to circa 1970 immediately following the "Golden Age of Comic Books" (1938–1950), represented a period of artistic advancement, commercial success, and innovation in the comic book superhero genre. Brown and Williamson rose to fame as Black superheroes were becoming familiar figures in comic books. African American comic book superheroes such as the western hero Lobo (debuting December 1965), the princely Black Panther

(July 1966), and the avian avenger Falcon (September 1969) emerged shortly after Jim Brown starred in his first motion picture, *Rio Conchos*.[17]

In the mid-'60s, Dell Comics was experimenting with new content. They hired writer Don Arneson and illustrator Tony Tallarico to create the medium's first African American comic book hero in his own series. *Lobo* chronicled the Wild West adventures of a wealthy unnamed African American gunslinger dubbed "Lobo" by the first issue's antagonists. Lobo was a hero people could admire. His series was set a full century in the past

FIGURE 3.1 A Western comic book hero, *Lobo* was the medium's first African American character to headline his own comic series.

(1865). Free from his duties as a Union soldier during the recent war, he is heading west with his horse, Midnight (which he bought for a sack of flour), looking for a life without killing. He soon finds that life as a cowboy means always proving himself to his white colleagues. Though he is tolerant and forgiving of unfair treatment, he defends himself and remains dignified, often humbling those who would humble him. Unfortunately, two of the cowboys that he meets accuse him of robbing and murdering the paymaster of their cattle drive; the real murderer is another cowpoke by the name of Johnson.

As Lobo goes on the run, hoping to prove his innocence, he meets a prospector who is drowning in a river. It is revealed that the prospector was also accused of a crime he did not commit and the two men form a bond. The prospector offers Lobo his fortune to fund his quest to prove himself innocent, but Lobo refuses, although he does take a pouch full of gold coins with the engraving of a wolf and the letter "L," a coin that becomes his trademark.

The two cowboys who have accused him of the crime (along with an accomplice of theirs) rob a local bank, and Lobo apprehends them and turns them into the sheriff. The sheriff declines to arrest Lobo after receiving one of the Lobo coins, saying, "I don't know; there was just something about him." Later he finds Johnson, the true robber, staked in the sun, punishment by a group of Apaches whose horse he tried to steal. Johnson dies and along with him Lobo's only chance at proving his innocence. He decides to ride back and visit the old miner who made his coins only to find him dying. The miner asks Lobo to take his fortune in gold and do some good with it, which is what he decides to do in the closing pages of issue number one.

From then on, Lobo has difficulty making friends and integrating into society. The name Lobo comes from his accusers calling him a *lobo*, or lone wolf. He decides that the name is appropriate and adopts it as his moniker. On the foreheads of vanquished criminals, Lobo leaves his calling card: a gold coin imprinted with the image of a wolf and the letter "L."[18] Lobo was arguably the first African American superhero.

According to Jeffrey A. Brown, only a few years later the comic book industry would be taking cues from blaxploitation precursors (e.g., *Sweet Sweetback's Baadasssss Song*, *Shaft*) and their bevy of imitators (e.g., *Super Fly*, *Top of the Heap*, *The Man*, *The Mack*, and *Black Caesar*).[19] But with *Lobo*, Dell Comics had created the first western comic book action figure and superhero. The conventional wisdom among graphic novel historians is that Black superheroes of DC Comics and Marvel Comics thereafter drew their inspiration from blaxploitation film characters. The unmistakable commonality between the two, writes Adilifu Nama, "exists because

Blaxploitation film characters *were* black superheroes." Nama continues by saying:

> Jim Brown, the retired football great, starred in numerous Blaxploitation films such as . . . *tick, tick, tick* . . . (1970), *Black Gun* (1972), *Slaughter* (1972), *Slaughter's Big Rip-Off* (1973), and *The Slams* (1973) and nearly became a genre by himself. Fred Williamson was no less prolific, starring in a series of dubiously titled films like *The Legend of Nigger Charley* (1972), *The Soul of Nigger Charley* (1973), *Boss Nigger* (1975), and *Bucktown* (1975). . . .
>
> For example, as a black western, the movie *Boss Nigger* (1975) is easily one of the most dreadful and uninspired films of the Blaxploitation era. But as a black superhero film, *Boss* is not as easy to dismiss. Rather than viewing *Boss* as a film about the real or imaginary place blacks occupied in the American Old West, I view *Boss* the way I view the infinite and parallel Earths that populate the comic book worlds of DC and Marvel.[20]

Nama indicates how different in tone the cynical revisionist 1960s and '70s Black westerns were from the emotionally naïve 1930s and '40s Black westerns with singing cowboys like Herb Jeffries or actor Clarence Brooks and riders like Bill Pickett. In some ways, Lobo belonged to a bygone era. He was written in the tradition of the sincere, upstanding loner characters and was less a civil rights era avenger than a lone hero.

The movies *Two Gun Man from Harlem, Harlem Rides the Range*, and *Bronze Buckaroo* were sepia imitations of Hollywood's white mounted heroes and their homespun sincerity. More disturbingly, Hollywood westerns created what Julia Leyda calls "strategic anachronisms" because they omitted Blacks, Mexicans, and Indians to skirt the complexities of having African Americans in imperialistic positions of authority vis-à-vis other people of color.[21] But the '60s and '70s movies were a breed apart. Gone were the contented sweet songs sung by kind Black cowboys like Herb Jeffries in *Two Gunman from Harlem* or white actor Gene Autry in *Tumbling Tumbleweed* (1935) and *Singing Cowboy* (1937). They were replaced by Black Panther metonyms, Black Power superheroes, and charismatic avengers who bucked white authority while moving to R&B rhythms.

The evolving civil rights movement and the Black comic book boom were two facets of the changing cultural landscape. The quest for Black civil rights and self-determination helped stimulate the second wave of the feminist movement. Second-wave feminism broadened the debate around women's rights and equal opportunity to include a wider range of concerns: gender roles, sexual liberation, patriarchal family structure, workplace politics, and reproductive rights. As Williamson debuted in films, the sexual revolution was under way. Millions of American women were using birth control

FIGURE 3.2 Lobo, the first African American comic book hero, on his trusty mount, Midnight. Lobo is a noteworthy fixture of Black western popular culture.

pills, as prohibitions around birth control had largely fallen by the wayside years earlier. The resulting sexual freedoms (which arguably impacted white women more than women of color[22]) occurred at a moment that corresponded with the Hays Production Code yielding to a new, more liberal Rating Administration. Films were no longer subject to prior restraint and were no longer required to be appropriate for all audiences.

The new film classification system did not remove all of the barriers that Hollywood faced regarding censorship. The new system relaxed existing codes forbidding obscenity, sexual slavery, interracial relations (formerly "miscegenation"), alcoholism, drug addiction, nudity, homosexuality, lustful kissing, and references to sexual "perversion." In all likelihood, the new system was partially attributable to the U.S. Supreme Court decision in 1969's *Stanley v. Georgia* (1969), a "right to privacy" decision that removed restrictions on possession of adult pornography.[23] Hoping to find another approach to controlling what many considered a threat to traditional American values, the U.S. Congress authorized $2 million to fund a presidential commission to study pornography in the United States. The commission's recommendations included a national sex education campaign, open discussion on issues relating to pornography, and generating additional information through research.

Whether they featured virile detectives and rogue cops as in *Shaft*, *Dirty Harry* (1971), and *The French Connection* (1971); recast the plight of the prostitute in relationship to members of the opposite sex like *Klute* (1971), *Sweet Sweetback's Baadasssss Song*, *McCabe & Mrs. Miller*, and *The Owl and the Pussycat* (1971); celebrated transgressive awakenings as in *Myra Breckinridge* (1970), *The Last Picture Show* (1971), and *Carnal Knowledge* (1971); addressed repressed queer subjectivity as in *Dog Day Afternoon* (1975) or *Midnight Cowboy* (1969); or depicted sexual violence as in *Straw Dogs* (1971) and *A Clockwork Orange* (1971), many motion pictures released in the early 1970s evinced some preoccupation with nontraditional sexuality. The year 1971 alone witnessed the release of over thirty lowbrow sexploitation features. This slightly more liberal, albeit often sexist, approach to cinematic subjects meant that movies could take license to push taboo boundaries in other ways.

Violence (*The Wild Bunch*), interracial relations (*100 Rifles*), sexual violence (*Last Tango in Paris*, 1972), pedophilia (*Lolita*, 1962), and other formerly forbidden subjects were now being explored. They were also treated less conservatively than before, since the subjects were now sometimes addressed with a campy sensibility.[24] Taken collectively, the aesthetically and politically unconventional films of the 1970s prefigured the social malaise of a decade cast in the shadow of Watergate and Vietnam; they also shared a preoccupation with cinematic excess in its various forms (e.g., blaxploitation, sexploitation, teensploitation, westploitation, and vigilantism).

The *Nigger Charley* Films

The *Nigger Charley* films emerged amid a confluence of events. In her well-researched 2011 essay "Death Proof," Amy Abugo Ongiri notes the convergence of those events when she writes, "In 1968, a year after Guy Debord published *The Society of the Spectacle* and Régis Debray published *Revolution in the Revolution*, Guevara would be killed in the jungles of Bolivia after failing to incite revolution there, and Larry Neal would declare the Black Arts movement 'the sister to the Black Power concept'."[25] Ongiri paraphrases Larry Neal to underscore how groups like the Symbionese Liberation Army (SLA) and the Black Panther Party (BPP) sought to release the stranglehold that the dominant media had over visual culture by disrupting existing image culture with a kind of politicized propaganda. The confluence of Black Power/ Black Arts sentiments, exploitation cinema aesthetics, sexual liberation, and widespread political discontent explains the tone, tenor, and brazenness of Fred Williamson's outlandishly titled blaxploitation western trilogy.

The three films told the story of an escaped slave named Charley. James Robert Parish and George Hill distinguish the *Nigger Charley* movies from Sidney Poitier's *Buck and the Preacher* (released a month earlier), noting that "unlike the Sidney Poitier–Harry Belafonte feature, which invested its six-gun tale with humanity, *The Legend of Nigger Charley* is exploitative to the hilt. . . . The teaser ad copy read: 'Somebody warn the West! Nigger Charley ain't running no more.'"[26]

The basis for the first movie was a story carried in 1966 by the *Los Angeles Examiner*.[27] According to the report, the skull of a free Negro man was dis-covered in Inyo County, eastern California. The bodily remains (supposedly belonging to a man who sacrificed himself to the Paiute Indians of Inyo County in 1863 to save a white woman) were studied at San Fernando Valley State College. Dr. Wesley L. Bliss, a renowned anthropologist/geologist and resident of Ojai,[28] theorized that the skull found near the town of Big Pine in Inyo County belonged to Charley Tyler. The escaped Charley was one of an estimated eight thousand Black cowboys, wranglers, and bronco busters in the Old West, constituting 25 percent of the frontier population.

Charley is believed to have given his horse to a woman during an Indian attack. After the attack, Charley was not seen again. According to folklore, the Paiutes tortured and burned him at the stake. The population of free slaves like Tyler (living on the Western frontier) expanded considerably after the Civil War when hundreds of thousands of Black refugees from slave states, who had no place to go, streamed to the West and built Black communities. There were no official Black marshals or sheriffs in California yet (Bass Reeves was in Arkansas and the Oklahoma Territory from 1838 to 1910), as these positions were exclusively held by whites, but there were Black bankers, businessmen, hotel operators, cattle ranchers, and even Black rustlers.

In the early 1970s, the film's producer, Larry Spangler, and director, Martin Goldman, completed a script based on the life of this legendary

Charley Tyler. It was supposedly after months of research on the subject of the Western frontier in the nineteenth century that Spangler committed to the film's concept. Because an adaptation of W. A. Chalfant's novel *The Story of Inyo* proved prohibitively expensive, Spangler, who was now aware of the obscurity of the Black cowboy, decided to write an original story instead.[29] Consequently, the eponymous Charley of the film *The Legend of Nigger Charley* became a composite of at least three different sources and time periods: (1) the historic pioneers for African American freedom such as Nat Turner, Frederick Douglass, and John Brown;[30] (2) traditional Hollywood heroes like Will Kane (played by Gary Cooper) in *High Noon*; and (3) real-life Black revolutionaries like Fred Hampton, Bobby Seale, Stokely Carmichael, and Huey P. Newton. This is not to mention the brutal Black buck stereotype that had long been central to the American cultural landscape and that the film revives. These tropes of Black masculinity infused the ethos of the film.

In a 1972 issue of *Sepia* magazine, African American journalist Earle Chisholm described the eponymous Charley as the repository of mainstream white American fears of Black American men:

> Charles Tyler was a "bad nigger" in the sense that he was irreconcilable, unconventional, and implacable in his ways. In that sense, many white Americans would describe as "bad niggers" so many of the leaders of today's black liberation movements ranging from Jesse Jackson to Julian Bond. And, it is significant that to play the "bad nigger" role in the new Paramount movie, the choice was actor Fred Williamson[,] who on many counts would fit that description. Bold, brash, frank and fearless, Williamson is a man who speaks his mind no matter who doesn't like it, black or white.[31]

According to scholar Erica James, the first *Nigger Charley* film was initially banned in several cities because the owners of movie houses feared promoting it. They worried that if they promoted the film on theater marquees, irate African Americans would riot and destroy the glass theater facades. Producer Larry Spangler claimed that the title was necessarily offensive within Black communities of the time. In press interviews, Williamson brazenly embraced the title on many occasions and described the movie as the "first honest black western."[32] Williamson and the producers claimed it was the first film to depict the raiding of Black tribes by other Blacks to capture people to be sold to white slave traders.

Journalist George Coleman covered the controversial title in his article "Nigger Charley Doesn't Bother Fred Williamson" for the *Atlanta Daily World*. Coleman opens his piece by paraphrasing the star: "The word nigger hardly seems controversial in 1972, except as the 'white man uses it to put us down,'" quips Williamson. "Black people have been calling each other nigger for years. There was nothing derogatory about it in their usage," he says. "It was the derogatory connotation the white man put on it that made it bad. He made it a bad word."[33] Nevertheless, *The Legend of Nigger Charley* was ultimately retitled *The Legend of Black Charley* for American broadcast television. But this title change was regional rather than global, according to Erica James, who observed that no deletions or title modifications were made for Caribbean audiences.[34] Despite limited distribution, Williamson's western became one of Paramount's highest-grossing films of 1972, earning over $12 million.[35] As a result, two sequels followed.

Released in rapid succession, the *Charley* sequels were salaciously titled *The Soul of Nigger Charley* and *Boss Nigger* (Jack Arnold, 1975). For historical spectators re-viewing the *Nigger Charley* trilogy today, the movies do not hold up. When they were released, they broke with conventions. But when viewed with perspective, the pictures are a hodgepodge of disparate western elements: formulaic action plots, naïve (rather than deliberate) camp aesthetics, shoestring budgets, and pseudo-political sloganeering clumsily scripted by out-of-touch writers. Still, in the 1970s, when the assassinations of Black leaders (Medgar Evers, 1963; Malcom X, 1965; Martin Luther King Jr., 1968; and Fred Hampton, 1968) were fresh on the minds of most African Americans, and many others, these films were a radical departure from the status quo. Black action heroes were new to the zeitgeist. Even Williamson knew as much when he told Earle Chisholm, "In the picture, Nigger Charley is a southern slave who, when his life is threated by the overseer, kills him and flees. A new breed of black man, Nigger Charley heads west accompanied by two other slaves, pitting themselves against tremendous odds while seeking their rightful place as men on the western frontier."[36]

The tropes associated with Black westerns were appealing across the U.S., and they were also appealing in the Caribbean. Perry Henzell's immensely popular *The Harder They Come*, which some scholars have described as a western, illustrates as much. The protagonist of Henzell's film watches the character Django on television and idolizes him. While Williamson considered himself an individualist rather than a civil rights activist, he nevertheless filled the void of activist/hero in the collective imagination.[37] And as is so often the case with celebrities, his physical body and sexuality were intimately linked to these roles. In his book on cult cinema, Louis Paul viewed the actor as a groundbreaking icon:

> In 1972, Williamson began appearing in gritty urban action-adventure films as the maverick hero and, in some cases, anti-hero. Barnstorming through roles with unmatched verisimilitude and glee, the world's first Black action

star was born. Most of the early films, defiantly anti-establishment, fulfilled the suppressed fantasies of millions of African American youths. . . .

In titles like *Hammer* (1972), *The Legend of Nigger Charley* (1972) and its sequel *The Soul of Nigger Charley* (1973), *Black Caesar* (1973), *That Man Bolt* (1973), *Hell Up in Harlem* (1973), *Black Eye* (1974), *Three the Hard Way* (1974), *Three Tough Guys* (1974), *Boss Nigger* (1975) and *Bucktown* (1975), Williamson meted out his own brand of justice. He had box-office success with his movies and earned himself a special place in the history of action films.[38]

Because Williamson had predecessors in Paul Robeson, Sidney Poitier, Woody Strode, and Jim Brown, he was not the first Black action star, but he was among the first Black actors to become both an action figure and an international sex symbol, according to European (i.e., Swedish) and American popularity polls. Such culture industry feedback was integral to his commercial marketability and reflected the changing sexual mores of 1970s popular culture in which Black masculinity was openly desirable.

Whereas Poitier's sexuality was constrained by the Hays Production Code and the intersection of gendered racism, Williamson's sex appeal was fodder for popular discussion in fanzines. Coverage included Jason Winter's *Black Stars* interview titled "Fred Williamson: The Sexy Superman!" In the interview, Williamson boasted, "I found my niche right away—I think because I was a physical star, an action star!" By the end of the interview, Winters is enamored:

> Uncertain. That's the best way to describe this writer's opinion of Fred Williamson's personality. Is he really arrogant and egotistical? Or, is it all a cleverly manipulated masquerade designed to fool the press and public? I don't know the answer but I do know that the charm, sensual good looks and old Hollywood style of glamour that Fred "The Hammer" Williamson brings to the screen is unsurpassed by any other star today—black or white, and that's what movie stars are supposed to be about. . . . Aren't they.[39]

In the United States, Williamson had been described as "one of America's most durable tough guys" by the New York *Daily News* and as "the Black Clark Gable" by the *New York Amsterdam News*. He quickly embraced references to classic Hollywood icons and began reproducing these himself. *Sepia* reporter Doris Black quoted Williamson saying, "I'm exciting, handsome, devastating—and any other attribute you want to think of . . . just like Gable."[40] The footballer-turned-actor seemed to have taken a page out of Muhammad Ali's braggadocio playbook. This would not be a surprise given that Williamson idolized Ali. But such adulation only reinforced the perception that Black stars were mere imitations of classical Hollywood's authentic white celebrities, since the praise was full of Eurocentric standards of beauty and art. For example, a *New York Times* article stated, "His face and physique look as though they were 'chiseled-to-order' in heaven by Michelangelo for some customer who had requested the perfect man."[41]

Embedded in the hyperbolic media coverage was the marketing of the *Nigger Charley* trilogy to a mainstream white America that likely needed permission to gaze at his body and contemplate his sexuality. However, this had happened before with Paul Robeson. Nevertheless, whereas the Black press (e.g., *Ebony*, *Sepia*, *Black Stars*, and *Our World*) emphasized his masculinity, the white press lauded his sexual desirability. The common denominator was that both praised him as the ideal actor to embody Charley on the basis of his manliness. Earle Chisholm, for instance, wrote that Williamson fit the personality of Charley to a tee. Chisholm felt the actor embodied what producer Spangler termed the feel, stamina, and virility of Nigger Charley.[42]

No one was more suited to succeed Melvin Van Peebles's portrayal of the sexually liberated revolutionary Sweetback than football star Fred Williamson. Together, *Sweetback* and *Shaft* set the tone for blaxploitation cinema. Though these films were heterosexist (even misogynistic at times), some African American audiences overlooked the gender politics because systemic, anti-Black racism made Black spectators more inclined to value missing elements of Black realism that were absent from earlier movies.[43] Thus, whereas Manthia Diawara identifies "New Black Realism" emerging in the 1990s, one could argue that the antecedents were planted by these western films.

They were antecedents for Black realism because westerns from *Django* (Sergio Corbucci, 1966) onward commented on white supremacy and criticized the "possessive investment in whiteness" often depicted in western films about the history of Black disenfranchisement.[44] One only need look as far as the Red Shirt movement in North Carolina for evidence of anti-Reconstruction, private terror units who adopted red shirts to make themselves more visible and threatening to Southern Republicans, both whites and freedmen. Red Shirts are central antagonists in *Django*. The eponymous hero is a former Union soldier who must defeat both a gang of Confederate Red Shirts (led by Major Jackson) and General Hugo Rodríguez's revolutionaries. This plot structure, with its emphasis on internal and external adversaries, outlines the blueprint for most African American–themed westerns that followed.

The fact that *The Harder They Come* features the movie *Django* as a film within the film and that Django fights Red Shirts is what leads some scholars to read Henzell's movie as a western.[45] The new, unrelated western titled *The Harder They Fall* only exacerbates this confusion. But for most film scholars, *The Harder They Come* will remain an example of revolutionary

Third Cinema (e.g., *The Battle of Algiers*, 1966; *The Hour of the Furnaces*, 1968; *Vidas Secas* [aka *Barren Lives*], 1963; *Memories of Underdevelopment*, 1968; *Le Noir de . . . [Black Girl]*, 1966; *Xala*, 1975; *Mandabi*, 1968), given their unique searing critiques of colonialism, underdevelopment, and myth-making.

With their penchant for a gritty cinematic realism, the *Nigger Charley* trilogy raised yet another social concern. Despite Williamson's avowed comfort with the title, the movies openly and unapologetically deployed the N-word throughout the films. Director Melvin Van Peebles had set the tone with the ending of *Sweetback*, which concluded with the prophetic warning *"WATCH OUT! A Baadasssss Nigger Is Coming Back to Collect Some Dues!"* The tremendous success of *Sweetback* enabled Van Peebles to set a mass-marketed, cinematic precedent for the reinterpretation of an otherwise ignominious racial slur. Like the counter-cultural movements that redesigned fashion, rewrote music, reformed politics, and reclaimed language, Van Peebles overturned the N-word, which then started to undergo resignification.

In his detailed etymology of the N-word, legal historian Randall Kennedy explains why the term "nigger" fascinates and titillates. Since it has been put to a variety of uses, it radiates an array of meanings, having undergone resignification multiple times. According to Kennedy, African Americans have used the term to lampoon slavery, to poke fun at the grisly phenomenon of lynching, to dramatize the tragic reality of Jim Crow subjugation, and to satirize "legal" disenfranchisement. When used by Black people among themselves, it is sometimes used as a term of endearment with undertones of goodwill. It might also be deployed as a compliment (e.g., "he played like a nigger") or a salutation (e.g., "This is my *main* nigger").[46]

Richard Pryor was one of the first professional comedians to bring the term to center stage in stand-up comedy at roughly the same time Fred Williamson's *Nigger Charley* trilogy emerged. Pryor's celebrated show *That Nigger's Crazy* won the 1974 Grammy Award for best comedy recording. The show is still fondly remembered for utilizing the racial epithet in unexpectedly innovative ways. For some, to proclaim oneself a "nigger" then was to identify oneself as real, authentic, uncut, unassimilated, and unassimilable. This was the opposite of a "Negro," someone whose rejection of "nigger" was seen as part of an effort to blend into the white mainstream.[47]

After *Sweetback* struck a chord with many and had earned millions, despite being made on a shoestring budget of approximately five hundred thousand dollars, the *Nigger Charley* trilogy producers (and filmmakers of Williamson's movies thereafter) sought to pick up where *Sweetback* left off. Using the word "nigger" was an attempt to capitalize on the cult movie allure of *Sweetback*. And when he reflected on making these movies, Williamson admitted that his use of the N-word was intentional.

Jim Brown's and Fred Williamson's western heroes differed from Melvin Van Peebles's Sweetback because they had proven their masculinity to other men in traditionally male arenas. Football was, and still is, analogous to the western because both establish male-dominated social realms where women are virtually sidelined. Both focus on rivalries (usually) between men for control and dominance.[48] Both rely on a theater of excess. Football celebrates excessive masculine physical strength like the western focuses on tales of extreme physical endurance in the face of insurmountable social and environmental challenges (e.g., tornadoes, floods, droughts, unfriendly Natives). Sport and western movies require nonparticipant observers (i.e., spectators) to witness narrated spectacles of dominance and defeat. Both football and the western present gladiator contests or showdowns ending in defeat for one contestant and victory for another. Both westerns and football are predicated on homosociality.

As Michael Kimmel notes, "Masculinity is a homosocial enactment." Manhood is demonstrated for other men's approval. Men evaluate the performance and authenticity of masculinity performed by one another in sports, at work, in domestic life, and even in the popular culture landscape of the western genre.[49] The western film, like the football game, has come to stand in synecdochically for masculinity itself. One could describe certain revisionist films as "feminist westerns" (e.g., *Johnny Guitar*; *Giant*; *Cat Ballou*; *Ballad of Little Jo*, 1993; *Bad Girls*, 1994; *Gang of Roses*, 2003; *Ride Sweet, Die Slow*, 2005), but such pictures tended to emerge as exceptions to the cinematic conventions that celebrated patriarchal, heterosexual (Black) masculinity.[50]

From Europe to the Caribbean (and beyond), the genre has held unique significance for men and boys in their socialization to homosocial and hetero-patriarchal masculine norms. For example, in Germany, the West German western *Der Schatz im Silbersee* (*The Treasure of Silver Lake*) was so popular that it subsequently inspired a series of Karl May adaptations to screen (seventeen of them between 1962 and 1968). As Tassilo Schneider notes, the film did not imitate American westerns as much as it adapted them to a specific national heritage: Karl May's romantic homosocial vision of the West, which also presented all-male narrative worlds.[51]

Moreover, since several of the West German westerns were co-productions with Italy (and Spain, France, West Germany, Britain, Portugal, Greece, Israel, and Yugoslavia), the movies are connected to spaghetti western filmmaking (even if the first German western—*The Treasure of Silver Lake*—was shot in 1962 before Sergio Leone had taken Europe by storm). Nevertheless, the global and cross-cultural emergence of the western in the Caribbean, Europe, and the United States underscores the symbolic power of the genre's codes and conventions and the appeal of those codes to audiences worldwide.

Similarly, in the Caribbean, local Jamaican film culture was galvanized by Perry Henzell's *The Harder They Come*. Henzell's movie, with its film-within-the-film references to Sergio Corbucci's iconic spaghetti western *Django*, was a hybrid western-crime story and critique of underdevelopment. Many people have mistakenly read *The Harder They Come* as a crime drama.

The Legend of Nigger Charley

The Legend of Nigger Charley begins with a bizarre prequel or prologue. The opening depicts images of scantily clad, spear-throwing African tribesmen. The tribesmen assemble at the coastline and some Africans are cast away in a dinghy supposedly sailing to the New World. The image of one infant passenger is seen in close-up before a freeze frame. The still image fades out into a superimposed image of a grown man named Charley (Williamson) toiling as a blacksmith in a barn. These images are absurdly stereotypical and racially offensive. They imply the Atlantic slave trade is a result of savage African warfare rather than the European colonial pillaging of continental resources, both human and natural. But the producers of *Nigger Charley* thought they were making something radical and progressive because it addressed slavery as ugly and brutal. In one article, a journalist quoted filmmakers saying, "Never before . . . have scenes been filmed that depict the raiding of a black tribe by other blacks to capture people to be sold to white slave traders. . . . Charley's father is killed in the action, and his mother dies giving birth to him after a long, forced march from the interior to the beach where the slave ship is anchored."[52]

The fade-in to the face of a grown man played by Williamson implies that he is the baby who has grown into a man. The camera pulls back to an aerial shot of a plantation where he works as a blacksmith. The film then cuts to an expensively appointed bedroom in the big house, where Charley's adoptive mother, Theo (Gertrude Jeannette), pleads with her ailing white master, Hill Carter (Alan Gifford), for her son's freedom. Initially he refuses because Charley is too valuable. But out of affection for Theo, Massa Carter eventually consents to free Charley. However, Carter's illness prevents him from running the plantation, which is now in the hands of the more violently racist overseer, Houston (John Ryan). Eager to maximize profit, Houston is determined to sell off every single "piece of property" from the plantation, including every slave, like Charley—despite his newly granted freedom papers. That night, Houston and the other overseers ambush Charley while he's making love to his girlfriend. They destroy his papers and imprison him. When he escapes, Charley accidentally kills Houston in self-defense. With the help of two fellow slaves, Toby (D'Urville Martin) and Joshua (Don Pedro Colley), Charley escapes on horseback, pursued by slave catchers.

The opening scenes of *The Legend of Nigger Charley* parallel the opening scenes of *Sweet Sweetback*. The narrative is also a blueprint for themes in Quentin Tarantino's *Django Unchained*. In both *Sweetback* and *Charley*, a Black man is brutally beaten by sadistic white supremacists. In both films, abused Black men successfully retaliate. The two narratives are propelled by their main character's flight from white supremacy and the egregious racial injustice endemic to American society. In both pictures, the eponymous character comes to a political awakening. However, *Charley* differs from *Sweetback* by giving its protagonist a cohort of companions—a posse or brotherhood that provides protection at the outset of his journey. The Charley films are neo-slave narratives as well as westerns.

Newly manumitted and emboldened by his escape from slavery, Charley greets the outside (white) world with unmitigated defiance and a display of Black pride rather than sheepish compliance. His behavior befits a Black superhero. For instance, after riding into town, Charley, Joshua, and Toby rest at a saloon, where Charley defies and intimidates the local whites who taunt him with racist epithets. He then goes on to chase these patrons out of the saloon. Holed up in the saloon, Charley tells Toby and Joshua, "I ain't never gonna be a slave again for no man!" Toby cautions Charley, saying, "There ain't never gonna be an end for us, Charley. There ain't never gonna be an end to the Black man's troubles." Despite Toby's fearful pessimism, Charley is undeterred, telling his companions, "I'm a free man, and that's how I'm gonna die." His expression of self-determination is interrupted by Sheriff Rhinehart (Jerry Gatlin), who enters the bar to warn Charley that he's being pursued by the notorious Niles Fowler (Keith Prentice), a ruthless professional killer for hire.

Before they can digest this information, a wiry, old, Black Indian man, calling himself Shadow (Thomas Anderson), shuffles into the saloon and introduces himself misleadingly as a "half-breed" who's part Indian. He tells Toby he's come to see the three Negro gunslingers the whole territory is talking about. Sheriff Rhinehart, who left after issuing his initial caution, quickly returns, warning Charley that Fowler is fast approaching. Unafraid, Charley, Toby, and Joshua refuse to flee and instead prepare to confront Fowler and his men. When a shoot-out ensues, Charley, Toby, and Joshua—aided by a new unnamed member of their posse—kill Fowler and his gunmen.

Moments after their stunning victory, white farmer Dewey Lyons (Douglas Rowe) sheepishly approaches Charley and offers all three men jobs as hired guns on his ranch. Lyons, a white homesteader, has grown fearful of a baddie known as the Reverend Jarvis Kissler (Joe Santos) and his racist posse. The Reverend Kissler and his henchmen have been robbing and raiding Lyons's farm and harassing his beautiful half-Cherokee wife, Sarah (Tricia O'Neil). Upon meeting Sarah, Charley is instantly attracted to her beauty, and she to him. Despite Sarah's attractiveness and Lyons's good nature, the white townsfolk refuse to defend Lyons because Sarah is half Indian. Initially Charley also rejects Lyons's offer and leisurely rides out of town with Toby and Joshua loyally in tow. But Charley can't shake his attraction to Sarah and finds himself longing for her.

Concern for, and attraction to, Sarah Lyons ultimately motivates Charley to double back and help the Lyons farm despite Joshua's insistence that Charley's going to get them all killed trying to help Dewey and his pretty young wife. While enjoying a home-cooked meal at the Lyons home, they listen to Dewey's sad story about his brother Will, who was hanged by Reverend Kissler and his men. Charley, Toby, and Joshua realize that colored folks (Black cowboys and Indians) aren't the only people vulnerable to the whims of wilding lynch mobs.

The next day, the Reverend's henchmen show up at the Lyons farm. When they laughingly dismiss Charley's warning, he pulls out a gun, shoots two men dead, and passes a message to the remaining thug: "Now, you tell this *Reverend*, if he sets foot—*one* foot—on this property, Nigger Charley will kill him!" This admonition marks a shift in the diegetic tone. For the first time in the film, Charley boldly embraces the racist moniker "nigger" as part of his new tough-guy (read: badass, vigilante) persona. In this speech act, Charley symbolically and prophetically transforms the racial epithet "nigger," forcing it to undergo resignification and imbuing it with a devil-may-care, badass sensibility reminiscent of *Sweetback*.

In the context of the narrative, "nigger" is transformed from a term of demeaning racial debasement into a part of Charley's radical war cry. He embraces the otherwise troublesome epithet as a source of Black (masculine) power and self-determination in the face of white supremacy. He also demeans his white adversaries by calling *them* "boy." He thereby reverses (if only rhetorically) the white patriarchal power structure and long-standing pigmentocracy under which Black men (and women) were historically infantilized as a part of the "racial contract."[53] It reverses the semiotic and discursive practices by which Black men were demeaned and interpolated as "boys" in society at large and in popular culture.[54] Fred Williamson's character is speaking diegetically to the other characters in the narrative world. The character's sentiments reverberate extradiegetically for Black audiences who are already tired of white supremacist language. Therefore, the film resonates with both the historical, post-antebellum era and the contemporary civil rights protests. Charley's unflinching masculinity is enacted homosocially as a warning demonstrated for other men to witness and heed as in many prior films, particularly Sergio Leone's *Dollars* trilogy and Sergio Corbucci's *Django*.

In the next scene, the Reverend rides up with his posse and calls Charley out to face justice. Reverend Kissler successfully provokes Charley with racist slurs, and a shoot-out ensues. With the help of his growing posse, Charley succeeds in killing many of the Reverend's men and drives him away. In this scene *The Legend of Nigger Charley* proves itself a conventional genre film. As John Cawelti has demonstrated, classical Hollywood westerns were films in which the hero or Westerner defended the personal, financial, and spiritual interests of the small family farmer, homesteader, or workaday white Christians. Inevitably, settlers were bedeviled by hostile Indians, big business interests (e.g., oil tycoons, railroad masters, or land barons), or greedy ranchers swallowing up smaller estates. The narrative structure of *Charley* is conventional because the eponymous hero/protagonist relents to defend the small family farmer's interests.

Charley's interest in Sarah proves both chivalrous and romantic. Later that night, after the shooting has ended, Sarah quietly enters the stable and gently asks Charley why he has returned to help them. She approaches him demurely and subtly reveals her sexual availability to him. In their exchange, Charley learns that she blames herself (or, more specifically, her Native Indian heritage) for the community's alienation of her and for Dewey's inability to secure backup for his fight before now. Taking pity on her, he embraces her and they kiss. But they are suddenly interrupted by the lone Indian member of the Reverend's thuggish gang. Charley defends her and instead of killing the attacker, mercifully releases him with a warning by saying, "My fight's not with you."

The next day, when the Reverend returns to settle the score, Charley's partner Toby is felled in battle, along with their teenage apprentice. As an incantation to battle, the Reverend uses biblical scripture and calls on the Tribes of Israel to justify his self-righteous, white supremacist violence. With an incantation to God, he tries to kill Charley but is killed instead, leading Charley to pronounce, "The lost tribes of Israel were *Black*!" With the Reverend dead, Charley and Toby ride off into the sunset. In the closing dénouement, Toby asks, "Where are we going now, Charley?" to which this comic book–style superhero responds, "Doesn't matter which way we go; there's trouble for *us* everywhere."

The music swells and the film concludes, having complied with the generic conventions of countless classic Hollywood westerns (*Stagecoach*,

FIGURE 3.3 D'Urville Martin, Fred Williamson, and Don Pedro Colley portray escaped slaves who buck the system in *The Legend of Nigger Charley*.

Rio Grande, *High Noon*, and *Shane*) in which the lonesome hero—himself an outsider—defends the manifest destiny of the everyman (or small family farmer) only to ride off into the sunset. The difference here is that in *The Legend of Nigger Charley*, the myth of the Westerner is refracted through the prism of Black masculine power rather than white male authority. By the film's dénouement, Charley has extricated himself from the challenges—in this case the chains that bound him, literally, as a slave. Second, he has protected the small family farmer from "the threat" hanging over an otherwise wholesome homestead. Third, he has led the charge, taking other men into battle with him (Toby and Joshua). Fourth, he rides into the sunset honorably, leaving undisturbed the virtue of the dutiful married woman with whom he shared a mutual physical attraction. Finally, with his loyal companion Toby alongside him, Charley remains an alpha male or leader among the men who are willing to follow him.

In its compliance with conventionally conservative generic tropes and traditionally masculine antics, *The Legend of Nigger Charley* set the stage for Fred Williamson's portrayal of Black western heroism. It was a fearlessness, self-determination, and moral probity for young African American spectators who were eager for role models who bucked white masculine authority. Charley was not a sex worker, pimp, or gigolo like Sweetback.

Charley was constructed as more respectable. He began his journey as a slave. The conservative moral ethos of this narrative enabled Williamson to leverage football fame and capitalize on name recognition. He converted his athletic capital into celebrity capital. Prior to the *Nigger Charley* trilogy, Williamson had made only guest appearances on a few television programs and one movie, *Tell Me That You Love Me, Junie Moon.*

"New *Nigger Charley* Film Opening at Local Theater"

Based on the box office success of *The Legend of Nigger Charley*, a sequel was released one year later. It was based on a screenplay by Harold Stone from a story idea developed by Larry Spangler. The sequel's success was a tribute to producer Spangler's promotional acumen and understanding of the market. Spangler benefited from the fact that by the 1970s, film audiences were so familiar with the phenomenon of Black-athletes-turned-actor that studios were promoting motion pictures with sports trivia connections.

The promotional campaign for the film included quiz game tie-ins. In one press kit the promotional campaign was captioned "SPECIAL BLACK WEST-ERNS HEROES CONTEST" and boasted "FREE PASSES AWARDED WINNERS OF BLACK WESTERN HEROES QUIZ." The contest asked newspaper readers and radio/television fans to name the athlete/actor based on a series of clues. The first five winners to call in were rewarded with free tickets to screenings of *The Soul of Nigger Charley*. There were also tie-ins to the soundtrack album. Music composed and conducted by Don Costa was sold on an MGM Records release. Included on the album were two new songs by popular artist Lou Rawls ("Sometime Day" and "Morning Comes Around"). Theater managers were encouraged to reach out to music stores and disc jockeys as well as key members of the Black media. Local radio stations were encouraged to sponsor "Soul Day" music festivals.

Theaters were encouraged to display antique Western weaponry and firearms in their lobbies. And Western-style clothing was also marketed.[55] One press kit boasted:

> Western fashions are always in style. Leather coats, vests, belts and boots have always been a stylish addition to any man's wardrobe. Fred Williamson, who stars in Paramount Pictures' *The Soul of Nigger Charley*, prefers the rugged look of Western clothes and his personal wardrobe includes many such garments that Williamson has personally designed. Arrange with the clothes stores in your area, particularly those that carry Western style apparel, to set up special displays in the windows and their shops utilizing scenes from *The*

Soul of Nigger Charley that reflect these exciting fashions. To add additional promotion strength to your engagement . . . have these stores set up special displays in your lobby prior to and during your playdate.[56]

The brazen commercialization of African American cultural idioms (e.g., music, fashion, vernacular, and machismo) indicates the extent to which the revolutionary ethos embodied by Charley was being commodified even as it was conceptualized. Charley was always already a product first and a revolutionary icon second.

This market sensitivity was evident in press kits, reviews, and articles that hailed producer-director Larry Spangler (a self-proclaimed high school underachiever) as having the "Midas Touch." Spangler had enjoyed previous success promoting celebrities Merv Griffin and Mike Douglas. While Spangler claimed it was his success making Williamson a star that engendered imitations of the *Nigger Charley* films, Columbia Pictures had already released Sidney Poitier's directorial debut, *Buck and the Preacher* in 1972. Moreover, Spangler could not legitimately claim a corner on the blaxploitation movie market, because the films of Jim Brown had emerged several years earlier. Spangler admitted that *The Soul of Nigger Charley* was not simply a sequel but, rather, was intended to make Charley a "four-dimensional man with a heart and a soul on top of all those muscles."[57]

The Soul of Nigger Charley

When *The Soul of Nigger Charley* begins, Charley and Toby are free men. They no longer fear for their lives and have managed to survive their enemies. The story unfolds in a post–Civil War western settlement. Some ex-Confederate soldiers in Mexico—led by Colonel Blanchard (Kevin Hagen)—are holed up in a lair where they've been plotting to capture freedmen and sell them back into slavery. The Confederate troops raid the town, killing everyone except young Marcellus (Kirk Calloway). Ode (George Allen), a powerful Black man who has been held captive in the troop's wagons, escapes during the raid but is recaptured when he tries to kill Blanchard. Ode is tortured and left to die after the soldiers burn the town. But two heroic Black men, Charley and Toby, ride into the settlement and discover the dead bodies. They immediately help young Marcellus and learn the identity of Blanchard's vicious henchmen when they free Ode.

The four men (Charley, Toby, Ode, and Marcellus) ride onto a Quaker commune, with its section of freed former slaves. The Quakers treat Ode's wounds while Charley learns about Blanchard's villainous intent to capture former slaves for General Marcus Hook. General Hook is living in Mexico with one hundred former members of the Southern aristocracy whom he has promised a restoration of the Confederacy, complete with working slaves.

Under General Hook they have set up a compound where captured freedmen are forced to work as slaves. Charley and Toby are trying to convince the free Blacks to leave the Quaker commune and join a fight against Blanchard when two strangers arrive. Elena (Denise Nichols) and Lee (Joe Henderson), an ex–Union Army sergeant, warn the people that Blanchard is headed their way. The Quakers refuse to take up arms to assist, but the Black community, with Fred (Robert Minor) leading the way, join Charley and Toby to prepare to ambush the raiders. They dig ditches and fill them with kerosene to entrap the troops when they attack. In the ambush, most of Blanchard's men are killed or captured by Charley.

Negotiating for his life, the captured trooper informs the Black community about a train carrying one hundred thousand dollars in gold for General Hook (and Hook's plans to use the money to re-enslave them). With Elena, Toby, and Marcellus, Charley and his followers decide to ride over the mountain and ambush the train. Charley's plan is to take the gold and use it to ransom the captured slaves' freedom from General Hook.

Charley and Toby take over the train, get the gold, and hide it in an abandoned mine. Meanwhile, Charley waits to make contact with General Hook's men. While waiting, Charley and Elena become romantic but are interrupted by Hook's ultimatum: "Give up the money or I'll kill all seventy-one slaves!" Charley and his men are forced to immediately attack Hook's fortress, Las Casas. When Blanchard anticipates Charley's strategy, most of Charley's men are killed and he blames himself. Luckily, a Mexican bandito named Sandoval (Pedro Armendáriz) comes to Charley's aid with a plan to infiltrate the general's fortress.

Together Sandoval and Charley form an interracial coalition and attack Hook's compound. The slaves are freed and Hook is forced to lead his aristocrats out of Las Casas. Suddenly, an injured Blanchard tries to shoot Charley but shoots and kills Elena instead. In the final scene, Charley, Toby, and Marcellus decide to stay in Las Casas, where they have buried Elena. They vow to build a community dedicated to African American people.

With its narrative emphasis on recapturing manumitted slaves, *The Soul of Nigger Charley* is another neo-slave narrative. In this iteration of a slave narrative, the Black western hero must defeat white supremacists and slave catchers. The diegesis reimagines the travails of Exodusters and their journey to freedom. It also animates the attempts of wagon masters to ensure the safety of freedmen settling out West. These films wed a Black nationalist ethos to historical revisionism in their attempt to reimagine, recreate, and re-spectacularize historical events. *The Soul of Nigger Charley* finds its cohort

FIGURE 3.4 Fred Williamson helps a group of men and women escape to freedom in *The Soul of Nigger Charley.*

with *Rio Conchos, Buck and the Preacher*, and, more recently, the made-for-TV Amazon miniseries *The Underground Railroad* (Barry Jenkins, 2021).

As Amy Abugo Ongiri observes in her work on trauma, memory, and Black Power–era imagery in contemporary visual culture, films of the Black Power era could be said to "mobilize Black Power images in formal as well as narrative challenges to conventions around race, gender, and sexuality. They question the notion that the historical past is effectively dead because of its seemingly fixed status as a static object in structures of nostalgia and memory."[58] The *Nigger Charley* films use the eponymous hero as a potential witness—and historical actor—who plays a key role in creating, bearing witness to, and effecting suppressed historical accounts of resistance, rebellion, and revolution.

In the case of the *Nigger Charley* trilogy, the movies are metaphors for two temporally distinct, but linked, historical moments: the Reconstruction era 1890s and civil rights era 1960s and '70s. The *Nigger Charley* westerns also remind us of activist organizations like the Black Panther Party and the Symbionese Liberation Army. As mentioned above, Ongiri notes that both organizations sought to shatter "the stranglehold dominant media and advertising had over visual culture by consciously disrupting existing image culture with a kind of propaganda shaped by the Black Arts movement belief that black culture should reflect a black aesthetic."[59]

The failed attack within *The Soul of Nigger Charley* is one of the most poignant moments in the film, because it resonates with three major setbacks experienced by Black Americans. First, there was the failed revolution inaugurated by the slain Fred Hampton, who had worked to build an interracial or Rainbow Coalition. His assassination dealt a tremendous blow to progressive politics. Second, there was the abbreviated presidential campaign of Shirley Chisholm in 1972. A few years prior, in 1968, she became the first Black woman elected to the United States Congress and represented New York's Twelfth Congressional District for seven terms from 1969 to 1983. In 1972 she was the first Black candidate for a major party's nomination for president of the United States and the first woman to run for the Democratic Party presidential nomination. The third setback was Bobby Seale's failed attempt to become mayor of Oakland, California. He and running mate Elaine Brown showed great strength in the polls, but they were beaten by incumbent mayor John Reading. Brown had also outpolled Seale, collecting nearly thirty-five thousand votes. By forcing a runoff in Oakland, the state's fifth largest city, Seale led the Black Panther Party's efforts to turn its image around. According to Earl Caldwell of the *New York Times*, "The Panthers in the last two years have abandoned their talk of revolution and have concentrated on what they call survival programs in the black community." These programs included widespread testing for sickle cell anemia and giving free groceries to needy Black families. These three events in the early 1970s were felt by millions of Black Americans. As reality checks and setbacks, they not only represented personal and political losses but also diminished hopes of effecting institutional change and dismantling structural inequality.

By 1974 the overdone Black action genre film was losing its appeal. As James Robert Parish and George Hill noted in their compendium *Black Action Films*, Allied Artists tried to revive this genre with the three-star, James Bond–style, action-packed vehicle *Three the Hard Way*, starring Jim Brown, Fred Williamson, and former martial artist Jim Kelly. This revival met with some success. Made on a budget of $1,400,000, it grossed $3,000,000 in domestic film rentals. The picture was practically a four-star vehicle because it was helmed by then celebrity director Gordon Parks Jr., who was now famous for his father's direction of *The Learning Tree* and *Shaft*, and for directing his own feature film, *Super Fly* (1972).

Jim Kelly was the only newcomer. He had appeared in *Melinda* (Hugh Robertson, 1972), *Enter the Dragon* (Robert Clouse, 1973), and *Black Belt Jones* (Robert Clouse, 1974) before making *Three the Hard Way*, but he was not a box office draw like Brown or Williamson.

Proof that the younger Parks was used as a major draw for the film (and that the producers were desperately seeking cultural cachet to promote it) was that the film's press kits boasted of Parks's privileged background attending upper-class private schools in Westchester, New York; a relocation to Paris; years spent residing in the South of France; and time spent at the home of Jean Renoir. Renoir was among the avant-garde and elite French filmmakers. For instance, one promotional article boasted:

> Aware of Parks' talent, French director Pierre Gaisseau of *The Sky Above and Mud Beneath* hired him to help still photograph and film a documentary on Africa called *Africa and I*. During their six months together Gaisseau taught him film photography and exposed him to the Dark Continent he came to love. Parks will return to Africa, when time permits, to be taken into the Maasai Tribe—one of only three Westerners to be so honored. Upon completion of the documentary, which won among other accolades, a Peabody Award, two events occurred to change Parks' career: the major market for still photography dried up and *Super Fly* was brought to his attention to direct.[60]

But Parks was not the only luminary whose celebrity persona was harnessed to market a genre that was rapidly losing its audience. Articles also appeared touting Jim Kelly's physical attributes and emotional conditioning due to his martial arts training.

Boss Nigger

The third installment of the *Nigger Charley* trilogy, *Boss Nigger*, was released on February 26, 1975. Its release came soon after Fred Williamson had teamed up with Jim Brown and Jim Kelly for the actioner *Three the Hard Way*. Further evidence that Williamson had been strategic all along about his use of the N-word to animate his Charley persona came decades later, in 2008, when *Boss Nigger* was rereleased on DVD. The VCI Entertainment disc opens with the following disclaimer from its leading actor:

> In 1972 I had just competed the *Legend of Nigger Charley* and *The Soul of Nigger Charley*. I made this sequel that you are about to see. I used the N-word to create sensationalism at the box office and all three films were a success. You have to remember that all who used that word against me in those films regretted it. Enjoy the movie. I approve the title and the song with dialogue intact. —Fred "The Hammer" Williamson, 2008.

With this proviso, Williamson dispelled uncertainties about his intentions with the racial epithet and repudiated the notion that it was unpopular with fans. However, by this time blaxploitation films were receiving criticism from organizations like the NAACP. Despite the growing disapproval of the Black intelligentsia, the film was produced by Jack Arnold and Fred Williamson himself. Unfazed by criticism, Williamson took to self-producing encore vehicles like the rape-and-rescue movie *Joshua*, which he wrote, produced, and starred in. *Joshua* was also a western in which a Black soldier returns from fighting for the Union Army only to find that his mother has been murdered by a posse of white thugs. He becomes a bounty hunter, determined to track down and kill the men who murdered his mother.

Williamson's co-star in *Boss* was actor-producer D'Urville Martin. Martin defended the *Nigger Charley* trilogy films against critics of exploitation cinema by citing the profit imperative. According to Martin, unless they proved profitable, Black-themed movies faced an existential threat. In an interview for the *New York Amsterdam News*, Martin told reporter Angela Smith:

> "Black films have to make money first. If they don't make money, they will never be made again. If a Nigger produces a film and it doesn't make money, he will never produce again. But if a white man produces a film and it does make money, he has the opportunity to do it again and again. The situation is not equal, and therefore, money has to be made. . . .
>
> "*Boss Nigger* is merely an entertainment vehicle that intends to show that Blacks were cowboys. It says that there were Black cowboys during that time, that's all. The rest is what we do. . . . If critics judge Black films on the same basis as white films, it's understandable they would not like it or by-pass it because a Black film is not done under the same equal situation as a white film in terms of the budget and the experience."[61]

D'Urville was speaking to the critical double standard that films addressing African American history face. He also alludes to the differing production values, which include the professional experience of those involved. Fifty and sixty years later, journalists were asking the same questions about newer superhero movies such as *Black Panther* (2018).[62] By closely reading the films—and the discourse around them—we gain a sense of the economic conundrums and existential challenges Black filmmakers face.

When *Boss Nigger* begins, the Charley and Toby names have been changed, but their roles are largely the same as in *The Soul of Nigger Charley*. They are now Boss and Amos, two prosperous bounty hunters who make an honest living collecting wanted white men and turning them in to the authorities (dead or alive) for a cash reward. In this regard, they recall real-life Black lawmen like Bass Reeves. Operating in concert with the law, they are no longer fugitives as they were in the first film. To that end, the British release title for the film—*The Black Bounty Killer*—was probably more accurate.

Set in the 1870s, the film begins when Boss (Williamson) and Amos (D'Urville Martin) kill several wanted bank robbers, including one recently appointed sheriff of San Miguel, Mexico. Boss and Amos decide to collect the bounty for the bodies. En route they rescue a pretty, young Black woman, Clara Mae (Carmen Hayworth), whose father has been shot by white gunmen. When they reach the nearest town, Boss appoints himself sheriff of San Miguel, much to the consternation of the mayor (R. G. Armstrong).

Boss Nigger periodically makes light of the ironic racial role reversal of Black bounty hunters turning in white outlaws. At one point, Amos tells the flummoxed mayor, "You all been hunting black folks for so long, we just wanted to see what it was like to hunt *white* folks." In the spirit of this reversal of fortune, Boss and Amos demand equality for all oppressed people in San Miguel. Boss marches a group of hungry Mexican children into the town square, where he takes food from the white grocery and gives it to the poor, paying for it himself. But the town is actually run by villain Jed Clayton (William Smith), who learns of these events and plots to remove Boss by killing him.

The next day, Jed Clayton's posse dynamites Boss's jailhouse to free Clayton's men and ambush Boss and Amos. They almost eliminate Amos. Worse still, they fatally wound five-year-old Pancho (Mark Brito), the son of Amos's Mexican girlfriend, Margarita (Carmen Zapata). Clayton and his men ride out of town and kidnap Clara Mae. Eager to avenge Poncho's death, free Clara Mae, and take down Jed Clayton, Boss agrees to meet Jed despite knowing he's walking into a trap.

When he is captured by Jed's men, Boss is shot and left wounded to bake in the sun. Later that night, while Clara Mae (also held captive at Jed's camp) waits on Jed and his posse of racist Rough Riders, Amos arrives. He furtively frees the badly wounded Boss and takes him to the home of Miss Pruitt (Barbara Leigh), a pretty, young schoolteacher. While Boss rests at Pruitt's home, the doctor pays a house call to treat his wounds.

Holed up at Miss Pruitt's house, Boss and Amos craft a plan to avenge Poncho's death by having gunmen lie in wait back in town to surprise Jed's posse. Boss succeeds, but Clara Mae is killed in the crossfire. When Boss finally comes face-to-face with Jed, the two men fight mano a mano but not before Jed says his piece. Cornered, wounded, and kneeling, Jed tells Boss:

"Go ahead and kill me, *nigger!*"
   "*Mister* Nigger to you," Boss replies.
   "Go to hell, Mister Nigger!"
   "To hell is where you're going. This is for Clara Mae!"

After this exchange, Boss unloads his shotgun on Jed and succeeds in killing him. By the end of their battle, Boss is also seriously wounded. He pleads with his partner, "Amos, don't let me die in a white folks' town." Amos quickly replies, "You ain't gonna die, Boss." Suddenly, Miss Pruitt runs up, collapses next to Boss, and declares her feelings for him. She announces her intent to join him when he leaves San Miguel. In response to Pruitt's declaration, Boss coolly replies, "Thanks schoolteacher, but a black man's got enough problems without having a white woman follow him around." Boss's deadpan dismissal of her passion is a comedic dismissal of the white female character specifically (and of white womanhood in general). It also evokes Woody Strode in *Sergeant Rutledge* when he realizes he should have taken care to avoid "white women business" because it often resulted in the lynching of Black men.

Boss's swift rejection of a relationship with the physically striking, sexually available white woman is an intentional ideological stance that speaks volumes about the kind of Black masculine hero proffered in *Boss Nigger*. The scene evokes Richard Dyer's landmark essay on the constructed image of the ideal white woman within heterosexuality.[63] Throughout the film, Boss shows awareness of Miss Pruitt's sexual curiosity. He even demonstrates his heterosexuality and capability by obliging her with a passionate kiss. But he quickly belittles her gestures and, by the end of the film, flatly rejects her advances. His behavior differs considerably from the blaxploitation characters of other films (e.g., Shaft, Sweetback, Priest, Goldie, et al.) and real world, non-diegetic African American men (e.g., Black Panthers, revolutionaries, and activists), some of whom never interrogated their preferential desire for white women and instead unthinkingly engaged in relations with white women during the civil rights movement.[64]

Moreover, Boss shows a respectable courtliness and gallantry toward the pretty, young African American woman Clara Mae, the maiden he and Amos rescued in the opening scene. It is important to note that the sexual and racial principles of *Boss Nigger* include a politicized rejection of white female beauty standards and idealized white womanhood, here delivered with a campy one-liner ("Thanks schoolteacher . . . but"). After Boss rejects Miss Pruitt, Amos loads up their wagon (complete with Jed's corpse for the bounty). Their wagon pulls off, the soundtrack swells, and Italian-style westploitation credits roll.

In his reference book *Black Action Films*, James Robert Parish observes that in *Boss Nigger*, statements about racial equality are rendered with satirical comedy. We can push Parish's reading further because throughout the *Nigger Charley* films, race relations are handled flippantly yet with a semi-serious air. Racial epithets are spoken and delivered with a camp sensibility reminiscent of the tone in, for example, Pam Grier's sexploitation and blaxploitation films. With satire and irony, camp and cult cinemas often employed references to race, racial fetishism, and violence in order to heighten spectators' awareness of social hierarchies being inverted. Female characters in Grier's pictures (e.g., *The Big Bird Cage*, 1972; *Women in Cages*, 1971; *The Big Doll House*, 1971) were often brutalized for strides toward (a figurative) liberation, a liberation metaphorically related to the women's movement and second-wave feminism.[65] Grier's characters would lash back at their racist white adversaries with campy phrases like "That's *Miss* Nigger to you." Similarly, in the *Nigger Charley* trilogy, the eponymous Charley/Boss is often assaulted for his strides toward liberation, a liberation metaphorically related to civil rights and Black Power. His final words to Jed Clayton ("*Mister* Nigger to you") echo the campy retorts of Grier's character Blossom in *The Big Bird Cage*, released two years earlier. Much of the appeal of blaxploitation and westploitation pictures was the fantasy of Black superheroism, which was delivered with heavy sarcasm and camp. The films gave audiences superheroes and larger-than-life metaphors for Black Power, chivalry, prized Black womanhood, and Black nationalism, often expressed—albeit not always—as a variant of racial solidarity. It was a solidarity valued on screen precisely because it was contained and suppressed in the real world.

Take a Hard Ride

By the mid-1970s, the marketplace that had initially been so receptive to Williamson's early film career and the *Nigger Charley* trilogy was saturated with blaxploitation content. Few films were returning the profit margins seen in the early '70s, and movies were now being advertised as general audience pictures. After five or six years of similar fare, the novelty was wearing off. Audiences were tiring of the formulaic narratives, one-dimensional characters, and hokey, predictable heroics. Civic and social organizations like the NAACP were becoming more vocal in their criticisms of the insipid, often stereotypical, nature of blaxploitation cinema.

Take a Hard Ride was a spin on the successful action hero antics featured in *Three the Hard Way* but with Italian-style western influences inspired by Italian director Antonio Margheriti (aka Anthony M. Dawson). Margheriti and screenwriter Eric Bercovici sought to take advantage of the atmosphere and location. Filmed on the Canary Islands, off the coast of West Africa (including Tenerife and Lanzarote), *Take a Hard Ride* was supposedly shot there because the director and screenwriter believed the Canaries would

FIGURE 3.5 Jim Brown, Jim Kelly, Fred Williamson, Lee Van Cleef, Catherine Spaak, and Harry Carey Jr. were cast in *Take a Hard Ride*.

add another character to the story. They hoped the setting would seem punishingly hard in the tradition of spaghetti western locations.

Take a Hard Ride was released on October 29, 1975. Like its pseudo prequel *Three the Hard Way*, *Take a Hard Ride* teamed Jim Brown, Fred Williamson, and kung fu star Jim Kelly. They were cast alongside western veteran bad man Lee Van Cleef, who had excelled in dozens of Hollywood and spaghetti western productions, including two films in the *Sabata* trilogy (dir. Gianfranco Parolini, 1969–1971).[66] Van Cleef was widely known by his nickname, "Angel Eyes," after his character in Leone's *The Good, the Bad, and the Ugly*. *Take a Hard Ride* enabled Van Cleef to reprise his stock-in-trade role as a merciless bounty hunter. Old Hollywood luminaries Dana Andrews (*The Ox-Bow Incident* and *The Best Years of Our Lives*, 1946) and second-generation western actor Harry Carey Jr. were also cast as supporting players.

In the movie, dying cattleman Bob Morgan (Dana Andrews) asks his foreman, Pike (Jim Brown), to deliver eighty-six thousand dollars from the sale of cattle in Abilene, Texas, to Morgan's widow at a ranch in Sonora, Mexico. Upon reaching Sonora, Pike is expecting to become a partner in the new ranch cooperative. The promise of advancement has Pike determined to make good on the delivery. And he wants to honor his dead boss, Morgan, who years before gave him a chance to lead a clean, decent life.

As Pike embarks on this challenging ride, he faces men of avarice and the brutality of Mother Nature. Shortly after setting out, he's ambushed by a group of white men who have heard about "the nigger carrying $86,000."

To Pike's surprise, a dandified, snake-throwing gambler named Tyree (Fred Williamson) comes to his aid with a six-shooter and a burlap sack of poisonous serpents. Tyree admits that he knows about the money and that the cash motivated him to help Pike fight off the greedy ambushers. Tyree proposes an alliance between the two of them against everybody else. Their pact proves to be useful. Various bad white men pursue them, but one by one they meet up with, and fall under, the coercive leadership of Keifer (Lee Van Cleef), a ruthless bounty hunter hoping to use Pike's checkered past (as a wanted man) to capture and steal the money from him.

One of Pike's would-be pursuers is Sheriff Kane (Barry Sullivan) of Abilene. Kane tries to pursue Pike alone but is quickly eliminated by Kiefer. Pike is also pursued by two of Mr. Morgan's bumbling cowhands: Dumper (Harry Carey Jr.) and Skave (Robert Donner). Dumper and Skave think they can kill Pike and capture the loot. While pursuing Pike, Dumper and Skave mistake Cloyd (Charles McGregor) and Cagney (Leonard Smith), two random African American travelers, for Pike and Tyree—simply because they're also African American. After them follows Halsey (Ronald Howard), a fanatical white Southern preacher crusading with a small army and a wagon carrying a machine gun (a prop that evokes Peckinpah's *The Wild Bunch*). Lastly, there's Calvera (Ricardo Palacios) and his gang of rogue bandits. They are recruited by Keifer when he grows frustrated by his inability to capture and rob Pike.[67] Much of the narrative pleasure of the film is supposed to derive from watching Williamson and Brown team up and defeat these adversaries.

In this regard, we might think of *Take a Hard Ride* as an early iteration of the *intra*racial buddy films that teamed African American actors. By this point in his career, Williamson was feeling comfortable enough with his box office appeal to generate genre pictures by himself. *Take a Hard Ride* was followed by *Adios Amigo* (1975), an episodic and totally incoherent oater about a frontier con man who tries to scam his partner. Released on December 25, 1975, nearly two months after *Take a Hard Ride*, *Adios Amigo* was written, directed, and produced by Fred Williamson with Richard Pryor as his zany co-star. *Take a Hard Ride* is the most coherent of the late '70s Black westploitation pictures as evidenced by its efforts at narrative closure.

In the film, Pike and Tyree press onward to Sonora but make newfound allies along the way. First there's a widow named Catherine (Catherine Spaak) whom they rescue from molestation. They also run into a mute, kung-fu-chopping Black Indian named Kashtok (Jim Kelly), who mysteriously travels alongside them on foot, unmounted for much of their journey. He's indebted to Pike and Tyree because they saved him from the same bandits who killed Catherine's husband. When Pike and Tyree are suddenly cornered by Halsey's men in the mountains, Catherine creates a diversion and sacrifices herself to free Pike and Tyree. Upon reaching their destination, thanks to Kashtok's tracking abilities, Pike and Tyree tussle over the money.

Before they can settle their dispute, their brawl is interrupted by Kiefer, Calvera, and his band. Unwilling to abandon Pike with Kiefer approaching, Tyree helps him send the money onward with Kashtok and young Chico (Robin Levitt), a little Mexican boy from a nearby town. In the final scenes, Pike and Tyree set a trap for Kiefer and Calvera with a stash of dynamite. They blow up a footbridge just as Calvera's men are crossing on horseback. Though wounded, Kiefer miraculously survives the explosion, but experiences a change of heart and decides not to pursue Pike and Tyree after all. As the lone Black heroes look at each other, thankful to have survived their journey, the credits begin to roll.

Film reviews of *Take a Hard Ride* were unenthusiastic. The response was understandable given the familiarity of formula films. Robert Parish observed that "Fred Williamson, Jim Brown and Jim Kelly had been teamed in *Three the Hard Way* to good result but such was not the case in this Spaghetti Western filmed on-the-cheap in the Canary Islands." Parish cited Vincent Canby of the *New York Times*, who dismissively wrote, "It goes on and on—it lurches, really—in fits and starts of inspiration from dimly remembered earlier movies."[68] And in a similarly glib tone, an *Independent Film Journal* critic found *Take a Hard Ride* wearisome. Despite the presence of its stars, he described *Hard Ride* as an "overlong formula western":

> *Take a Hard Ride* takes a very standard Western scenario that a decade ago would have served as a lower-case Audie Murphy vehicle, spruces it up with handsome production values and loads the marquee with a melting-pot cast. . . .
>
> The fireworks that might have been expected from this high-powered cast never materialize, all but one of the stars lending a minimum of energy and even less conviction. Basically, what's wrong with the film is its failure to come up with any new angles or variations to flesh out a very skeletal, tired plot. . . .
>
> The combination of lackluster performances and a threadbare script— further handicapped by Anthony Dawson's leisurely direction—makes for a very, very long ride.[69]

Tom Milne of *Monthly Film Bulletin* gave it a mixed review, calling it a "formulary Spaghetti Western," "with a few pleasant conceits." He extolled Williamson's performance, calling him "outstanding as the laconic gambler who is perversely constrained to make a last-minute play for the money."[70] It is a bit perplexing that the Italian-style westerns, which were just as repetitive and formulaic, were praised by the same critics who found *Take a Hard Ride* tiresome. The racial climate in America was one of many factors impacting these reviews, but it's unclear whether these Black westerns were any less positively reviewed than their mainstream Italian and German counterparts.

The African American press, such as *the New Pittsburgh Courier*, the *Afro-American*, and the *Chicago Defender*, reviewed *Take a Hard Ride* more favorably than the mainstream (read: white) press. Such discrepancies between reviewing patterns are explicable given the African American press's position vis-à-vis mainstream media, and their understanding of the marginality of Black filmmaking in the entertainment industry. For example, the *New Pittsburgh Courier* critic praised Jim Brown and the film in general, saying that Brown appears in what some consider his best performance in a motion picture to date. Kelly and Williamson were found to "add character and dimension to the story and film."[71]

In fairness to both sides of the critical divide, Jim Brown always seemed a bit wooden or stiff in his western performances, a fact partially attributable to Italian-style western filmmaking. Fred Williamson, by contrast, often seemed to be playing a campy or exaggerated version of himself as super-sexy man Fred. Both actors were shaped by the amalgamation of blaxploitation cinema and spaghetti westsploitation, in which actors tended to be stoic or less expressive. Sergio Leone, for instance, cut considerable dialogue from *A Fistful of Dollars* to shape Clint Eastwood's character. "In my opinion," Leone explained, "the more the main character speaks, the more he loses in charisma and the more the strength of the movie is lost. . . . Every single sequence of *A Fistful of Dollars* is marked by an almost liturgical solemnity that emerges in the dialogues as well as the images."[72] Like Eastwood, actor Franco Nero (*Django*) relied on the same stoicism and impassiveness, a coldness and unfeeling remoteness that many others—arguably including Brown and Williamson—imitated.

Curiously, few critics, barring Vincent Canby of the *New York Times*, identified *Take a Hard Ride*'s specific homages to prestige westerns such as *Butch Cassidy and the Sundance Kid* or ultraviolent Vietnam-era oaters like *The Wild Bunch* or even Italian series like the *Sabata* trilogy. Few mention the *Sartana* series, beginning with *If You Meet Sartana, Pray for Your Death* (Gianfranco Parolini, 1968). But just as the Pam Grier–Margaret Markov women-in-prison pictures (*Black Mama, White Mama* and *The Arena*) were homages to Sidney Poitier and Tony Curtis in *The Defiant Ones*, the movie *Take a Hard Ride* was an homage to *Butch Cassidy and the Sundance Kid*. Evidence of this referencing is in Fred Williamson's character, Tyree. Like Robert Redford's Sundance, Tyree is a master poker player and card gambler whose sharpshooter abilities are initially concealed. Pike is clearly the thinking man who functions as an analog to Paul Newman's contemplative character, Butch.

A more recognizable homage comes at the end of *Take a Hard Ride*. On the lam from a posse that includes renowned Indian tracker Lord Baltimore and lawman Joe Lefors, Butch and Sundance finally elude their pursuers by jumping from a cliff into a river far below, but not until Harry Longabaugh (aka the Sundance Kid) initially refuses to jump because—as he famously confesses—he can't swim. Similarly, in *Take a Hard Ride*, Tyree and Pike must jump off a cliff into rapid waters. Initially Tyree refuses to jump because, to Pike's surprise, as Tyree admits, he can't swim. The setting, the mise-en-scène, and the framing of these two scenes are identical. In both movies, the two men are framed in a medium close-up with their backs against the stone mountain wall, itself a metaphor for masculinity. And in both films the men jump and survive. Only Canby's dismissive review tacitly noted the similarities to *Butch Cassidy and the Sundance Kid*. Canby wrote that "Mr. Williamson works hard to achieve a light touch but all his efforts are immediately absorbed by Mr. Brown, whose impassive performance acts as a kind of blotter. . . . The two have a long way to go before they give Paul Newman and Robert Redford any competition."[73] Clearly, Canby's quip was his way of acknowledging the intentional similarities between these motion pictures.

Take a Hard Ride also pays homage to Sam Peckinpah's *The Wild Bunch*. Peckinpah's revisionist western stars William Holden as Pike Bishop, the leader of a gang of aging outlaws seeking retirement after one final score: the robbery of a railroad office containing a cache of silver. The gang is ambushed by Pike's former partner, Deke Thornton, who is leading a posse of bounty hunters. At the end of the film, a mounted machine gun becomes a "weapon of mass destruction" (WMD) and a character in its own right. Thus, both films feature a leading character named Pike looking to retire to a quieter, more righteous life. Both films cast Pike as the moral leader among men who is nonetheless pursued by dangerously immoral gangs. Both films introduce the figure of the bounty hunter as a cold-blooded killer willing to stop at nothing to get what he wants. Finally, both films introduce the mounted machine gun as a signifier of a new, more violent modern era, the beginning of an age characterized by the deployment of machine guns or WMDs in which mass carnage becomes the new normal in warfare. Gone are the conventional standards of decency, chivalry, and honor that the Hays Production Code required along with mythic depictions of the Old West.

The themes of death, destruction, inequality, and brutality related to the existential experiences of African Americans in the post–World War II civil rights era. Black Americans, who had fought for victory against fascism abroad, had come home to a country that was virulently racist. Jim Brown and Fred Williamson clearly intended for these western star vehicles to enhance their careers first and encourage African Americans viewers to see themselves in the historical context of movies about the Old West second. These were stories of Black empowerment, African American heroism, and masculine chivalry. Williamson's next western star vehicle, *Joshua*, was a solo venture in which he would save a damsel from a vicious posse. As a lone hero, Joshua could have been taken from the pages of the comic book *Lobo* (were it not for the explicit rape-and-rescue violence it depicted). And Jim Brown claimed that his films of this era made a significant difference in the genre and industry.

In press interviews, Brown was asked if the presence of a Black hero marked the "maturing" or evolution of the western genre. He replied, "Since I came into the industry there has been a change. What are known as black films are being made. In all my films, I've worked with white and black actors, and *Take a Hard Ride* isn't a black film. It's a western. It's not a film about get whitey or a ghetto situation, but simply a good outdoor adventure we hope the total public will consume."[74]

Brown and Williamson were only a few of the actors diversifying and politicizing the genre. The 1970s also witnessed the rise of Black rodeo culture. In addition to Brown's and Williamson's superhero-like films, other iterations of African American western culture emerged during these years, including *The McMasters* (Alf Kjellin), *Man and Boy* (E. W. Swackhamer, 1971), *Skin Game* (Paul Bogart), and director Jeff Kanew's extraordinary documentary *Black Rodeo*. Clearly, the football-star-turned-action-hero motion pictures were only one iteration of an ever-evolving and deeply contradictory genre.

4

Harlem Rides the Range

Nobody Told You There Were
Black Cowboys

> Americans have always idealized cowboys as a symbol of strength,
> courage and manhood; the cowboy has symbolized man's struggle
> against insurmountable odds—says Bud Bramwell, rodeo champ
> and President of the American Black Cowboy Association. In rodeo
> contests from Cheyenne to Madison Square Garden, it is easy to
> spot Bud—he's Black. To most Americans who are used to seeing
> and thinking of cowboys only as white, Bud comes as a revelation—
> since so few Americans, Black or white, know anything about the
> important role Blacks played in helping to settle the American West.
> Yes, there are Black Cowboys. Proof positive is *Black Rodeo*—a new
> motion picture.
>
> —American Black Cowboy Association

On February 1, 1939, an all-Black-cast singing cowboy film
titled *Harlem Rides the Range* (dir. Richard Kahn), starring Herb Jeffries
and Spencer Williams, was produced by Hollywood Pictures and released
by Sack Amusement Enterprises. One of three Black cowboy films made in
close succession, *Harlem Rides the Range*—like *Harlem on the Prairie* (Sam
Newfield, 1937) and *Bronze Buckaroo* before it—was commercially successful
with audiences. Thirty-two years later, an actual all-Black-cast rodeo would
come to Harlem and be filmed in real time.

"On September 4th, 1971—at Randall's Island Park in New York City—a
major event took place: a bronco-busting-bull-riding rodeo, complete with
a traditional wild west show. But this was not an ordinary rodeo. It was
unlike the others because all of the cowboys and cowgirls were Black!" So
reads the press kit advertising *Black Rodeo*, a cinema vérité–style documentary directed by twenty-seven-year-old neophyte filmmaker Jeff Kanew.[1]

Promotional materials and reviews boasted of special guest appearances by Woody Strode and Muhammad Ali. They touted appearances by competitive riders in rodeo events (e.g., bronco riding, calf roping, steer wrestling, and bull riding) competing for a piece of the six-thousand-dollar purse. Muhammad Ali, the world-famous activist and pugilist known for his charmingly alliterative oratory, turned up as a surprise visitor. But director Kanew later revealed he had invited the boxer to make a guest star appearance.[2]

Kanew paid Ali five thousand dollars to appear at a time when the athlete needed the money. On June 20, 1967, Ali had been convicted of draft evasion, sentenced to five years in prison, fined ten thousand dollars, and stripped of his boxing license. He had refused military service on religious grounds as a practicing Muslim. Eventually Ali's conviction was overturned by the U.S. Supreme Court in 1971. Charges and appearance fees notwithstanding, Ali was also personally interested in the rodeo as a fellow athlete and as a Black man interested in seeing what he jokingly called "brother cowboys."

Whereas Muhammad Ali clearly increased the documentary's celebrity quotient with his appearance, it was Woody Strode who endowed the film with authenticity. Strode was the only Black actor widely recognized for his work in western films. After all, Herb Jeffries had not appeared in westerns for thirty years. Sidney Poitier had appeared in only two westerns. Strode was the Black actor most closely associated with the American West in the popular imagination. After his work with John Ford, he represented African American cowboys, usually excluded from motion pictures. Strode was pleased that a "real rodeo," featuring Black cowboys, had come to Harlem. He happily endorsed the documentary by accepting Kanew's invitation to be its narrator.[3]

This chapter offers a reading of Jeff Kanew's documentary, viewing it as additional cultural evidence of African American Western idioms. By situating *Black Rodeo* as part of this book, and putting it in dialogue with other films, we can examine connections and differences between fictional features about Black Westerners and a documentary about actual Black cowboys and cowgirls observing folkways associated with frontier life. Exodusters were people who left a legacy of traditions, practices, and community engagement. The objective of these close readings is to juxtapose fictional and nonfictional texts to learn what they reveal about the cultural and political climate of the 1970s.

Black Rodeo was the first feature-length film of Utopia Productions Incorporated, and it was produced in cooperation with the American Black Cowboy Association (ABCA), a labor union of Black rodeo riders from across the country. The workers association was formed in 1970 by George Richardson of New York City; Bud Bramwell of Stillwater, Oklahoma; rodeo announcer

Charles Evans of Tulsa, Oklahoma; and Professional Rodeo Cowboys Association (PRCA) member Marvel Rogers.[4] According to their mission statement, in addition to being a labor union, the ABCA was a cultural organization designed "to remind people of *all* races of the black heroes American history books forgot to include." The organization provided much of the historical information presented in Kanew's documentary.[5] Their legacy continues to the present. Today the Cowboys of Color Rodeo is one of the largest multicultural rodeos in the country and promotes the contributions of African American, Hispanic American, and Native American (as well as European) cultures to the settling of the American West.[6]

In May 1972, the same year *Black Rodeo* appeared in theaters, Sidney Poitier's directorial debut, *Buck and the Preacher*, was released by Columbia Pictures. Coincidentally, 1972 was also the year *The Red, White, and Black* (first released in 1970) was rereleased as *Soul Soldier*. As discussed earlier, it was also the year Paramount released director Martin Goldman's *The Legend of Nigger Charley*, the first film in what became the westploitation *Nigger Charley* trilogy. In January of that same year, Warner Bros. released *The Cowboys*, starring Roscoe Lee Brown and John Wayne (who was now sixty-five years old). Only six months earlier, in June 1971, Columbia Pictures released *Man and Boy*, a Bill Cosby and Gloria Foster star vehicle about a Black family on the prairie, directed by E. W. Swackhamer. In its focus on Exodusters, *Man and Boy* bore a weak resemblance to Gordon Parks's autobiographical *The Learning Tree*, which is not really a western but rather a coming-of-age drama about adolescence, puberty, and hard lessons learned by youth in Kansas.

Nineteen seventy-two was a watershed year for several reasons. It marked the concurrent release of at least five African American–themed westerns (and similar films co-starring Black characters) and major events in the political sphere, such as the first Black National Convention and Shirley Chisholm becoming the first Black candidate for the presidency. These events were indicative of the convergence of cultural and political developments. The steady release stream also suggests that earlier Black-themed westerns (e.g., *Rio Conchos*, *100 Rifles*, and *El Condor*) performed well enough at the box office to indicate continued commercial viability for the genre. Their box office success was a sign that Black-themed westerns resonated with audiences. Their appeal, especially among African American audiences, was a function of the narratives containing Black stars. But appeal was also a function of the themes of racial uplift, African American empowerment, civil rights discourse, Black economic enfranchisement, and counter-cultural narratives of a Black nationalism contesting white supremacy. Black westerns structurally altered the politics and poetics (in other words, the ideology and the construction) of traditional westerns through a dramaturgical reinterpretation of the genre's myths, conventions, and conceits. Such films reconstructed a Black national imaginary or imagined community of Exodusters who persevered, and even triumphed, against the difficulties of the frontier.

Instead of heroic white male saviors, African American–themed westerns presented embattled Black men (and women) negotiating structural racism, fighting systemic disenfranchisement, and confronting inequality endemic to American society in the nineteenth and twentieth centuries. These narrative and documentary films shifted focus away from Anglo-American settlers (and their claim to manifest destiny) and onto African American Exodusters searching for liberty and the pursuit of justice. The revisionist, ironic, and sometimes campy mythmaking of African American–themed westerns provided particularly meaningful metaphors in the revolutionary 1960s and '70s. As Brian Henderson notes in his seminal essay on *The Searchers*, westerns (like most genre pictures) typically reveal more about the politics of the moment when they were produced than about the historical moment they purport to represent. Black westerns responded directly and metaphorically to the political tumult of the 1960s and '70s rather than the colonial history from which they were a century removed. This was clearly expressed in the reemergence of the genre during the civil rights era.

The western regained appeal among African American audiences during these years for specific cultural and sociopolitical reasons. Beginning in 1964, Black Americans began making headway as performers in actual rodeos. For example, Myrtis Dightman became the first Black cowboy to compete in the National Finals Rodeo in 1964. Historians were seemingly prompted to follow suit in addressing the role of Western Blacks.

In 1965 historians Philip Durham and Everett Leroy Jones published *The Negro Cowboys*, one of the first books to document the experiences of Black ranchers in the West. In 1966 Jim Brown began appearing in the genre's movies following Woody Strode's lead. In 1970 Charles Evans—known as "the voice of Black rodeo"—assisted in establishing the American Black Cowboys Association, which staged Black rodeos nationwide, raising awareness of Black cowboy culture and the part Black cowboys played in the history of the American West. The association was not created to be a segregated alternative to predominantly white associations but rather to work alongside mainstream rodeos to promote the overall good of the sport. Collectively, these African American rodeo riders, history books, competitive rodeos, and mythmaking movies evince the existence of Black Western history, idioms, and the malleability of western cinema.

As much as the legacy of Black westerns was meaningful in the '60s and '70s, it remains meaningful today. The second decade of the new millennium witnessed yet another renaissance of Black Western idioms in mainstream popular American culture with the releases of movies like *Django Unchained* and *The Harder They Fall*. Interest in twenty-first-century Black Western idioms began years earlier in the cinematic, musical, and rodeo culture, as well as in the riding clubs like the Black Cowboy Federation or, more recently, the Compton Cowboys from California.

Throughout the 1990s there was a slow but steady drip of Black western movies on offer. In 1993 the revisionist western *Posse*, directed by Mario Van Peebles, was released. This film, in concert with several movies from the New Black Cinema movement, spurred a renaissance in filmmaking and historical content. In February 1997 the historical drama *Rosewood* emerged. Directed by John Singleton, *Rosewood* was based on the true story of the 1923 massacre of African Americans in Rosewood, Florida. Though set in Florida, the film relied on the visual vocabulary and syntax of western cinema. Later that year, in December 1997, Charles Haid released the made-for-TV-movie *Buffalo Soldiers*, starring Danny Glover, Carl Lumbly, Glynn Turman, Clifton Powell, and Mykelti Williamson. Outside the movie houses and beyond screens, African American cowboys provided a touch of the Wild West in Brooklyn's East New York neighborhood. Along with lessons in horseback riding and horse care, the Black Cowboy Federation sought to educate the public on the contributions of African American cowboys of the Old West.[7]

In 2002 the renowned L.A. Rebellion school filmmaker Larry Clark released *Cutting Horse* about an aging Black cowboy revisiting his past. In 2012 Quentin Tarantino released his highly stylized homage to blaxploitation and spaghetti westerns, *Django Unchained*. A tribute to 1966's *Django*, Tarantino's homage also draws on the *Nigger Charley* trilogy pictures starring Fred Williamson, which in their own way were Black spaghetti westerns decades before Tarantino's remake of Corbucci's film.

In the extradiegetic real world, the Compton Cowboys emerged and grew. They started as an outgrowth of the Compton Jr. Posse riding club,[8] which had been active since the 1980s. Today the Compton Cowboys actively participate in political events and protests on horseback. Their presence is being felt in the elite hunter-jumper world, where sport clothing brands like Ariat feature Compton Cowboy advertisements.

In 2013, unbeknownst to the film industry, Stanford E. Moore began publishing *Black Reins* magazine, a glossy online lifestyle zine for African American cowboy enthusiasts. Moore wanted to start a magazine for several years and make it accessible. Today *Black Reins* has a social media presence on platforms including Instagram and Facebook. And, finally, beginning in the 2010s, possibly due to a gradual increase in representation, news outlets began interviewing some of the retiring Black cowboys like Larry Callies and Edward J. Dixon. Callies was featured in Dillon Hayes's documentary op-ed, which paralleled Callies with the late country-western singing cowboy Charlie Pride.[9] Taken collectively, these events, rodeos, and films render a documentary like *Black Rodeo* even more relevant today. The film is part of the connective tissue between twentieth-century Black Western idioms (e.g., film, music, rodeo, and riding clubs) and twenty-first-century idioms or practices.

The mainstream music industry was also impacted by the new country/hip-hop syncretism when popular recordings by Blanco Brown, Lil Nas X, and Travis Scott bolstered the zeitgeist. Beginning in August 2014, popular rap artist Travis Scott released his second mixtape, titled *Days before Rodeo*. One year later, on September 4, 2015, Scott's debut studio album, *Rodeo*, was released. He opened the door for other "country/hip-hop" artists to follow. By 2019 a mélange of country-rap songs (aka "country-trap"[10]) were being released and mentioned in popular periodicals such as *Billboard* and *Time*. These artists were broadening a musical genre historically considered to have an exclusively white character and ethos.[11] Journalist Andrew Chow claims, "More and more, in recent years, hip-hop has been merging with country music, a genre long associated with white conservatism."[12] In popular culture, Western idioms (e.g., frontier folklore, western movies, country music) have typically been associated with white illiberalism, xenophobia, and a nostalgic ethnocentrism reminiscent of manifest destiny.

Nevertheless, a chief participant of the country shift in popular rap was Lil Nas X, with his debut single, "Old Town Road." The single was released independently in December 2018. *Time* magazine cited the song as "the defining sound of the year." Shortly thereafter, Lil Nas X signed with Columbia Records. By March 2019 the song had reached number nineteen on *Billboard*'s "Hot Country Songs" chart before the magazine disqualified it from being included on the grounds that it did not fit the country genre. This reclassification led to some debate and discussion about the definition of country music. By August 2019 "Old Town Road" was the longest-running number one song at the time. It occupied the top spot on the *Billboard* "Hot 100" for five months, and it has streamed more than a billion times on Spotify alone.

Billy Ray Cyrus was criticized by Nashville's insular country music community for having crossed the ethnomusical divide and agreeing to record a new verse for the remix Lil Nas X desired. Cyrus and Lil Nas then released an "old school" Western outlaw video that evoked the visual lexicon of African American western movies with a crafty trickster figure added in. The music video mimicked Black western movies by recreating the mise-en-scène of western cinema complete with "guest star" appearances,[13] stylized cowboy costumes, horses under Western saddles, and prairie vistas. The song, the music video, and its Western apparel gained attention and landed twenty-year-old rap artist Lil Nas X on the cover of *Time* magazine.

Despite the popularity of the song and its featurette music video (with over 300 million YouTube views), the double-voiced syncretism continued to be a source of dispute over its authenticity as *country* music. Some diehard country music fans threatened, for instance, to boycott Wrangler jeans for hiring Lil Nas X as a spokesperson for the denim brand.[14] Nevertheless, "Old Town Road" enabled Lil Nas X and Billy Ray Cyrus to expand their fan base and break new ground by proving that seemingly antithetical genres and idioms (Black urban vernacular and white Western dialect) can coexist harmoniously and lead to commercial success. African Americans—and mainstream American viewers—have enjoyed, and continue to enjoy, a cultural investment in the history, mythology, and imagery of the Old West and frontier landscape (however parodic, ironic, campy, or complex this imagined community and landscape may be).

The popularity of "Old Town Road," with its focus on a dandified, anti-authoritarian, quick-witted, self-proclaimed "queer" Black cowboy, can be seen as a reminder of—and a metaphor for—the commercial success of Black western movies specifically and Black Western folk culture generally. It could also be viewed as a tribute to the legacy of singing Black cowboys like actor Herb Jeffries and musician Charley Pride. While film stars such as Woody Strode, Jim Brown, and Fred Williamson (or the riders in *Black Rodeo*) would not have self-identified as *sexually* queer, they did represent a cultural rewriting of the reel Western mythology and dominant cinematic vocabulary by unmooring the western genre from its predetermined colonialism, white supremacy, and ethno(musical)centrism.

In 2019 two collections of Black Western rodeo photographs were published. Melodie McDaniel published a book of realist urban photography documenting the Compton Jr. Posse of Black western and English riders in *Riding through Compton*.[15] Rory Doyle captured Mississippi's Delta Hill Riders in his photography.[16] Both photographers reflected part of the legacy of Exodusters. Viewed collectively, the "country-trap" musicians, Compton Cowboy riders, Delta Hill Riders, and community organizations can be viewed as threads in the same sociopolitical-cultural movement.

The films, these horseback riders, and these musicians are coheirs to a legacy of Black westerns (and Westerners, or people who helped settled the West). Collectively, they reproduce a Western imaginary and an Afro-diasporic Southwestern affinity in which Black life and culture are amalgamated: rural and urban, folksy and urbane, traditional and modern, apolitical and activist.

The political nature of Black Western culture was evident in the 2020 protests against systemic police brutality evident in the murders of George

Floyd, Breonna Taylor, Eric Garner, Freddie Gray, Philando Castile, Ata-
tiana Jefferson, Dominique Clayton, Tamir Rice, Sandra Bland, and many
others. In the wake of the George Floyd killing by Minnesota police officer
Derek Chauvin on May 25, 2020, protesters took to the streets across the
globe. Some protesters rode on horseback in cities including Houston and
Compton to demonstrate against police brutality. Videos of the protesters
on horses spread across social media, showing riders wearing shirts that
read "Black Cowboys Matter."[17] In Houston, Black cowboys participated in
protests on horseback as part of a Houston urban trail riding club called
Nonstop Riders. In Compton, the Compton Cowboys invited fellow equestrians to join protests.[18] The presence of these activist groups, and the
attention they garnered, speaks to their political relevance within Black
communities. Here the relationship with one's horses enables protesters
to inhabit public space peacefully while making a powerful—and highly
visible—statement about their entitlement to inhabit space, land, and the
public sphere.

Just as we find precursors to Lil Nas X's visual imaginary in everyday
lifestyles and fashions of *Black Rodeo* riders like Bud Bramwell (real name
Archie Wycoff), Cleo Hearn (Clarence Gonzalez), Skeets Richardson (Pete
Knight), Billy the Kid (Moses Fields), Outlaw Kid (Cornell Fields), and Rocky
Watson (Marvel Rogers), we also see the reemergence of an affinity for
horses, rodeos, riding, and rodeo training in the cultural practices of the
Compton Cowboys and the Houston Trail Riders.

We also witness a longing for African American Western history among
the people of Harlem in *Black Rodeo* who comprised the pre-rodeo parade
performers and spectators at the opening of Jeff Kanew's documentary.
Kanew's film is the first nonfiction visual record of ordinary people living
out their extraordinary fantasies of rodeo stardom and cowboy legend.
It is understandable that one of the ABCA's first projects was to assist in
the production of Kanew's *Black Rodeo* in New York City, which included a
parade through Harlem.[19]

Inasmuch as the 1960s was an era of political empowerment for champions of civil rights, an era marking the emergence of the Black Arts movement, and Black protests against the racial state apparatus, it was also an era
of cultural revolution. This revolution enabled alterative, underrepresented,
and suppressed epistemologies and ontologies of Black life to gain expression, including Black Southwestern cultural practices and hybrid identities
and syncretism. The documentary *Black Rodeo* gave audiences, particularly
Northeasterners (where the film was in limited release), a glimpse of equine-
and livestock-based agrarian lifestyles practiced by African Americans who
bred, raised, trained, and rode livestock and horses.

Black Rodeo

Even before the opening credits roll, *Black Rodeo* begins with a sepia-toned montage of still photographs of white male film stars like Roy Rogers, Tom Mix, Gene Autry, Hop-Along Cassidy, and John Wayne rolling along to a twangy rendition of "Home on the Range." As the montage concludes, the film cuts to a black screen with large white letters reading BLACK RODEO. The R&B rhythms of Sammy Turner's bass guitar theme song, "The History of the Black Cowboy," swells as a different set of images appears. On screen is a brightly colored, live-action montage of New York City street scenes, filmed by a roaming camera immersed in Harlem traffic. The rapid, cinema verité–style shots focus, fleetingly, on the African American cowboys dressed fancily for rodeo performance in colorful shirts, Stetson hats, bolo neckties, cowboy scarves, silver belt buckles, and shined cowboy boots. Riders are filmed as they busily engage in preparations for the rodeo. Many are shown grooming their horses. One man, wearing a red shirt and a black hat while mounted on a gray horse, is seen loping down the street. The horse's moves are graphically matched to the beat of the soundtrack as he maneuvers through heavy traffic between cars and buses.

The synchronization between the bass rhythms, the horse's loping movements, and the rider's body evokes the opening images of Gordon Parks's *Shaft*, when Richard Roundtree makes his entrance from the subway to the beat of Isaac Hayes's award-winning score. Both films use beat, tempo, and rhythmic editing to convey ideas about masculinity, mastery, and control. Next, *Rodeo* cuts to a beautiful chestnut horse in full Western tack. The horse jumps down from a trailer onto the street, and the camera quickly cuts to two attractive young women riders, each mounted on their own horses standing patiently at a traffic light. The camera swish-pans back and forth at a busy intersection as if trying to follow the cacophonous mélange of people, horses, cars, buses, pedestrians, and riders as they move frenetically through the crossroads. Infants are shown carefully perched on horseback by parents holding them tightly around the waist as if on a pony ride at a petting zoo.

The opening montage, set on the Harlem streets, concludes as the camera stops moving. In a static shot the camera lingers to focus on a group of young African American boys gazing excitedly into the camera. The cameraman asks them, "Have you been on a horse before? Have you ever seen a rodeo before? What do you think a rodeo is all about?" The children joke and giggle while bobbing over each other, trying to see the camera and to be interviewed by a camera operator. Meanwhile adults stand by, waiting and watching as their children stare in awe of the horses, riders, and their costumes. Parents and adults are asked their opinions of the rodeo. In reply, they laud the riders as good role models for the Harlem neighborhood kids. One proud parent boasts, "We were out in the West too. . . . You never see it on TV, but we were out there. . . . We helped put it together." Reviving, reenacting, and restoring the legacy of Black cowboys, as the rodeo riders do, calls attention to the suppressed history of Black American frontier culture and the political economy of the Western frontier.

When asked how he feels about the rodeo, one parent replies, "I think it's a very good idea; I think it advances the country more when you can show both sides of the picture instead of just one side of the picture." Featuring these testimonials, Kanew seeks to demonstrate the political awareness of bystanders. Next, the camera finds another man dressed in a rodeo outfit. An off-screen voice asks him, "What's your name?" A tall, lean, handsome man with a deep baritone voice replies. He's Rocky Watson, originally from Montana but currently living in Chicago. Rocky directly addresses the camera, explaining that he's a full-time rodeo athlete specializing in bull riding, which he's been doing since he was seventeen. The film rapidly cuts to a slow-motion scene of Rocky riding a large white bucking bull. In the voice-over narration, Rocky assures the audience that "the danger goes down when you've been in it for a while. . . . I ain't got a whole lot to say, but I'm glad we can make folks aware of it."

During Rocky's interview, the film crosscuts from his image to that of an attractive, young female pedestrian as she walks purposefully down a Harlem sidewalk clad in a mishmash of contrasting fashions. With her hair plaited into two braids, she wears a beaded Indian headband, a beaded Indian necklace, yellow-tinted sunglasses, and a pink tie-dyed tank top. Her creolized Afro-Indian fashion suggests that she is part of the rodeo. And, indeed, she will appear later as one of the parade float ladies or exhibitors. Her fashion combines flower-child freestyling and Native Indian jewelry, pulled together in an Afro-kitsch pastiche. Her image is juxtaposed against Rocky Watson's image and interview.

In juxtaposition, the two subjects come into a visual relationship. The woman's Afro-hippie-Native fashioning and Watson's rodeo performing evoke the history of Exodusters of the 1870s with their Afro-Indian syncretism and reimagined blackness. Just as Exodusters created a sense of Black identity from African American, Native Indian, and Anglo-Saxon settler frontier cultures (formed around style, fashion, livestock, cattle ranching, horseback riding, and farming), so too Rocky and the unidentified parade float exhibitor recreate a Black West. They invite spectators to contemplate the hodgepodge of Afro-hippie tie-dye fashion and how the Black Power and Black Arts movements encouraged young people to also pay homage to Black

Western culture in their sartorial habits. The subjects present alternative ways of constructing the self not only as urban, metropolitan, postmodern, city dwellers but also as folksy, agrarian, traditional, agriculturalists. In their fashions these young people evoke Michel Foucault's "technologies of the self," whereby individuals effect operations on their own bodies, thoughts, conduct, and ways of being to transform themselves.[20] Rocky Watson and the unidentified female exhibitor engage in techniques of self-imaging that produce new, alternative aesthetics of cultural experience.[21]

Next the camera pauses on Gordon Hayes, who first appears with Sonda, one of his two gray vaulting horses. Gordon tells the director of photography that both of his horses (Sonda and Sonora) perform in the rodeo. The film uses evidentiary editing to crosscut between images of Gordon riding and performing (sitting astride one horse while keeping the second in hand) and his interview. He explains that he has trained trick horses for fifty years. The film cuts to rodeo clown Billy the Kid (Moses Fields) as he jokingly shakes hands with, and introduces, other rodeo riders.

These unscripted, cinema vérité–style street scenes and spontaneous interviews introduce the documentary subjects: the real-life people of the film. The scenes also recall classic cinema verité movies like Jean Rouch's *Chronicle of a Summer* (1961) and the way verité filmmakers captured the unfiltered, impromptu feelings ordinary people have about their surroundings. More significantly, the scenes capture what Stuart Hall describes when he discusses cultural identities in the cinema: "Cultural identities come from somewhere, have histories. But, like everything which is historical, they undergo constant transformation. Far from being eternally fixed in some essential past, identities are subject to the continuous 'play' of history, culture and power."[22] The reclamation of rodeo culture, as one facet of Exoduster history, is consistent and coterminous with an African American transformation and reimagination of Black presence in the West and Black Indian creolization.

The film then turns its gaze upon the colorfully clad Afro-Caribbean parade of rodeo riders marching and prancing down Adam Clayton Powell Boulevard past 142nd Street in Manhattan. Complete with dancing girls, marching bands, flag carriers, and banner wavers, the marchers move along. They are followed by Harlem residents—parade watchers careening for a glimpse of the excitement, entertainment, and syncretism of Black Western rodeo pageantry. The parade musicians marching down the avenue play African folk music. Their song is a rendition of "Dianka Bi," a ballad by Festival Music of the Princess of Dahomey. Dancers dressed in the colors of the Pan-African flag undulate in unison with the traditional West African melody, which slowly fades out, giving way to drumming, and then fades back to Sammy Turner's R&B theme song, "The History of the Black Cowboy."

Next, the film follows a trail of spectators traveling to Randall's Island Stadium for the actual rodeo, intercutting cinema verité interviews with direct cinema's passive observations. As spectators file into the stadium, a sound bridge connects the images. A rodeo announcer says:

> We got a lot of people outside coming in. We certainly want everyone to see the rodeo. Most of the people unaware of the black cowboys are the black people in the early part of this country. And this is what we're all about. So, sit back, relax, and get ready as we swing down to the gates for the first event on the program this afternoon. Ladies and gentlemen, our grand entry![23]

Two riders, one carrying an American flag, the other carrying a Pan-African flag, ride through the arena gates and open the rodeo. Several mounted riders follow behind in single file. Some are clad in Native American outfits with full Indian headdress and mounted bareback on Appaloosas (a breed often symbolically associated with Native peoples). Other performers are dressed as Ninth and Tenth Cavalry officers in uniform, and some wear conventional everyday Western gear: chaps, cowboy boots, and Stetson hats.

Director Jeff Kanew's six camera operators capture the spectacle of the performers' entry into the stadium from distant establishing shots and nearby and low-angle medium shots. Lee Dorsey's folksy rendition of the popular anthem "Yes We Can" plays over the opening rodeo footage.

> Now's the time for all good men
> to get together with one another.
> We got to iron out our problems
> and iron out our quarrels
> and try to live as brothers.
> And try to find a piece of land
> without stepping on one another.
> And do respect the women of the world.
> Remember you all have mothers.
> We got to make this land a better land
> than the world in which we live.
> And we got to help each man be a better man
> with the kindness that we give.
> I know we can make it.
> I know darn well we can work it out.
> Oh yes we can, I know we can can
> Yes we can can, why can't we?
> If we wanna get together we can work it out.

FIGURE 4.1 The Buffalo Soldiers Riding Club on parade in *Black Rodeo*.

"Yes We Can" is a clever choice for this scene because it signifies literally on the contemporary context and symbolically on the historical background. A popular song, with messages of brotherhood, self-determination, racial uplift, and self-improvement, it connects—intentionally or otherwise— African American political struggles of the 1860s and '70s with contemporary civil rights struggles of the 1960s and '70s by implying that social justice battles for Black inclusion are ongoing. The call to "make this world better" resonates with the rhetoric employed by Black religious, political, and revolutionary leadership. The song implies that knowing "our" history is part of making the world better for posterity.

As each rodeo performer is introduced, they gallop through the arena gates to the sound of the announcer's introduction and the band's cue. First comes Cornell Fields, then Joanne Eason; next there's rodeo president Bud Bramwell followed by Marvel Rogers. Then the rodeo officially begins. But instead of singing the national anthem or reciting the Pledge of Allegiance, a common practice at rodeos, the announcer asks everyone to stand in prayer. They remove their hats and bow their heads.

When the prayer concludes, the camera pans across the field of spectators and lands squarely on the face of actor Woody Strode—the Black star of *Sergeant Rutledge*—in and among the crowd. Swarmed by spectators, Strode is shown signing autographs. The film cuts away from the public space of the rodeo to a small room where Jeff Kanew interviews Strode on how he, serendipitously, learned about the rodeo and decided to remain in New York to see it. It crosscuts between the stream of rodeo contestants and Woody Strode's on-camera explanation of the history of Exoduster culture. One after another, the contestants mount up and ride into the arena. Their rodeo names evoke the lore of the Old West. Billy the Kid, Clarence Gonzales, and fellow riders (from as far away as Oklahoma City, Bay City, Dallas, and Montana) follow each other.

Director Kanew then changes the tempo of action and rhythmic montage. He uses a slow-motion montage of bronco riders—one rider after another—undulating atop the massive waves of an unbridled bucking horse. Kanew underscores the soulfulness of this communally Black rodeo showcase with African American music. He uses B. B. King's 1969 blues song "Get Off My Back Woman," followed by Aretha Franklin's "Good to Me as I Am to You," on the soundtrack. The music plays over the slow-motion images of the rider using brute strength to surf the wave of a bucking bronco. As the King song gives way to the voice of Aretha Franklin, Kanew interpolates or reaches out to the African American viewing audience with the music and lyrics. He knows this music will register with them and capture their imaginations. Traditional blues historically addressed various personal and political themes, including lost love, bigoted law enforcement, racism,

FIGURE 4.2 Woody Strode signs autographs in *Black Rodeo*.

and hard financial times. In true blues tradition, both King's and Franklin's lyrics express the personal woes experienced in a world of harsh realities.

The music on the soundtrack signifies both literally and figuratively. On the image track, horses are shown literally bucking riders off their backs. The song also resonates symbolically. The lyrics signify on the historic and systemic exploitation of Black labor under American capitalism. A subaltern socioeconomic group, African American labor has historically been exploited on Southern plantations, Western ranches, and in metropolitan factories. The lyrics on the soundtrack suggest the relentless grinding drudgery of manual labor under the yoke of carceral capitalism. In addition to a close rapport with one's trusted animals, Black rodeo culture offers riders the liberating sensations of control, mastery, and freedom from everyday concerns. As a form of physical recreation and emotional cathartics, rodeo performance becomes a place to express pride, dignity, and racial solidarity.

> Yeah, you get off of my back, baby
> Can't you tell you're choking me
> Oh I ain't no pony, baby
> Can't you tell you're choking me
> Yeah, you just get off of my back, baby
> Can't you see you're hurting me
> Well, I don't mind helping you, baby

FIGURE 4.3 Skeets Richardson rides a bull.

Every now, now and then
Yes, you ain't helped yourself, baby
Since God knows when
So you just get off of my back now, baby
Can't you see you're hurting me

Director Jeff Kanew quickly returns the camera's gaze to the audience for testimonials of their impressions. Repeatedly, adults and parents affirm the value of role modeling and the need for inclusive history. The camera pans and lingers—temporarily—on random faces in the crowd. Families and children are shown on the screen, staring in awe at the riders. Non-diegetic voice-overs express the pride of spectators. For example, one woman says, "Of course . . . I'm from Texas, so I knew they were here all the time but the kids need to know." Next, a male voice is heard saying, "Now . . . when they look at television, they won't have to wonder if there were really Black people living in that era." Assertively, another man claims, "They'll get the impact of this years from now." Yet another woman assures, "It means they'll learn more about Blacks and that there's more than just *whites* out there." Finally, one observer quips, "Frankly, I think the grownups are

FIGURE 4.4 Cowboy
Charles Lewis
demonstrates
quick draw.

enjoying it more than the kids." Repeatedly, the non-diegetic voice-over testimonies of adults are used to express appreciation for the historical framework that the rodeo offers Black youth.

After several endorsements, the documentary cuts to another rodeo event: barrel racing, again accompanied by non-diegetic R&B vocals. The song is by artist Dee Dee Sharp singing "Ride," which was a crossover hit that had reached number five on pop charts and number seven on the R&B charts in 1962. Barrel racing is the only event in which a young Betsy Bramwell (cowboy Bud Bramwell's pre-teen daughter) also competes. Although brief, her presence in the film is significant. Her barrel racing, along with the music, conveys the feeling of carefree youth, throwing caution to the wind, and bold ambition. She represents the spirit of unchecked possibilities and opportunities. The young barrel racer proves these rodeos are family-friendly events with role models for viewers of all ages. Her ride also demonstrates that young Black girls ride competitively. In recent years, social media organizations attested to the fact that African American men and women participate in equestrian activities (e.g., the Black Female Equestrians, We Ride Too, Outdoorsy Black Women, *Black Reins* magazine, and the Compton Cowboys). Nearly fifty years (1971–2021) before the hashtag "#weridetoo" emerged, young Betsy Bramwell was demonstrating that Black girls participate in competitive equestrian sports, whether English or Western in discipline. Her appearance debunks the falsehood that equestrian activities are exclusively white Anglo-Saxon pursuits.

FIGURE 4.5 Betsy Bramwell rides in the rodeo.

Kanew's film then crosscuts between the rodeo and his interview with Woody Strode, in which the actor reflects on his relationship with horses, riding, and how riding helped him secure a role in a John Ford western. Shortly after making the Korean war picture *Pork Chop Hill*, Strode began working with Ford. Sitting in a dimly lit room with Jeff Kanew, Strode addresses the camera, saying,

> The Black rodeo has been very close to me ever since I got involved with John Ford back around 1959. I never thought I'd get involved in motion pictures. He picked me up when I was doing *Pork Chop Hill*. He called me in to do a picture called *Sergeant Rutledge*. It was originally called *The Buffalo Soldiers*. He had a big fight because they wanted *named* stars, like you would normally. And he told them, "They're not tough enough." But nobody realized what he wanted his Black star to do. I don't believe I could have gotten started if I couldn't ride horses. People asked me, "Were people prejudiced?" Well, I look at it another way. It was expedient at that time for a Black [person] to be able to *do* something. Maybe that was an excuse for letting me put on these cowboy clothes. They said, "Woody knows how to ride; he knows how to shoot. He knows how to use a bow and arrow." In other words, I almost had to be Superman to get started. They said they'd have to get a white actor to stunt-double me because no one could. Who would that be? With me being *born* in the West, [casting me] made it like a rabbit being thrown in a briar patch. . . .
>
> I had to do everything without a double; it was a very unique job. And I understood what he meant when he said they weren't tough enough. . . .
>
> I've always said that Blacks should have been put on the screen from the Western side. But when they brought us into the contemporary, they brought us into the race riots, into the competition against whites, instead of showing how we helped build the country.[24]

Black Rodeo links the rigorous work of rodeo performance with Woody Strode's film performances. Strode concludes that had he not been able to ride, shoot, and do archery, he might not have been cast by John Ford in Hollywood films. In actuality, Ford was aiming to cast an unknown actor in *Sergeant Rutledge* rather than overcome the cultural baggage accompanying the use of a well-known film star like Sidney Poitier. Nonetheless, Strode's interview underscores the link between land/livestock ownership and how such access begets future financial and professional opportunities. Strode serves as an authenticating voice, a professional "talking head" who connects the documentary to everyday economics, politics, history, and political economy—all the "discourses of sobriety" that Bill Nichols has outlined in his seminal work on modes of documentary practice.[25] Strode's claim of possessing "real skills" reverberates beyond the artistic realm of filmmaking (either industrial or independent, documentary or fiction) into social and economic opportunities for Black Americans, both past and present. Strode's interviews function as an ideological linchpin linking the mythology of cinema and representational discourse to everyday practices routinized by ordinary people.

Problematically, however, Woody Strode's on-camera, first-person account of Western history fails to address the genocide wrought upon Indian civilizations. His recitation of American history reveals an underdeveloped and sometimes jingoistic view of American colonialism. Instead of censuring the colonial government's military campaigns against Native Indians, Strode looks into the camera and hails Colorado Expedition champions like Esteban de Dorantes (aka Esteban the Moor), the tenacious African slave who would reportedly be the first non-Native person to visit the southern reaches of the Colorado Plateau. Similarly, Strode recalls historical figures like Cherokee Bill, Deadwood Dick, and Bill Hodges, among others known from frontier folklore. In this interview setting, Strode explains the etymology of the term "Buffalo Soldier" as the nickname given to Black cavalrymen by Native Indians. As a documentary, *Black Rodeo* calls attention to the complex, contradictory, and colonialist role that Black Americans played on the frontier, but it does not address the complicity and collusive nature of African American participation in the destruction of Indian civilizations.

The film's representation of African American–Native American cultural hybridity in the form of Black participation complicates an otherwise simplistic reading of the documentary as merely reproducing dominant cultural idioms (e.g., bull riding). For instance, one participant appearing in full Indian headdress tells bystanders about the Navajo Indian linguistic codes used during World War II. Laying claim to his own Seneca Indian heritage, he asserts that everyone should know the history of the Navajo people so that they might receive proper recognition for their contribution to America's defeat of European fascism. In these spontaneous conversations, *Black Rodeo* not only opens up opportunities to acknowledge fissures and gaps in the historical record but also advocates for American pluralism.

Following a thematic emphasis on lessons learned from this rodeo, Kanew cuts back to scenes of children offering their views on the Black cowboys and rodeos. In response to how the rodeo makes them feel, the boys enthusiastically respond in unison:

"Do you all like cowboys?"
    "Yeah!"
"Did you wear cowboy hats when you were little?"
    "Yeah!"

"Did you all have guns?"
  "Yeah!"
"Did you all watch cowboys on TV?"
  "Yeah."
"But most of those were all white cowboys on television, right?"
  "Yeah."
"Do you dig seeing Black cowboys here?"
  "Yeah!"
"How does it make you feel?"[26]

Black Rodeo uses evidentiary editing and the personal testimony of these boys to convey the pleasure they take from seeing cowboy role models. But one of the most revealing comments comes from an off-screen adult male subject lamenting another stereotype of blackness, who says:

> A lot of people don't believe Black people have horses. We have 'em. That's a fact. That's something that's true. We go riding. When we do, some people look at us like its *real* strange. It's like we're not supposed to be able to ride horses. The only people who are supposed to be able to ride horses are white folks. And this [rodeo] is something that's really great because we need it. It's a way of life.[27]

These statements render visible the invisibility of Black disenfranchisement from land proprietorship, farming, and ownership of livestock. It renders

FIGURE 4.6 Rodeo clowns are official cowboy lifeguards.

visible the pleasures many African Americans take—and have historically taken—in owning and caring for their land and animals.

The deeply rewarding nature of relationships with one's animals—particularly with horses—is documented in the realist urban photography of Rory Doyle and Melodie McDaniel. In their photographs, they capture the western horsemanship of African Americans living in the Mississippi Delta and in the city of Compton, California, respectively. In 2019 Doyle began displaying his photographic show titled *Delta Hill Riders*. That same year, McDaniel published *Riding through Compton*, documenting the equestrians of the Compton Jr. Posse. Viewed together with *Black Rodeo*, the contemporary Doyle and McDaniel images present a more comprehensive picture of African American Western cultural experience. Much of this experience has been erased from American history, hidden from present-day record, and suppressed from Hollywood's cinematic mythmaking. Black Western idioms reveal a connection between (1) the real presence of Exodusters and their descendants within historical discourse, (2) the everyday practices of the Western lifestyle, and (3) the cultural myths of the West in mainstream movies. Distinct yet overlapping discourses (e.g., the historical, the everyday, the cinematic) speak volumes about the sustained invisibility of Black life in America.

In the final scenes of *Black Rodeo*, Kanew concludes by giving Strode and Muhammad Ali a final nod. First he captures Ali's playful interaction with riders as he meets and pets the trick horses and greets their owners. When asked if he would bullfight, Ali responds with characteristic quick-wittedness, saying, "Joe Frasier is enough bull for me to fight." In response, bystanders chuckle at his disarmingly lighthearted humor regarding rodeo bull riding, barrel racing, horseplay, and boxing.

Kanew then replaces the ambient voices with the theme song for *Black Rodeo*. In these loose closing moments, the director allows the sound recorder and camera operator to be seen on film recording Ali's jocular horseplay. It's one of several brief moments of cinematic reflexivity that fits in organically with the observational and vérité style of *Black Rodeo*. Playing along, Ali allows the riders to dress him in chaps, a Stetson, and boots as he prepares to sit on a bull and be led around the arena. Using a graphic match-on-action in which the same chaps are worn by another rider, we see a bull leap out of his pen as the announcer calls out a rider's name and the film cuts away from Ali and back to rodeo footage. A montage of bull riders rolls on screen and Kanew uses Little Richard's song "Slippin' and Slidin'," on the soundtrack.

The film's final words are spoken by the disembodied voice of an off-screen man who reminisces by saying, "I'm glad I've lived to see them today.

I'm seventy-one years old and I'm proud to see what it means for a man to live under the sun and make a place for himself under the sun equal to all men." The camera freezes on a frame of a mounted cowboy whose face is silhouetted by the sun. As his silhouette fills the screen, Sammy Turner's song "The History of the Black Cowboy" returns until the screen fades to black. Kanew's choice of closing remarks summarizes principal themes and symbols embedded in *Black Rodeo*: the ability to tame, train, and ride one's animals is an integral part of independence, self-determination, and prosperity in America.

Skin Game

Skin Game, directed by Paul Bogart and Gordon Douglas, is an interracial buddy film and comedy-western released a few months before *Black Rodeo*. At the time, Paul Bogart was one of television's most prominent directors and winner of numerous Emmy Awards. Cinematography was shot by Fred Koenenkamp and the picture was scored by David Shire. A feature-length comedy, it assumes a decidedly different tone than previous Black western dramas and the nonfiction documentary *Black Rodeo*. *Skin Game* paired James Garner (who secured his Western persona portraying Bret Maverick in the hit television show *Maverick*) and Lou Gossett, who made his first screen appearances in the social problem pictures *Take a Giant Step* (1958) and *A Raisin in the Sun*.

As early as 1966, producer Harry Keller was slated to make *Skin Game* at Universal Studios. Perhaps it was Keller's intention to follow up on the success of *Duel at Diablo*, in which Garner had successfully co-starred with Sidney Poitier. But *Skin Game* was dropped by Universal. By September 1970, Keller announced that the film would be made by James Garner's production company, Cherokee Productions, for distribution by Warner Bros.[28]

Set in the pre–Civil War West, con man Quincy Drew (James Garner) and his well-educated friend Jason O'Rourke (Louis Gossett), a Black man from New Jersey, are longtime friends. Together they have a successful business partnership as con men who bilk slave owners out of their ill-gotten gains. Traveling throughout smaller hamlets of Kansas and Missouri, Drew pretends to offer up O'Rourke for sale at a slave at auction and then rescues him later that evening after collecting payment. Once Jason is freed, he and Quincy depart for the next unsuspecting town and scam the gullible slave owners out of their money.

For Quincy and Jason, work is profitable and life is relatively carefree until they meet their match in the form of an attractive young pickpocket named Ginger (Susan Clark) who wants in on their swindle. Along their travels, Jason meets a beautiful, young enslaved woman named Naomi (Brenda Sykes) and insists that Quincy purchase her freedom. Initially all seems well, but no sooner have they teamed up with their lady companions than Ginger steals their money and she and abolitionist John Brown (Royal Dano) abscond with all the Black people, including Jason and Naomi. What would ordinarily be liberating to most enslaved persons proves inconvenient for freeman Jason and Naomi, who now carry out a charade of being enslaved so that John Brown's men don't suspect that they're faking enslavement. At this juncture, *Skin Game* proves a full-throttle send-up. It plays like the *Blazing Saddles* of westploitation narratives.

In a comedy of errors, Quincy must rescue Jason and Naomi from John Brown (who was busily liberating the enslaved). Once reunited, Quincy and Jason plan one bigger scam (to recover the money Ginger stole from them) before they retire to enjoy their spoils.[29] Their traveling con game continues smoothly until they again cross paths with a sadistic slave dealer and tracker named Plunkeet (Edward Asner) whom they had earlier swindled. Seeking revenge and looking to profit, Plunkeet imprisons Quincy on sight. Fortuitously, a remorseful Ginger—feeling guilty about stealing Quincy and Jason's "skin-game" money—resurfaces. She breaks Quincy from jail, returns half their money, and together Ginger and Quincy return to Calloway's (Andrew Duggan) ranch to rescue Jason and Naomi from servitude. Only, despite their temporary re-enslavement, Jason has joined forces with a tribe of newly arrived Songhai Africans. When Quincy and Ginger arrive at Calloway's to free Jason and Naomi, they are too late. Aided by the Songhai, Naomi and Jason have already mastered their escape from Calloway's ranch. When the four friends reunite, the longtime buddies Jason and Quincy sever their brotherly partnership and decide to go their separate ways; Jason and Naomi depart for Mexico (to escape the American slavocracy) while Quincy and Ginger embrace an uncertain path.

Skin Game was not a small film. It was released with pomp and circumstance. It was the fifteen-hundredth motion picture released by Warner Bros. and enjoyed a gala world premiere on September 30, 1971, at the famous Grauman's Chinese Theatre. The film's release was part of a weeklong salute to Warner Bros., culminating in a benefit premiere of the film. Though an important film to Warner Bros., and an attempt to critique American plantocracy and lampoon slavery, *Skin Game* proved to be just a run-of-the-mill comedy, evidenced by its mixed critical reviews.

On one hand, the picture's mediocrity was captured by critics writing for the *New York Times* and *Chicago Tribune*. But the movie was also applauded by writers for the *L.A. Times* and *Washington Post*. For example, Roger Greenspun saw *Skin Game* as a "race relations comedy that['s] really

meant to be about how people relate to one another . . . [but] isn't a very
consistent movie, and its comedy misses much more often than it hits."[30]
In the *Chicago Tribune*, Gene Siskel summed it up, saying, "I think the script
is unnecessarily burdening itself when it tries to be both educational and
humorous. The equality issue would have been the natural product of any
situation comedy in which black and white are equal partners."[31] But *Los
Angeles Times* critic Kevin Thomas lauded the movie. "What could have
easily been the most tasteless picture of the year turns out to be one of the
funniest," he wrote. In the *Washington Post*, Gary Arnold offered tempered
praise: "*Skin Game* is surprisingly buoyant and likable, an attempt at light
entertainment that, for the most part, proves light and entertaining."[32]
These lukewarm reviews are put into context when we consider the African
American press and their coverage of the film in newspapers. For instance,
New York Amsterdam News critic Willie Hamilton wrote:

> The idea is workable but at the same time a great many Blacks who have a
> hang-up about the "nigger" or slavery aspect of the picture may be highly
> offended. . . .
>   Not too much else to say about this one. If you are not really sensitive
> and can laugh about previous conditions, see it.[33]

If *Skin Game* achieved anything, it was that it enabled James Garner
to once again co-star with an African American actor in a western, as he'd
successfully done in *Duel at Diablo* with Sidney Poitier in 1966. But the film
was an unfunny parody lacking memorable moments, beautiful vistas, or a
novel use of humor. Instead, it plays more like a made-for-television western
comedy than a substantive feature. A similar sentiment was captured by
Howell Raines in his review for the *Atlanta Constitution*. "Such improbable
plots," wrote Raines, "seem to work nicely for Garner[,] who plays them with
the tongue-in-cheek style he developed back in his days on the television
series 'Maverick'."[34] Perhaps this was because it was shot in twelve weeks
on a Burbank backlot on hastily constructed cover sets.[35]

Both director Paul Bogart and co-star James Garner had spent so much
time working in television that the filmmakers brought out small-screen
sensibilities rather than widescreen grandeur. Furthermore, the film over-
played the jocular camaraderie between its leads. Either way, it possessed
none of the solemn moral dilemmas or "crises of conscience" characteristic
of memorable pictures. Instead, it was a light send-up of both Western
generic elements and 1970s race relations. In the end, *Skin Game* has more
in common with the light humor of the classic parody *Blazing Saddles* than
the somber *100 Rifles* or the gloomier (albeit similarly unseasoned) *The
McMasters*.

Nevertheless, the film remains important. The comedic pranks, banter, and seemingly genuine camaraderie between Lou Gossett's Jason and James Garner's Quincy further set the stage for interracial buddy comedies that would emerge a few years later, particularly the Richard Pryor–Gene Wilder vehicles *Silver Streak* and *Stir Crazy*. Some cultural critics—chief among them being James Parish—viewed *Skin Game* as a continuation of the interracial buddy picture that began with *The Defiant Ones*.[36] It is important to recall that *Duel at Diablo* (which paired Garner with Poitier on more equal footing) was also a crucial step along the road to interracial buddy comedies released in the 1980s. Moreover, the serious "social problem picture" tone of a drama like *The Defiant Ones* is considerably dissimilar from the comedic antics and relaxed posture of a parody like *Skin Game*, which spoofed the genre, its wooden characters, and even its antebellum Americana setting.

To that end, Parish quotes *Essence* magazine writer Maurice Patterson saying, "Your eyes do not deceive you, the film really does make a mockery of 200 years of terror and agony—but not without scoring serious points along the way."[37] More than the *Defiant Ones*, however, *Skin Game* marked a perceptible shift in the tone of race relations on screen.

FIGURE 4.7 Louis Gossett's Jason O'Rourke and James Garner's Quincy Drew on the run in *Skin Game*.

In the wake of the profitability of blaxploitation, New Hollywood–era producers believed mainstream films could joke about slavery and racial injustice. And in some ways they could. It was the tonal shift in these movies that also set the stage for later comedies such as Eddie Murphy's interracial-buddy star vehicles *48 Hours*, *Trading Places*, *Beverly Hills Cop*, and the sequels *Beverly Hills Cop 2* (1987) and *Beverly Hills Cop 3* (1994).

The McMasters

Among the numerous but lesser-known African American–themed westerns to emerge in the early '70s was *The McMasters*. Only months before *Skin Game* was released, the Swedish film-actor-turned-director Alf Kjellin released the film in 1970. A quirky and little-known oater, it starred Brock Peters as a lone Black cowboy returning to his prairie home after the Civil War.

Peters had appeared in the prestigious films *Carmen Jones* (1954), *Porgy and Bess* (1959), and *To Kill a Mockingbird* (1962) as well as successful television programs: *Rawhide* (1965), *Mission Impossible* (1967), and *Gunsmoke*, among others. He was a highly respected actor with impressive credits to his name. In *The McMasters* he was placed in familiar company alongside genre veterans Jack Palance, Burl Ives, and David Carradine. Carradine would go on to star in *Kung Fu*, which began airing on television in 1972 and introduced the action-adventure martial arts Western drama. Carradine's father, John Carradine, made an appearance playing the town preacher. And Hong Kong–born former ballet dancer Nancy Kwan (star of *The World of Suzie Wong*, 1960; and *Flower Drum Song*, 1961) was cast in her familiar role as a vulnerable ingénue caught between disparate worlds. However, the strong cast alone was insufficient connective tissue for this otherwise uninspiring film.

The *McMasters* story is set after the Civil War around the fictional town of Ironwood. A young Black man named Benjie (Brock Peters) returns to the Southwest, having fought for the Union Army up north. His homecoming brings him to the ranch of Neal McMasters (Burl Ives) a friendly old Santa Claus of a man who raised Benjie from childhood. Upon Benjie's return, Neal sells him half of the ranch and together they try to make a go of it. Benjie's lifelong dream is to own land. In his ambition of land ownership, he is the repository for African American dreams of racial uplift and enfranchisement. When Neal has a serious accident, the workload becomes too much for Benjie alone. Because Benjie is Black, none of the white ranch hands will work for him. But an act of kindness to local Indians inadvertently saves him. Benjie befriends White Feather (David Carradine) when he prevents Kolby (Jack Palance) from lynching several Indians falsely accused of cattle stealing. Instead, Benjie orders Kolby off his land and gifts some of McMasters's cattle to the starving Indian tribe.

Indebted to Benjie for his acts of kindness, Chief White Feather returns with his tribe to help Benjie with a laborious cattle roundup on the McMasters ranch, and he offers his sister, Robin, to Benjie as cook and comfort woman. Initially appalled by the offer of her servitude, Benjie begrudgingly accepts but remains ill at ease with her presence. Having not been around women in years, he is gruff and agitated by her femininity. Torn between desire and repression, Benjie suddenly loses control and rapes Robin in a bizarre fit of anger. His actions are jarringly unmotivated and out of character, as he is depicted as an otherwise gentle soul. Immediately horrified by his erratic behavior, he expresses contrition. Oddly, the film's script puts the character (and the audience) through an emotional roller coaster that seems disjointed from the film's other intentions.

The dutiful, stereotypical Indian woman, Robin (played by Nancy Kwan in redface) forgives Benjie and eventually accepts his invitation to move into the McMasterses' ranch house. Over time, Benjie's guilt and remorse gradually change him. Witnessing Benjie's remorse, Neal McMasters encourages Benjie to "say something nice to her." Fortuitously, their conversation leads to a proposal in which Benjie offers Robin his adopted name in marriage.

News of their impending marriage causes more waves in Ironwood, but the ceremony goes forward. However, their honeymoon is cut short—in a narrative maneuver that references *High Noon*—when Benjie is told that his herd of cattle has been scattered and that some were poisoned. He

FIGURE 4.8 Burl Ives and Brock Peters are *The McMasters*.

discovers the culprits pouring arsenic into the cattle feed and shoots one of the perpetrators as they flee. But his actions evoke even greater retaliation. One night he comes home to find some of his Indian ranch hands dead, old McMasters slumped at the table, and Robin violated. He takes Robin back to White Feather for safekeeping and asks for help. But White Feather refuses to get involved in "Black and white man problems." Here the narrative of *The McMasters* precludes an African American–Native American alliance against white settler colonialism, marking a key difference between *The McMasters* and *Buck and the Preacher*. Buck offers an inversion of this relationship in which the Mescalero Indian tribe supports and rescues the Black wagon train of Exodusters seeking refuge from white supremacists.

The McMasters is not an outlier in its treatment of the main female character, but it is significant that Robin (who stands in metonymically for women) is raped not once but twice in the film. Kwan's character is not scripted the way Black women are often scripted in revisionist Black westerns, wherein women of color are usually being rescued from white male aggressors (e.g., *The Legend of Nigger Charley, Buck and the Preacher, Thomasine & Bushrod*) rather than abused by Black male characters. The misogyny embedded in this film's diegesis (not to mention the general emphasis on machismo in many westerns) is a disturbing reminder of the extradiegetic cultural backlash against women at a time when they were making political strides with the second wave of the feminist movement.

Filmmakers and audiences alike openly acknowledged the ascent and popularity of Black male protagonists in blaxploitation (and westploitation) as a response to seventeen years (1950–1967) of Poitier's asexual, assimilated, integrationist screen persona. Earlier films featured the ascent of Jim Brown—and later Fred Williamson—as super-sexy, badass revolutionaries. But with this ascent came the collateral effect of a deeply misogynistic "Black Macho," to use Michele Wallace's term.[38] While 1972 and the years immediately preceding it were deeply politicized, they were also painfully negating for Black women. Black feminist and cultural historians Angela Davis, Michele Wallace, Toni Morrison, Alice Walker, and others explained in their prose and poetry that these were extremely difficult years. Wallace was one of the first feminists to capture the cultural events and their impact on the zeitgeist:

> Around the time that Shirley Chisolm [*sic*] was running for President in 1972, Redd Foxx, the black comedian and television star, made a joke about her. He said that he would prefer Raquel Welch to Shirley Chisolm [*sic*] any day. The joke was widely publicized in the black community, and thought quite funny. There was something about it that made black men pay attention, repeat it, savor it. . . .

She had shown by her congressional record, her fiery speeches, and her decisions to run a spunk that America hadn't seen in a black woman since Fannie Lou Hamer. The black political forces in existence at the time—in other words, the black male political forces—did not support her. In fact, they actively opposed her nomination.[39]

Redd Foxx's comedic reference to Raquel Welch is not arbitrary. It marks a direct allusion to her sex scene with Jim Brown in *100 Rifles*. Theirs was the first interracial love scene ever depicted in mainstream cinema. More specifically, according to Wallace, Redd Foxx's comment was backlash against Black women's empowerment. His comedy made it clear that some Black men were more interested in sleeping with Raquel Welch than in having an African American woman president.[40]

The abuse endured by Nancy Kwan's character in *The McMasters*—and the narrative trajectory requiring Benjie to prove his manhood through his dominance over Robin—seems relevant to the masculinity matrix of the late 1960s and '70s as outlined by Wallace. African American men wanted freedom and equality, but they also wanted to be recognized as men. At least initially, Benjie's masculinity seems to depend on his dominance over and access to Robin. Significantly, *The McMasters* is one film in which the Black male character remorsefully atones for his treatment of women.

In the final climactic scenes, Benjie prepares for the worst after taking Robin to safety. He goes back to the ranch, which is now besieged, and finds Neal McMasters murdered. Ambushed, Kolby's men tie Benjie to a stake and burn his ranch. They plan to burn him next. Thankfully, Chief White Feather and his braves finally ride to the rescue. Days later, Spencer tries to persuade Benjie and Robin to leave, but Benjie resists and White Feather abets him. The Indians take him to their encampment, where Robin nurses his wounds. Once he's healed, Benjie and Robin return to their ranch. He tells White Feather, "We gotta go home." As they move off down the canyon, White Feather shouts after them with frustration, "You like us. . . . You ain't got no home."

For all of its technical shortcomings, aesthetic weaknesses, and formulaic storytelling, *The McMasters* makes several important political statements throughout its diegetic use of the character Benjie. First, it suggests that Black soldiers who fought in American wars will return home, an important recognition of service. Second, its narrative implies that these war veterans will stake a claim on land, liberty, and civil rights as promised by the founding fathers. Here the reel diegetic Civil War and World War I veterans stand in metaphorically for the real extradiegetic World War II, Korean War, and Vietnam War spectators viewing the film. Third, *The McMasters* conveys the sentiment that re-enfranchised African Americans will defend their property and build a political coalition with other oppressed peoples (e.g.,

Native American, Latinos, Asian Americans). Fourth, through its narrative, *The McMasters* proffers that African Americans also have the right to bear arms and engage in self-defense. Finally, the film leaves audiences with the haunting reality of continued Black disenfranchisement and dispossession voiced via Carradine's White Feather but thwarted by Benjie's dogged determination to survive. Even though the movie was not popular with broad audiences, it did resonate with the political upheavals of the 1960s and '70s, and it resonates with today's climate as well. For all of these reasons, the film stands out as a kind of revisionist western.

Thomasine & Bushrod

In 1974, forty-five years before Melina Matsoukas's feature film debut, *Queen & Slim*, director Gordon Parks Jr. released *Thomasine & Bushrod*, which marked the first African American cinematic homage to *Bonnie and Clyde*. A blaxploitation western, *Thomasine & Bushrod* stars Max Julien (Goldie from *The Mack*, 1973) and Vonetta McGee (*Hammer*, 1972; *Melinda*, 1972; *Blacula*, 1972; *Shaft in Africa*, 1973; *Detroit 9000*, 1973) as the eponymous young lovers on the lam.

Set in 1911, *Thomasine & Bushrod* opens with long shots of a lone rider. As the camera zooms in and the figure approaches, it becomes clear the rider is a woman. Watching her stalk and capture her outlaw bounty, we discover that it's Thomasine, a successful bounty huntress. While cashing out with the sheriff, she learns that her former lover, Bushrod, is still alive but has given up living on the wrong side of the law. Bushrod has turned to breaking horses to earn his living. Unable to forget him, Thomasine embarks on a journey to find Bushrod. When she locates him, they start a new life together. But their past comes back to haunt them when Adolph Smith (Jackson Kane), who years earlier assaulted Bushrod's sister, goads Bushrod to exact his revenge, making him a wanted man again.

Fugitives from injustice, and sorely in need of money, Thomasine and Bushrod begin robbing banks. Stealing from the banks, they share their spoils with the poor, handing out cash to destitute Indians, Mexicans, and poor whites in local villages. These acts of charity make them folk heroes in one town after another. Hot on their trail, however, the vindictive sheriff Bogardie (George Murdock) wants revenge for Bushrod's humiliation of him during a previous encounter.[41]

One day, while resting at an encampment, Thomasine and Bushrod meet a blind gypsy woman, Pecolia (Juanita Moore), who warns them of impending trouble. Suspecting it will lead them into another trap, they do not heed her advice. Shortly thereafter, when they run into trouble, their old Jamaican friend, Jomo (Glynn Turman), arrives to save them. Significantly, this is one of the only African American westerns in which an Afro-Caribbean character appears. His Caribbean identity marks a shift in the narrative scope of Black westerns by acknowledging the African diasporic coalition against white supremacy. No sooner does Jomo appear and reunite with his friends, however, than he is gunned down by Bogardie, who has been in hot pursuit of Thomasine and Bushrod.

Tired of running from Bogardie and his posse, a now pregnant Thomasine and Bushrod decide to face off with their adversary and his backward henchmen. Unfortunately, Thomasine and Bushrod are outnumbered. Ambushed by dozens of Bogardie's men, the young couple proceed unafraid. Thomasine advances first and is ripped apart by a hail of bullets, one of which pierces her abdomen. Bushrod follows her and is also mortally wounded but manages to kill Bogardie before dying. The film delivers this tragic ending as though it was the inevitable—or even expected—outcome spectators would have anticipated. Clearly, *Thomasine & Bushrod* is formally and stylistically indebted to self-reflexive cinema vis-à-vis *Bonnie and Clyde*, *Butch Cassidy and the Sundance Kid*, and *The Wild Bunch*.

In all of these pictures, audiences witnessed the spectacular slow-motion deaths of the leading characters with whom spectator identification was

FIGURE 4.9 Vonetta McGee and Max Julien as *Thomasine & Bushrod* are reunited lovers.

FIGURE 4.10 Max Julien and Vonetta McGee are Black and beautiful in *Thomasine & Bushrod*.

closely aligned. Thomasine's and Bushrod's deaths—much like the deaths of Bonnie and Clyde or Queen and Slim—are rendered with spectacle. The state-sanctioned violence against them obliterates their bodies and makes a display of their annihilation. The state's display against youth (who challenge the criminal justice system) and against Black "outlaws" articulates the fury of a white supremacist, heteropatriarchal, "carceral capitalism" that will not tolerate dissent.[42] These excessive displays recall the premodern European practice of having bodies drawn and quartered in public squares to punish the guilty for crimes against the monarchy or state (as Michel Foucault has aptly demonstrated) and to discipline onlookers and instill fear to ensure their future compliance.[43]

The African American diegetic audience for films such as *Black Rodeo*, *Thomasine & Bushrod*, *The McMasters*, *Skin Game*, and *Man and Boy* at least enjoyed the visual pleasure, albeit fleeting, of knowing that their feelings toward the repressive state apparatus were not unwarranted or unsupported. One can easily relate the deaths of these cinematic folk heroes to the real-life assassinations of actual political heroes (Medgar Evers, Martin Luther King Jr., Fred Hampton, Huey P. Newton, Malcolm X) whose teachings of political resistance threatened America's racial contract.

5

Westerns and Westploitation

Brothas and Sistas at the O.K. Corral

> It is thanks to Corbucci that 1966 became an all-important year in
> the history of the Italian western. It was in this year that he directed
> his masterpiece, *Django*, a film which, just like *A Fistful of Dollars*, was
> to become a prototype for future Italian westerns and, at the same
> time, the first incredibly violent western in the history of cinema.
> It was with this film that Corbucci came into his own, just as it was
> with this film that a previously little heard of actor, Franco Nero,
> began to leave his mark on the screen, first as the Italian answer
> to Clint Eastwood and later as an independently successful actor.
> No wonder Corbucci was often heard to say: "John Ford has John
> Wayne, Sergio Leone has Clint Eastwood, and I have Franco Nero."
> —Antonio Bruschini and Antonio Tentori, *Western all'Italiana:*
> *The Specialists*

In 1975, movie studios—large and small—were experimenting
with different varieties of the western genre to find a formula that would
revive its popularity with audiences. *Take a Hard Ride*, a western done in
the Italian style, teamed former football icons Jim Brown and Fred Williamson. They were joined by veteran western villain Lee Van Cleef. Van
Cleef's appearance in dozens of westerns, from Fred Zinnemann's *High Noon*
to Sergio Leone's *Dollars* trilogy, established him an iconic figure, known
worldwide simply as "Angel Eyes." His casting guaranteed that audiences
would recognize *Take a Hard Ride* as an Italian American spaghetti western
with *soul*. Or better yet, if spaghetti westerns were made in Italy, and paella
westerns were shot in Spain, sauerkraut westerns heralded from Germany,
and sukiyaki westerns were from Japan, then *Take a Hard Ride* qualified as a
soul food western. It was made in the same tradition of pastiche and bricolage.

More importantly, the dual billing of Brown and Williamson assured African American audiences that the picture would contain popular icons portraying cowboys and convey Black Power sentiments. In the vein of these intraracial buddy films, the two actors presented authoritative, Black masculinity unified against a common white adversary. The intraracial buddy formula had worked before and infused various blaxploitation movies whether they were women-in-prison pictures, campy horror films, crime dramas, or mafioso-style gangster tributes (e.g., *Black Mama, White Mama*; *Blacula*; *Coffy*, 1973; *Cleopatra Jones in the Casino of Gold*, 1973; *Scream Blacula Scream*, 1973; and *The Black Godfather*, 1974). *Take a Hard Ride* sought to tap into the same audience as *Three the Hard Way*, which had teamed Jim Brown, Fred Williamson, and Jim Kelly. It also sought to compete with the box office earned by sequels like *Shaft's Big Score* (Gordon Parks, 1972) and *Shaft in Africa* (John Guillermin, 1973).

By 1973 many film critics and scholars questioned the cultural relevance of westerns. Philip French, Virginia Scharff, and Neil Campbell (among others) adopted the term *postwestern* to address everything from metacritical to metaphysical elements of the genre's idioms in a media landscape that was increasingly embracing an intergalactic frontier. Sci-fi movies had been popular since the inception of narrative cinema (e.g., *A Trip to the Moon*, 1902; *The Golem*, 1915; *Metropolis*, 1927). But science fiction movie and television production exploded in the 1950s and '60s.[1] *Lost in Space* first aired on September 15, 1965. *Star Trek* began airing on September 8, 1966. Such programs made the spectacle of interplanetary travel domestically available on TV screens and more quotidian. With space as the new final frontier, the western seemed irrelevant. African American audiences, being "resisting spectators,"[2] had long questioned the accuracy and relevance of the western's imperial imaginary.

For audiences of color, the western was always already a constellation of politically motivated, ideologically determined fantasies, rewritten, reimagined, and rescripted.[3] Never consistent or factually based on real cowboys who settled the frontier, the western's politics evoked "scenes of subjection" that were spectacularized in many films and experienced in real life by Native Indians, African Americans, Asian Americans, and Mexican Americans. Western films evoked the racism of American life and the everyday abuses that Saidiya Hartman discusses in her *Scenes of Subjection: Terror, Slavery, and Self-Making in Nineteenth-Century America* (1997).[4] The genre's malleability and its manipulation of truth heightened African American audiences' desire to see themselves represented in this landscape. As *The Harder They Fall* director, Jeymes Samuel, told journalist

Marcus Jones, "When you cut out a period, or a people, you change the culture and there's no right version of wrong history."[5]

The African American press, exemplified by periodicals like the *Afro-American, New Pittsburgh Courier, Amsterdam News, Chicago Defender*, and the *Atlanta Daily World*, understood the appeal of Black-themed western pictures—even if some of these movies were "Black westploitation."[6] Comprised of various genres (e.g., the western, the martial arts actioner, film noir, and drama) and revisionist films, Black-themed westerns had a lasting impact. Twenty years after their release, some Black westerns were still influencing popular film culture, specifically New Black Cinema of the 1990s. Directors Mario Van Peebles, John Singleton, and Quentin Tarantino all made westerns early in their careers. And veteran L.A. Rebellion school filmmaker Larry Clark made a western too. Except for Clark's modern-day story, these directors created pictures (e.g., *Posse* by Mario Van Peebles; *Rosewood* by John Singleton; *Cutting Horse* by Larry Clark; and *Django Unchained* by Quentin Tarantino) that referenced westerns preceding them.

Secondarily, there was also a rash of lesser-known pictures that have since fallen into near obscurity, including Clark's independently produced *Cutting Horse*; the big-budget flop *Wild Wild West* (Barry Sonnenfeld, 1999) with Will Smith and Kevin Kline; the made-for-TV-movie *Buffalo Soldiers* (Charles Haid) featuring Danny Glover; and the ensemble picture *Silverado*, also featuring Danny Glover along with Kevin Costner and Kevin Kline. The more memorable and impactful Black westerns, however, resonated with the politics of the zeitgeist, bore the stylistic imprint of earlier films, and possessed production values sufficient to capture audiences.

In the late 1980s and early '90s, the zeitgeist was ablaze with the culture wars.[7] The '80s witnessed the rise of the New Right and a concomitant shifting of political tectonic plates. First, there was Reaganomics, with its reduction of governmental programs for those living in substandard conditions and the redistribution of wealth to the already affluent. Second, President Reagan installed a team of officials and cabinet members who were primarily business-oriented and largely unconcerned with the struggling underclass.[8] In his 2015 book, *A War for the Soul of America: A History of the Culture Wars*, Andrew Hartman argues, like many others, that the culture wars should be seen as a right-wing backlash against the gains of the 1960s cultural revolution (much like Donald J. Trump's presidency was a backlash against the gains of Barack Obama's two-term presidency).

Also at the top of Reagan's culture war agenda was the "War on Drugs." Reagan reinforced, and expanded, Nixon's War on Drugs policies. In 1984 Reagan's wife, Nancy, launched the "Just Say No" campaign intended to highlight the dangers of drug use. Ronald Reagan's refocus on drugs and enacting severe penalties for drug-related crimes in Congress and state legislatures led to a significant increase in incarcerations and longer sentences for nonviolent drug crimes. In 1986 Congress passed the Anti–Drug Abuse Act, which established mandatory minimum prison sentences for certain drug offenses. This law is now widely recognized as racist because it allocated longer prison sentences for offenses involving the same amount of crack cocaine (used disproportionately by African Americans and people of color) as opposed to powdered cocaine (used disproportionately by white Americans and wealthier people).[9] There is considerable activism and literature challenging mass incarceration and the predatory state apparatus. Scholars in the fields of prison studies and critical carceral studies have been combating what Jackie Wang, among many scholars, has termed "carceral capitalism" since the civil rights era.[10] Wang outlines the "interrelatedness of the economy, policing and municipal finance."[11] But the laws and policies still require reform. Wang's work dovetails with S. Craig Watkins's description of the use of hip-hop in Black cinema.[12] Both Wang and Watkins explore the relationship between urban youth idioms and carceral capitalism.

The conservative backlash of the 1980s extended beyond legal policy and into cultural policy, where funding to produce transgressive and avant-garde art was under assault. Protests over the National Endowment for the Arts' funding for Andres Serrano's *Piss Christ* (1987), panic over Madonna's 1989 "Like a Prayer" music video, the religious fundamentalist outrage against Robert Mapplethorpe's homoerotic adult photography, anger at Karen Finley's risqué performance art, and Roman Catholic protests of Martin Scorsese's *The Last Temptation of Christ* (1988) represented the outcry during the culture wars. During the Reagan administration, anti-Black racism and police brutality intensified. The Reagan presidency (which initiated the "Make American Great Again" slogan and social backlash that continued through Donald Trump's term) was known for a surge in acts of white supremacy and anti-immigrant xenophobia.

For instance, the 1980s witnessed a surge of clashes. One of the first incidents involved Eleanor Bumpurs, who was shot by an officer from the New York Police Department (NYPD) on October 29, 1984. The police were present to enforce a city-ordered eviction of Bumpurs. In requesting NYPD assistance, housing authority workers told police that Bumpurs was emotionally disturbed, had threatened to throw boiling lye, and was using a knife to resist eviction. When Bumpurs refused to open her door, police broke in. In the struggle to subdue her, one officer fatally shot Bumpurs twice with a twelve-gauge shotgun. She was an elderly, mentally unstable African American woman living in public housing in the Bronx.

Eleanor Bumpurs's murder was one of several deaths that inflamed racial tensions in the 1980s. Similarly tragic incidents included the fatal beating of Willie Turks in 1982.[13] Mr. Turks's killing was followed by the 1983 arrest and death of Michael Stewart while he was in police custody.[14] That event was followed by the subway shooting of four Black men by Bernhard Goetz in 1984.[15] Then there was the fatal assault on Michael Griffith in 1986.[16] Another tragedy involved the shooting of six NYPD officers by Larry Davis (aka Adam Abdul Hakeem) in self-defense in 1986. On November 19, 1986, nine New York City police officers, with nearly twenty outside the building, raided the Bronx apartment of Davis's sister. In the ensuing shootout, Davis escaped uninjured. All six officers who had been shot survived. Police explained the raid as an attempt to question Davis as a suspect in a multiple murder.

In the 1988 political campaign, George H. W. Bush and his adviser Lee Atwater exploited white people's fears of African American men, specifically the perception of them as criminals. Of particular significance was the Bush campaign's use of Willie Horton and his image. Horton was a convicted felon who, while on furlough from prison in Massachusetts, committed assault, armed robbery, and rape before being recaptured. During the presidential election campaign, Bush played upon mainstream white American fears of the Black brute stereotype by frequently invoking Horton as an example of what could happen to whites if, he, Bush, was not elected.[17] Beginning on September 21, 1988, the Americans for Bush arm of the National Security Political Action Campaign (NSPAC), under the auspices of Floyd Brown, began running a campaign ad titled "Weekend Passes," using the Horton case to attack Democratic candidate Michael Dukakis. The ad was produced by media consultant Larry McCarthy, who had previously worked for Fox News's Roger Ailes. After clearing the ad with television stations, McCarthy added a mug shot of Horton.

In many ways this was a symbolic return to D. W. Griffith's *The Birth of a Nation* and the infamous trope of the Black rapist (Gus) pursuing white womanhood (Little Sister). A narrative trope linking blackness and white peril persisted in movies of the next decade as well. Beyond the 1990s, studios were releasing movies with the Gus-and-Little-Sister construct such as *True Romance* (Tony Scott, 1993), *Black and White* (James Toback, 1999), *Traffic* (Steven Soderbergh, 2000), *Requiem for a Dream* (Darren Aronofsky, 2000), and *Storytelling* (Todd Solondz, 2001). The public policies, cultural policies, and repressive policing policies constituted the crux of the culture wars of the racial state in which African American lives were expendable.

George H. W. Bush reinforced the mythology that Black men posed a clear and present danger to white women. This climate of anti-Blackness normalized racial violence against African Americans and even impacted youth like sixteen-year-old Yusef Hawkins. Hawkins was killed by a mob in Bensonhurst, New York, on August 23, 1989, because the mob believed he was romantically involved with a white girl who lived in the neighborhood.[18] Spike Lee dedicated his film *Jungle Fever* (1991) to the memory of Hawkins.

Although the Willie Turks, Michael Griffith, and Yusef Hawkins murders uncorked a torrent of racial tension and protest marches in the ensuing weeks, little changed in the policing practices of the carceral state. White-on-Black police brutality and vigilante violence nationwide continued unabated. One of the highest-profile cases of the decade involved the brutal beating of twenty-five-year-old unarmed driver Rodney King in 1991. King was severely beaten by Los Angeles Police Department (LAPD) officers after a high-speed chase during his arrest for drunk driving on California's I-210. Fourteen officers were present at the scene when King suffered this beating, which resulted in King sustaining a broken right leg, serious cuts, a swollen face, bruises on his body, and burns to his chest where he had been jolted with a 50,000-volt stun gun. A civilian, George Holliday, fortuitously filmed the incident from his nearby balcony and sent the footage to local news station KTLA. The filming of this incident blindsided the law enforcement establishment, as the footage clearly shows an unarmed King on the ground being brutally beaten by four officers simultaneously. The incident was covered by news media around the globe and understandably led to public dismay.

In 1997 Abner Louima was assaulted, brutalized, and sexually abused by NYPD officers after being arrested outside a Brooklyn nightclub. His injuries were so severe as to require three major surgeries. And in the early hours of February 4, 1999, twenty-three-year-old Guinean immigrant Amadou Diallo was shot and killed by four NYPD plainclothes officers (Sean Carroll, Richard Murphy, Edward McMellon, and Kenneth Boss).

These and other viciously racist incidents occurring throughout the '80s and '90s happened in various parts of the country. They reflected the U.S. government's attitude toward state-sanctioned carceral management of African Americans and revealed the national racial climate in which Black lives did *not* matter. Presidents Ronald Reagan and George H. W. Bush made little effort to strike a different political tone or make meaningful changes in how law enforcement interacted with communities of color.

Out of this tumultuous atmosphere emerged the New Black Cinema of the 1990s, with its realist aesthetic and socially conscious critique. New Black Cinema critiqued (1) deindustrialization with its decline in urban manufacturing jobs, (2) trickle-down Reaganomics, (3) the influx of crack cocaine to urban communities, (4) the impact of Rockefeller drug laws, (5) police corruption, and (6) mass incarceration.[19] The first wave of realist films performed well enough commercially to inspire market confidence in a second wave. That second wave of films included Neo-Black westerns of the mid-1990s, which emerged on the coattails of—and in tandem with—New Black Cinema. For instance, Mario Van Peebles's hybridized gangster noir film *New Jack City* (1991) earned $47 million on a budget of $8 million. It was one of the defining pictures of New Black Cinema,[20] advancing the careers of actors including Wesley Snipes, Ice-T, Chris Rock, Michael Michele, and Russell Wong. As a result, Van Peebles made a leap from urban-centered social problem pictures to historic period pictures when he addressed racial injustice on the western frontier in *Posse*. And John Singleton did well enough with *Boyz N the Hood* (1991), *Poetic Justice* (1993), and *Higher Learning* (1995) to make *Rosewood*.

Van Peebles seemed to be informed or influenced by Manning Marable's seminal tome, *How Capitalism Underdeveloped Black America* (1983), when he connected the history of African American disenfranchisement and abolitionist struggles for Western frontier justice.[21] In *Posse*, Van Peebles reconnected frontier Reconstruction-era struggles (against the Black Codes, Jim Crow laws, convict work programs, land appropriation, and racial intimidation occurring nationwide, particularly in towns where African Americans were beginning to prosper) to economic underdevelopment.

In interviews, actor/director Van Peebles pointed out that Black "desperadoes in the Old West were driven to lawlessness because not everyone can dribble his way out of poverty like a pro-basketball player."[22] In his anachronistic comment, Van Peebles was trying to connect the history of African American struggle against disenfranchisement in the 1890s with the popular myth of Black enfranchisement in the 1990s through professional sports. His statement marks the intersection of Manning Marable's text on capitalist expropriation of Black labor and John Hoberman's *Darwin's Athletes: How Sport Has Damaged Black America and Preserved the Myth of Race* (1997).[23] Both call attention to the fact that sports is not a real avenue of economic opportunity because so few individuals can expect to have careers as professional athletes.

In his film and promotion, Mario Van Peebles forged a link between previous Black westerns and *Posse* through formal and stylistic cinematic choices. Chief among these choices was the decision to enlist actor Woody Strode as *Posse*'s omniscient narrator. Significantly, both the documentary *Black Rodeo* and the narrative feature film *Posse* utilized the diegetic and cinematic persona of actor Woody Strode to invoke the non-diegetic real lives of African American Westerners. In both *Posse* and *Black Rodeo*,

Strode—who portrayed many western characters over several decades—is
the authenticating voice bearing witness to an African American presence
on the frontier by recalling the names of *real* Black settler-cowboys, gunslingers, and lawmen like Nat Love, Eisen Dart, and Cherokee Bill. Van
Peebles also forged a linked between the liberationist ethos of *Posse* and the
rebellious spirit of *Sweet Sweetback's Baadasssss Song* by casting his director
father, Melvin Van Peebles.

Posse

Like other Black westerns before it, *Posse* bears resemblance to the Italian
westerns that preceded it. Chief among them is director Giulio Questi's
Django, Kill . . . If You Live, Shoot! (1967). In addition to its homage to Questi's
film, *Posse* employed an ensemble cast notable for success in music, film,
and television and with brand-name recognition. The cast included western veteran Woody Strode, iconoclastic indie director Melvin Van Peebles,
singer/songwriter/actor Isaac Hayes, action figure Pam Grier, Grammy-
winning rapper Big Daddy Kane, NBC TV drama star and rom-com heart-
throb Blair Underwood, comedian Nipsey Russell, R&B vocalist/musician
Aaron Neville, and actor/director Stephen Baldwin. That's not to mention
a cameo appearance by renowned director/producer brothers Reginald and
Warrington Hudlin.

To Mario Van Peebles's credit, *Posse* utilizes the cultural sign value of
these performers, and it relies on audience recognition of their individual,
extradiegetic personae to enrich *Posse*'s diegesis with Black popular cultural
references. Though most of these performers are supporting players (e.g.,
Pam Grier, Isaac Hayes, Nipsey Russell, Aaron Neville), with few spoken
lines, each enriches the mise-en-scène with a performance repertoire or
idiolect and an oeuvre of work that interpolates (or hails) the audience
to recall these performers' contributions to watershed moments in Black
popular culture. Van Peebles sought to recreate a multigenerational, Black
popular cultural sphere within the film. Regardless of whether *Posse* succeeds as a western, the film succeeds in recreating—and thereby reinforc-
ing—this cornucopia of Black cultural references.

As *Posse*'s opening credits roll to the ominous sounds of an organ and
brass instruments, the first image dissolves to a silhouette of an elderly
man (Woody Strode) teetering in a rocking chair in a dimly lit room while
handling a Remington 1875 Army revolver. He begins his narration by
reminiscing about a Colt .45 firearm dubbed "The Peacemaker." Many
have pointed out that he's holding a different firearm than is mentioned
by Strode. Nonetheless, his soliloquy begins in earnest with a critique of

dominant historiography and its whitewashing of the Western frontier experience:

> Pictures are a funny thing. They got us believing that Columbus discovered America when the Indians were already here. That's like, me telling you, while you're sitting in your car, that I discovered your car! Then, they want to call them the "evil red savages" because they didn't give up the car soon enough. . . . People forget that almost one out of every three cowboys was black. 'Cause when the slaves were free, a lot of them headed out West and built their own towns. Shit, they didn't have much choice. In fact, over half of the original settlers of Los Angeles were black. But for some reason, we never hear of *their* stories. Stories like Jesse Lee and his posse. That was the gambler, Father Time. This here was Crazy Little J. The big man was Obobo. He was Jesse's enforcer. And then there was Weezie and Angel. And then, of course, there was the leader: Jesse Lee. Yeah, man, these cats was the *original* posse. I'm gonna tell you, it all started at the Spanish-American War on the front line.[24]

Thus begins the movie with its introduction of characters and chronological framework. The storyteller's critique of the dominant historical narrative invokes the journey traveled by thousands of Exodusters who had few choices but to migrate west to escape persecution and then settle their own farms.

The storyteller's monologue bridges a flashback to the Spanish-American War. The intertitle reads "Cuba, 1898." The film stock fades from sepia to full color and transitions from still photos to live action. We meet Jesse Lee and the men of the Tenth Cavalry in medias res, being berated by the narcissistic, racist white Colonel Graham (played with deliberate camp by Billy Zane). Knowing that Black soldiers are more easily victimized, Graham coerces the Tenth to accept a suicide mission: steal a chest full of Spanish mint gold coins while *not* wearing their uniforms. When they return with the gold, Graham tries to frame them for treason, capture the gold, and jail the posse on charges of theft and desertion. To avoid certain death, Jesse's men shoot their way past the colonel and his men. Graham is wounded in the face as the posse makes a narrow escape, now fugitives from the white army's injustice.

Escaping to the United States from Cuba, Jesse Lee and his posse travel to New Orleans by posing as corpses in caskets en route to the mainland for burials. They land in New Orleans during Mardi Gras, and the men dabble in some of the local vices (women, booze, cards). But before long, Colonel Graham's gang tracks Jesse Lee's posse down. Together, Jesse's men—Father Time (Big Daddy Kane), Crazy "Little J." Teeters (Stephen

FIGURE 5.1 Billy Zane's Colonel Graham tries to frame Mario Van Peebles's Jesse Lee in *Posse*.

Baldwin), Weezie (Charles Lane), Obobo (Tommy "Tiny" Lister), and Angel (Tone Loc)—ride west attempting to outrun the colonel's band. Out on the range, they happen upon dilapidated railroad construction camps, where starving Indians and overworked Chinamen labor in deplorable working conditions.[25]

Along this route, Jesse has a flashback to his past. Raised in the all-Black settlement of Freemanville, next door to the all-white village of Cutterstown, Jesse Lee learned from his minster father, Dr. Reverend King David. A "race man" in the tradition of educator/orator/businessmen like Booker T. Washington, Marcus Garvey, and W.E.B. Du Bois, Reverend David was a peace-loving clergyman. He suffered a fatal beating at the hands of Cutterstown Klansmen who clubbed him to death for preaching that "Education is Freedom" and for instilling hope in the people of Freemanville.

Arguably, the *Posse* narration is structured to utilize the death-by-clubbing narrative trope rather than death-by-lynching (a more common convention in antebellum period pictures depicting white supremacist violence), because it resonated with the extradiegetic, real-life beating of Rodney King in the 1990s and contemporary audiences more than with the historical era of the 1890s. Van Peebles, and the studio (PolyGram Filmed

Entertainment), would have recognized the value of this timely connection for audiences. The film made repeated allusions to the Rodney King incident. Later in the film, Stephen Baldwin's character, Little J. Teeters, dies at the hands of Sheriff Bates's deputies when they club him to death for defending Weezie. And, during the climactic final shoot-out, Nipsey Russell's character, Snopes, rhetorically asks, "Can't we all just get along?" in a reflection of Rodney King's now oft-quoted plea.

Despite the fact that Rodney King's beating was captured on video by George Holliday, verified as legitimate by news outlets, and submitted as evidence of excessive police force, it did not prove effective in court. The acquittal in a state court of the four defendants (Officer Lawrence Powell, Sergeant Stacey Koon, Timothy Wind, and Theodore Briseno), charged with using excessive force, provided the spark that led to the 1992 Los Angeles riots. Within hours of the acquittals, the riots began, lasting six days. African Americans nationwide were outraged by the verdicts and began protesting; some rioted along with Latino and other communities. Smaller protests and riots occurred in San Francisco, Las Vegas, Seattle, and as far east as Atlanta and New York City. A minor riot even erupted in Toronto, Canada.

During these riots, on May 1, 1992, Rodney King made a television appearance pleading for an end to the disturbances. Recordings of his statement abound in social media and online: "I just want to say—you know—can we all get along? Can we, can we get along? Can we stop making it horrible for the older people and the kids?"[26] Although Mr. King was well-intentioned, his platitude rang hollow because it was designed to quell legitimate resentment over continued police brutality and dampen outrage at the police state (which routinely brutalizes and incarcerates African Americans). Director Mario Van Peebles and PolyGram Entertainment knew that the phrase "Can't we get along" would resound with audiences and reanimate frustrations over injustice. It was a clever—if not very subtle—use of Rodney King's clichéd lament. And it's probably no accident that the line was given to comedian Nipsey Russell, who could deliver it with double entendre and comedic camp. It was one of several references that *Posse*'s filmmakers used to allude to the Rodney King incident. And it explains why the culture wars and climate of the '90s were relevant to movie content.

As Jesse continues to elude Colonel Graham, the film descends deeper into Jesse's troubled past. On the open prairie, he and his posse encounter a stalled covered wagon bound for Freemanville. Inside they discover a sleeping child and his (several days dead) parents. This image takes Jesse Lee back to memories of his own traumatic youth when the Ku Klux Klan murdered his father in Freemanville. Looking at the orphaned boy reanimates Jesse's desire to settle this old score and avenge his father's death. So instead of riding past the town, Jesse Lee carries the boy to safety and tracks down the Klan members responsible for his father's murder. Reluctant, but steadfastly loyal, the posse accepts Jesse's new mission.

Riding into Freemanville, Jesse can't believe his eyes: his father's dream of a thriving Negro settlement has become a reality. No sooner does he arrive than he meets and drinks with his childhood friend Carver (Blair Underwood). Carver is now Freemanville's first Black sheriff. And all seems well. After seeing Carver, Jesse rides to the outskirts of town and reconnects with his mentor, Papa Joe (Melvin Van Peebles), to learn more about what he has missed. It would not be lost on *Posse*'s extradiegetic audience that Jesse and Papa Joe are portrayed by real-life father-and-son filmmakers.[27] Such casting would invite comparison between the radical ethos of *Sweetback* ("a badass is coming to collect some dues") and the liberationist sentiments of *Posse*. Nevertheless, Papa Joe's alluring daughter, Lana (Salli Richardson), is Jesse's teenage sweetheart. While Lana and Jesse are getting intimately reacquainted, she tells him about the new "grandfather clause" being used to deny Black people suffrage.[28]

Meanwhile, back in town, the rest of the posse carouse at the Promised Land Inn saloon. Before they get too comfortable, the sadistically racist Sheriff Bates (Richard Jordan), responsible for lynching Jesse's father, comes

FIGURE 5.2 Mario and Melvin Van Peebles portray Jesse Lee and Papa Joe in *Posse*.

looking to capture Jesse Lee. Finding Jesse absent from the saloon, Bates terrorizes the other Black townspeople and then singles out Little J. (the only white man in Jesse's posse) for defending Weezie against their abuses. Bates's men bludgeon Little J. to death in a scene that recalls the Rodney King beating, even though Little J. is white. In fact, the scene is clearly shot in a manner that evokes the Rodney King tape shot by George Holliday.

Jesse Lee returns from a rendezvous with Lana to find Little J. dead, Obobo and Angel in jail, and the Promised Land Inn destroyed. Jesse and Father Time free Obobo and Angel from jail. Jesse finally realizes what's really at stake with the railroad coming through: property values will soar in Freemanville. He then prepares the townspeople to fight back against Bates's plan to invoke the grandfather clause and reclaim property deeds to dispossess Freemanville's Black residents of their settlements. Back at the jailhouse, Sheriff Bates returns to find *his* men imprisoned and Obobo and Angel gone. Just then, Colonel Graham shows up with men and joins forces with Bates to capture Jesse.

Once convinced of the dangers posed by Bates and his men, the townspeople are themselves motivated to join the fight. In a standoff with Bates and his deputies, Black residents prevail until Colonel Graham and his goons arrive with a wagon-mounted Gatling gun. The scene in which the Gatling gun is unveiled recalls the famous climactic shoot-out in Sam Peckinpah's *The Wild Bunch*, in which a hail of bullets from a Gatling gun rip through a sea of men.

The scene marked a turning point in American cinema. *The Wild Bunch* had upped the proverbial ante on screen violence and excessive carnage, marking a point of no return. It was a shift that enabled American westerns to keep pace with the carnage on display in Italian-style westerns. Peckinpah claimed that his intent was to shock and induce catharsis in 1969's movie audiences. Some film historians speculate he was recalling the brutality he witnessed in China as a marine. Regardless, Peckinpah is not the original author of this watershed moment of increased violence or for the narrative device of a machine gun playing a central role. Both Peckinpah's *The Wild Bunch* and Van Peebles's *Posse* pay homage to Sergio Corbucci's *Django*. In *Django* the eponymous character, a former Union soldier, uses a machine gun hidden in his coffin to battle Confederate Red Shirts and a band of Mexican revolutionaries.[29]

Nevertheless, in Van Peebles's 1993 western, the Gatling firearm reverberates with other instances of non-narrative extreme force—namely, excessive police force and the assassinations of Black Panther Party members like Fred Hampton,[30] or, more concurrently with the film, the murder of citizens like Eleanor Bumpurs.

In a heroic last stand, Jesse blows up the Gatling with a stick of dynamite and fights Colonel Graham mano a mano to rescue Lana and keep Freemanville free, Black-owned, and self-governed. Narratively, *Posse* is a double-voiced film because it employs historical references literally and symbolically. References to the grandfather clause, to "Reverend King's" assassination, to hints about gerrymandering, and to discourses of racial uplift evoke the history of Reconstruction-era struggle and activism during the 1960s civil rights movement.

The film has a Bakhtinian double-voiced, or multilayered, pattern of articulation. At one level it speaks to the 1890s diegetic story content of the Wild Western frontier. At another level it speaks to the 1990s extradiegetic political content, which it uses to arouse contemporary audiences. In the denouement, Jesse finally finishes Colonel Graham by running him through with a saber and then shooting him dead. Once the final battle is over, the town is safe from Sheriff Bates (who is gunned down in the shoot-out) and the ruthless Colonel Graham. Jesse decides to use the booty of Spanish gold (which resonates with the spoils in countless other westerns) to rebuild the Afro-Indian town of Freemanville, thereby fulfilling his father's (Reverend King's) dream.

Admittedly, *Posse* is somewhat formulaic. And a few of the casting choices stand out as anachronistic. Reviewing the film for a Criterion showcase, one *Pitchfork* staff critic wrote:

> In director Mario Van Peebles' revisionist western *Posse* . . . Tone Loc seemingly has absolutely no idea he's in late-1800s New Orleans, and that's part of the charm of his performance. While shady cowboys, conniving outlaws, and dirty colonels are stomping around, Tone Loc acts as if he's in a Death Row music video. "Who the fuck is you?" he says to one of the movie's villains, holding a cigar in his hand as if it's a blunt and sipping straight from a bottle of liquor before he gets blown to bits.
>
> Meanwhile, Big Daddy Kane, who became a pillar of rap's late-'80s golden age with a flashy persona that made him out to be a real-life blaxploitation antihero, is perfectly suited to play the cartoonish gambler Father Time. Kane might be the best part of *Posse*: He carries himself with a regal presence that's over-the-top without being goofy. Unlike Tone Loc, who would rack up dozens of film credits across the next two decades, Kane didn't go on to do much else on the silver screen. It feels like a missed opportunity.[31]

Due to some conventional casting and reliance on narrative formulas, *Posse* calls attention to its construction. It also has a few set design blunders and over-orchestrated pyrotechnics. For instance, not only does it mistake a Remington 1875 firearm for a Colt .45 in the opening scene, but also, in the climactic battle, the colonel's eye patch keeps moving to reveal actor Billy Zane's *un*injured eye. Second, Jesse fantastically storms the Gatling gun holding a lit stick of dynamite in his mouth, a firearm in one hand, reins in the other hand, all while galloping, unharmed, through a crossfire of bullets. Upon reaching the Gatling, he manages to toss the dynamite with perfect precision. Finally, while it is commonplace for mainstream studio pictures to depict formidable, physically tenacious villains, Colonel Graham practically returns from the dead after Jesse runs him through with a saber, calling attention to the hokey heroics the film imagines. But *Posse* is not more fantastic or formulaic than other American or Italian westerns before or after it. Rather, it is in tandem with standard narrative tropes but reproduces—for African American audiences—the fantastic displays of masculine heroism, bravery, marksmanship, and nobility of character that are commonplace in the generic lexicon.

Made on a budget of approximately $10 million, *Posse* grossed $19 million worldwide, making it a commercial disappointment when compared with the resounding success Van Peebles scored with *New Jack City*, which had earned six times its $8 million budget only two years prior. Nevertheless, Van Peebles planned a second western. In 2019 the director announced his intentions to direct and star in *Outlaw Posse*, a new western for which he had written the script. *Outlaw Posse* was to be set against the rolling hills and the lawless towns of the American Wild West in the late 1800s. Van Peebles was to play Chief, leader of a posse of Black cowboys in search of truth and justice. But long before Van Peebles's sequel, John Singleton's film *Rosewood* emerged.

Rosewood

No story is more tragic or more indicative of the racial terrorism that is endemic to the United States than the true events that inspired John Singleton's *Rosewood*. For the narrative, Singleton returned to the hamlet of Rosewood, Florida, during the fateful week of January 1923 when a thriving African American community was destroyed and the lives of many African Americans and two white men were taken. According to historian R. Thomas Dye, the incident created headlines in Florida newspapers and the national—especially Black—press but interest waned, and the events faded from historical record until the 1980s.[32] In 1982 *St. Petersburgh Times* investigative reporter Gary Moore and surviving residents and descendants publicly conveyed the story.[33] A decade later, in 1994, the Florida legislature took up the incident and passed a bill to compensate the Rosewood victims for loss of property resulting from the state's failure to prosecute responsible persons. The Rosewood bill was the nation's first compensation package for African Americans who had suffered from past racial injustices.[34] It was based, in part, on the results of a study conducted by a team of historians commissioned by the Florida House.

The Rosewood incident, writes Dye, provides an example of a fully functional and economically viable Black community that was destroyed as a result of white rage. During World War I and immediately after, racial tensions escalated because African Americans challenged segregation customs of Southern society and many others moved north. African Americans who had served in the armed forces during World War I expected to be welcomed home and treated as full citizens. They were disabused of those expectations by rampant violence (e.g., the Ku Klux Klan in 1915 and the riots during the Red Summer of 1919). History will not forget the Red Summer of 1919, which has been well documented:

> The ink had barely dried on the Treaty of Versailles, which formally ended World War I, when recently returned black veterans grabbed their guns and stationed themselves on rooftops in black neighborhoods in Washington D.C., prepared to act as snipers in the case of mob violence in July of 1919. Others set up blockades around Howard University, a black intellectual hub, creating a protective ring around residents.
>
> White sailors recently home from the war had been on a days-long drunken rampage, assaulting, and in some cases lynching, black people on the capitol's streets. The relentless onslaught proved contagious, escalating in dozens of cities across the U.S. in what would become known as The Red Summer.
>
> The racist attacks in 1919 were widespread, and often indiscriminate, but in many places, they were initiated by white servicemen and centered upon the 380,000 black veterans who had just returned from the war. Because of their military service, black veterans were seen as a particular threat to Jim Crow and racial subordination. . . .
>
> During the Red Summer, massive anxiety became mass violence. Between April and November of 1919, there would be approximately 25 riots and instances of mob violence, 97 recorded lynchings, and a three-day long massacre in Elaine, Arkansas during which over 200 black men, women, and children were killed after black sharecroppers tried to organize for better working conditions. The Ku Klux Klan, which had been largely shut down by the government after the Civil War, experienced a resurgence in popularity and began carrying out dozens of lynchings across the south.[35]

The state of Florida was not exempt from these events. Florida witnessed its own rash of anti-Black lynchings and mass murders. Thomas Dye noted that a few weeks before the events in Rosewood, a Black man was burned alive at the stake in Perry; two others murdered; and a local Black church, school, and meeting hall burned following the murder of a white school-teacher: "The destruction of Rosewood has been described as a massacre, a race riot and even a holocaust by some journalists. The entire town was burned out and never rebuilt. At least eight people were killed, and an undetermined number were injured."[36]

By 1890, when all the red cedar had been harvested and the Cedar Key pencil mills closed, most white families moved out of Rosewood and sold (or leased) their land to Blacks. By 1900 the Black community had become the majority. Black-owned and -operated businesses such as M. Goins and Brother Naval Stores Company took advantage of the white exodus and prospered through distilling turpentine and rosin from the pine trees in the area. Many families owned their own homes and worked farms raising hogs and poultry.

Sadly, Rosewood's quiet community was shattered on the morning of January 1, 1923, when Fannie Taylor, a white woman and resident of Sumner, claimed she was attacked by a Black man in her home. Whether or not she was actually raped has never been determined, but most white residents, including her husband, James Taylor, believed she had been sexually assaulted and that an escaped Black convict, Jesse Hunter, was responsible. However, the Black community of Rosewood maintained that Mrs. Taylor's assailant was her white lover, a railroad employee who came to see her that morning after her husband had left for work.[37] Rumors that whites would meet resistance from prominent African Americans led by Black homeowner and businessman Sylvester Carrier provoked violent action and mobilized the white community.

On Thursday evening, January 4, twenty to thirty armed vigilantes descended upon Rosewood bent on taking matters into their own hands. Surrounding the Carrier house, the angry white mob riddled it with rifle and shotgun fire, killing Sylvester's mother, Sarah Carrier. But Sylvester engaged in self-defense and shot two men as they tried to enter his home. The exchange ended when the white vigilantes had expended their ammunition. Leaving their two dead companions on the front porch of the Carrier home, the white mob retreated, returning to Sumner, the neighboring white town. The idea that African Americans in Rosewood had taken up arms against whites was unthinkable in the Deep South. As a consequence, armed white folks subsequently descended on Levy County from across the state to seek retribution for the deaths of Henry Andrews and Poly Wilkerson—the two dead men who had joined the mob that descended on the Carriers. On foot, by horseback, in wagons, and driving Model Ts, a mob of more than two hundred whites attacked Rosewood.[38]

The events that transpired in Florida proved fodder for John Singleton's 1997 period picture, *Rosewood*. Singleton had already demonstrated an ability to select actors who worked well together. Whether it was Laurence Fishburne and Angela Bassett in *Boyz N the Hood*, Janet Jackson and Tupac Shakur in *Poetic Justice*, or Ice Cube and Omar Epps in *Higher Learning*, his direction helped the casting choices cohere on screen. The same is true of *Rosewood*, which features seasoned players Ving Rhames, Don Cheadle, Jon Voight, Esther Rolle, Michael Rooker, and Robert Patrick Jr. among others. However, the central question remaining is whether *Rosewood* is, generically speaking, a western. The film's form, narrative content, and themes render it identifiable as a western despite its setting in the deep, rural American South.

First, *Rosewood* is a western because Ving Rhames's character, Mister Mann, is an archetypal lone (st)ranger who rides into Rosewood from nowhere to defend the small African American hamlet from the tyranny of an unjust white supremacist lynch mob. His status as a "loner" willing to risk his life for others makes Rhames's "Mann" analogous to countless other western heroes while simultaneously positioning him as the proverbial "every*man*" who stands in synechdochically for ordinary men willing to do extraordinary things. Mann is a unique character and a character who evokes Michael Rohmer's 1964 realist film *Nothing but a Man*, whether intentionally or inadvertently.

Second, like the definitive western hero, Mann is a uniquely skilled marksman. He is a talented gunslinger and war veteran, a trained combatant prepared to lead and defend ordinary family men. He reminds spectators of post–World War II hybrid genre films that featured combat-veteran western heroes (e.g., *Dark Command*, 1940; *Border Patrol*, 1943; *Django*). An outsider to both the Black and white communities, Mann conceals his mysteriously troubled past. Eventually the audience discovers that he has already survived one attempted lynching.

Third, *Rosewood* is a western because—main character notwithstanding—it structurally triangulates the competing interests of (1) the settler/homesteader; (2) the "threat," which is embodied by a white supremacist lynch mob determined to oust the (Black) family farmers and businessmen; and (3) the defending gunslinger who, like Jesse Lee in Van Peebles's *Posse*, fights, righteously, for Black self-determination, equal opportunity, and justice. Finally, *Rosewood* resonates with western genre films because it relies on the mise-en-scène of props, costumes, signifiers, and cinematic conventions typically associated with these genre movies.

Singleton's film opens with the sounds of singing birds. This peaceful soundtrack bridges a transition to the rusty earth-toned images of a warm and calming hamlet: Rosewood, Florida. The intertitle reads "December 31, 1922." As the camera pans across a landscape, it reveals a thriving African American farming village, complete with a railroad station, the First A.M.E. Church, bountiful gardens, thriving businesses, a one-room schoolhouse full of children, and cordial relations between coloreds and whites. The less prosperous town of Sumner sits next door, a small, working-class white settlement. Into this milieu rides the striking Mr. Mann (Ving Rhames), a handsome, well-built, and dignified man riding astride his jet-black horse, "Booker T." Just then, as he rides past the Sumner sheriff's office, a white deputy named Earl (Jaimz Woolvett) mistakes Mann for an escaped convict. "There goes Jesse Hunter," he tells Sheriff Walker. But Walker, who is less overtly racist and considerably more intelligent, quickly admonishes the dimwitted Earl: "Put down your gun. He's no more off a chain gang than I'm governor of Florida."

As Mann rides out of Sumner and on into Rosewood, he meets Sylvester Carrier (Don Cheadle), a prosperous farmer and talented musician, who invites Mann to New Year's Eve dinner at the Carrier home. There Mann learns of the bounty of Rosewood and that colored folks own all the nearby land with prosperous businesses outperforming the white town of Sumner next door. After dinner the Carrier family attends Rosewood's New Year's Eve party, where Sylvester's cousin, a pretty young schoolteacher nicknamed "Scrappie" (Elise Neal), flirts with Mann after some encouragement from Aunt Sarah (Esther Rolle). Initially it seems that Mann has found not only the ideal hamlet in which to settle down but also, possibly, an attractive young woman as his companion.

The next day, Mann heads to an auction, where he outbids John Wright (John Voight) (the only white general store owner in Rosewood) for a parcel of land next door to the town store. But trouble is brewing next door in Sumner, where an adulterous Fanny Taylor (Catherine Kellner) is in a postcoitus fit of anger. She accuses her lover (Robert Patrick) of cheating on her and strikes him from behind. He retaliates by viciously beating Fanny, leaving bruises and welts over her entire body before quickly fleeing—but not before he's been spotted by Aunt Sarah Carrier (Esther Rolle), Fanny's housekeeper. Her abusive lover, an unnamed character, flees one mile down the road to nearby Rosewood, where he conscripts assistance from fellow Freemasons Aaron Carrier (Phil Moore) and blacksmith Sam Carter (Kevin Jackson).[39] Because of their fraternal association, Aaron feels beholden to their oath despite Sam's warning that helping a strange white man means trouble.

Meanwhile, an embarrassed and ashamed Fanny tries to cover up her transgressions and assuage her battered ego by blaming her bruises on a

Black assailant. Fanny cleans herself up, puts on a dress, and calmly walks outside of her house to begin hysterically screaming, "Help me, please help! . . . *Nigger* . . . it was a *nigger*. . . . He broke into my house and he beat me up. It was a nigger, it *was*!"

Director John Singleton is signifying on the cinematic apparatus, which has failed to fully interrogate its foundation in white supremacist narratives of early cinema like *The Birth of a Nation*. The film is also a commentary on both the sociopolitical machinations or racial state, in which Black and brown men (and women) are unjustly funneled through the criminal justice system, and the intersectional privilege of white women. Historically speaking, John Singleton also references the real-life practice of lynching African American men (often falsely accused) of raping white women. By cinematically alluding to that archetypal narrative of Gus and Little Sister inherited from Griffith's *The Birth of a Nation*, Singleton enables *Rosewood* to expose the perversity of white racial hysteria over Black masculinity and Black male sexuality.

Trouble is exactly what Aaron and Sam encounter when word spreads. It starts when young Emmett, a white resident of Sumner, tells Sherriff Ellis Walker, "Fanny Taylor done got raped by a nigger!" The news sets off a chain reaction of events leading to a white lynch mob descending upon the town of Rosewood. Ellis tries in vain to keep the enraged mob focused on alleged—but yet unseen—escaped convict Jesse Hunter. The irrational and uncontrollable nature of the white folks' rage against the peaceable (and prosperous) Black townsfolk of Rosewood succeeds in casting doubt on Hunter's guilt *and* on the entire infrastructure of the criminal justice system with its haphazard machinations and hastily deputized white folks. In this deftly played plot point, *Rosewood* succeeds in paying homage to classic western tragedies like *The Ox-Bow Incident* (William Wellman), which focused on the destructive nature of mob mentality.[40] As in *The Ox-Bow Incident*, "The Law" (manifest in the character of Sheriff Walker), proves useless against hysterical, untamed frontier violence. Walker heeds the threats and warnings that if he seeks reelection, he had best not defend "nigger law."

Irrationally and relentlessly pursuing cause for a lynching, the white mob is primed to kill. Bloodhounds lead them first to Aaron Carrier and then to Sam Carter, whom they torture for information about Jesse Hunter's whereabouts. John Wright tucks Aaron away in a Sumner holding cell for protection and the mob moves on. By the time they reach Sam Carter, the mob has spun out of control. After beating Sam senseless, they insist he reveal the whereabouts of the (now) phantom rapist Jesse Hunter. Convinced he's going to die, Carter brazenly tells recently deputized Duke Purdy (Bruce McGill), "You can kill me, but you can't eat me," evoking the Seminole Indian admonition to white folks. Since former slaves often settled nearby and intermingled with Native Americans, they created cultural amalgamations and hybrid identities. Sam's admonition implies that he is part Seminole.[41] Doubling down on his vengeance, Purdy quickly responds, "You *ain't* no Seminole, *boy!*" just before he shoots him and strings him up. Witnessing this unthinkable savagery from the woods nearby, Mann lies in hiding until he and Sylvester can cut Carter's corpse down.

Sylvester and the preacher (Andrew "J. R." Tarver) hold a town meeting for the colored community at the church to plan their defense. Realizing he's a newcomer and likely to be scapegoated as escaped Jesse Hunter, Mann leaves Rosewood, explaining to the community, "I just come from one war, friend; I ain't looking for another." His departure is viewed as a betrayal of the community (and the Carrier family) that welcomed him so warmly the previous night. Mann's departure is a ruse. The townsfolk and the film's audience later learn his true plan is to return to Rosewood.

The next morning, the massive manhunt continues across Levy County, Florida. Men are let off work early to scour the countryside. But inside of Aunt Sarah's quiet house, she explains to Miss Scrappie why she won't bother telling the truth about Fanny's beating: that Fanny Taylor's assailant was "as *white as butter.*"

> Child, you don't think they gonna listen to old Aunt *Sarah*? They'd just as soon string me up like they did Sam Carter. You ain't never *seen* crackers act the way *I know*. When I was a little girl, about 7, still on the Willowbrook Plantation, old Massa's son stole $20 out of the family chest for a cockfight. Massa knew he took it. As blue as Jesus's eyes he knew. But just the same, he whipped my daddy half to death. It don't matter what man was beating on Fanny Taylor. . . . *Nigger* is just another word for *guilty.*"[42]

Scrappie and Aunt Sarah's conversation accomplishes multiple goals for the *Rosewood* diegesis and for the extradiegetic movie audience.

Within the narrative, and for spectators, it establishes the tradition of passing down slaves' survival stories from one generation to the next. The scene also functions to teach young people that bravery takes many forms, including abstention from intervention. Historically, for African Americans it has been imprudent to be entangled with the criminal justice system in any capacity, even as an otherwise uninvolved witness. The scene aptly demonstrates that the irrationality of white supremacy particularly in the Deep South could not be underestimated, especially after World War I and the Red Summer of 1919. White Americans, especially working-class white folks, now had to compete for jobs with skilled African American workers in the post–World War I era. This exacerbated existing racial and class tensions. Working-class whites relied on white supremacy for their sense of self-worth. They even used false accusations and legal instruments to take out frustrations on African Americans with whom they were in conflict but could no longer subjugate through slavery.

Further, this scene establishes the long-standing nexus between what Frantz Fanon termed "The Fact of Blackness" and the fact of one's guilt in the eyes of "the Law."[43] From slavery to Jim Crow, to the New Jim Crow of the twenty-first century, numerous scholars (e.g., Angela Davis, Michelle Alexander, Elizabeth Hinton, Alex Lichtenstein, Loïc Wacquant, David Theo Goldberg, Jordan Camp, Jackie Wang, and filmmaker Ava DuVernay) have endeavored to explain how blackness and guilt have been made synonymous under the surveilling panopticon of the racial state.[44]

Finally, this scene in *Rosewood* is significant because it foreshadows the final tragedy of the film, in which Aunt Sarah (Esther Rolle) is murdered on her front porch for finally speaking truth to power. It is a pivotal moment and a narrative tipping point. The character resonates with audiences diegetically as the gentle grandmother/nanny/mammy within the story and extradiegetically with the film's theater audience as the beloved grand matriarch of African American actors (in theater, film, television, and documentary voice over). Singleton uses Sarah's tragic and sudden death to mark the film's most solemn note.

After Aunt Sarah is murdered, her son Sylvester responds by killing Henry Andrews (Muse Watson) and Poly (Mark Boone Jr.), two white men who enter his house. The mob responds by descending on the Carrier home, burning it down. Thus the stage is set for Ving Rhames's Mann to make his heroic return as the western hero. As whites across the county join the manhunt, even churchgoing whites load their guns, don KKK robes, and join the Klan's parade to raid Rosewood. In the afternoon Sumner is a three-ring circus far beyond Sheriff Ellis Walker's control. By evening, all of Rosewood is in flames and hanging corpses dress the landscape. Into this inferno of hatred, Mann rides to the rescue. He rounds up the children and moves them—with young Arnett Carrier's help—deeper into the swamp.

The next morning, John Wright and Mann devise a plan to move the children (who've been hiding in the swamp) out of Rosewood via train at nearby Kelly's Pond station. But moving past Sumner to meet the train proves nearly impossible. And when the train breaks down, the situation worsens. Whether intentionally or not, Mann is caught by Sherriff Walker and his posse of rednecks. They hang Mann from a tree, insisting he's the wanted Jesse Hunter. Just then, a brawl breaks out among the mob over

FIGURE 5.3 Ving Rhames is valiantly the lone hero in John Singleton's *Rosewood*.

whether Fanny lied about her attacker being colored. Their fight diverts attention from Mann, who manages to cut himself loose. Mann's miraculous escape from the noose evokes an iconic scene from Sergio Leone's *The Good, the Bad, and the Ugly*, in which Clint Eastwood's Blondie frees Eli Wallach's Tuco from hanging by miraculously shooting the rope at exactly the right point and time to free him from strangulation. Just as Tuco is freed in Sergio Leone's film, John Singleton's Mann goes free. In the woods, Mann calls to his horse, rides to the children, and together they board the train for Tallahassee.

With the angry mob in pursuit of the children, the film makes an interesting narrative maneuver. Director Singleton expands the scope of racial terrorism for the extradiegetic audience by revealing dozens of men emerging one by one from the woods. They come running for the train like hunted animals, fleeing gun-toting whites. To defend these men, Mann returns fire from the moving train he has just boarded. Witnessing Mann's shots, John Wright calls out, "What are you doing?" Mann responds, "It's a war; we're in the *trenches*!" Mann thereby reminds Wright—and both the diegetic audience of bystanders and the extradiegetic audience of spectators—of his service and the sacrifices of more than twenty thousand African American soldiers during World War I.[45]

The film's closing intertitles summarize the political, ideological, and formal interventions *Rosewood* makes as a mainstream motion picture that corrects the historical record of the 1920s and resonates with the culture wars of the 1990s:

> In 1993, 70 years after the massacre, the Florida House of Representatives granted reparations to the Rosewood families, spearheaded by Philomena's son, Arnett Doctor. The success of the case was due largely to the sworn testimony of several SURVIVORS, who were children at the time of the events, and to the deposition of one WHITE citizen who testified on behalf of the victims.
>
> The official death toll of the Rosewood massacre, according to the state of Florida, is eight . . . two WHITES and six BLACKS. The survivors, a handful of whom are still alive today, placed the number anywhere between 40 and 150, nearly all of them AFRICAN AMERICAN.

The final scenes, with terrified fugitive Black men running from armed lynch mobs, stand in metonymically (as a part for the larger whole) for Black men and women brutalized by unchecked racial terrorism. These scenes remind audiences of unarmed Black men (and women) who perished due to racism, white supremacy, and excessive policing during the Jim Crow era. The film also evokes the current climate marred by the New Jim Crow of mass incarceration and carceral capitalism.[46] *Rosewood* seeks to make cinematic reparations by relaying the story of the Rosewood massacre and by offering up a western-style hero for public consumption. It offers a mythological, sacred, and sanctified legend as historical redress by telling the tragic story of how African American and Black Seminole lives were devastated in the twentieth century. Van Peebles and John Singleton were not alone in bringing these restorative myths to screen.

Cutting Horse

In 2002 director Larry Clark released the revisionist western *Cutting Horse*. The film was Clark's second independent feature film. But he was already part of a collective of influential filmmakers known for radical cinematic interventions. At UCLA Clark became a member of the L.A. Rebellion school of filmmakers (including directors Julie Dash, Charles Burnett, Haile Gerima, Shirikiana Aina, Billy Woodbery, Carroll Parott Blue, and Zeinabu Irene Davis). Taught by Elyseo Taylor, UCLA Film School's first Black faculty member, these graduate students were influenced by the political tumult of 1968, an activist-oriented curriculum developed by Taylor and Colin Young, and events in global cinema.[47]

Politicized by the 1965 Watts riots and activism at UCLA, the filmmakers sought to make thoughtful, rather than commercial, films about African American life. Their pictures were described by Clyde Taylor as "manifesto films."[48] They rejected blaxploitation aesthetics in favor of realism. Their concept of realism was informed by Italian neorealism and the revolutionary "Third" cinemas from Africa and Latin America (i.e., Brazilian Cinema Novo, postrevolutionary Cuban cinema, and independent Senegalese cinema).[49] Given Elyseo Taylor's training in Heidelberg, Germany, their work would also have been informed by New German cinema's radical Oberhausen Manifesto (1962).[50] Like the revolutionary films informing them, these L.A. filmmakers used location shooting, nonprofessional actors, natural lighting, improvised dialogue, jump cuts, dialectical montage editing, surrealism, migration narratives, Africanisms,[51] and the history of slavery to inform cinematic storytelling.

Cutting Horse is Clark's modern-day western about the ambitious dreams of struggling African American and Mexican American horse trainers. While the film was shot in and around Portville, California, the narrative is set in an unspecified Western locale. The story's protagonist is Tyler, a strong, taciturn man. He is supposed to be as stalwart as the freed slaves who once worked with Mexican cattle-herding vaqueros in the Old West. Tyler's return home is narrated by Alejandro Sanchez (Cesar Flores) and is told as a flashback. Alejandro sits down to write in his journal and recalls the day when a talented rider named Tyler (Albert Harris) returned home after spending fifteen years in Canada.

Upon returning, Tyler goes to work on Doc Pete's (Roberto Bethel) farm as a horse trainer. A folksy old-timer, Doc Pete has long dreamed of owning a champion cutting horse.[52] Tyler is the trainer who Doc hopes can get him into the winner's circle. But Doc's aspirations are felled when his horses mysteriously get sick and die suddenly. It turns out that the horses were poisoned by the hazardous waste dumped by Stone Chemical, a local chemical company owned by a wicked old rancher named Neil Stone (Rufus Norris). After the industrial accident, Stone schemes to buy up all the surrounding smaller ranches. The only way for Stone Chemical to evade paying penalties imposed by the Environmental Protection Agency (EPA) is to acquire neighboring land so that previous leaks of waste are unreported and he has additional deep storage space for dumping.

Thus, Larry Clark sets the stage for the African American (Doc Pete) and Mexican American (Sanchez) ranchers to resist Stone's attempt to acquire their land. They hope to stop Stone Chemical from contaminating the environment and evicting farmers from their homes but have no way to intervene. No sooner do Sanchez and Doc Pete join forces than they meet with terrible luck. First, they lose their prize cutting horse when Sanchez's son-in-law, Ray Wilson (Robert Earl Crudup), goes deeper into debt. Ray was part owner of one of the horses that died. With no hope of selling the dead animals, Ray's debts start piling up. He takes another horse jointly owned by himself and Doc Pete and sells it to Neil Stone. Next, Ray has a near-fatal car accident when he falls asleep at the wheel. Then, toxic chemicals begin welling up on the surface of Doc's and Sanchez's farmland. Just when life couldn't get any worse, there's a reversal of fortune. Tyler wins second place in a cutting horse competition, receiving twenty thousand dollars in prize money. When Stone's own henchmen unintentionally set off an explosion at the chemical storage facility, it bankrupts the company, ruining old man Neil Stone.

With the Stones' dynasty bankrupt, the future looks promising for the community. Doc Pete has the winning cutting horse he always dreamed of owning, and Sanchez has renewed hope they can clean up their contaminated farms. The chemical accident forces the Stone family to face difficult truths, and regulatory consequences, that they've long avoided. Even Neil's browbeaten son, Toby Stone (Christopher Upham), eventually regrets his abuse of Sanchez's daughter, Rosa (Mellisa Cellura), whom he molested years ago during their youth.

Cutting Horse is aesthetically distinctive in tone and style from other New Black Cinema westerns. Clark sought to bring the realism of the L.A. Rebellion school of filmmaking to the western and worked toward sincerity, naturalism, and simplicity in the diegesis. Through the character of Tyler (who stands up to Ray when he bullies, diligently trains horses, and withstands the Stones' intimidation tactics), *Cutting Horse* emphasizes traditional values of bravery, honesty, fidelity, and diligence. Tyler is a sharp contrast to Ray, who is cowardly; deceitful; unfaithful to his wife, Rosa; and generally ineffective. But Clark unites Doc Pete, Sanchez, Tyler, and Ray against their common foe: Stone Chemical. *Cutting Horse* is a traditional western insofar as it casts big business, or corrupt corporations, as presenting an existential threat to small family farmers. And it deploys Tyler as the everyman-hero whose championship riding helps save the day.

Cutting Horse delivers tidy—and somewhat hackneyed—resolutions and comeuppances characteristic of the western genre in the '50s. Some critics viewed the film as delivering stereotypical white villains and wooden strawmen. While that's not entirely fair, it would be an error to view any of these characters as nuanced or complex. While Clark may have been trying for an unvarnished realism, he created a diegesis that is naïve. It lacks generic reflexivity or awareness of conventions. Consequently, *Cutting Horse* plays like an *ABC Afterschool Special* with simplistic good guys and obvious baddies written for youth audiences.[53] Critics who faulted director Larry Clark for creating stereotypical (i.e., blaxploitation-style) white villains missed the point.[54] It is not only the white characters that are wooden but the film itself, which, strangely, harkens back to a bygone era of generic development. However clichéd and caricatured the characters, narrative, and dénouement might be, director Clark clearly tried to alter the western's form with an African American–centered and realist narrative.

To Clark's credit, the film eschews the artifice of other pictures and focuses on the lives of ordinary people rather than legendary gunslingers (e.g., Bass Reeves, Nat Love, Wyatt Earp, Jesse James, Annie Oakley, Billy the Kid, Calamity Jane). The message conveyed is that hard work and integrity will eventually pay off for salt-of-the-earth, workaday farmers. Like many of the other westerns discussed herein, *Cutting Horse* seeks to tell the sacred and sanctified legend of the Western lifestyle from a multiracial perspective but without the veneer of Hollywood sensationalism or blaxploitation antics.

Perhaps the most significant difference between *Cutting Horse* and other Black westerns is that *Cutting Horse* was a low-budget production. Reportedly made on a shoestring budget of eighty thousand dollars (less than some of today's music videos), it lacks the production value of costlier professional period pieces. Consequently, it also lacks the polish of such productions. The modest budget evidently dictated unfortunate artistic choices regarding locations, casting, continuity editing, and sound equipment. The budgetary constraints speak volumes about the necessity of African American–directed films obtaining adequate financial support. It also underscores how impressive most L.A. Rebellion school films are (e.g., *Killer of Sheep*, 1978; *Illusions*, 1982; *Diary of an African Nun*, 1977; *Sankofa*, 1993) given their modest production values.

Django Unchained

Unlike several other African American–themed westerns, there is no shortage of scholarly critical engagement dedicated to the close analysis of Quentin Tarantino's self-reflexive, Black westploitation mashup *Django Unchained*. Essays, articles, books, and commentary on the film from scholars across the disciplinary spectrum abound. Engaging *Django Unchained* analytically, scholars in various disciplines realized that this film—and by extension westerns generally—is not about history but rather historical erasures from cinema, from national mythology. Yarimar Bonilla says as much when he writes, "Tarantino himself is quick to point out, his movie is not 'History with a capital H.' In fact, in many ways Tarantino is engaged in a conversation about cinematic history as much, if not more so than, American history."[55] Scholars of cinema have asserted this for years.[56]

The critical attention lavished on *Django Unchained* raises questions about why Quentin Tarantino's film received more critical attention than *Posse* or *Rosewood*.[57] In fact, it may have received more attention than the original *Django* from which it draws. Yet the critical response was uneven. Perhaps this is partially attributable to the nature of the source material. *Django Unchained*, and dozens of other sequels, is based on Sergio Corbucci's *Django*, which was an enormously impactful film in markets around the world. A commercial success upon release, *Django* garnered a cult following outside of Italy and was widely regarded as one of the better Italian-style westerns ever produced. Corbucci's direction, Franco Nero's minimalist performance, Luis Bacalov's haunting soundtrack, and the artwork were frequently praised. It was so popular that it inspired a franchise that included approximately six films. The name Django is referenced in over thirty supposed sequels from the time of the film's release in 1966 until the early 1970s. All were films attempting to capitalize on the success of the original. Most of these films were unofficial reproductions and imitations featuring neither director Corbucci nor lead actor Nero, for whom this was a breakthrough role as the laconic eponymous hero.

Like Sergio Leone's *A Fistful of Dollars*, Corbucci's *Django* is considered a loose, unofficial adaptation of Akira Kurosawa's samurai classic *Yojimbo* (1961).[58] Both inspire and are venerated texts that were tremendous box office hits worldwide. Even today, *Django* is considered a cult classic because it revised the samurai myth and defied the generic conventions of respectability politics regarding what was acceptable in mainstream cinema.

In the film, Nero co-starred alongside Loredana Nusciak, Jose Bodalo, Angel Alvarez, and Eduardo Fajardo. The film established Corbucci (together with Leone) as one of the greatest creators of the Italian western. If Leone was responsible for the birth of the spaghetti western, Corbucci was responsible for transforming it by creating an important and precise style. Corbucci added various formal elements that not only would ensure the subgenre's worldwide success but also influenced imitators at home and abroad. Though his first film dates to 1964 and was co-directed with Albert Band and Franco Giraldi (*Massacre at Grand Canyon*), *Django* earned Corbucci a reputation as a master director of one of the "most violent films" produced at the time. The violence was remarkable because (like the parallel demise of the Hays Production Code in 1967), the film's intensity and viciousness pushed against the hegemony of what was considered acceptable in cinema. It pushed back against the dominance of an otherwise bourgeois cinema, which was outdated, unrealistic, and disconnected from the violence, political turbulence, and sexually liberated 1960s.

With dozens of sequels, many of which did *not* star Franco Nero, *Django* proved profitable nonetheless. It became a franchise unto itself. In market terms, the original *Django* is analogous to tent-pole blockbusters like *Black Panther* (Ryan Coogler, 2018). Although *Black Panther* was a more commercial product and based on the Marvel comic book characters, it's like Black westerns because it offers a reimagining of heroic Black masculinity. It reframes the heroic myths from the standpoint of Black empowerment, generic revisionism, and critical African American spectatorship.

Tarantino's considerable cult following and stature as a director of offbeat, oddly disturbing, popular arthouse cinema is a major factor in the reception and cult following of *Django Unchained*. He is celebrated as a pastiche artist par excellence, an originator of nothing, a sampler of everything.[59] He is also an immensely capable savant of cinema, gifted at deftly interweaving (1) martial arts movie allusions, (2) exploitation cinema aesthetics, (3) graphic novel iconography, (4) blaxploitation's racial tropes, and (5) grindhouse excess.

The critical attention given to *Django Unchained* is also attributable to the creative license Tarantino consistently takes with racial stereotypes, African American representation, and Black vernacular. For example, his frequent use of the N-word in *Reservoir Dogs* (1992), *Pulp Fiction* (1994), and *Jackie Brown* (1997) made him the subject of controversy for fostering the belief that it's acceptable for white people to use racial epithets (liberally). Moreover, his films sometimes offer an unhealthy titillation and flirtation with anti-Black rhetoric and anti-Black violence. Rather than identifying white supremacist taboos embedded in his use of exploitation cinema signifiers, scholars have embedded their enchantment with Tarantino's aesthetics in scholarly cinephilia. They have failed to hold him accountable for overtly offensive content. With *Django Unchained*, however, it was as if Tarantino sought to make amends for past films. In some ways, *Jackie Brown* had already performed some of that work. Nevertheless, as an amalgamation of exploitation genres, *Django Unchained* utilizes operatic theatrics from Corbucci's *Django*, Black westploitation language from the *Nigger Charley* trilogy, and "slavesploitation" antebellum settings from movies like *Mandingo* (1975) and *Drum* (1976).[60] But he gives them a revisionist twist: Black empowerment and anti–white supremacist narrative closure.

In an interview with historian Henry Louis Gates Jr., Tarantino was asked if he intended to riff on *The Legend of Nigger Charley*. He responded affirmatively, saying, "Yes, exactly. . . . The thing is, that actually is an empowering movie. And it wants to be a good movie, but they had no money. Nonetheless, it stands alone."[61]

When *Django Unchained* opens, the setting is 1858, three years before the Civil War. The location is "Somewhere in Texas," according to the intertitle. The very first images on screen are of an unidentified rocky desert landscape. The inhospitable terrain evokes the spaghetti and sauerkraut westerns of the '6os. Over this barren landscape the credits roll, listing Jamie Foxx, Christoph Waltz, Kerry Washington, Leonardo DiCaprio, and Samuel L. Jackson. The camera pans downward to the right as an ill-fated group of half-dressed slaves, shackled together, shuffle into the frame.

Chained together, the enslaved men are marched across the arid desert by the Speck brothers. These slave traders take the men over hilly mountains and wooded terrain, making an arduous journey from Mississippi to Texas for market. In this context, the bullwhip heard on the soundtrack is no longer symbolic as it was in Italian-style westerns. Here it evokes the physical presence of real whips, used during slavery to discipline and punish slaves and to create "scenes of subjection."[62] In these opening images of *Django Unchained*, the sound of a cracking whip becomes part of the "mise-en-scène of subjection," allowing Luis Bacalov's haunting ballad, sung by Rocky Roberts, to transform the opening diegesis into a world where subjugation, oppression, and hopelessness pervade the diegesis.

One cold evening, the Speck brothers slave traders are met by Dr. King Schultz (Christoph Waltz), a well-dressed, impeccably mannered German immigrant pretending to be a dentist. Schultz's true identity is that of a bounty hunter seeking a slave from the Carrucan plantation who can identify the Brittle brothers. In his detailed, close reading of the Schultz character, scholar Robert Dassanowsky aptly notes that we never learn the true first name of Dr. Schultz but that his nickname, "King," is "part of the complex and reflective dualism that runs through Tarantino's films." Clearly, Tarantino playfully references both the future Dr. Martin Luther King and—with Django's wife, Brunhilde von Schaft (here presented as Broomhilda von Shaft)—evokes the blaxploitation character John Shaft.[63]

After confirming Django's identity (and his ability to ascertain the Brittle brothers), Schultz liberates Django from his captors, employing force as a last resort. The next day, as they ride into the fictional town of Daughtrey, Texas, white townspeople gaze in shock. When Schultz asks, "What's everybody staring at?" Django replies, "They ain't never seen no nigger on a horse before." Thus begins *Django*'s self-reflexive inversion of western movie conventions, complete with Ennio Morricone's "The Braying Mule" song playing in the background to evoke the Clint Eastwood–Shirley McClaine vehicle *Two Mules for Sister Sara* (Don Siegel, 1970). Like many

Black westerns before it, *Django Unchained* subverted the semiotic convention in which only white men were mounted. It was unusual—threatening
to white supremacy even—to see an armed Black man riding on horseback
during the antebellum era. Even Black cavalry officers were expected to
dismount when riding through white villages and towns.

In Daughtrey, Schultz and Django enter a bar and are having drinks when
Schultz discloses to Django that he's a bounty hunter. "The way the slave
trade deals in human lives for cash, the bounty hunter deals in corpses. . . .
Like slavery, it's a flesh for cash business," Schultz explains. Thus begins
Schultz's mentorship of the newly manumitted Django.

Significantly, the casting of Christoph Waltz as a dentist-turned-bounty-
hunter is an intertextual inversion of Waltz's role as Standartenführer Hans
Landa (aka "The Jew Hunter") in Tarantino's *Inglorious Bastards* (2009). For
Waltz, the role of Schultz proves an opportunity to shed the image of a
murderer and fascist, which he portrayed brilliantly. It also provides ironic
continuity between the German officer from *Inglorious Basterds* and the German liberal in *Django Unchained*. Disclosing his personal disgust of slavery,
Schultz enters into an agreement with Django. He enlists Django's help in
capturing the Brittle brothers in exchange for his freedom, and Schultz
will receive twenty-five dollars per head as his cut of the Brittle brothers'
bounty. First, however, they must collect their reward in Daughtrey so that
Django can learn the ropes before beginning their partnership in earnest.

The next morning, when Schultz asks Django where he'll go once freed,
Django explains that he'll search for his wife and buy her freedom. He tells
Schultz that his wife was raised by a German mistress, speaks German, and
that her name is "Broomhilda von Shaft" (aka Hildie). In addition to the
allusion to *Shaft*, *Django* implicitly evokes actor Samuel L. Jackson's role
in John Singleton's 2000 remake. It also establishes a connection between
Broomhilda and Schultz, who, out of loyalty to his German heritage, feels
duty-bound to help Django find his ladylove.

Dassanowsky interprets these references as Tarantino's allusions to the
German revolutions of 1848, which were essentially democratic and liberal
in nature, with the aim of removing the old monarchial structures and
creating independent nation-states. Dassanowsky aligns Schultz's class
consciousness with his abolitionist beliefs. While the history of German
class consciousness may be attributed to the backstory of Dr. King Schultz
in *Django Unchained*, we should keep in mind that the Berlin Conference
of 1884–1885 (*Westafrika-Konferenz*) regulated European colonization and
trade in Africa during the New Imperialism period and coincided with Germany's sudden emergence as an imperial power. The conference's outcome
can be seen as the formalization of the "Scramble for Africa." Germany's

participation in the colonization of Africa demonstrates that, as in many nations, German class consciousness at home did not necessarily translate into a critique of white supremacy or anti-Black German racism abroad.

Another, perhaps more productive way to interpret the King Schultz character is to consider the German films that Tarantino would have certainly watched, studied, and sampled—namely, the sauerkraut westerns of the early '60s. *Django Unchained*'s use of German characters and culture (e.g., Schultz, Broomhilda, folkloric storytelling) is just as likely a thinly veiled reference to the German sauerkraut westerns (i.e., Karl May–inspired), which were (1) decidedly pro–Native American, (2) anti–white colonial settler, and (3) deeply folkloric. These sauerkraut westerns also influenced the directors of Italian-style westerns that followed behind the German films. Moreover, Leone and Corbucci had acknowledged the work of other Europeans making westerns in Spain, Germany, and Yugoslavia.

Once Schultz and Django arrive in Tennessee, Schultz prepares Django for the theatrical ruse they'll be performing at various plantations until they locate Broomhilda (Kerry Washington). He invites Django to select his costume for the journey, one that will enable him to masquerade as a valet. The seventeenth-century apparel Django selects is strange, comical and inappropriate. For the film, the actual costume was inspired by Thomas Gainsborough's 1770 oil painting *The Blue Boy* and is thought to be a portrait of Jonathan Buttle (1752–1805), the son of a wealthy hardware merchant. The youth in his seventeenth-century apparel is regarded as Gainsborough's homage to painter Anthony van Dyck and is reminiscent of the artist's portraits of Charles II as a boy.

Within the antebellum narrative world of *Django Unchained*, Django's aristocratic attire is strangely anachronistic, functionally inappropriate, and bizarrely comical. Even the dim-witted young servant Betina (Miriam F. Glover playing an homage to Butterfly McQueen) asks Django, "You mean you *wanna* to dress like that?" Outside the film's narrative, however, in the extradiegetic real world, the eighteenth-century costume is perfect for Tarantino's carnivalesque subversion of class hierarchies and western genre conventions.

Consistent with Mikhail Bakhtin's explanation of "the carnivalesque" spirit in early Europe,[64] *Django Unchained* performs several carnivalesque functions in which there's a reversal of power, albeit temporarily, as happens in traditional forms of carnival. First, the narrative unites the unlikeliest of characters (i.e., the German immigrant/dentist Dr. Schultz and the enslaved Django). It encourages the interaction in unity of these two men as they work in tandem as bounty hunters and abolitionists. Second, the diegesis allows eccentric and otherwise unacceptable behaviors to go unchallenged (e.g., slavery, vigilantism, Mandingo fighting, and bloodshed) only to subvert them. Third, *Django* ensures that strict rules of Anglo-Saxon piety, plantation hierarchy, and the sacred are stripped of their power with blasphemy, obscenity, and corporeal bloodletting. In a carnivalesque subversion of conventions, Django rides on horseback, he wears nobleman's clothes, he reclaims his wife, and he enacts retribution and destruction upon Calvin Candie's plantation and family.

Carnivalesque inversion has significance outside the narrative world of the film as well. In these contexts, Tarantino uses the Django trope first to undermine the myths of the Enlightenment (during which Europeans still traded slaves). Second, the carnivalesque inversion of power condemns slavery as an institution, and the tropes of slavesploitation cinema (e.g., Mandingo fighting, racial caricatures like Uncle Tom/Stephen, the sexual exploitation of slaves, incest between Candie and his sister, Laura) while still allowing Tarantino to exploit the spectacle on screen. Third, it is through Django that Tarantino imagines a tougher, more vengeful version of Corbucci's original Django, the lonesome, anti-Confederate Union man who battled Red Shirts and won. All of these represent reversals of power.

Upon reaching the Bennett plantation in Tennessee, owned by "Big Daddy" Bennett (Don Johnson), Django locates the Brittle brothers, who now go by the alias surname Schaffer. This occasions a flashback for Django, who remembers when Big John Brittle (M. C. Gainey) opened up Broomhilda's back with a bullwhip. Django interrupts John as he's setting up to thrash Little Jodie. He shoots Big John through the heart and brutally whips fellow overseer Lil Raj senseless. This spectacle of retribution provides one of the many ironic visual pleasures of slavesploitation cinema. It advances the inversion of power hierarchies visualized in the narrative. Not only are the Brittle brothers slain by Django, but they are also beaten with instruments reserved for the terrorization and subjection of slaves. Big Daddy attempts to ambush Django and Schultz's wagon later that night with a mounted posse of thirty hooded horsemen. But Schultz and Django have already laid a trap. They blow up their own wagon and pick off Big Daddy's men from a distance with rifle fire.

Relaxing over an evening campfire, Schultz tells Django the legend of Broomhilda, the most popular of all German legends—or so he claims. At this moment, the two men form a more intimate bond. Their relationship is forged less by the homoeroticism typical of westerns than by the (cultural) paternalism of Schultz over the narrative.

> SCHULTZ: "Broomhilda is a princess. Daughter of Wotan, god of all gods. Her father is mad at her. I can't remember why. . . . She disobeyed him in some way. He puts her on top of a mountain."

DJANGO: "There's a mountain?"

SCHULTZ: "It's a German legend. There's always a mountain somewhere. He puts a dragon to guard the mountain. And he surrounds her in a circle of hellfire. And there, Broomhilda shall remain unless a hero arises brave enough to save her."

DJANGO: "Does one arise?"

SCHULTZ: "Yes, Django . . . a fella named Siegfried."

DJANGO: "Does Siegfried save her?"

SCHULTZ: "Quite spectacularly so. He scales the mountain because he's not afraid of it. He slays the dragon because he's not afraid of him. And he walks through hellfire because Broomhilda's worth it."

DJANGO: "I know how he feel."

SCHULTZ: "I think I'm starting to realize that."[65]

The retelling of this mythic legend highlights the significance of German culture to *Django Unchained*. It underscores Tarantino's awareness of Karl May–inspired German westerns of the early 1960s and their anti-colonialist, abolitionist, pro–Native American ideological tone. These films were themselves palimpsests upon which earlier German legends were graphed, including *Der Schatz im Silbersee* (*The Treasure of Silver Lake*), a West German film from 1962, based on Karl May's novel, which was an overwhelming commercial success throughout Europe and generated a series of Karl May adaptations (seventeen between 1962 and 1968).[66]

As Tassilo Schneider and Joe Hembus note, "*Der Schatz im Silbersee* was the first continental post-war film that did not imitate the American Western but instead adapted it to a specific national heritage—here Karl May's romantic vision of the West."[67] Schneider and Hembus are not alone in recognizing (revisionist) westerns as having roots in national allegories. For example, Clifford Manlove read *Django* (and by extension *Django Unchained*) through the lens of the Jamaican movie *The Harder They Come*. In that movie, Manlove finds evidence of a Babylonian conspiracy/connection between church, commerce, and government that he also sees at work in Sergio Corbucci's *Django*.[68] By following this trail of global connections, we can see a relationship between German westerns (e.g., *The Treasure of Silver Lake*), Italian westerns (*Django*), Jamaican westerns (*The Harder They Come*[69]), and American revisionist westerns (*Django Unchained*). All manifest national allegories for their respective countries and contain, as well as portray, abolitionist sentiments.

It was Karl May's films, released before the Italian westerns of Leone or Corbucci, that indicated the West's existence as a fluid/floating signifier onto which various national crises and conditions could be repeatedly scribed like a palimpsest. More significantly, May's films demonstrated the potential for redressing fascism and the ideological deployment of cinema. The implicit references to revisionist and politically progressive West German westerns through the Schultz character further aligns *Django Unchained* with a pro-Black, abolitionist, anti-colonialist stance. Moreover, the connection underscores the subversion of the iconographic conventions of slavery (and even African American representation) in mainstream movies.

Moved by Django's devotion for Broomhilda, Schultz proposes they join forces over the winter as bounty hunters and search for her in the spring.[70] Initially Schultz appears much like a traveler, in the tradition of Alexis de Tocqueville. An educated, worldly European traveler and abolitionist, Schultz philosophizes the contradictions of democracy in America and pontificates about his personal aversion to slavery. Mentoring Django into greater self-awareness with the detachment of a social scientist, Schultz helps Django devise and implement a plan to rescue his wife.

During one of their conversations, Django asks, "Why do you care what happens to me?" Schultz replies in a manner suggesting the paternalism he feels toward Django and the ownership he claims over the narrative trajectory of their quest. Schultz replies, "I've never given anyone their freedom before. So, I *kinda* feel responsible for you. Plus . . . when a German meets a real-life Siegfried, that's kind of a big deal. As a German, I'm *obliged* to help you on your quest."[71] Thus begins their formal partnership and mission to rescue a captive young woman in the tradition of John Ford's *The Searchers*. Unlike Ford's film, however, *Django Unchained* pays homage to the tradition of interracial buddy alliances in westerns like *Duel at Diablo*, *100 Rifles*, *Skin Game*, and even the parodic *Blazing Saddles*. *Django Unchained* has the most in common with *Skin Game*, though they are completely different in tone. However, both *Unchained* and *Skin Game* pivot on a series of racial ruses complete with costumes, carnivalesque masquerades, and inverted hierarchies.

At this point in the film, Tarantino employs the soundtrack to signpost generic nostalgia for the bygone New Hollywood–era westerns like *McCabe & Mrs. Miller* by using Jim Croce's folk-rock melody "I've Got a Name." The song was popularized by its use on *The Last American Hero* (1973) movie soundtrack. More relevantly, the film's theme song, as sung by Croce, became a best-selling single and a folk ballad synonymous with the Rocky Mountain sound. The song marks a tonal shift in social relations between Django and Schultz, who set out for a winter of bounty hunting as equal partners in a mise-en-scène evoking the vistas of *Jeremiah Johnson* (Sydney Pollack, 1972) or *Pat Garrett and Billy the Kid* (Sam Peckinpah, 1973). The music also marks a shift in the emotional tone of the film. This is a period of cool, quiet calm before the brutal, heated storm that will follow when they finally engage Calvin Candie.

Following this wintry montage set to Croce's song, an intertitle reads, "After a cold and profitable winter, Django and Schultz came down from the mountains and headed for . . . Mississippi." In the South, they discover that Calvin J. Candie, owner of Candyland ("the 4th largest cotton plantation in Mississippi"), has purchased Broomhilda. The ironically named Candyland has both diegetic and extradiegetic resonance. Narratively, it is simply ironic, as nothing could be more rancid than a slave plantation. Extradiegetically, it evokes Toni Morrison's novel *Beloved* and Jonathan Demme's cinematic adaptation. In *Beloved* the plantation from which Sethe has escaped is known as Sweet Home. At one point, in both the novel and the film, Sethe remarks, "There was nothing sweet about it."

To find Broomhilda, Schultz and Django develop a new ruse. They will pose as prospectors interested in Mandingo fighting as a means of gaining an introduction to Candie. Schultz agrees to pose as a gambling investor looking to buy a fighter. Django will play the Mandingo-handling trainer. A definitive feature of the carnivalesque is the recurrent theme of transformation. Through these multiple masks, masquerades, and transformations, *Django Unchained* performs carnivalesque reversals of structure and social order.

They finally meet Calvin Candie for the first time at the Cleopatra Club in the Julius Caesar room, where he's watching a Mandingo fight in medias res. Actor Franco Nero, the original star of *Django*, makes a cameo in this iconic scene playing Amerigo Vessepi,[72] the owner of an enslaved man (played by Clay Donahue) fighting Big Fred (Escalante Lundy), owned by Candie. Before departing, Vessepi orders a tequila and sits next to Django at the bar. During their brief exchange, Vessepi asks:

VESSEPI: "What's your name?"
DJANGO: "Django."
VESSEPI: "Can you spell it?"
DJANGO: "D. J. A. N. G. O. . . . The 'D' is silent."
VESSEPI: "I know."[73]

The scene, like many in Tarantino's oeuvre, is an example of how overtly self-reflexive and intentionally campy these baroque cinematic flourishes are. Tarantino uses audiovisual hyperbole to encourage a cult-following audience by rewarding loyal spectators for watching movies and recognizing intertextual references between films. It's a moment when Tarantino puts both *Django* and *Django Unchained* into a more explicit dialectic relationship. Moreover, it offers a momentary comedic reprieve from the emotional intensity and brutality depicted seconds earlier when Big Fred rips out his challenger's eyes before bludgeoning him to death. Following the Mandingo

FIGURE 5.4   Jamie Foxx and Franco Nero are *Django* dopplegangers.

fight, Schultz and Django secure Candie's attention by offering an obscene amount of money to purchase the fighter. The offer earns them a trip to the ironically, and sardonically, designated Candyland.

En route to Candyland, they gain a glimpse of the daily horrors over which Calvin Candie lords. On the plantation outskirts, the caravan encounters D'Artagnan (Ato Essandoh), a runaway slave whom Candie feeds to his German shepherds to test Django. Upon arrival at the plantation, Django and Schultz find a scorched Broomhilda, who is retrieved from the "hot box" where she has been tortured for hours for her recent attempt to escape.[74]

During dinner, Calvin Candie lectures about phrenology and puts on airs as if he were a sophisticated Frenchman. But he cannot even speak the language and he lacks basic manners. Again the film calls attention to masquerades—both real and pretend. Just as Shultz and Django pretend to be Mandingo shopping, Candie appears to be something he is not: a cosmopolitan, well-mannered gentleman. Midway through dinner, Uncle Stephen (Samuel L. Jackson) furtively calls Candie into the library, where he secretly informs him that Schultz and Django are not who they pretend but rather imposters seeking to liberate Hildie. The relationship between Calvin and Stephen is oddly close. Too close. And it becomes clear that Stephen, who served Calvin's father, is pulling the strings.

Enraged by their subterfuge, Calvin takes the opportunity to transform the dinner into a morbid lecture on race and phrenology. In doing so, he again reveals his true inner monster—as earlier when he fed D'Artagnan to his German shepherds. He forces Schultz to purchase Broomhilda immediately to save her from an imminent, skull-cracking death. Just as Schultz attempts to leave, with Django and Broomhilda in tow, Candie insists on one last handshake. But the handshake proves a bridge too far for Schultz, who has grown weary of Candie's depravity, which is adorned with a contorted deployment of European culture as justification for white supremacy. A shoot-out ensues.

In a baroque generic flourish, Tarantino orchestrates a scene that rivals Italian western carnage. Both Candie and Schultz die in the gunplay, leaving only Django to battle the remaining henchmen and save Hildie. When he's cornered, Django surrenders his life in exchange for hers.

The next morning, we find Django hanging upside down in the barn.[75] With Schultz dead and Django captured, it appears their quest has ended in failure. Billy Crash (Walton Goggins) has been sent to castrate Django. But just as he's about to be snipped, Stephen walks out to the barn and intervenes. It turns out that death by castration is too quick. Instead, Calvin's widowed sister, Miss Lara Lee Candie-Fitzwilly (Laura Cayouette), chooses to turn Django over to the Le Quint Dickey Mining Company, where he will surely experience an even slower demise and more painful death.

But Django outsmarts the Australian Le Quint Dickey Mining Company employee (Quentin Tarantino, who appears in a Hitchcockian-style cameo) by tricking him into returning to Candyland to collect the unpaid bounty for the Smitty Bacall gang. Using the familiar script Django has learned from his now dead partner, Schultz, he says, "I've got the handbill right here in my back pocket." No sooner does Django get a gun than he kills all three mining employees and doubles back to Candyland to save Hildie.

Returning to the plantation, Django rescues Hildie and descends upon the family funeral procession inside Calvin's mansion. Capitalizing on the element of surprise, he dispenses with Billy Crash, Lara Lee, and all remaining henchmen. He shoots Stephen in the knees before blowing up the big house with dynamite. As we watch a flame moving quickly along the dynamite's long fuse, Stephen, groaning in pain, offers his final admonishment to Django: "Django! You *uppity* son-of-a-*bitch*!"

This final line would be recognizable to western genre fans because it's a direct allusion to the final line in Sergio Leone's *The Good, the Bad, and the Ugly*. Having destroyed the antebellum house of horrors, Django mounts his horse alongside Broomhilda on her mount. Together they ride off into the night. But first he spins his horse in a moment of revelry, and the song "Trinity" from the Italian western comedy *They Call Me Trinity* (1970) plays on the soundtrack. Broomhilda and Django ride off into the vast dark night with a bright future ahead.

In his foreword to the illustrated book *Western all'Italiana: The Specialists*, actor Franco Nero outlined an important distinction between Italian and American westerns: "Differently from the American western, the Italian western was a kind of adventurous and black comedy, where the hero was often not completely positive but instead a son-of-a-bitch. Not the spotless hero of the classic American western, but a more contradictory and much more human character."[76] *Django Unchained* is yet another successful installment, albeit significantly revised, in a franchise predicated on the elements and ethos Franco Nero describes.

The film is one part revisionist western, one part carnivalesque parody, and one part horror story in which the subjugated returns to exact revenge. It is also a campy mashup of the Black westploitation, martial arts action films Tarantino has sutured together in a bricolage. At its core *Django Unchained* presents the eponymous character as a deeply righteous and seriously wronged man. In this iteration of the Django legend, the lead character represents a "return of the oppressed,"[77] the revenge of the enslaved, and the rejection of America's ignominious national heritage (i.e., racial injustice, structural inequality, and the carceral state). It is the literal replacement of an Italian Amerigo with an African American Django. Like African American western heroes before him, Django is a dignified multidimensional gunslinger who subverts hierarchies of power in a spirit of carnivalesque inversion. The film is less about how the West was won and more about the need to dispel the pernicious sacred and sanctified legends or myths of the past so that we might imagine something yet unseen.

Concrete Cowboy

Django Unchained would not be the last of the new millennium Black westerns. Beginning in 2020, two African American–themed westerns—both starring Idris Elba—were released to streaming platforms. *Concrete Cowboy* premiered worldwide at the Toronto International Film Festival on September 13, 2020, and was digitally released on Netflix on April 2, 2021. Like the movie *Cutting Horse*, *Concrete Cowboy* is a modern-day western but set in present-day inner-city Philadelphia. Inspired by the Fletcher Street Urban Riding Club, the film is based on the novel *Ghetto Cowboy* by Greg Neri, which was about the urban, African American horse-riding culture of Philadelphia, and the fact that the Fletcher Street Riding Club has been in existence for over one hundred years.

Given its focus on inner-city life, *Concrete Cowboy* is not a traditional western as much as it is a throwback to the 'hood genre of the late 1980s and early '90s. Films about inner-city African American life first emerged in the 1970s and '80s. They included social problem pictures such as *The Education of Sonny Carson* (1974); *Cooley High* (1975); *Cornbread, Earl, and Me*; *Brothers* (1977); *Youngblood* (1978); and *Stand and Deliver* (1988). In the '90s these "coming-of-age-in-the-'hood" films experienced a renaissance with the release of features by John Singleton, Mario Van Peebles, the Hughes brothers, Spike Lee, Darnell Martin, and Allison Anders. In form and content, *Concrete Cowboy* evokes the New Black Cinema trendsetting pictures *Boyz N the Hood*, *South Central* (Stephen Millburn Anderson, 1992), *New Jack City*, and *Menace II Society* (Allen and Albert Hughes, 1993). All were big box office successes, made for relatively low budgets but earning significant profits.

In the tradition of the 'hood films, *Concrete Cowboy*'s narrative focuses on the perils and pitfalls of being young, Black, male, and poor in the inner city during this era of late carceral capitalism. Black urban youth disproportionately face poverty, unemployment, AIDS, and incarceration.[78] With its emphasis on a tenuous father-son relationship that is negotiated through the love of horses, *Concrete Cowboy* bears strong resemblance to *Man and Boy*, one of the earlier Black westerns, featuring Bill Cosby portraying the stern father figure and George Spell playing his son.

Like *Boyz N the Hood* before it, *Concrete Cowboy* begins when fifteen-year-old Cole (Caleb McLaughlin) is sent to live with his estranged cowboy father, Harp (Idris Elba), for the summer. Cole (like the protagonist Tre Styles in *Boyz*) has been kicked out of school. Worse still, he's been expelled from many schools. Fed up, his mother sends him from Detroit to North Philly to live with his dad. The move proves even more difficult when Cole realizes that Harp lives with a horse. To Cole's surprise, he finds the horse standing in the living room, and the refrigerator and cupboards are empty. A dedicated horseman and tough disciplinarian, Harp spends his money and time taking care of his animals. Refusing to accept his father's strict rules, Cole starts hanging out with his childhood friend Smush (Jharrel Jerome), who is now a drug dealer. But without anywhere to live, Cole eventually accepts his father's rigorous lifestyle and begins to bond with the horses boarded nearby.

Life slowly improves when Cole learns to ride and develops a bond with "Boo," an untamed horse that won't let anyone else near him. Cole spends his days learning how to muck stalls under the instructions of Paris, a wheelchair-bound rider who lost his legs in a drug-related shooting. Eventually, Harp reveals to Cole that he also used to deal drugs and had spent time in prison before Cole was born, thus explaining their longtime estrangement. When Cole pulls away from Smush, Smush justifies his actions. He tells Cole he used to be a rider too but began dealing drugs to save money to buy a ranch out West.

Back at the stables, Animal Control has arrived to seize all the horses due to neighborhood complaints and poor conditions. Harp explains that there's nothing they can do, and Cole calls him a coward. A grieving Cole turns to Smush again, and they go on another drug deal. This time Smush gets shot, and Cole flees. Harp searches for Cole, eventually finding him hiding in the stables. Washing the blood off Cole's hands, Harp tells his son that Smush needs a proper memorial.

That night they break into the municipal stables and free the horses for the memorial ride. Everyone mounts up to ride their horses through the neighborhood to the cemetery, where Cole places Smush's cowboy boots on his grave and then stands up on his horse's back in a memorial moment. Days later, the Black community watches as the stables are demolished by city workers. But Harp vows that they will keep riding even without their beloved stables. At summer's end, Cole's mother returns to Philadelphia, and Harp thanks her for sending Cole to live with him. Thus, the film concludes almost as quickly as it began.

One of the most moving aspects of *Concrete Cowboy* is how much it is grounded in an aesthetic of realist cinema. The film is one part realist cinema (in the tradition of L.A. Rebellion films), one part ghettocentric Hollywood feature (with star Idris Elba and producer Lee Daniels at the helm).[79] And it evokes the cinema verité documentary style of surveying everyday riders used in *Black Rodeo* by Jeff Kanew. For instance, most of the cast is comprised of nonprofessionals, with ten of the twenty-five speaking roles played by members of the local community. Made on a modest budget of $10 million, *Concrete Cowboy* was shot on location in the North Philly neighborhood that Fletcher Street riders call home.[80] The actors did their own horseback riding. And the entire picture was filmed in only twenty days by debut director Ricky Staub.

Staub stumbled upon the Fletcher Street Urban Riding Club the same way Jeff Kanew stumbled upon a traveling Black rodeo in Harlem. Like Jeff Kanew, Ricky Staub also initially planned a documentary for his production. According to reporter Brent Lang, Staub was inspired by what Chloe Zhao achieved in her 2018 release, *The Rider*, a western about the Lakota Sioux residents of the Pine Ridge Reservation.[81]

Like an embedded anthropologist conducting participant observation, the director immersed himself in the Philadelphia riding community after he became captivated by a horse and buggy (with a subwoofer and speakers) ambling down the streets of North Philly. Staub's encounter and Neri's *Ghetto Cowboy* were inspiration for the film. But Staub experienced numerous challenges bringing the concept to fruition. It was delayed five years. Fortunately, Lee Daniels learned about the project. Daniels, who was born and raised in Philadelphia only blocks from the stables, reviewed the project and was impressed.

The most poignant aspect of the film—and its production history—is that it speaks to the relationship between African Americans and their horses. The love of horses and horseback riding has long existed in African American communities nationwide. Sadly, however, the history of economic disenfranchisement, exploitation, and land appropriation has left many

African Americans without the resources to maintain and properly care for their animals. Though it is partially a coming-of-age story, the subtext for *Concrete Cowboy* is the history of gentrification and dispossession of African American communities that have lost access to their land. In this regard it is actually a poignant story.

The Harder They Fall

The Harder They Fall, not to be confused with the Jimmy Cliff star vehicle *The Harder They Come*, is a visually stunning film. It marks a return to more fanciful western moviemaking. Whereas *Concrete Cowboy* is modern, urban, and deals with inner-city poverty, *The Harder They Fall* is historical, rural, and imagines a community of legendary gunslingers and badass bank robbers.

Set in 1890, the film opens on an idyllic homestead complete with a mother, a father, and a young boy. Into this calm walks an imposing nameless and faceless villain. A strange man enters the house and summarily kills the comely mother and devoted father, leaving their little boy the sole survivor. Years later, outlaw Nat Love (Jonathan Majors) assembles a posse to take revenge on Rufus Buck, who murdered his parents in cold blood in front of him. Fresh out of prison, Rufus (Idris Elba), a bandit, has taken over a town with his ruthless gang. Rufus kidnaps Nat's girlfriend, Stagecoach Mary (Zazie Olivia Beetz), when she tries to infiltrate his posse. A badass bandit, Rufus uses Mary as barter, forcing Nat to rob a bank to pay for her safe recovery. Rufus, it turns out, considers himself a "race man," dedicated to contributing to the betterment of Black people—or so he believes. His accumulation of capital is part of an uplift plan to build a Black mecca, where folks can live safely and economically—independent from white prejudice and discrimination.

At this juncture, director Jeymes Samuel takes an Expressionistic detour. Nat Love's gang rides into a white town to commit the bank robbery. But for this scene, Samuel has the entire set completely whitewashed in an Expressionistic cinematic flourish. Every plank, sign, and stoop has been so conspicuously painted white that audiences find themselves noticing just how artificial the entire white town looks.[82] The scene calls to mind parodies like *Blazing Saddles*, in which set pieces and cardboard backdrops were lampooned as unrealistic and hokey. *The Harder They Fall* uses set design to convey how the characters feel about the world around them. And since Expressionism is anti-realist, the white-washed mise-en-scène signifies on the surreal diegesis created for *The Harder the Fall*. It calls attention to the film's inversion of racial relations. Extradiegetically, the set also critiques the cinematic unreality typically depicted in conventional westerns, which have normalized all-white social environments in mainstream cinema. This scene mocks the hundreds of western movies that completely erased people of color and, by extension, all color. It's a cinematic joke that may never have occurred to audiences, particularly if they have not seen Mel Brooks's send-up *Blazing Saddles*.

After robbing the bank, Nat and his gang return to Redwood City, a frontier town bursting with color. In Redwood all the residents are people of color, and many are female. Both diegetically and extradiegetically, Redwood is in intertextual relationship with *Rosewood*. Rufus's dream of economic self-determination for Redwood recalls the actual economic independence of Rosewood, Florida. But whereas Rosewood was a real location with actual families, Redwood stands in symbolically for the heartland generally.

Chief among the formidable women in Redwood are Stagecoach Mary; her gender-neutral bodyguard, Cuffee (Danielle Deadwyler); and "Treacherous" Trudy Smith (Regina King). Every woman is strong and independent. And the women take sides along with the men in the showdown between Nat Love and Rufus. Riding into Redwood, Nat meets up with Rufus, where he and his gang prepare to battle. The film delivers a clash of the titans–style battle as Rufus and Nat Love come to terms with who they really are and the family connections that brought them together.

Contrasted with *Concrete Cowboy*, *The Harder They Fall* was not steeped in realism but rather in the generic revision and Expressionism. It has more in common with spaghetti westerns and westploitation mashups like *Django Unchained* than with *Concrete Cowboy* or *Cutting Horse*. For example, the picture opens with the disclaimer that it is not a true story but that the people depicted were real.

Clearly influenced by Tarantino and Leone, Jeymes Samuel had a principal goal in mind: making an epic western in which Black people were not subservient. Samuel said as much to an *Entertainment Weekly* reporter: "My wish is that any director who makes a western movie with a Black person in it doesn't give a reason why they're there. . . . I don't need a reason. We existed in that time and place."[83] It is disappointing that twenty years into the new millennium, an upcoming director needs to attest to the existence of African Americans living on the frontier. It is an indication that mainstream cinema is still struggling to correct the omissions of our mythological past.

Multiple reviewers remarked that Samuel favored style over story in his effort to make a political statement about film history. *Variety* reviewer Peter Debruge wrote, "Samuel's two biggest influences seem to be Sergio Leone and Quentin Tarantino, which makes for a very style-forward presentation, sometimes at the expense of a clean, straightforward story."[84]

And *Sight and Sound* acknowledged the film's slick, glossy aesthetic, as when reviewer Leila Latif wrote:

> Where many recent westerns have striven for gritty authenticity in sweat-stained leather, Samuel gives *The Harder They Fall* a hyper-stylized polish: everything (from Elba's gold pistols to Zazie Beetz's many layered outfits) looks plucked from the pages of *Vogue*. The action is set to reggae and dub, which works well for the most part but occasionally distracts, tipping the film into music video territory.... *The Harder They Fall* is as realistic a depiction of life for Black people in the West as Moulin Rouge was of Victorian sex work; Samuel's lens is unashamedly modern, colorful and cool. It's an imperfect but wonderfully fun debut that's a welcome respite from seeing the Black experience dictated by its proximity to whiteness, on and off screen.[85]

While Samuel's aesthetic choices are understandable, Latif correctly observes that the movie has one foot in the music industry. After all, the movie marks a directorial debut for British singer/songwriter/music producer Jeymes Samuel (aka The Bullitts). Samuel is the younger brother of Grammy Award–winning musician Seal and reportedly "sees the world in symphonic terms." He speaks rhythmically and often launches into a cappella renditions of songs, drumming on his chest or the table during interviews.[86] Samuel co-wrote the script with screenwriter Boaz Yakin. Together they agreed to engage Jay Z for the soundtrack.

The Carter family product tie-ins don't stop with the music, however. In August 2021, Adidas and Beyoncé Knowles presented the latest Adidas and Ivy Park Rodeo collection of clothing and sneakers. Supposedly inspired by the style and influence of Black cowboys and cowgirls, the collection honors the impact of Black men and women on American Western culture. The collection was marketed to highlight the hidden history of Black pioneers within cowboy and cowgirl culture and their continued influence on the American rodeo. The pop star's line of clothing revealed Jay Z's participation in Samuel's film as a fortuitous choice. Taken together, the movie, the soundtrack, and the clothing line harken back to the promotional materials that accompanied the *Nigger Charley* trilogy back in the '70s. The promotional campaign for the *Charley* films included quiz game tie-ins, highlighted a "special black westerns heroes contest," and boasted "free passes awarded to winners of [the] black western heroes quiz." The first five winners to call in to radio programs were awarded free tickets to screenings of *The Soul of Nigger Charley*. More relevantly, there were soundtrack album tie-ins for the music composed and conducted by Don Costa, as sold on an MGM Records release. Perhaps the biggest shift marked by *The Harder They Fall* is that African Americans are at the center of American media production and commodification circulated to a global market.

Monetarily speaking, *The Harder They Fall* was better funded than most Black-themed westerns, following closely behind Tarantino's film in subsidy. Whereas *Django Unchained* cost $100 million, *The Harder They Fall* received a generous Netflix-backed budget of $90 million. Shot in Santa Fe, New Mexico, it features a star-studded cast headlined by Idris Elba, Delroy Lindo, LaKeith Stanfield, Jonathan Majors, and recent Oscar winner Regina King. But its box office return on investment will be tougher to gauge, because *The Harder They Fall* received a limited release on October 22, 2021, before streaming on Netflix beginning on November 3, 2021.

According to reporter Angelique Jackson, it was Tendo Nagenda, Netflix's vice president of original film, who guaranteed that the movie would come to fruition. In mid-March of 2020, the coronavirus pandemic began to impact the entertainment industry. Netflix put all of its productions on hold, but Nagenda remained committed to this production.[87]

Eventually, *The Harder They Fall* was produced and successfully released. It marks another installment in the ongoing movement toward more inclusive, and ultimately corrective, American filmmaking. That there are currently new Black western movies in production and preproduction speaks volumes about the desire to fill the void left by historical and cinematic erasures. Studied collectively, we can learn about the history they purport to represent and the social climate in which they were conceived. Both the actual history and the cinematic mythmaking give us a richer understanding of cinematic history and our shared American reality.

Appendix

Interview with Jeff Kanew

For better or worse, social media has made communication easier. I am not a frequent Twitter user. But in my desperate search to find the director of the documentary *Black Rodeo*, I found myself scrolling through Twitter one day. Low and behold, I found the name of the man for whom I was searching: Jeff Kanew. I thought to myself: "It's something of an unusual name. . . . Could it be him?" I reached out with a single tweet by identifying myself as a fan of his film, which I had seen at the Library of Congress. Thankfully, he responded warmly and confirmed that he was the film's director. We had a wonderful exchange during our call. And I am grateful that Mr. Kanew was willing and able to speak with me openly about the production of this very special documentary. The following is an account of our conversation.

MIA MASK (MM): While researching my book about the tropes and cinematic conventions of the African American western, I discovered your film *Black Rodeo*. But at the time I first discovered it, *Black Rodeo* was not yet on DVD. It was only available at the Library of Congress—if you can believe that.

JEFF KANEW (JK): I had to send the print there.

MM: Okay. So you knew it was there?

JK: It might be the only print in existence at this point.

MM: Can you tell me what inspired you to make this film? On the audio commentary, you mentioned you were working on a western that was trumped by Fred Williamson's *Legend of Nigger Charley*. What were you working on and how did you come to *Black Rodeo*?

JK: My involvement in the movie industry began in 1963. I was in the process of dropping out of Columbia or getting kicked out of Columbia, and

I got a job working at a movie company. And somehow through the process there, I became aware of editing trailers. It wasn't really an industry yet, but I got a job editing movie trailers. They made me the assistant to the guy who did movie trailers for United Artists. That was the company.

I was doing that, but I wanted to be a musician or a rock star. I wasn't a movie historian or a film student. I discovered that editing movie trailers and writing copy for movie trailers was sort of related to writing stupid doo-wop songs that I used to do. I was kind of floating around within this world, and then I got lucky and got to do some trailers on some movies that were successful, and all of a sudden I was the trailer maker. I was working on some pretty good things.

It became my focus and suddenly I was aware of making movies and started thinking maybe I want to make one. It was just about the time that *Shaft* and *Super Fly* were starting to take off and people discovered blaxploitation films. People were discovering that there really was a Black movie audience. Becoming aware of that, I thought, *What kind of movies, for the Black audience, haven't been made yet?* One of the things I thought of was the western. I wasn't very knowledgeable about the western—Black or white. Except I was familiar with Roy Rogers, Gene Autry, and Hop-Along Cassidy. I looked into it and I sort of got a sense that there is a history there, I don't know much about it, and I decided I would write a movie about a runaway slave who becomes a gunfighter, which is exactly, I think, what *Legend of Nigger Charley* turned out to be.

I started working on this script, and a friend called me and said, "You know that thing you're working on, the Black cowboy thing? Well, I just saw some signs on the streets of New York saying there's a Black rodeo coming to Manhattan." I went out and found some signs, and I wrote down the names of the Black rodeo cowboy association. I got in touch with them and thought maybe I should film it. I spoke to a congressman from New Jersey. We made a deal for me to film the Black rodeo. I put film crews together, and it was filming at Randall's Island in a stadium outside the East River between Queens and Manhattan.

MM: I'm a native of Brooklyn, born and raised. I know Manhattan well. But when I found your film, I was surprised. I didn't know anything about this rodeo or much about the stadium.

JK: This was happening, and I plunged into it not really having made a documentary, thinking, *I'll just film it and see what I end up with*. It snowballed. I had five cameras there to cover the rodeo, and then I found out that Muhammed Ali was in town, because I happened to share the same lawyer he had. This was the perfect time because Ali couldn't fight. He had refused induction into the U.S. Army and was immediately stripped of his heavyweight title.[1]

MM: Sure, as a protest of the Vietnam War.

JK: I knew he was around, and the word was he needed money. He was doing a Broadway play. I called Bob Alan, who was the lawyer, and said, "Do you think Ali would show up for an hour or so at the Black rodeo?" And he said, "I'll call you back." He called me back and said, "Yeah, he'll do it for five grand." I said, "Wow, all right. Done!" The next day was a Saturday and we arranged to start filming on 125th outside the Apollo Theater. I had the cowboys come over with their horses. Ali was there. He got out of a Rolls Royce, got on a horse, started riding around, interacting with the cowboys. It was really magical, and for the next couple of hours he was interacting with the guys. He was so fun and charismatic. I knew that whatever length of time he was in the movie, it would dominate the whole picture. It was great.

MM: You have a lot of wonderful moments in this film. You talk about being an inexperienced filmmaker, but you do a couple of things that are so smart. You have an opening montage of images of all the celebrated white cowboy stars. I love what you say on the DVD commentary about this. You said, "I wanted to juxtapose them as being nerdy or dorky and juxtapose the dorkiness of the music with the cool hip [Black] aesthetic" that at the time was a result of *Shaft*, *Sweetback*, and *Coffy*. Those films were taking off thanks to music written by people like Isaac Hayes, Aretha Franklin, B. B. King, Ray Charles, and Little Richard. You also have a cinema verité visual style. Did you have an aesthetic that informed your thinking? Whether it was Albert and Alfred Maysles or D. A. Pennebaker. Was it *Gimme Shelter*, maybe?

JK: I wasn't enough of a student of film to even know about those things. I only knew we needed as many cameras as possible, because we don't know what's going to happen and we're going to have to cover it from many angles. And we need coverage of spectators. I know you can't take six positions on tripods. It was going to be handheld. I had to trust the cameramen to get the best stuff they could get. At that point in my talent or craft with editing, I knew I was going to have to edit it together and figure out what to do with it. There wasn't a shooting style.

One of the cameramen was really good and steady. Another one was a little jerky. Another one, John Stevens, specialized in the high-speed shot. And there were two other guys we got stuck with by the union. At the last minute the IA [International Alliance of Theatrical Stage Employees] came in. I had hired random guys who I had heard about, and they said, "You have a mixed crew. That's not good. We're going to shut you down." I had to get rid of two of my cameramen. They let me keep three, and then I had to hire two of their guys. I think they gave me guys who were unemployed at the time, so they weren't the greatest.

MM: They wanted you to go with the same union?

JK: Yeah. There were two unions in New York at the time. One was called IA and the other was called Maybin. They were competitive unions in the film business, and they tried to block each other out. If you had a Maybin crew, you couldn't hire IA people. If you had an IA crew, you couldn't hire Maybin. I was kind of naïve about all of this, so I was stumbling along. So, we had these five people, and we had several sound people, and they would be there and cover as much as possible. With the Muhammad Ali thing, he was in Harlem and we were there and filming, and all of a sudden, very spontaneously, we got into his car and he wanted to drive across the stadium, and we didn't have a camera in the car. But I was holding one of the sound recorders, so I jumped in the backseat of the car, so I got sound for that but no images. It was very hectic. It was also great.

MM: You had five crews or five cameramen. How much did this cost you? Because you had to pay Muhammad Ali five grand. How much did the film cost you?

JK: I don't remember exactly, but it was in the neighborhood of $120,000.

MM: What were your returns? Do you know anything about the film's domestic gross?

JK: I don't really. . . . It was released by a company called Cinerama Releasing, which eventually went out of business, but it's not unheard of in the movie business for [documentary] films to never return any money. Most of them return no money.

MM: Especially documentaries. It's a really hard market.

JK: No, I never got a penny back on that movie. At least I got it into theaters and people wrote some reviews. I didn't do it as a moneymaking thing as much as to get started as a filmmaker.

MM: Of course. I'm interested in this for my students, for film history, for documentary history. I teach courses on African American cinema and on documentary. Let's follow with that. You talk about the film not doing well commercially. You've mentioned how it's different from *Shaft* and *Super Fly*.

On the audio commentary you said maybe the audience wasn't interested in something as sincere and sensitive as this. But to be fair to the audience, do you think part of the problem was that audiences didn't know about it? You had a very special and unusual film. It was unlike anything in Hollywood, even in the era of blaxploitation, sexploitation, and westploitation. Did marketers understand it?

JK: I think so. I've been around the business for most of my life. G-rated, non-animated films are never what studios are trying to market. Mostly because people can see that on TV unless it's Disney. Audiences were not running to see those movies until they got bigger than life. Now parents run out with their kids [on] opening weekends because on the big screen the animation looks great. The techniques are better. But back then, families were not considered a great investment. I don't know if it's still like that other than the big tent-pole Disney movies. Although, I think somehow it did change. But back then it was not considered a hot item.

MM: Hopefully, there's more of an art house and documentary market now. A niche art house market for cinephiles, documentary filmgoers, and all kinds of people who are interested in films that are outside the mainstream. What instructions, if any, did you give your five main cameramen?

JK: To the two main guys that I knew the best and trusted the most, I said, "You guys try to get as many interviews as you can, but try also to cover the action whenever it's happening." I had two main interview cameramen. They would basically go through the stands and talk to the parents, kids, cowboys, and everybody. That was their marching order. They all participated in shooting the events in progress. I had John Stevens, who was the slow-motion guy, and he knew that was his job. I don't exactly remember what I told the additional two guys other than "Don't just sit there and point your camera at the sky." I think that's what one of them was doing.

MM: On the DVD commentary you said that approximately three thousand people attended. What's your guesstimate? Would you stick with that number?

JK: It was two days. I don't think it was more than that. It might have been more like fifteen hundred a day. It wasn't a lot. That's why, if you notice, there weren't a lot of shots of the stands except close-ups. It would make it feel like there was a bigger audience than there actually was. The audience loved it, I will say. At the beginning, when everybody was filing into the stadium, it felt like there was an energy, excited anticipation in the streets of Harlem.

I was a commuter from Long Island for a good part of my life. If you drove across the Tri-Borough Bridge, you went down East River Drive, but you never went to Harlem, because it was too scary. Then I went to Columbia University and they tell you, "Don't go down Morningside Heights into Harlem or you'll die." I was fearful of Harlem, but once I had the energy that I was going up there to make this film, I just let go of that, and for those two days it was an eye-opening experience. It was all these people interested and excited and out in the streets. It was such a positive vibe. I spent two great days in Harlem. It was the first two days I ever spent there.

MM: You said it completely changed you forever.

JK: You have to give up whatever preconceived notions you have about individuals or groups of people. They're usually based upon ignorance and not having any real exposure to them, and suddenly all I could see was smiling people looking out their windows and getting down on the streets. It really did change me. It took away fear I brought to my New Yorker ways.

MM: That's great. Let's talk a little about access to the music. You said that wasn't difficult because of your lawyer. Why was it relatively easy?

JK: I had a good industry lawyer, and for some reason it wasn't as hard then. Later on, I did a film called *Revenge of the Nerds*, and I was paying thirty-five thousand dollars for thirty seconds of Talking Heads, or Michael Jackson, or whatever. But back then I literally paid for Ray Charles, Aretha Franklin, and Little Richard. I think across the board we paid thirty-five hundred dollars a record. It wasn't bad.

MM: That's amazing. If you had to do it over again, what do you think you would do differently? Are there any things you would change?

JK: I didn't shoot Woody Strode properly. Two things I did wrong was it was not lit well. And he was on a wooden rocking chair that squeaked the whole time. I had to worry about that, but that's the only thing I would have done differently. I loved having Woody Strode. I happened to know *Sergeant Rutledge*. I will say . . . I don't know if I talked about this on the DVD. The first guy I went to, to be the spokesperson was Bill Cosby. He decided not to do it. Woody was next, and I was happy about that because he's a really good person.

MM: I want to come back to the point about Strode. But you talked a little bit about the sound crews and that you would have made the rodeo sounds more realistic or true to the experience of what cowboys were feeling. I'm assuming you would have made it sound more painful.

JK: At that budget, I didn't have a budget for really going back in and doing . . . when you're filming you go back in and lay down all-new sound effects, and it gets a richer feeling to it. I didn't have that. I just used whatever sound we recorded on location, so it wasn't great. It was okay, but the music was kind of the star so I wasn't too worried about it.

MM: I think it works really well when you put it up against cinema verité of that era. You talk about Wiseman, you talk about Maysles, you talk about Pennebaker and all of those folks who were doing cinema verité in the '60s.

They were just using diegetic or ambient sound. It's great from that perspective. On another note, I want to commend you on the interviews that you conducted with parents regarding the Black pride that they experienced and wanted for their youngsters. Did you expect to hear that? Was that all new for you in the moment when it was happening?

JK: It kind of was. I didn't know what I was going to get. Just from the looks on people's faces, as they were coming into the stadium with their kids. I knew that there was going to be a really nice energy, and that was there. Pretty much anyone you spoke to had something very positive to say. That was not a hard thing to gather. Some people were really nice and articulate and energetic. Some people would giggle. It was all there. That whole parental pride was something I didn't anticipate. I didn't have that. I was a little kid who watched cowboy movies, but I never connected to them as a part of my history.

MM: As you may know, there is a rebirth of Black rodeo culture. There's a new magazine called *Black Reins* magazine. On social media there is a bit of both presence on Facebook and Instagram and these outlets for *Black Reins* and Black rodeo culture or organizations. It's actually fascinating. It's not so much on the East Coast, but there are still multicultural rodeos that have primarily people of color performing in them because rodeo culture tends to be segregated. It's interesting to see that there's a reemergence of this culture.

JK: I'm not aware of that, but that's great. I did get a call recently from a little film festival or something in Houston in November that deals with the same theme. They asked if I'd come down and show the film down there, so I might. There is more interest now than there ever was before.

MM: Do you think you would have had a feature-length film without Woody Strode? You said on the audio commentary that you think that it would have been tricky to flesh it out.

JK: I think so. I had references to a lot of material and photographs and whatever. But with Woody, he could tell stories about Deadwood Dick and some of these other characters and his own experiences, so it gave me an extra twenty to twenty-five minutes of material just because of who he was.

MM: Yes, absolutely. I feel like there is a little bit of an homage to your film in *Posse*. Have you seen the movie *Posse*?

JK: The one with Mario Van Peebles?

MM: Yeah, Mario Van Peebles. Doesn't it begin with Woody Strode talking about the Old West in the credit sequence?

JK: That movie was a while ago.

MM: 1993. You wouldn't necessarily remember it, but go watch the opening credit sequence. I almost felt like there was a way in which it was an homage to your film, but I think you're right. Woody Strode adds an amazing component, and having looked at his autobiography, *Goal Dust*, it's been fascinating to learn more about his career, and as you said earlier, you have Mohammed Ali here. It's so amazing to have the two of them in this film. I guess you really wanted to also have the images of Ali. Did you save any of the sound from that car ride from the theater to the stadium?

JK: Unfortunately that was 1972 and Cinerama had the negatives and the original material, and they went out of business God knows when. I tried to track down all that material, and it seemed to have disappeared off the face of the earth, so I don't have anything.

MM: Have you had any other sort of interest, people calling you or talking to you expressing interest and curiosity about this film in relationship to other Black westerns? This is my own curiosity.

JK: No, not in relation to the making of any other films. Quentin Tarantino didn't call me. No, the only person that did was a boxing documentarian named Leon Gast. Leon called me once and asked if he could use some of the Ali stuff. I told him he could. I don't know if he ever did.

MM: I do remember hearing you talk about that on the audio commentary, but I think you said that since your film was made before he made that film, there wasn't much still left or available for him to use.

JK: Yes, that's true.

MM: I'm working right now with the Criterion Collection. The Criterion Channel is interested in working with me to maybe program some films, and I would love for your film, *Black Rodeo*, to be part of that. I hope that they'll be reaching out to you soon. I have to submit a list of films that I'd like for them to put into a program, and I'm sure they'll be amenable to your documentary as part of this slate. I hope, Jeff, that you and I will be in contact again in the coming months.

JK: All right, we can and we will.

MM: Thank you! You know to reach me by email, and I just hope that I can reach out to you and we can talk more if I have any follow-up questions.

JK: Okay, great.

Notes

Preface

1. Ice became a mass-market commodity by the early 1830s with the price of ice dropping from six cents per pound to a half of a cent per pound. In New York City, ice consumption increased from twelve thousand tons in 1843 to one hundred thousand tons in 1856.

2. Dr. Graceland Santos, "Who Remembers Riding Horses on Staten Island?" *SiLive. com*, April 27, 2019. John Franzreb III served as a ringmaster at top-tier equestrian competitions everywhere from the Florida circuit to Devon, the Washington International Horse Show, and the National Horse Show, as well as points west. He died in 2020 at age seventy-nine. Despite having done his job for decades, he never lost his enthusiasm for playing such a key role on the sporting scene. https://www.silive .com/life-and-culture/g66l-2019/04/6d42c125047425/who-remembers-riding-horses -on-staten-island-vintage-photos-of-clove-lake-stables.html/.

3. Diana Shaman, "An Enduring Place for Horses Amid the Urban Welter," *New York Times,* October 2, 1977.

4. Pete Daniel, *Dispossession: Discrimination against African American Farmers in the Age of Civil Rights* (Chapel Hill: University of North Carolina Press, 2013); Samuel Bowles and Herbert Gintis, "The Inheritance of Inequality," *Journal of Economic Perspectives* 16, no. 3 (2002): 3–30.

5. Leah Douglas, "African Americans Have Lost Untold Acres of Land Over the Last Century," *The Nation,* June 26, 2017; Dillon Hayes, "A Black Cowboy Confronts the Whitewashed History of the West," *New York Times*, June 16, 2020.

6. Douglas, "African Americans Have Lost Untold Acres."

7. Dania V. Francis, Darrick Hamilton, Thomas W. Mitchell, Nathan A. Rosenberg, and Bryce Wilson Stucki, "Black Land Loss: 1920–1997," *American Economic Association: Papers and Proceedings* 112 (May 2022): 38.

8. Jess Gilbert, Spencer D. Wood, and Gwen Sharp, "Who Owns the Land? Agricultural Land Ownership by Race/Ethnicity," *Rural America* 14, no. 4 (2002): 55.

9. Francis et al., "Black Land Loss: 1920–1997," 38–42.

10. Richard Rothstein, *The Color of Law: A Forgotten History of How Our Government Segregated America* (New York: Liveright Publishing), vii.

11. Manning Marable, *How Capitalism Underdeveloped Black America* (Boston: South End Press, 1983, 2000, 2015).

12. Melodie McDaniel and Amelia Fleetwood, *Riding through Compton* (Seattle, Washington: Minor Matters Books, LLC, 2018). See also the following sites: https://www.awesomefoundation.org/en/projects/3735-compton-jr-posse-youth-equestrian-org; https://www.comptonjrequestrians.org/about; and https://www.theplaidhorse.com/2017/06/01/compton-jr-posse-changing-the-course-of-kids-lives/.

13. For example, Eric Schaefer, *Bold! Daring! Shocking! True! A History of Exploitation Film, 1919–1959* (Durham, NC: Duke University Press, 1999). See also Nick Cato, *Suburban Grindhouse: From Staten Island to Times Square and All the Sleaze Between* (London: Headpress Books, 2020); Alan Betrock, *I Was a Teenage Juvenile Delinquent Rock 'n' Roll Horror Beach Party Movie Book: A Complete Guide to the Teen Exploitation Film, 1954–1969* (Medford, NJ: Plexus Publishing, 1988).

Introduction

1. The oldest of thirteen children born to former slaves, Bill Pickett (1870–1932) helped pave the way for Black rodeo stars, film actors, and stunt professionals. As America's first Black cowboy movie star and the greatest rodeo star of his era, Pickett is credited with inventing the sport of "bull dogging," the predecessor to today's steer wrestling. Born in Taylor, Texas, Pickett was of African, white, and Cherokee descent. He attended school through the fifth grade, leaving to take up ranching work to help support his family.

2. Barbara Tepa Lupack, *Richard E. Norman and Race Filmmaking* (Bloomington: Indiana University Press, 2014), 86. After observing trained bulldogs corral stray steers by gripping the most sensitive areas of their faces, Pickett created his most famous stunt: he would jump from a moving horse onto a steer, which he wrestled to the ground and then immobilized with a strong bite to its lip. The signature move earned Pickett the nickname "The Bulldogger." Richard Norman later boasted of him, "Bill Pickett was the colored man who invented bull-dogging."

3. Ibid., 1.

4. "Bill Pickett," Norman Studios, http://normanstudios.org/films-stars/norman-players/bill-pickett/.

5. Sarina Pearson, "Cowboy Contradictions: Westerns in the Postcolonial Pacific," *Studies in Australasian Cinema* 7, nos. 2/3 (2013): 153.

6. Mary Ellen Higgins, Rita Keresztesi, and Danya Oscherwitz, eds., *The Western in the Global South* (London: Routledge, 2015), xiv.

7. Cynthia J. Miller and A. Bowdoin Van Riper, eds. *International Westerns: Relocating the Frontier* (Lanham, MD: Scarecrow Press, 2014), xii.

8. Cynthia J. Miller and A. Bowdoin Van Riper, eds. *Undead in the West: Vampires, Zombies, Mummies and Ghosts on the Cinematic Frontier* (Lanham, MD: Scarecrow Press, 2012), xii. See also Elise M. Marubbio, *Killing the Indian Maiden: Images of Native American Women in Film* (Lexington: University of Kentucky Press, 2006).

9. Michael S. Kimmel, "Masculinity as Homophobia: Fear, Shame, and Silence in the Construction of Gender Identity," in *Theorizing Masculinities*, ed. Harry Brod and Michael Kaufman (Thousand Oaks, CA: Sage Publications, 1994).

10. Miller and Van Riper, *Undead in the West*, xi.

11. "Revisionist Western," *Wikipedia*, https://en.wikipedia.org/wiki/Revisionist_Western/.

12. "Black westploitation" is a term used throughout this book to refer to exploitation westerns. It is a term applied to specific films made during this period but not all of them. It refers to a particular mode of production and a resulting cinematic style. "Blaxploitation" is a subgenre of exploitation film that emerged during the early 1970s. The films, while popular, suffered backlash for their disproportionate numbers of stereotypical characters showing bad or questionable motives, including roles as criminals. However, the films ranked among the first in which Black characters and communities were the heroes and subjects of film and television rather than sidekicks, villains, or victims of brutality. Blaxploitation films were originally aimed at urban African American audiences, but the genre's audience appeal broadened, traversing across racial, ethnic, and class lines. Film studios realized the potential profit of expanding the audiences for blaxploitation films across racial lines. "Westploitation" is a subgenre of Westerns. They were cheaply made, low-quality, B-western movies; produced quickly; and recycled familiar themes, characters, plot devices, and cinematic clichés. They often utilized deliberate camp aesthetics with an emphasis on failed seriousness. The use of these familiar and "exploitation cinema" devices attracted critical attention and garnered a cult following among audiences. Therefore, Black westploitation films (or "blaxploi-westerns") fused the two. The terms "Black westploitation" and "blaxploiwestern" are used interchangeably in this book and refer to the fusion of some blaxploitation themes, actors, and political rhetoric with westploitation filmmaking practices. In this book I am referring to the production of a series of Black westploitation films including, but not limited to, the *Nigger Charley* trilogy.

13. Antonio Bruschini and Antonio Tentori, *Western All'italiana: The Specialists*, ed. Stefano Piselli and Riccardo Morrocchi (Florence: C. E. Nerbini, 1998), 11–12.

14. Homi K. Bhabha, *Nation and Narration* (New York: Routledge, 1990).

15. Black nationalism was a political and social movement prominent in the 1960s and early '70s in the United States among some African Americans. The movement, which can be traced back to Marcus Garvey's Universal Negro Improvement Association of the 1920s, sought to acquire economic power and to infuse among Blacks a sense of community. Many adherents to Black nationalism assumed the eventual creation of a separate Black nation by African Americans. As an alternative to being assimilated by the American nation, which is predominantly white, Black nationalists sought to maintain and promote their separate identity as a people of Black ancestry. With such slogans as "Black Power" and "Black is beautiful," they also sought to inculcate a sense of Black pride.

W.E.B. Du Bois's Black nationalism took several forms, the most influential being his pioneering advocacy of Pan-Africanism—the belief that all people of African descent have common interests and should work together in the struggle for their freedom. Du Bois was a leader of the first Pan-African Conference in London in 1900 and the architect of four Pan-African Congresses held between 1919 and 1927. Second, he articulated a cultural nationalism. As the editor of *The Crisis*, he encouraged the development of African American literature and art and urged his readers to see "Beauty in Black." Third, Du Bois's Black nationalism is seen in his belief that colored folks should develop a separate "group economy" of producers' and consumers' cooperatives as a weapon for fighting economic discrimination and poverty. This doctrine became especially important during the Great Depression of the 1930s and precipitated an ideological struggle within the National Association for the Advancement of Colored People (NAACP).

16. The first period of Black nationalism began when poor Africans were brought to the Americas as slaves through the American Revolutionary period. The second period of Black nationalism began after the Revolutionary War. This period refers to the time when a sizeable number of educated Africans within the colonies (specifically within New England and Pennsylvania) had become disgusted with the social conditions that arose out of the Enlightenment. The third period of Black nationalism arose during the post-Reconstruction era, particularly among various African American clergy. Separated circles were already established and accepted because African Americans had long endured the oppression of slavery and Jim Crow in the United States. The clerical politicization led to the birth of a modern form of Black nationalism that stressed the need to separate African Americans from non-Blacks and build separate communities that would promote racial pride and collectivize resources. "Black Nationalism," *Wikipedia*, https://en.wikipedia.org/wiki/Black nationalism/.

17. Kimmel, "Masculinity as Homophobia."

18. In the 1972 "Gary Declaration: Black Politics at the Crossroads," the leaders of the movement shared the following pronouncement on the state of Black America: "Our cities are crime-haunted dying grounds. Huge sectors of our youth—and countless others—face permanent unemployment. Those of us who work find our paychecks able to purchase less and less. Neither the courts nor the prisons contribute to anything resembling justice or reformation. The schools are unable—or unwilling—to educate our children for the real world of our struggles. Meanwhile, the officially approved epidemic of drugs threatens to wipe out the minds and strength of our best young warriors. Economic, cultural, and spiritual depression stalk black America, and the price for survival often appears to be more than we are able to pay. On every side, in every area of our lives, the American institutions in which we have placed our trust are unable to cope with the crises they have created by their single-minded dedication to profits for some and white supremacy above all."

19. "Exodusters" was a name given to African Americans who migrated from states along the Mississippi River to Kansas in the late nineteenth century as part of the Exoduster movement or the Exodus of 1879. It was the first general migration of Black people following the Civil War. The movement received substantial organizational support from prominent figures, including Benjamin Singleton of Tennessee and Henry Adams of Louisiana. As many as forty thousand Exodusters left the South to settle in Kansas, Oklahoma, and Colorado.

20. Olivier Driessens, "The Celebritization of Society and Culture: Understanding the Structural Dynamics of Celebrity Culture," *International Journal of Cultural Studies* (September 18, 2012): 641–57. Driessens states that celebrification captures the transformation of ordinary people and public figures into celebrities, whereas "celebritization" is conceptualized as a meta-process that grasps the societal and cultural changes implied by celebrity. Celebritization addresses the societal and cultural embedding of celebrity, which can be observed through its democratization, diversification, and migration. It is argued that these manifestations of celebritization are driven by

three separate but interacting molding forces: mediatization, personalization, and commodification.

21. Ibid., 643.

22. See note 12.

23. The Big Five major studios were Metro-Goldwyn-Mayer, Paramount Pictures, 20th Century Fox, Warner Bros., and RKO Pictures. The Little Three majors were United Artists, Columbia Pictures, and Universal Studios. The top four Poverty Row studios were Grand National, Republic Pictures, Monogram Pictures, and Producers Releasing Corporation.

24. Republic Pictures was created in 1935 when Herbert J. Yates combined six other established Poverty Row companies—Monogram, Mascot Pictures, Liberty Pictures, Majestic Pictures, Chesterfield Pictures, and Invincible Films—with his Consolidated Film Laboratories. "Republic Pictures," *Wikipedia*, https://en.wikipedia.org/wiki/Republic_Pictures/.

25. Julia Leyda, "Black-Audience Westerns and the Politics of Cultural Identification in the 1930s," *Cinema Journal* 42, no. 1 (2002): 60–61.

26. This movie was initially released under the title *The Red, White, and Black*.

27. Skerry quoted in Neil Campbell, *Post-Westerns: Cinema, Region, West* (Lincoln: University of Nebraska Press, 2013), 19–55.

28. Ethan Persoff, "Lobo," *Comics with Problems*, http://www.ep.tc/problems/70/.

29. Philip Durham and Everett L. Jones, *The Negro Cowboys* (Lincoln: University of Nebraska Press, 1965), 2.

30. John H. Nankivell, *Buffalo Soldier Regiment: History of the Twenty-Fifth United States Infantry, 1869–1926* (Lincoln: University of Nebraska Press, 1927), ix.

31. Ward Churchill, *Fantasies of the Master Race: Literature, Cinema, and the Colonization of American Indians* (Monroe, ME: Common Courage Press, 1992), 233.

32. Ibid., ix.

33. John Lenihan, *Showdown: Confronting Modern America in the Western Film* (Chicago: University of Illinois Press, 1979), 56–58. See also Tim Lucas, "Western Promise," *Sight & Sound* 21, no. 7 (2011): 88.

34. Neil Campbell, "'Coming Back to Bad It Up': The Posthumous and the Post-Western," in *The Western in the Global South*, eds. Mary Higgins, Rita Keresztesi, and Dayna Oscherwitz (New York: Routledge, 2015).

Chapter 1. Football Heroes Invade Hollywood

1. Michael Johnson, "Cowboys, Cooks, and Comics: African American Characters in Westerns of the 1930s," *Quarterly Review of Film and Video* 22, no. 3 (2005): 227. Johnson summarizes the way the all-Black-cast movies like *Harlem Rides the Range* revised mainstream westerns by creating a "private" space within the mise-en-scène where African American entertainers or comics could perform free from the intrusive presence of white evaluation. The films differ from mainstream movies by presenting Black comic figures whose wit is purposeful, knowing, and clever. See Johnson, p. 234.

2. Donald Bogle, *Toms, Coons, Mulattoes, Mammies, and Bucks: An Interpretive History of Blacks in American Films* (New York: Continuum, 1994).

3. Ed Guerrero, *Framing Blackness: The African American Image in Film* (Philadelphia: Temple University Press, 1993); Yvonne Sims, *Women of Blaxploitation: How the Black*

Action Film Heroine Changed American Popular Culture (Jefferson, NC: McFarland: 2006); Novotny Lawrence and Gerald Butters, *Beyond Blaxploitation* (Detroit: Wayne State University Press, 2016); Christian Metz, *Film Language: A Semiotics of Cinema* (Cambridge, UK: Oxford University Press, 1974).

4. Cynthia J. Miller, "Tradition, Parody, and Adaptation: Jed Buell's Unconventional West," in *Hollywood's West: The American Frontier in Film, Television, and History*, ed. Peter C. Rollins and John E. O'Connor, 65–80 (Lexington: University of Kentucky Press, 2009).

5. A "singing cowboy" was a subtype of the archetypal cowboy hero of early western films. It references real-world campfire-side ballads of the settler culture. In some of these, the cowboys sang of life on the trail with all the challenges, hardships, and dangers encountered while pushing cattle for miles up the trails and across the prairies. This continues with modern vaquero traditions and within the genre of western music and its related New Mexico, Red Dirt, and Texas country styles. Many songs have been written and popularized by groups like Riders in the Sky and by individual performers such as Gene Autry, Herb Jeffries, Roy Rogers, Tex Ritter, and Bob Baker.

6. Miller, "Tradition, Parody, and Adaptation."

7. Clayton R. Koppes and Gregory D. Black, *Hollywood Goes to War: How Politics, Profits, and Propaganda Shaped World War II Movies* (Berkeley: University of California Press, 1987), 16.

8. Ibid., 33–34.

9. "Vertical integration" here refers to the combination in one company of two or more stages of production that are normally operated by separate companies. A company may achieve vertical integration by acquiring or establishing its own suppliers, manufacturers, distributors, or retail locations rather than outsourcing them.

10. Koppes and Black, *Hollywood Goes to War*, 84.

11. Jeanine Basinger, *The World War II Combat Film: Anatomy of a Genre* (New York: Columbia University Press, 1986), 14.

12. Ibid., 266.

13. A "social problem film" is a narrative film that integrates a larger social conflict into the individual conflict between its characters. In the context of the United States and of Hollywood, the genre is defined by fictionalized depictions of social crises set in realistic American domestic or institutionalized settings. Like many genres, the exact definition is often in the eye of the beholder; however, Hollywood did produce and market several topical films beginning in the 1930s. By the 1940s the term "social problem film" or "message film" was conventional in its usage among the industry and the public. Characteristics that have grown to define the social problem film revolve around the perceived consciousness of the nation about a certain social issue and integrating that issue into a narrative. An important fact of the social problem film is its ability to react to and display a social problem that is relevant to the current era. It specifically addresses an issue while the issue is still part of the national consciousness, often forming an argument for what the problem is through the narrative and character development. Early social problem films blended ideological feelings of the time into a narrative that translated it into a message for audiences to absorb. This can be evidenced within certain sociological experiments that occurred revolving around the ability of a film to change public perception. A prime example of this is the representation of anti-Semitism within the film *Gentleman's Agreement* or racism within *Blackboard Jungle*.

Peter Roffman, *The Hollywood Social Problem Film: Madness, Despair, and Politics from the Depression to the Fifties* (Bloomington: Indiana University Press, 1981).

14. Formed from the wreckage of a failed California Pro Football League, the Pacific Coast Professional Football League (PCPFL) showcased the Los Angles Bulldogs and the Hollywood Bears. The league became the "home" of African American football stars (including Kenny Washington, Woody Strode, and, briefly, Jackie Robinson), as the NFL had developed and enforced a color barrier in 1934, which was extended until 1946.

15. Woody Strode and Sam Young, *Goal Dust: The Warm and Candid Memoirs of a Pioneer Black Athlete and Actor* (Lanham, MD: Madison Books, 1990), 4.

16. Ibid., 5–6.

17. Ibid., 181–99.

18. Both the Ninth and Tenth Cavalry Regiments participated in dozens upon dozens of skirmishes and larger battles of the Indian Wars as America became obsessed with westward expansion. For instance, the Ninth Cavalry was critical to the success of a three-month unremitting campaign known as the Red River War against the Kiowas, the Comanches, the Cheyenne, and the Arapahoe. It was after this battle that the Tenth Cavalry was sent to join them in Texas.

19. "Buffalo Soldier, dreadlock Rasta / There was a Buffalo Soldier / In the heart of America / Stolen from Africa, / brought to America / Fighting on arrival, fighting for survival / I mean it, when I analyze the stench / To me, it makes a lot of sense / How the dreadlock Rasta was the Buffalo Soldier / And he was taken from Africa, brought to America / Fighting on arrival, fighting for survival / Said he was a Buffalo Soldier, dreadlock Rasta / Buffalo Soldier, in the heart of America / If you know your history / Then you would know where you coming from / Then you wouldn't have to ask me / Who the heck do I think I am / I'm just a Buffalo Soldier / In the heart of America / Stolen from Africa, brought to America / Said he was fighting on arrival / Fighting for survival / Said he was a Buffalo Soldier." "Bob Marley—Buffalo Solider Lyrics," http://www.songlyrics.com/bob-marley/buffalo-soldier-lyrics/.

20. Strode and Young, *Goal Dust*, 200–201.

21. Ibid., 204.

22. Brian Henderson, "*The Searchers*: An America Dilemma," in *Movies and Methods: An Anthology*, vol. 2, ed. Bill Nichols (Berkeley: University of California Press, 1985), 429–49. Henderson writes, "The emotional impact of *The Searchers* can hardly come from the issue of the kinship status and marriageability of an Indian in white society in 1956. This issue cannot be the locus of that unconscious conflict in knowledge or social life that activated every effective myth and fixes the attention of its listeners, according to Levi-Strauss. It becomes explicable only if we substitute black for red and read a film about red-white relations in 1868–1873 as a film about black-white relations in 1956" (444).

23. Joseph McBride and Michael Wilmington, "*Sergeant Rutledge*," *Velvet Light Trap: A Critical Journal of Film and Television* 2 (August 1971): 16–18.

24. Cheryl I. Harris, "Whiteness as Property," *Harvard Law Review* 106, no. 8 (1993): 1707–1791.

25. McBride and Wilmington, "*Sergeant Rutledge*," 17.

26. Daniel O'Brien, *Black Masculinity on Film: Native Sons and White Lies* (London: Palgrave Macmillan, 2017), 95.

27. Frank Manchel, "Losing and Finding John Ford's *Sergeant Rutledge* (1960)," *Historical Journal of Film, Radio, and Television* 17, no. 2 (1997): 246.

28. Ibid.

29. Richard Dyer, *White: Essays on Race and Culture* (New York: Routledge, 2017), 127–30. Reprint ed. See the entire chapter titled "The Light of the World" for a full discussion.

30. Manchel, "Losing and Finding John Ford's *Sergeant Rutledge*," 247.

31. O'Brien, *Black Masculinity on Film*, 96.

32. Brian Henderson, "*The Searchers*: An American Dilemma," *Film Quarterly* 34, no. 2 (1980–1981): 9–23. Reprinted in *Movies and Methods: An Anthology*, vol. 2, ed. Bill Nichols (Berkeley: University of California Press, 1985), 429–49.

33. See Manchel, "Losing and Finding John Ford's *Sergeant Rutledge*," 247. The term "Supermasculine Menial" is from Eldridge Cleaver, *Soul on Ice* (New York: Dell Publishing, 1968), 164–67. In Cleaver's spiritual and intellectual autobiography, four types of people are distinguished as occupying positions in the social hierarchy of American society: the Omnipotent Administrator (white men), the Ultrafeminine Doll (white women), the Supermasculine Menial (Black men), and the Amazon (Black women). The Supermasculine Menial, in Cleaver's schema, is the social strata or group reserved for Black men in America who, within the logic of white supremacy he describes, were given the attributes of masculinity associated with the body rather than intellect associated with the mind. They were associated with strength, brute power, and muscle. They were athletes, laborers, and menials who were expected to rely on their physical strength to survive. In this position, Black men were considered lowly, viewed as unintelligent, and symbolically degraded. In myth the Supermasculine Menial functions as the proverbial unrestrained id, often driven by uninhibited bodily needs, wants, desires, and impulses, rather than the rational ego or moral superego.

34. Heather J. Hicks, "Hoodoo Economics: White Men's Work and Black Men's Magic in Contemporary American Film," *Camera Obscura* 53, vol. 18, no. 2 (2003): 27–55. In American cinema the Magical Negro is a supporting stock character who comes to the aid of white protagonists in a film. Magical Negro characters, who often possess special insight or mystical powers, have long been a tradition in American fiction. A familiar convention, the term "Magical Negro" was popularized in 2001 by film director Spike Lee while discussing films with students during a tour of college campuses, in which he said he was dismayed at Hollywood's decision to continue employing this premise; he noted that the films *The Green Mile* (1999) and *The Legend of Bagger Vance* (2000) used the "super-duper magical Negro." The word "Negro" is used because the trope is considered archaic, and usually offensive, in modern English. This underlines their message that a "magical Black character" who goes around selflessly helping white people is a throwback to stereotypes such as the "Tom," the "Coon," the "Sambo," or the "noble savage."

35. McBride and Wilmington, "*Sergeant Rutledge*," 17.

36. Manthia Diawara, "Black Spectatorship: Problems of Identification and Resistance," in *Film Theory and Criticism: Introductory Readings*, ed. Leo Braudy and Marshall Cohen, 672–80 (New York: Oxford University Press, 2016).

37. "Football Heroes Invade Hollywood: Filmland Entices Black Grid Pros to Trade Yardage for Footage," *Ebony*, October 1969, 195.

38. McBride and Wilmington, "*Sergeant Rutledge*," 17.

39. Hicks, "Hoodoo Economics," 28.

40. Jeffrey A. Brown, "Comic Book Masculinity and the New Black Superhero," *African American Review* 33, no. 1 (1999): 28.

41. Keith Harris, *Boys, Boyz, Bois: An Ethics of Black Masculinity in Film and Popular Media* (New York: Routledge, 2006), 66–69.

42. A world-renowned athlete before turning to motion pictures, Rafer Johnson noted that his role in *Soul Soldier* was the first role ever offered to him as a Black actor rather than as a Black athlete. The major difference between this feature and others is that this film is about a part of Black history that has never before been told. The Tenth Cavalry was a Black regiment, mostly former slaves. The six-foot-four-inch Johnson studied drama in high school and acted in stage productions at UCLA (where he also captained the track team and was elected president). He has appeared in numerous feature films, including *The Games* (1970), *The Last Grenade* (1970), *None but the Brave* (1965), *Pirates of Tortuga* (1961), and *Wild in the Country* (1961). See the press kit for *Soul Soldier*, courtesy of Schomburg Center for Research in Black Culture.

43. Brown, "Comic Book Masculinity," 32.

44. John Cawelti, "Chinatown and Generic Transformation in Recent American Films," in *Film Theory and Criticism: Introductory Readings*, ed. Leo Braudy and Marshall Cohen, 7th ed. (New York: Oxford University Press, 2009), 498–511.

45. Mike Freeman, *Jim Brown: The Fierce Life of an American Hero* (New York: HarperCollins e-books; reprint ed., 2009), 108.

46. Ibid., 142–44. The basic principle was simple: when a potentially Black-owned business could not receive funding from traditional means, such as white-owned banks, the NIEU would either provide those monies or arrange backing from an institution that could.

47. Dave Zirin, *Jim Brown: Last Man Standing* (New York: Blue Rider Press, 2018), 116.

48. Freeman, *Jim Brown: The Fierce Life*, 151.

49. Jim Brown, *Out of Bounds* (New York: Kensington Publishing Group, 1989), 142.

50. Freeman, *Jim Brown: The Fierce Life*, 172.

51. Ibid.

52. Simon Gelten, "*Rio Conchos* (1964)," *Westerns on the Blog: A Blog Dedicated to Western Movies*, http://westernsontheblog.blogspot.com/2014/06/rio-conchos-1964.html/, June 30, 2014.

53. "Greaser" was a derogatory term for a Mexican in what is now the U.S. Southwest in the nineteenth century. The slur likely derived from what was considered one of the lowliest occupations typically held by Mexicans: the greasing of the axles of wagons. They also greased animal hides that were taken to California, where Mexicans loaded them onto clipper ships (a greaser). The term was in common usage among U.S. troops during the Mexican-American War and was actually incorporated into an early California statute, the Greaser Act (1855), an expression of a virulent form of anti-Mexican sentiment among many Anglo Californians. For more discussion of this caricature in cinema, see the 2002 documentary *The Bronze Screen: 100 Years of the Latino Image in American Cinema*, directed by Susan Racho, Alberto Dominguez, and Nancy De Los Santos-Reza.

54. Presidio is a city in Presidio County, Texas. It stands on the Rio Grande on the opposite side of the U.S.–Mexico border from Ojinaga and Chihuahua. The junction

of the Rio Conchos and Rio Grande at Presidio was settled thousands of years ago by hunting and gathering peoples. Local Native Americans adopted agriculture and lived in small, closely knit settlements, which the Spaniards later called pueblos. "La Junta Indians" is a collective name for the various Indians living in the area known as *La Junta de los Rios* ("the confluence of the rivers": the Rio Grande and the Conchos River) on the borders of present-day West Texas and Mexico. In the eighteenth century, the Spanish set up missions in the area and the Native Americans gradually lost their tribal identifications. After suffering severe population losses through infectious disease, the Spanish slave trade, and attacks by raiding Apaches and Comanches, the La Junta Indians disappeared. Some intermarried with Spanish soldiers, and their descendants became part of the Mestizo population of Mexico; others merged with the Apaches and Comanches; still others departed to work on Spanish haciendas and in silver mines. "Ojinaga," *Wikipedia*, https://en.wikipedia.org/wiki/Ojinaga/.

55. NGC was the successor of 20th Century Fox theater division (with 550 theaters when it spun off in 1951 and reduced in half, by court order, six years later). Fox recycled talent at both ends of the spectrum. For example, producer Marvin Schwartz was contracted to film "four high-budget features for 20th Century Fox release, the first of which was *100 Rifles*." See the press kit for *100 Rifles* courtesy of Schomburg Center for Research in Black Culture.

56. Steven Cohan and Ina Rae Hark, *Screening the Male: Exploring Masculinities in Hollywood Cinema* (London: Routledge, 1993) 14–15.

57. Bruschini et al., *Western All'Italiana*, 58.

58. Angela Aleiss, *Making the White Man's Indian: Native Americans and Hollywood Movies* (Westport, CT: Greenwood Publishing, 2005). Aleiss's book is an excellent analysis of Native American stereotyping in mainstream cinema.

59. Spike Lee, dir., *Jim Brown: All American*, HBO Sports, 2002.

60. Vito Russo, *The Celluloid Closet: Homosexuality in the Movies* (New York: Harper and Row, 1981). This book, along with scholarship by intellectuals like Richard Dyer, was fodder for a 1995 American documentary film directed and written by Rob Epstein and Jeffrey Friedman.

61. Camp is an aesthetic style and sensibility that regards something as engaging because of its bad taste and ironic value. Camp aesthetics disrupt many notions of what art is and what can be classified as "high art" by inverting aesthetic hierarchies of beauty, value, and taste. Camp can also be a social practice. It is considered a style and performance identity in film, television, social media, GIFs, cabaret, and music videos. Where high art necessarily incorporates beauty and value, camp necessarily needs to be lively, audacious, and dynamic. Camp aesthetics delight in impertinence, impropriety, and inversion of social hierarchies. According to the *Oxford English Dictionary*, it denotes "ostentatious, exaggerated, affected, theatrical," or "effeminate behavior, and by the middle of the 1970s, the definition included banality, mediocrity, artifice, and ostentation . . . so extreme as to amuse or have a perversely sophisticated appeal." Much of the understanding of camp derives from Susan Sontag's seminal essay "Notes on Camp" (1964), which emphasized its key elements as artifice, frivolity, naïve middle-class pretentiousness, and *excess*. Sontag writes, "Allied to the Camp taste for the androgynous is something that seems quite different but isn't: a relish for the exaggeration of sexual characteristics and personality mannerisms. For obvious reasons, the best examples that can be cited are movie stars. The corny flamboyant female-ness of Jayne Mansfield,

Gina Lollobrigida, Jane Russell, Virginia Mayo; the exaggerated he-man-ness of Steve Reeves, Victor Mature. The great stylists of temperament and mannerism, like Bette Davis, Barbara Stanwyck, Tallulah Bankhead, Edwige Feuillière" (4).

62. Harry Benshoff, *Monsters in the Closet: Homosexuality and the Horror Film* (Manchester, UK: Manchester University Press, 1997).

63. Terry Clifford, "Burt Reynolds, Who Plays Half-Breeds Stoic about Roles," *Chicago Tribune*, April 6, 1969, F14.

64. Racho et al., *Bronze Screen*.

65. Melvin Donalson, *Masculinity in the Interracial Buddy Film* (Jefferson, NC: McFarland, 2006).

66. One *Variety* review read, "**Rio Conchos** is a big, tough, action-packed slam-bang western with as tough a set of characters as ever rode the sage. It is Old West adventure at its best. Producer David Weisbart has woven fanciful movement along with lush settings via on-the-spot color lensing in Arizona. To this, Gordon Douglas has added his own version of what a lusty western should be in the direction, getting the most from a batch of colorful characters." Variety Staff, "Rio Conchos," *Variety*, December 31, 1963, 82.

67. The brute caricature portrays Black men as innately savage, animalistic, destructive, and criminal—deserving punishment, maybe death. Black brutes are depicted as terrifying predators who target helpless victims, especially white women. A specific permutation of the brute is the Black buck. Donald Bogle was one of the first film historians to catalog stereotypes of African Americans in film. The buck caricature, as typified by Gus in D. W. Griffith's *The Birth of a Nation*, was shown to be sexually predatory and promiscuous—preying on, or seeking out, white women as his most desired prey. Within independent Black cinema, a new permutation of Black masculinity emerged in *Sweet Sweetback's Baadasssss Song*. Rather than conforming to previous mainstream representations of the Black buck, Melvin Van Peebles's representation of Sweetback takes the previous racist illustration and adapts it for his own revisionist purpose. Instead of the buck being a negative representation to both white Americans and African Americans, the African American audiences found a new hero in a Black man who stood up to his white oppressors and who did what he felt was right and enjoyable. Two years before *Sweet Sweetback*'s release, Jim Brown incarnated and revised the buck stereotype by playing a brawny Black masculine hero desired by the white actress playing a Mexican woman in *100 Rifles*. Joshua Gleich spends time deciphering what happened to Jim Brown's film persona. Joshua Gleich, "Jim Brown: From Integration to Re-segregation in *The Dirty Dozen* and *100 Rifles*," *Cinema Journal* 51, no. 1 (2011): 2.

68. Ibid.

69. Gleich writes, "The interracial sex scene at the center of *100 Rifles* precluded a similarly cohesive promotion and production. The film had to be advertised as a sex film in the North and a Western in the South. Yet the ad campaign failed insofar as the film appeared too tame for certain northern audiences and too controversial for certain southern audiences. The film itself was convoluted, as the filmmakers struggled to place Brown within the racial structures of the Western genre and the sexual taboos of race in late 1960s Hollywood. In 1967, Brown had succeeded as an integrationist action hero, but by 1969, his sexuality proved incompatible with Hollywood filmmaking and American audiences." Ibid., 5.

70. Brown, *Out of Bounds*, 152–54.

Chapter 2. Black Masculinity on Horseback

1. Richard Slotkin,

2. Ibid., 19.

3. Churchill, *Fantasies of the Master Race.*

4. Joanna Hearne, "The Cross-Heart People: Race and Inheritance in the Silent Western," *Journal of Popular Film and Television* 30, no. 4 (2003): 181.

5. John Cawelti, *The Six Gun Mystique Sequel* (Bowling Green, OH: Bowling Green State University Popular Press), 1999.

6. Basinger, *World War II Combat Film*, 4.

7. For further reference, see David Meuel, *The Noir Western: Darkness on the Range, 1943–1962* (Jefferson, NC: McFarland, 2015). Meuel demonstrates generic pliability, as do noir films like *The Pursued*, 1947; *The Treasure of the Sierra Madre*, 1948; *The Furies*, 1950; *Rancho Notorious*, 1952; and *Man in the Shadow*, 1957. There are other variants as well: the gunfighter western (*The Man Who Shot Liberty Valance*, 1962; *A Fistful of Dollars*; *The Wild Bunch*; *Butch Cassidy and the Sundance Kid*; *Unforgiven*), the melodrama (*Duel in the Sun*, 1946; *Johnny Guitar*; *Giant*, 1956; *The Searchers*, *Unforgiven*; *Flaming Star*), the musical comedy (*The Harvey Girls*, 1946; *Annie Get Your Gun*, 1950; *Calamity Jane*, 1953; *Seven Brides for Seven Brothers*), or star vehicles like those made for Black singing cowboys Herb Jeffries in the 1930s or Elvis Presley in the 1960s. Feminist westerns (*Johnny Guitar*; *Cat Ballou*; *The Ballad of Little Jo*, 1993; *Gang of Roses*, 2003) often challenge basic assumptions about the genre's political malleability.

8. *The Dick Cavett Show: Harry Belafonte and Sidney Poitier*, Season 4, Episode 219, air date May 1972.

9. Lester Keyser and Andre Ruszkowski, *The Cinema of Sidney Poitier: The Black Man's Role on the American Screen* (San Diego: A. S. Barnes, 1980), 92. "I agreed to make it soley [*sic*] because I would have a role as a Negro Cowboy. . . . No one knows the Negro contribution to the building of the West. . . . I also did the film because it gave me an opportunity to give a hero imagery to Negro children who love Westerns." Keyser and Ruszkowski cite "Poitier Shows What Films Teach," *Catholic Standard and Times*, July 28, 1967, 3.

10. Carol Bergman, *Sidney Poitier* (New York: Chelsea House Publishers, 1990), 25.

11. Ella Shohat and Robert Stam, *Unthinking Eurocentrism: Multiculturalism and the Media* (New York: Routledge, 1994,) 137.

12. Churchill, *Fantasies of the Master Race*; Shohat and Stam, *Unthinking Eurocentrism*; Aleiss, *Making the White Man's Indian*; Jacquelyn Kilpatrick, *Celluloid Indians: Native Americans and Film* (Lincoln: University of Nebraska Press, 1999).

13. Christine Bold, "Where Did the Black Rough Riders Go?" *Canadian Review of American Studies* 39, no. 3 (2009); 273–97; Quintard Taylor, "African American Men in the American West, 1528–1990," in *In Search of the Racial Frontier: African Americans in the American West, 1528–1990* (New York: W. W. Norton, 1998), 119–202.

14. Bold, "Where Did the Black Rough Riders Go?" 274.

15. Taylor, "African American Men in the American West," 103.

16. Stuart Hall, *Encoding and Decoding in the Television Discourse* (Birmingham, UK: Centre for Cultural Studies, University of Birmingham, 1973), 507–517.

17. These films are also critical of big business, the American government, masculine figures (including the military and their policies), and a turn toward historical authenticity.

18. R. Philip Loy, *Westerns in a Changing America, 1955–2000* (Jefferson, NC: McFarland), 35.

19. Richard Slotkin, *Gunfighter Nation: The Myth of the Frontier in Twentieth-Century America* (Norman: University of Oklahoma Press, 1992).

20. Henderson, *"The Searchers*: An American Dilemma."

21. Andrea Levine, "Sidney Poitier's Civil Rights: Rewriting the Mystique of White Womanhood in *Guess Who's Coming to Dinner* and *In the Heat of the Night*," *American Literature* 73, no. 2 (2001): 365.

22. Writer and composer Neal Hefti arranged for some of the biggest names in jazz and popular music and was the composer and conductor of the music for *Duel at Diablo*. See the film's press kit available at the Schomburg Center for Research in Black Culture.

23. Deborah Allison, "Title Sequences in the Western Genre: The Iconography of Action," *Quarterly Review of Film and Video* 25 (2008): 107–115.

24. "3D Film," *Wikipedia*, https://en.wikipedia.org/wiki/3D_film#Revival_(1960%E2%80%931984)_in_single_strip_format/. Martin Quigley Jr., ed., *New Screen Techniques* (New York: Quigley Publishing, 1953), 55–59. (See https://archive.org/details/newscreentechniq00mart/page/6/mode/2up?q=natural+vision.)

25. "Comin' at Ya! 3D Films through the Ages," *Matchbox Cine*, May 15, 2016, https://matchboxcineclub.com/tag/space-vision-3d/.

26. Allison, "Title Sequences in the Western Genre," 108.

27. Buffalo Soldiers originally were members of the U.S. Army's Tenth Cavalry Regiment, formed on September 21, 1866, at Fort Leavenworth, Kansas. The nickname was given to the "Negro Cavalry" by the Native American tribes they fought; the term eventually became synonymous with all of the African American regiments formed in 1866.

28. This movie could also be noted as an early precursor to movies like *Skin Game* with Louis Gossett, *100 Rifles*, *Silver Streak*, and several decades later the *Lethal Weapon* franchise with Danny Glover and Mel Gibson.

29. Shohat and Stam, *Unthinking Eurocentrism*.

30. Ralph Nelson quoted in Keyser and Ruszkowski, *Cinema of Sidney Poitier*, 92.

31. Durham and Jones, *Negro Cowboys*.

32. See the film's press kit courtesy of the Schomburg Center for Research in Black Culture.

33. Guerrero, *Framing Blackness*, 72.

34. Clifford Mason quoted in Alvin H. Marill, *The Films of Sidney Poitier* (Secaucus, NJ: Citadel Press, 1978), 141.

35. Steven Cohan, *Masked Men: Masculinity and the Movies in the Fifties* (Bloomington: Indiana University Press, 1997), 201–263. See the chapter "Why Boys Are Not Men."

36. Scott Simmon, *The Invention of the Western Film: A Cultural History of the Genre's First Half Century* (New York: Cambridge University Press, 2003), 110–12.

37. Ibid.

38. See the press kit for *Duel at Diablo* at the Schomburg Center for Research in Black Culture.

39. Lee Grant, dir. *Sidney Poitier: One Bright Light, American Masters*, Thirteen/WNET, 2000.

40. Keyser and Ruszkowski, *Cinema of Sidney Poitier*, 150. The authors are citing a *Variety* magazine article titled "U.S. Black Settlers of Wild West Pic Had to Be Directed by Poitier," *Variety*, March 17, 1971.

41. Kimberlé Crenshaw, "Demarginalizing the Intersection of Race and Sex: A Black Feminist Critique of Antidiscrimination Doctrine, Feminist Theory, and Antiracist Politics," *University of Chicago Legal Forum*, vol. 1 (1989): 139–67. I am not suggesting the western is feminist but that Poitier and Belafonte recognized the need for an intersectional perspective on the issues raised in the film.

42. George Goodman, "Durango: Poitier Meets Belafonte. Two Wary Rivals Patch Up a Fight to Make a Movie Together," *Look*, August 24, 1971, 56–61.

43. Ibid.

44. Keyser and Ruszkowski, *Cinema of Sidney Poitier*, 146.

45. "U.S. Black Settlers of Wild West Pic Had to Be Directed by Poitier," *Variety*, March 17, 1971.

46. Ibid.

47. Walter Price Burrell, *"Buck and the Preacher," Black Stars*, February 1972, 58–60.

48. Wanda Hale, "Movies, Sidney Poitier—A Star's Director," *New York Daily News*, March 26, 1972, S7.

49. Keyser and Ruszkowski, *Cinema of Sidney Poitier*, 146.

50. "The Rising Attack on Nixonomics," *Time*, February 2, 1970. http://content.time.com/time/subscriber/article/0,33009,878183,00.html/.

51. The Wounded Knee Occupation, also known as Second Wounded Knee, began on February 27, 1973, when approximately two hundred Oglala Lakota (sometimes referred to as Oglala Sioux) and followers of the American Indian Movement (AIM) seized and occupied the town of Wounded Knee, South Dakota, on the Pine Ridge Indian Reservation. The protest followed the failure of an effort of the Oglala Sioux Civil Rights Organization (OSCRO) to impeach tribal president Richard Wilson, whom they accused of corruption and abuse of opponents. Additionally, protesters criticized the United States government's failure to fulfill treaties with Native American people and demanded the reopening of treaty negotiations to hopefully arrive at fair and equitable treatment of Native Americans. See "Wounded Knee Occupation," *Wikipedia*, https://en.wikipedia.org/wiki/Wounded_Knee_Occupation/.

52. "President Obama Presents the Presidential Medal of Freedom to Sidney Poitier in Washington," United Press International, August 12, 2009.

53. Burrell, *"Buck and the Preacher."*

54. Keyser and Ruszkowski, *Cinema of Sidney Poitier*, 146.

55. Guy Flatley, "Be Thankful You're Not as Handsome as Harry," *New York Times*, July 2, 1972; section D, page 7.

56. Vincent Canby, "Poitier Directs *Buck and the Preacher*," *New York Times*, April 29, 1972, L 19.

57. Ibid.

58. Sidney Poitier, *This Life* (New York: Alfred A. Knopf, 1980), 198.

59. Bogle, *Toms, Coons, Mulattoes*, 335–36.

60. Hale, "Movies, Sidney Poitier—A Star's Director."

Chapter 3. Blaxploitation versus Black Liberation

1. Yvonne Tasker, *Spectacular Bodies: Gender, Genre and the Action Cinema* (New York: Routledge, 1993), 97.

2. Press kit for *Three the Hard Way*, Schomburg Center for Research in Black Culture.

3. Louis Paul, "Fred Williamson," in *Tales from the Cult Film Trenches: Interviews with 36 Actors from Horror, Science Fiction, and Exploitation Cinema* (Jefferson, NC: McFarland, 2014), 279.

4. Chris Wyse, "Fred Williamson . . . A Special Brand of Man," *Black Stars*, December: 56.

5. Paul, "Fred Williamson," 280.

6. "How to Survive in Hollywood between Gigs," *Ebony* 33, no. 12 (October 1978), 34.

7. Paul, "Fred Williamson," 280.

8. Woody Strode was the first to emerge. In addition to westerns and action movies, he was cast as a kind of circus strongman in movies with animal titles like *The Lion Hunters* (1951), *Bride of the Gorilla* (1951), *Androcles and the Lion*, and similarly themed jungle pictures. In the 1940s and '50s, Hollywood hadn't shed the overt racism of equating Black people with animals. Strode was usually the brawny object of the spectator's gaze within the mise-en-scène; his characters possessed a tough exterior on the outside but were usually longing for recognition of their humanity. Jim Brown was the next African American action hero to become a mainstream crossover moviestar strongman. He was the first to have an interracial love scene with a white woman (Raquel Welch in *100 Rifles*). And he emerged as an athlete-activist-turned-actor at the height of the civil rights movement in 1960.

9. In 1971 there were thirteen African American members of Congress. For comparison's sake, as of November 2021, there were fifty-eight African Americans in Congress.

10. Shirley Chisholm, *Unbought and Unbossed* (Boston: Houghton Mifflin, 1970). Decades later, filmmaker Shola Lynch titled her documentary about Shirley Chisholm's bid for the presidency *Chisholm '72: Unbought & Unbossed* (Realside Productions, 2004).

11. Paulo Freire, *Pedagogy of the Oppressed*, trans. Myra Bergman Ramos (New York: Herder and Herder, 1970).

12. She formally announced her presidential bid on January 25, 1972.

13. "By any means necessary" is a translation of a phrase used by Fanon in his 1960 Address to the Accra Positive Action Conference, "Why We Use Violence." In this address, Fanon said, "Violence in everyday behavior, violence against the past that is emptied of all substance, violence against the future, for the colonial regime presents itself as necessarily eternal. We see, therefore, that the colonized people, caught in a web of a three-dimensional violence, a meeting point of multiple, diverse, repeated, cumulative violences, are soon logically confronted by the problem of ending the colonial regime by any means necessary." Frantz Fanon, "Why We Use Violence," part 3, chapter 22, in *Alienation and Freedom* (London: Bloomsbury Academic, 2015); originally published 1960. The phrase had also been used by French intellectual Jean-Paul Sartre in his play *Dirty Hands* (1948). Later it entered the popular civil rights culture through a speech given by Malcolm X at the Organization of Afro-American Unity founding rally on June 28, 1964. It is generally considered to leave open all available tactics for the desired ends, including violence.

14. See the documentary *The Murder of Fred Hampton* and the film *Judas and the Black Messiah* (Shaka King, 2021).

15. Robin Wood, *Hollywood from Vietnam to Reagan and Beyond* (New York: Columbia University Press, 2003). See the chapter titled "The American Nightmare."

16. Earle Chisholm, "The Legend of the Bad Nigger," *Sepia*, July 1972, 62.

17. Adilifu Nama, *Super Black: American Pop Culture and Black Superheroes* (Austin: University of Texas Press, 2011), 37.

18. Don Markstein, "Lobo" (1965 character), Toonpedia, October 31, 2011, http://www.toonopedia.com/lobo1.htm/.

19. Jeffrey A. Brown, *Black Superheroes, Milestone Comics, and Their Fans* (Jackson: University Press of Mississippi, 2000), 3–4.

20. Nama, *Super Black*, 37–38.

21. Leyda, "Black Audience Westerns," 60–61.

22. Michele Wallace, *Black Macho and the Myth of the Superwoman* (New York: Dial Press, 1978). In her discussion of the sexual politics of the era, Wallace discusses the denigration of Black women both within the Black community and without. She bases her interpretation on views and publications by men like Leroy Jones, Eldridge Cleaver, and others. Wallace makes the argument that Black men sought to realize and actualize their manhood through relationships with white women. While Black women were increasingly considered less desirable as partners, they were gradually viewed as undesirable or culturally abject—that which needed to be jettisoned, cast off. Wallace writes, "She was too domineering, too strong, too aggressive, too outspoken, too castrating, too masculine. She was one of the main reasons the black man had never been properly able to take hold of his situation in this country. The black man had troubles and he would have to fight the white man to get them solved but how would he ever have the strength if his own house was not in proper order, if his wife, his woman, his mother, his sisters, who should have been his faithful servants, were undermining him at every opportunity" (91).

23. In *Stanley v. Georgia* (394 U.S. 557), the U.S. Supreme Court ruled that simply possessing obscene material was not a crime, thus implying a right to privacy.

24. In this case, "camp" refers to deliberately exaggerated characters or theatrical style. It might involve performance designed for humorous effect. "Camp" usually describes theatrical, well-mannered, hyper-macho, or flamboyantly effeminate portrayals of gender roles or those that are deliberately embellished in behavior or style.

25. Amy Abugo Ongiri, "Death Proof: Trauma, Memory, and Black Power–Era Images in Contemporary Visual Culture," *Journal of Contemporary African Art*, no. 29 (Fall 2011): 42–49.

26. James Robert Parish and George Hill, *Black Action Films: Plots, Critiques, Casts, and Credits for 235 Theatrical and Made-for-Television Releases* (Jefferson, NC: McFarland, 1989), 201.

27. E. Chisholm, "Legend of the Bad Nigger," 56.

28. Obituaries: Wesley L. Bliss; Anthropologist, Geologist, July 18, 1996. "Wesley L. Bliss, a renowned academic and 45-year Ojai resident, died Saturday. He was 91. Born on a farm in Greeley, Colo., Bliss attended college in the same city, graduating with a bachelor's degree in geography. In the 1930s, Bliss worked on several paleontological and archeological sites around the western hemisphere, including a stint at the La Brea Tar Pits in Los Angeles, a paleontological survey of Mexico, and an exploration of the Bering Straits in search of evidence of early man's crossing into the Americas. Bliss graduated from the University of New Mexico in 1936 with a master's degree in anthropology. It was at the university that he met his future wife, Shirley. They married in 1938. In 1942, Bliss traveled to Pittsburgh to help locate the remains of

Fort Pitt, which had been buried under city streets. The site was later turned into a park." (*L.A. Times*, July 18, 1996)

29. E. Chisholm, "Legend of the Bad Nigger," 56.

30. Obviously, John Brown was not African American, but he was a pioneer for Black freedom. A pioneer is commonly defined as someone who develops or is one of the first to use or apply a new method, an area of knowledge, or activity. A pioneer is also someone who redefines our relationships to ideas, techniques, and knowledge.

31. E. Chisholm, "Legend of the Bad Nigger," 62.

32. Ibid., 54.

33. George Coleman, "Nigger Charley Doesn't Bother Fred Williamson," *Atlanta Daily World*, July 6, 1972, 3.

34. Erica Moiah James, "*Every Nigger Is a Star*: Reimagining Blackness from Post–Civil Rights America to the Post-independence Caribbean," *Black Camera* 8, no. 1 (2016): 55–83. James's excellent essay considers the relationship between the *Nigger Charley* trilogy and a missing but intriguing Caribbean blaxploitation film titled *Every Nigger Is a Star* (Calvin Lockhart, 1974).

35. Doris Black, "Hollywood's New King of Ego," *Sepia* 22, August 1973, 37–43. There are competing accounts of how much money the film earned at the box office. According to James Robert Parish and George Hill, the film earned $3,000,000 in domestic film rentals on an estimated production cost of $400,000. See their book *Black Action Films*. However, journalist Doris Black reported that the film earned $12 million. Black's figures probably include foreign rentals.

36. E. Chisholm, "Legend of the Bad Nigger," 56.

37. According to George M. Coleman of the *Atlanta Daily World*, "He [Williamson] does not consider himself a civil rights activist. 'I'm a Fred Williamson fighter,' he said. . . . When the chips are down, I feel that each person fights for survival regardless of all the talk about helping others. . . . I figure that by doing my own thing somebody else can follow and this benefits racial progress." See Coleman, "Nigger Charlie Doesn't Bother Fred Williamson," 3.

38. Paul, "Fred Williamson," 280.

39. Jason Winters, "Fred Williamson: The Sexy Superman," *Black Stars*, February 1978, 20–24.

40. Black, "Hollywood's New King of Ego," 37–43.

41. Paul, "Fred Williamson," 279.

42. E. Chisholm, "Legend of the Bad Nigger," 54–60, 62.

43. Realist films often define themselves as being in opposition to dominant commercial cinema. But in the case of blaxploitation movies, we see a combination of realist and commercial Hollywood cinematic practices. Films that inscribe themselves within the realist tendency often challenge the rules of verisimilitude that dominate Hollywood realism. Realism brings to the screen individuals and situations often marginalized by mainstream cinema and society. Realism makes visible unseen groups, and makes audible unheard voices. In this sense, realism has been considered a fundamentally political art form. If cinema participates in the construction of what a society knows and says about itself, realist films make visible individuals and situations previously left unseen. Showing actors, faces, people who had rarely or never been shown on the screen, or who had only been seen through stereotypes, was part of cinematic realism's way of reconfiguring the world. Realism situates its characters

socially and economically, and economic hardship is often one of the motivating forces of the realist films' plot. To the extent that it shows characters and situations usually unseen, blaxploitation movies are striving for realism. But they also feature conventional narratives, observe rules of continuity, privilege heterosexual male protagonists, objectify women as objects of the gaze, and feature spectacle rather than contemplation. Hence blaxploitation's commercialism.

44. The phrase "possessive investment in whiteness" is from George Lipsitz, *The Possessive Investment in Whiteness: How White People Profit from Identity Politics* (Philadelphia: Temple University Press, 1998). "Disenfranchisement movements are of great importance to all who are concerned with the nature of black-white encounters in America. During this era African Americans were experiencing acute social and economic repression, while political freedom faded after the brief Reconstruction experiment. With the 'Grandfather Clauses,' Mississippi, South Carolina, and Louisiana were able to abrogate 'the national commitment to black citizenship with clever circumvention of the Fifteenth Amendment.'" Leon Prather, "The Red Shirt Movement in North Carolina, 1898–1900," *Journal of Negro History* 62, no. 2 (1977): 174.

45. Clifford Manlove, "From *Django* to *Django Unchained*: Love Narratives in the Global South," in *The Western in the Global South* ed. Mary Ellen Higgins, Rita Keresztesi, and Dayna Oscherwitz, 60–78 (London: Routledge, 2015).

46. Randall Kennedy, *Nigger: The Strange Career of a Troublesome Word* (New York: Pantheon Books, 2002), 34–43.

47. Ibid.

48. Excluding the group of female-centered westerns, of which there are several. Titles include, but are not limited to, *Destry Rides Again, Johnny Guitar, Cat Ballou, The Ballad of Little Jo, Gang of Roses*, and *Ride Sweet, Die Slow*.

49. Kimmel, "Masculinity as Homophobia," 214.

50. Women in classic westerns released before 1960, whether cheerleaders or damsels in distress, functioned as a kind of currency between men. But revisionist (read: Black and feminist) westerns like Poitier's *Buck and the Preacher*, Nicholas Ray's *Johnny Guitar*, and George Stevens's *Giant* cast women and people of color as protagonists and agents of action.

51. Tassilo Schneider, "Finding a New Heimat in the Wild West: Karl May and the German Western of the 1960s," in *Back in the Saddle: New Essays on the Western*, ed. Edward Buscombe and Roberta Pearson, 141–59 (London: British Film Institute, 1998).

52. E. Chisholm, "Legend of the Bad Nigger," 59.

53. While Lynn is referring to the Caribbean and Latin America, his framework and understanding applies to race relations in North America, specifically the United States. Lynn writes, "The term 'pigmentocracy' has recently been adopted by social scientists to describe societies in which wealth and social status are determined by skin color. There are numerous pigmentocracies throughout the world, and they all have the remarkable characteristic that invariably the light-skinned peoples have the highest social status. These are followed by the brown-skinned, who occupy intermediate positions, and finally by the black-skinned who are at the bottom of the social hierarchy." Richard Lynn, "Pigmentocracy: Racial Hierarchies in the Caribbean and Latin America," *Occidental Quarterly* 8, no. 2 (2008): 25–44; Charles W. Mills, *The Racial Contract* (Ithaca, NY: Cornell University Press, 1999).

54. Harris, *Boys, Boyz, Bois*.

55. Readers of these press junkets could contact the Field Advertising and Publicity Department at Paramount Pictures. Paramount Pictures press kit courtesy of the Schomburg Center for Research in Black Culture, Manuscripts Division, New York Public Library.

56. See the press kit for *The Soul of Nigger Charley*.

57. See film press kit, courtesy of Schomburg Center for Research in Black Culture.

58. Ongiri, "Death Proof," 42–49.

59. Ibid., 44.

60. See the "Official Campaign Material from Allied Artists," press kit, courtesy of the Schomburg Center for Research in Black Culture.

61. D'Urville Martin quoted in Angela E. Smith, "Producer of *Boss Nigger* Just That," *New York Amsterdam News* (March 1, 1975), D17.

62. Bryan Rolli, "'Black Panther' Proves, Yet Again, That Diversity Sells in Hollywood," *Forbes*, February 19, 2018, https://www.forbes.com/sites/bryanrolli/2018/02/19/black -panther-proves-diversity-sells-hollywood/?sh=5c49e9e63198/. See also Ashton Yount, "Black-Oriented Films Can Be Highly Profitable When Marketed to All Audiences, Study Finds," Annenberg School of Communications research study, published online April 26, 2018, https://www.asc.upenn.edu/news-events/news/black-oriented-films -can-be-highly-profitable-when-marketed-all-audiences-study-finds/.

63. Dyer, *White: Essays on Race and Culture*, 122. See the section "The Glow of White Women" (122–42). For best results, see the twentieth-anniversary edition of the book.

64. Wallace, *Black Macho and the Myth of the Superwoman*. Wallace offers a well-known critique of the fractured relations between Black men and women in this tome.

65. Mia Mask, *Divas on Screen: Black Women in American Film* (Urbana: University of Illinois Press, 2009), 70–78.

66. *Sabata* (Gianfranco Parolini, 1969) and *Return of Sabata* (Gianfranco Parolini, 1971). The middle film in the trilogy is *Adiós, Sabata* (Gianfranco Parolini, 1970) but Lee Van Cleef did not appear in that film.

67. Tom Milne, "*Take a Hard Ride*," *Monthly Film Bulletin*, January 1, 1975, 244.

68. Vincent Canby cited in Parish and Hill, *Black Action Films*, 300.

69. B. G., review of *Take a Hard Ride*, *Independent Film Journal* 76, no. 12 (November 12, 1975): 9.

70. Milne, "*Take a Hard Ride*," 244.

71. "*Take a Hard Ride*: A Challenge for Right," *New Pittsburgh Courier*, City Edition, September 20, 1975, 17. See also the reviews "Smooth Talking Gambler in *Take a Hard Ride*," *Afro-American*, August 30, 1975, 11, and "Take a Hard Ride Coming," *Chicago Defender*, July 31, 1975, 14. The *Pittsburgh Courier* was an African American weekly newspaper published in Pittsburgh, Pennsylvania, from 1907 until October 22, 1966. By the 1930s the *Courier* was one of the top Black newspapers in the United States. It was acquired in 1965 by John H. Sengstacke, a major Black publisher and owner of the *Chicago Defender*. He reopened the paper in 1967 as the *New Pittsburgh Courier*, making it one of his four newspapers for the African American audience.

72. Leone quoted in Bruschini et al., *Western all'Italiana*, 29.

73. Vincent Canby, "'*Take a Hard Ride*': Black Western Goes on in Fits and Starts," *New York Times*, October 30, 1975.

74. "*Take a Hard Ride* with Jim Brown," *Atlanta Daily World*, August 26, 1975.

Chapter 4. Harlem Rides the Range

1. Director Jeff Kanew also edited the film because for years before making his first picture, Kanew had been writing, producing, and editing trailers, TV spots, and radio spots for major film companies under the auspices of Utopia Productions.

2. See the transcript of my interview with Jeff Kanew in the appendix.

3. See the press kit for *Black Rodeo*, available at the Schomburg Center for Research in Black Culture located in Harlem, New York.

4. The PRCA is the largest rodeo organization in the world. It sanctions events in the United States, Canada, Mexico, and Brazil, with members from those countries as well as others. Its championship event is the National Finals Rodeo. The organization was created in 1936 when a group of cowboys walked out of a rodeo at Boston Garden to protest the actions of rodeo promoter W. T. Johnson, who refused to add the cowboys' entry fees to the rodeo's total purse.

5. See the press kit for *Black Rodeo*, available at the Schomburg Center for Research in Black Culture located in Harlem, New York.

6. "Remembering Muhammad Ali and His Role in Cowboys of Color," *Wrangler Network*, June 10, 2016, http://wranglernetwork.com/portfolio-view/remembering -muhammed-ali-and-his-role-in-cowboys-of-color/.

7. Corey Kilgannon, "Black Cowboys Ride the Range in Queens, and Keep a Sharp Lookout for Traffic," *New York Times*, October 10, 2006. See also Kristen Sollee, "Brooklyn's Black Cowboys," *Stay Free!* no. 24, 20. The Federation of Black Cowboys is an organization that keeps alive the heritage of the forgotten Black horsemen of the Old West. They keep their horses at the Cedar Lane Stables, at the junction of Conduit Avenue and Linden Boulevard. *Stay Free!* was a Brooklyn-based nonprofit magazine about the politics of culture. It was founded in 1993 by Carrie McLaren. In March 2007, McLaren announced that *Stay Free!* would no longer be published in print, although it would continue online. The last print issue appeared in 2008, and the website is no longer online. In 2009 Carrie McLaren and Jason Torchinsky of *Stay Free!* released the book *Ad Nauseam: A Survivor's Guide to American Consumer Culture* (New York: Faber and Faber, 2009).

8. In 1988 Mayisha Akbar founded the Compton Jr. Posse to provide local youth with a safe alternative to the streets, one that connected them with the rich legacy of Black cowboys in American culture. From Mayisha's youth organization came several cowboys of today: Black men and women from Compton for whom the ranch provides camaraderie, respite from violence, trauma, and recovery from incarceration.

9. Dillon Hayes, "A Black Cowboy Confronts the Whitewashed History of the West," *New York Times*, Opinion: Op-Docs, June 16, 2020, https://www.nytimes .com/2020/06/16/opinion/all-i-have-to-offer-you-is-me-black-cowboys.html?search ResultPosition=1/.

10. Andrew Chow, "Old Town, New Road: How 20-Year-Old Upstart Lil Nas X Used the Internet to Beat Nashville at Its Own Game," *Time*, August 26, 2019, 54–59. According to Chow, this new "country-trap concoction" is a combination of country-trap (a Southern-born hip-hop subgenre propelled by vicious bass and crawling tempos) with more familiar or traditional country music.

11. Jon Meacham and Tim McGraw, "Whose Country? The Distinctive American Music," *Time*, August 26, 2019, 50–53.

12. Chow, "Old Town, New Road," 54–59.

13. Chris Rock, Haha Davis, Rico Nasty, Diplo, Young Kio, and Vince Staples appear in the "Old Town Road" music video.

14. Country music fans reportedly boycotted the Wrangler brand due to their recent partnership with rising star Lil Nas X. The jeans brand launched its new "capsule collection" with Lil Nas X. The line was inspired by a lyric from the rapper's number one hit "Old Town Road." In the song he sings, "Cowboy hat from Gucci / Wrangler on my booty." To paraphrase the *Vibe* article, it was unclear whether fans were boycotting because they believed Lil Nas X was mocking country music or because they resented the musical syncretism between country and rap. https://www.vibe.com/2019/05/lil-nas-x-partnership-wrangler-boycotted-angry -country-music-fans/.

15. Melodie McDaniel, *Riding through Compton* (Seattle, WA: Minor Matters, 2018). The press release for the book read as follows: "According to the US Census Bureau, one-third of the population of Compton, California is under the age of eighteen and one-fourth of its population lives at or below the poverty line. Despite the latter statistic, Compton has been home to significant athletes, musicians, scientists, writers, and pioneering public officials. Over decades young people have found a way to overcome the socioeconomic odds against them when their life begins in this city. For the last thirty years, the streets of Compton have been the stomping grounds of a youth riding and equestrian program under the leadership of Mayisha Akbar." https://www.comptonjrposse.org/?mc_cid=c2f5b3f4ba&mc_eid=cf040a72dd/.

16. Rory Doyle was born October 15, 1983. He is an American photographer based in Cleveland, Mississippi. Doyle's ongoing project, *Delta Hill Riders*, about African American cowboys and cowgirls, won *Smithsonian* magazine's annual Photo Contest and the Zeiss Photography Award at the Sony World Photography Awards.

17. Matthew Impelli, "Black Texas Cowboys on Horseback Protest George Floyd's Death in Viral Video," *Newsweek*, June 3, 2020. Also see Walter Thompson-Hernández's *The Compton Cowboys: The New Generation of Cowboys in America's Urban Heartland* (New York: Harper Collins, 2020).

18. Kristina Bravo, "Compton Cowboys Ride Alongside Marchers to MLK Memorial in Demonstration against Police Violence," KTLA broadcast, June 7, 2020, https://ktla .com/news/local-news/compton-cowboys-hundreds-others-march-to-mlk-memorial -in-protest-against-police-violence/.

19. Tim Stanley, "Tulsan Charles Evans, 'The Voice' of Black Rodeo, Dies at 88," *Tulsa World*, August 31, 2018.

20. Luther H. Martin, Huck Gutman, and Patrick H. Hutton, eds., *Technologies of the Self: A Seminar with Michel Foucault* (Amherst: University of Massachusetts Press, 1988).

21. Carol Tulloch, *The Birth of Cool: Style Narratives of the African Diaspora* (London: Bloomsbury), 128–33.

22. Stuart Hall, "Cultural Identity and Cinematic Representation," *Frameworks: The Journal of Cinema and Media*, no. 36 (1989): 68–81.

23. *Black Rodeo* (Jeff Kanew, 1972).

24. Ibid.

25. Bill Nichols, *Representing Reality: Issues and Concepts in Documentary* (Bloomington: Indiana University Press, 1992).

26. *Black Rodeo* (Jeff Kanew, 1972).

27. Ibid.

28. Cherokee Productions was first incorporated by James Garner in 1965 and has continued to be a recognized domestic and international brand. For more information, see the company's website, now run by Garner's daughter Gigi Garner. https://www.cherokeeproductions.com/.

29. Parish and Hill, *Black Action Films*, 266–67.

30. Roger Greenspun, "White and Black Play the *Skin Game* in Film," *New York Times*, October 1, 1971, 34.

31. Gene Siskel, "*Skin Game*," *Chicago Tribune*, October 19, 1971, A5.

32. Gary Arnold, "On *Skin Game*," *Washington Post*, October 9, 1971, C1.

33. Willie Hamilton, "If Your Sensitivity Shows, Don't See *Skin Game*," *New York Amsterdam News*, October 9, 1971, B10.

34. Howell Raines, "Con Artist, Tricks Key *Skin Game*," *Atlanta Constitution*, November 8, 1971, 12A.

35. "Master-Slave Bid to Swindle Big Money Is Theme of the New Film Here," *Philadelphia Tribune*, October 5, 1971, 16.

36. Parish and Hill, *Black Action Films*, 267.

37. Ibid. See also Maurice Peterson's article in *Essence* magazine, 1972.

38. Wallace, *Black Macho and the Myth of the Superwoman*.

39. Ibid., 28–29.

40. Ibid., 30. She writes, "The black man of the 1960s found himself wondering why it had taken him so long to realize he had an old score to settle. Yes, yes, he wanted freedom, equality, all of that. But what he really wanted was to be a man. America had made one point painfully clear. As long as the black man did not have access to white women, he was not a man."

41. Parish and Hill, *Black Action Films*, 308.

42. Jackie Wang, *Carceral Capitalism* (South Pasadena, CA: Semiotext(e), 2018).

43. Michel Foucault, *Discipline & Punish: The Birth of the Prison* (New York: Random House, Inc. 1995, originally published in France as *Surveiller et Punir: Naissance de la prison* [Paris: Editions Gallimard, 1975]).

Chapter 5. Westerns and Westploitation

1. These science fiction movies include *The Thing from Another World* (Christian Nyby, 1951); *Them* (Gordon Douglas, 1954); *The Day the Earth Stood Still* (Robert Wise, 1951); *When Worlds Collide* (Rudolph Mate, 1951); *Cat Women of the Moon* (Arthur Hilton, 1953); *Forbidden Planet* (Fred Wilcox, 1956); *Invasion of the Body Snatchers* (Don Siegel, 1956); *She Devil* (Kurt Neumann, 1957); *The Incredible Shrinking Man* (Jack Arnold, 1957); *The Invasion of Saucer Men* (Edward L. Cahn, 1957); *Attack of the 50-Foot Woman* (Nathan Juran, 1958); *The Blob* (Irvin Shortess Yeaworth, 1958); *I Married a Monster from Outer Space* (Gene Fowler, 1958); *Teenagers from Outer Space* (Tom Graeff, 1959); *The Wasp Woman* (Roger Corman, 1959); and *The World, the Flesh & the Devil* (Ronald MacDougall, 1959). These titles exemplify of the proliferation of sci-fi cinema in the 1950s. In terms of science fiction on television at the time, *Captain Video* ran from 1949 to 1955 on the DuMont Television Network; *Tom Corbett Space Cadet* was one of only six TV series to appear on all four networks (ABC, CBS,

NBC, and DuMont Television at the same time) from 1950 to 1955; *Buck Rogers* had a failed debut in 1950; and *Rod Brown of the Rocket Rangers* ran from 1953 to 1954 on CBS.

2. Manthia Diawara, "Black Spectatorship: Problems of Identification and Resistance," *Screen* 29, no. 4 (1988): 66–79. This essay has been rewritten, revisited, and widely anthologized and is cited elsewhere in this book. However, I cite this version here to make the point that Diawara's thesis has been available for academic film studies for several decades.

3. Churchill, *Fantasies of the Master Race*.

4. Saidiya Hartman, *Scenes of Subjection: Terror, Slavery, and Self-Making in Nineteenth Century America* (New York: Oxford University Press, 1997).

5. Jeymes Samuel, "There No Right Version of Wrong History," *Entertainment Weekly*, Issue 1619/1620, November 2021, 112. *The Harder They Fall* writer-director Jeymes Samuel loves westerns, but note here how the genre's history is marred by acts of omission.

6. As mentioned earlier, "Black westploitation" is a term used throughout this book to refer to exploitation westerns. It is a term applied to specific films made during this period but not all of them. It refers to a particular mode of production and a resulting cinematic style. "Blaxploitation" is a subgenre of exploitation film that emerged during the early 1970s. The films, while popular, suffered backlash for their disproportionate numbers of stereotypical characters showing bad or questionable motives, including roles as criminals. However, the films ranked among the first in which Black characters and communities were the heroes and subjects of film and television rather than sidekicks, villains, or victims of brutality. Blaxploitation films were originally aimed at urban African American audiences, but the genre's audience appeal broadened, traversing across racial, ethnic, and class lines. Film studios realized the potential profit of expanding the audiences for blaxploitation films across racial lines. "Westploitation" is a subgenre of Westerns. They were cheaply made, low-quality, B-western movies; produced quickly, and recycled familiar themes, characters, plot devices, and cinematic clichés. They were often utilizing deliberate camp aesthetics with an emphasis on failed seriousness. The use of these familiar and "exploitation cinema" devices attracted critical attention and garnered a cult following among audiences. Therefore, Black westploitation films (or "blaxploi-westerns") fused the two. The terms "Black westploitation" and "blaxploiwestern" are used interchangeably and refer to the fusion of some blaxploitation themes, actors, and political rhetoric with westploitation filmmaking practices. In this book I am referring to the production of a series of Black westploitation films including, but not limited to, the *Nigger Charley* trilogy.

7. A culture war is a conflict between social groups and the struggle for dominance of their values, beliefs, and practices. It commonly refers to hot-button topics on which there is general societal disagreement and polarization in societal values is seen. The term "culture war" is often used to describe contemporary politics in the United States with issues such as abortion, feminism, sexuality, pornography, multiculturalism, and other cultural conflicts based on values, morality, and lifestyle being described as the major political cleavage. Roger Chapman and James Ciment, eds., *Culture Wars in America: An Encyclopedia of Issues, Viewpoints and Voices* (London: Routledge, 2014).

8. Among his appointees was Donald T. Regan as secretary of the treasury, who had been Merrill Lynch chairman; Malcolm Baldridge as secretary of commerce, who had

served as chairman of the profitable Scovill Inc.; construction millionaire Raymond Donovan as secretary of labor; and James Watt, an anti-environmentalist lawyer, who became secretary of the interior. For further reading, see Arthur L. Tolson and Q. R. Hand Jr., "Reaganomics and Black Americans," *Black Scholar* 16, no. 5 (1985): 37–49. Or read Maurice A. St. Pierre, "Reaganomics and Its Implications for African-American Family Life," *Journal of Black Studies* 21, no. 3 (1991): 325–40.

9. Editors, "War on Drugs," History.com, https://www.history.com/topics/crime/the-war-on-drugs, May 31, 2017; updated December 17, 2019.

10. Wang, *Carceral Capitalism*.

11. Ibid., 19.

12. S. Craig Watkins, *Representing: Hip Hop Culture and the Production of Black Cinema* (Chicago: University of Chicago Press, 1998).

13. On June 22, 1982, Turks, a Black New York City transit worker, and two Black co-workers were in the Gravesend section of Brooklyn. During a stop at a bodega, the men were confronted by a group of white men. To avoid a conflict, Turks and his friends tried to get away when their car broke down. The mob of white men, which had grown to about fifteen to twenty individuals, dragged Turks out of the car and fatally beat him with clubs and bats.

14. Artist Michael Stewart was arrested for spraying graffiti at the First Avenue station on the L train's Brooklyn-bound platform. Transit police officer John Kostick found Stewart scrawling "RQS" on the wall and had him arrested. Doctors confirmed he was brain dead and had hemorrhaged in a way that suggested he had either been choked or strangled. Stewart died on September 28, 1983, thirteen days after his arrest.

15. On December 22, 1984, four men (Barry Allen, Troy Canty, Darrell Cabey, and James Ramseur) were shot and wounded by Bernhard Goetz after they approached him on a New York City subway train in Manhattan.

16. On December 20, 1986, a young man was murdered (and another severely beaten) in Howard Beach, Queens, New York, in a racially charged incident that heightened racial tensions in the city. The murdered man was twenty-three-year-old Michael Griffith (March 2, 1963–December 20, 1986), who was from Trinidad, had immigrated to the United States in 1973, and lived in Crown Heights, Brooklyn. He was killed after being hit by a car as he was chased onto a highway by a mob of white youths who had beaten him and his friends. Griffith's death was the second of three infamous racially motivated killings of Black men by white mobs in New York City in the 1980s. The other two incidents involved victims Willie Turks in 1982 and Yusuf Hawkins in 1989.

17. For a brief but thorough explanation of this image, see either Donald Bogle, *Toms, Coons, Mulattoes, Mammies, and Bucks* or the Jim Crow Museum at Ferris State University in Big Rapids, Michigan. The museum website has posted a description that references literature and film: "The brute caricature portrays black men as innately savage, animalistic, destructive, and criminal—deserving punishment, maybe death. This brute is a fiend, a sociopath, an anti-social menace. Black brutes are depicted as hideous, terrifying predators who target helpless victims, especially white women. Charles H. Smith (1893), writing in the 1890s, claimed, 'A bad negro is the most horrible creature upon the earth, the most brutal and merciless' (p. 181). . . .

"During slavery the dominant caricatures of blacks—Mammy, Coon, Tom, and picaninny—portrayed them as childlike, ignorant, docile, groveling, and generally harmless. These portrayals were pragmatic and instrumental. Proponents of slavery created and promoted images of blacks that justified slavery and soothed white consciences. If slaves were childlike, for example, then a paternalistic institution where masters acted as quasi-parents to their slaves was humane, even morally right. More importantly, slaves were rarely depicted as brutes because that portrayal might have become a self-fulfilling prophecy.

"During the Radical Reconstruction period (1867–1877), many white writers argued that without slavery—which supposedly suppressed their animalistic tendencies—blacks were reverting to criminal savagery. The belief that the newly-emancipated blacks were a 'black peril' continued into the early 1900s. Writers like the novelist Thomas Nelson Page (1904) lamented that the slavery-era 'good old darkies' had been replaced by the 'new issue' (blacks born after slavery), whom he described as 'lazy, thriftless, intemperate, insolent, dishonest, and without the most rudimentary elements of morality' (pp. 80, 163). Page, who helped popularize the images of cheerful and devoted Mammies and Sambos in his early books, became one of the first writers to introduce a literary black brute. In 1898 he published *Red Rock*, a Reconstruction novel, with the heinous figure of Moses, a loathsome and sinister black politician. Moses tried to rape a white woman: 'He gave a snarl of rage and sprang at her like a wild beast' (pp. 356–358). He was later lynched for 'a terrible crime.'" Dr. David Pilgrim, "The Brute Caricature," Jim Crow Museum, Ferris State University, https://www.ferris.edu/HTMLS/news/jimcrow/brute/homepage.htm/.

This stereotype exists today in many other iterations, including but not limited to O. J. Simpson, Willie Horton, or any Black man, whether criminal or not, who, as a result of the "fact of his blackness," to use Fanon's phrase, is perceived as a threat.

18. Yusef Hawkins was a sixteen-year-old Black teenager from East New York, Brooklyn, who was shot to death on August 23, 1989, in Bensonhurst, a predominantly Italian American working-class neighborhood in the New York City borough of Brooklyn. Hawkins and three friends were attacked by a crowd of ten to thirty white youths, with at least seven of them wielding baseball bats. One, armed with a handgun, shot Hawkins twice in the chest, killing him. Hawkins had gone to Bensonhurst that night with three friends to inquire about a used 1982 Pontiac automobile that was for sale. The group's attackers had been lying in wait for Black youths whom they believed had dated a neighborhood girl. Hawkins and his friends walked onto the ambushers' block unaware that local residents were preparing racist attacks against Black youth. After the murder of Hawkins, police confirmed that he had not in any way been involved with the neighborhood girl whom the killers believed Hawkins was dating.

19. Manthia Diawara, "Black American Cinema: The New Realism," in *Black American Cinema,* ed. Manthia Diawara, 3–25 (New York: Routledge, 1993).

20. I am placing this film in a cohort of films along with *Boyz N the Hood, Menace II Society, Mi Vida Loca* (Allison Anders, 1993), and *Set It Off* (F. Gary Gray, 1996).

21. Manning Marable, *How Capitalism Underdeveloped Black America: Problems in Race, Political Economy, and Society* (Boston: South End Press, 1983).

22. John Clark, *"Posse," Premiere* 6 (1993), 84.

23. John Hoberman, *Darwin's Athletes: How Sport Has Damaged Black America and Preserved the Myth of Race* (Boston: Houston Mifflin, 1997).

24. *Posse* (Mario Van Peebles, 1993).

25. "Beginning in the early 1870s, railroad construction in the United States increased dramatically. Prior to 1871, approximately 45,000 miles of track had been

laid. Between 1871 and 1900, another 170,000 miles were added to the nation's growing railroad system. Much of the growth can be attributed to the building of the transcontinental railroads. In 1862, Congress passed the Pacific Railway Act, which authorized the construction of a transcontinental railroad. The first such railroad was completed on May 10, 1869. By 1900, four additional transcontinental railroads connected the eastern states with the Pacific Coast. . . . Railroad construction crews were not only subjected to extreme weather conditions, they had to lay tracks across and through many natural geographical features, including rivers, canyons, mountains, and desert. Like other large economic opportunity situations in the expanding nation, the railroad construction camps attracted all types of characters, almost all of whom were looking for ways to turn a quick profit, legally or illegally. Life in the camps was often very crude and rough." "Railroads in the Late 19th Century," Library of Congress, https://www.loc.gov/classroom-materials/united-states-history-primary-source-timeline/rise-of-industrial-america-1876-1900/railroads-in-late-19th-century/#:~:text=Life%20in%20the%20camps%20was,generally%20tied%20the%20country%20together.

26. "May 1, 1992: Rodney King Asks, 'Can We All Get Along?'" *New York Times*, May 1, 2012. See https://learning.blogs.nytimes.com/2012/05/01/may-1-1992-victim-rodney-king-asks-can-we-all-get-along/. "By the time law enforcement, the California Army National Guard, the United States Army, and the United States Marine Corps restored order, the riots had resulted in 63 deaths, 2,383 injuries, more than 7,000 fires, damage to 3,100 businesses, and nearly $1 billion in financial losses." For more, see "Rodney King," *Wikipedia*, https://en.wikipedia.org/wiki/Rodney_King/.

27. Melvin Van Peebles is best known for *Story of a Three-Day Pass* (*La Permission*) (1967), *Watermelon Man* (1970), and *Sweet Sweetback's Baadasssss Song*, but he has several other writing and directing credits as well.

28. The term "grandfather clause" originated in late nineteenth-century legislation and constitutional amendments passed by a number of U.S. Southern states, which created new requirements for literacy tests, payment of poll taxes, and/or residency and property restrictions to register to vote. The clauses restricted voter registration, effectively preventing African Americans from voting. States in some cases exempted those whose ancestors (grandfathers) had the right to vote before the Civil War, or as of a particular date, from such requirements. The intent and effect of such rules was to prevent poor and illiterate African American former slaves and their descendants from voting but without denying poor and illiterate whites the right to vote. Although these original grandfather clauses were eventually ruled unconstitutional, the terms "grandfather clause" and "grandfather" have been adapted to other uses. The original grandfather clauses were contained in new state constitutions and Jim Crow laws passed between 1890 and 1908 by white-dominated state legislatures, including Alabama, Georgia, Louisiana, North Carolina, Oklahoma, and Virginia. They restricted voter registration, effectively preventing African Americans from voting. Racial restrictions on voting in place before 1870 were nullified by the Fifteenth Amendment.

29. Prather, "Red Shirt Movement," 174–84. "The Red Shirts were white supremacist paramilitary terrorist groups that were active in the late 19th century in the last years of, and after the end of, the Reconstruction era. Red Shirt groups originated in Mississippi in 1875, when anti-Reconstruction private terror units adopted red shirts to make themselves more visible and threatening to Southern Republicans, both whites and freedmen. Similar groups in the Carolinas also adopted red shirts. . . .

During the 1876, 1898, and 1900 campaigns in North Carolina, the Red Shirts played prominent roles in intimidating non-Democratic Party voters." "Red Shirts (United States)," *Wikipedia*, https://en.wikipedia.org/wiki/Red_Shirts_(United_States)/. See also articles documenting white supremacist riots, such as "White Men Show Their Determination to Rid Themselves of Negro Rule: A Thousand Red Shirts," *Morning Star*, November 2, 1898, *Special Star Telegram* (Wilmington, NC), 1.

30. In December 1969, Fred Hampton was shot and killed in his bed during a pre-dawn raid at his Chicago apartment by a tactical unit of the Cook County State's Attorney's Office in conjunction with the Chicago Police Department.

31. Alphonse Pierre, "An Introduction to Milwaukee's Fast-Emerging Rap Scene," *Pitchfork*, March 5, 2021, https://pitchfork.com/thepitch/milwaukee-rap-biggie -netflix-papoose-cereal/. For more discussion of the formal and stylistic similarities between rap and westerns see chapter 5 of Blake Allmendinger's *Imagining the African American West* (Lincoln and London: University of Nebraska Press, 2005), 79. Allmendinger writes: "The similarities between Westerns and rap music are broadly superficial as well as highly specific. Both genres typically feature male protagonists (gun slingers, urban "cowboys" or "gangstas"). These heroes—or anti-heroes—have uneasy relationships with frontier civilization and with contemporary urban society. They glorify violence and vigilante behavior (in Westerns, a "posse" is a deputized mob; in hip hop it refers to a street gang or, more benignly, to a group of male associates). Both cowboys and homeboys tend to be territorial. Cowboys ride the unfenced range, protecting their turf from invading railroaders, farmers and Native Americans. Gangs stake their claim to urban locations, challenging the authority of rival gangs, local police and neighborhood residents."

32. R. Thomas Dye, "Rosewood, Florida: The Destruction of an African American Community," *The Historian* 58, no. 3 (1996): 605–622. For additional reading, see Edward González-Tennant, *The Rosewood Massacre: An Archaeology and History of Intersectional Violence* (Gainesville: University of Florida Press, 2018).

33. Gary Moore, "The Rosewood Massacre," *St. Petersburg Times*, July 27, 1982.

34. Dye, "Rosewood, Florida," 605.

35. Abigail Higgins, "Red Summer of 1919: How Black WWI Vets Fought Back against Racist Mobs," History.com, July 26, 2019, https://www.history.com/news/ red-summer-1919-riots-chicago-dc-great-migration/.

36. Dye, "Rosewood, Florida," 607.

37. Ibid., 611.

38. Ibid., 615.

39. Freemasonry or Masonry consists of fraternal organizations that trace their origins to the local fraternities of stonemasons that (from the end of the fourteenth century) regulated the qualifications of stonemasons and their interaction with authorities and clients. Freemasonry evolved from the guilds of stonemasons and cathedral builders of the Middle Ages. With the decline of cathedral building, some lodges of operative (working) masons began to accept honorary members to bolster their declining membership. From a few of these lodges developed modern symbolic or speculative Freemasonry, which particularly in the seventeenth and eighteenth centuries adopted the rites and trappings of ancient religious orders and of chivalric brotherhoods. In 1717 the first Grand Lodge, an association of lodges, was founded in England.

40. "[Walter Van Tilburg] Clark's first published novel, *The Ox-Bow Incident* (1940), was successful and is often considered to be the first modern Western, without the usual clichés and formulaic plots of the genre. The novel is a story about a lynch mob mistaking three innocent travelers for cattle rustlers suspected of murder. After the travelers are hanged, the lynch mob finds that they killed the wrong suspects. The novel's themes include an examination of frontier law and order, as well as culpability. . . . In 1943 [it] was adapted into a movie starring Henry Fonda and Harry Morgan." "Walter Van Tilburg Clark," *Wikipedia*, https://en.wikipedia.org/wiki/Walter_Van_ Tilburg_Clark/. It's a film that has been aptly described as "a master class in dramatic escalation." Andy Crump, Derek Hill, Joe Pettit Jr., Amanda Schurr and Paste Staff, "The 100 Best Western Movies of All Time," *Paste*, June 20, 2016, https://www.paste magazine.com/movies/the-100-best-westerns-of-all-time/#27-el-topo/.

41. "Together with the Choctaws, Chickasaws, Creeks and Cherokees, the Seminoles were called 'The Five Civilized Tribes.' The name was coined because these tribes in particular adopted many ways of the white civilization. They lived in cabins or houses, wore clothes similar to the white man and often became Christians. Another habit many of the other tribes acquired from the whites was that of slavery. Though some of the tribes owned African slaves, the Seminoles never did. Indeed, many black Africans escaping from slavery in the Carolinas and Georgia came to Florida and built settlements near the Seminoles. They formed a union with the Seminoles based upon their mutual fear of slavery. This union was a strong one which surpassed attempts by the U.S. to break them apart. Intermarriages and friendships were common. In fact, they were so closely allied that the blacks became known as the Black Seminoles." Dru J. Murray, "The Unconquered Seminoles," Florida History, FunandSun.com, http:// funandsun.com/1tocf/seminole/semhistory.html/.

42. *Rosewood* (John Singleton, 1997).

43. Fanon, *Black Skins, White Masks*.

44. Alex Lichtenstein, *Twice the Work of Free Labor: The Political Economy of Convict Labor in the New South* (New York: Verso, 1996); Loïc Wacquant, "From Slavery to Mass Incarceration," *New Left Review* 13 (January 1, 2002): 41; David Theo Goldberg, *The Racial State* (London: Wiley Blackwell, 2001), Jordan Camp and Christina Heatherton, eds., *Policing the Planet: Why the Policing Crisis Led to Black Lives Matter* (New York: Verso, 2016), Wang, *Carceral Capitalism*. See also Ava DuVernay's documentary film *13th* (2016).

45. "With the entry of the United States into the Great War in 1917, African Americans were eager to show their patriotism in hopes of being recognized as full citizens. After the declaration of war, more than 20,000 blacks enlisted in the military, and the numbers increased when the Selective Service Act was enacted in May 1917. It was documented on July 5, 1917, that over 700,000 African Americans had registered for military service. However, they were barred from the Marines and served only in menial roles in the Navy. Blacks were able to serve in all branches of the Army except for the aviation units." "African-American Participation during World War I," HCA: Delaware Historical & Cultural Affairs, https://history.delaware.gov/african -americans-ww1/.

46. Michelle Alexander, *The New Jim Crow: Mass Incarceration in the Age of Colorblind- ness* (New York: New Press, 2012). See also Wang, *Carceral Capitalism*.

47. Allyson Nadia Field, Jan-Christopher Horak, Jacqeline Najuma Stewart, eds., *L.A. Rebellion: Creating a New Black Cinema* (Oakland: University of California Press, 2015), 6.

48. Clyde Taylor quoted in ibid., xxxi.

49. Fernando Solanas and Octavio Getino's "Towards a Third Cinema" has been widely anthologized. One of the first U.S. publications was *Movies and Methods: An Anthology*, ed. Bill Nichols (Phoenix: University of Arizona Press 1976), 44–64.

50. First published as "Oberhausener Manifest" (aka "Oberhausen Manifesto") at the 8th Oberhausen Short Film Festival, February 28, 1962. Also published in English in Eric Rentschler, ed., *West German Filmmakers on Film: Visions and Voices*, trans. Eric Rentschler (New York: Holmes and Meier, 1988), 2. The Oberhausen Manifesto was a declaration by a group of twenty-six young German filmmakers at the International Short Film Festival Oberhausen on February 1, 1962: Bodo Blüthner, Boris von Borresholm, Christian Doermer, Bernhard Dörries, Heinz Furchner, Rob Houwer, Ferdinand Khittl, Alexander Kluge, Pitt Koch, Walter Krüttner, Dieter Lemmel, Hans Loeper, Ronald Martini, Hansjürgen Pohland, Raimund Ruehl, Edgar Reitz, Peter Schamoni, Detten Schleiermacher, Fritz Schwennicke, Haro Senft, Franz-Josef Spieker, Hans Rolf Strobe, Heinz Tichawsky, Wolfgang Urchs, Herbert Vesely, and Wolf Wirth. The International Short Film Festival Oberhausen, founded in 1954, is one of the oldest short film festivals in the world. It is one of the major international platforms for the short form.

51. Melville J. Herskovits, *The Myth of the Negro Past* (New York: Harper and Brothers, 1941). Herskovits intended to debunk the myth that African Americans lost their African culture due to their experience of slavery. He argued that African Americans had retained their heritage from Africa in music, art, social structure, family life, religion, and speech patterns.

52. A cutting horse is typically an American Quarter Horse, bred and trained for cutting, a modern equestrian competition requiring a horse and rider to separate a single cow from a herd of cattle and prevent it from getting back to the herd. One of the desired qualities in a cutting horse is "cow sense," described as an innate ability to read a cow, eye to eye, in anticipation of each move.

53. The American Broadcasting Company coined the term "after school special" in 1972 to refer to a television anthology series that aired from October 4, 1972, to January 23, 1997. The movies usually aired in the late afternoon on weekdays. As a series of television films, most episodes dramatically presented controversial, socially relevant situations of interest to school-age children and teenagers. Topics included illiteracy, substance abuse, and teenage pregnancy. They were broadcast four to six times during the school year, preempting local programming that would follow the network schedule in the late afternoon hours.

54. Jan-Christopher Horak, "Tough Enough: Blaxploitation and the L.A. Rebellion," in Field et al., *L.A. Rebellion*, 155n61.

55. Yarimar Bonilla, "History Unchained," *Transition*, no. 112, *Django Unpacked* (2013): 68–77.

56. See Vivian Sobchack, *The Persistence of History: Cinema, Television, and the Modern Event* (New York: Routledge, 1995). Or see Brian Henderson's 1979 essay on *The Searchers*.

57. The journal *Transition* dedicated a special issue to *Django Unchained* in 2013 titled "The *Django* Issue." *Black Camera: An International Film Journal* devoted space to a series of "close-up" articles on the film in Spring 2016. Bloomsbury published *Quentin Tarantino's Django Unchained: The Continuation of Meta-Cinema*, edited by Oliver Speck in 2014. Clifford Manlove has published a comparative analysis of Corbucci's *Django* (1966) and Tarantino's *Django Unchained* (2012) as post-western love stories in "From

Django to *Django Unchained*: Love Narratives in the Global South," published in the anthology *The Western in the Global South*, which was released in 2015. While there are references to other Black westerns in the aforementioned publications, there's little sustained engagement regarding the intertextual relationships between Black-themed westerns. There is little to no discussion of the way earlier Black westerns seek to address film history.

58. Christopher Frayling, *Sergio Leone: Something to Do with Death* (London: Faber and Faber, 2000).

59. Patrick McGee, *From Shane to Kill Bill: Rethinking the Western* (Malden, MA: Blackwell Publishing, 2007).

60. See Simon Abrams *Indiewire* article, "5 Spaghetti Westerns & 5 Slavesploitation Films That Paved the Way for 'Django Unchained,'" https://www.indiewire.com/2012/12/5-spaghetti-westerns-5-slavesploitation-films-that-paved-the-way-for-django-unchained-249928/. Slavesploitation, according to various sources, is a subgenre of blaxploitation in literature and film that flourished briefly in the late 1960s and 1970s. As its name suggests, the genre is characterized by sensationalistic depictions of slavery. Abrams maintains that Quentin Tarantino's *Djanjo Unchained* finds its historical roots in the slavesploitation genre and observes that slavesploitation films are characterized by "crassly exploitative representations of oppressed slave protagonists." I am arguing that it sits at the intersection of slavesploitation and Blaxploiwestern because it utilizes so many elements of the western. Moreover, most spectators would recognize the film more readily as a Blaxploiwestern or Black westploitation than a slavesploitation because of its use of exploitation cinema. But all of these cinemas are in tandem with exploitation aesthetics Eric Schaefer discusses in his book *Bold, Daring, Shocking, True: A History of Exploitation Films, 1919–1959* (Durham, NC: Duke University Press, 1999). One early antecedent of the slavesploitation genre is *Slaves* (1969), which Mikal Gaines notes was "not 'slavesploitation' in the vein of later films" but featured graphic depictions of beatings and sexual violence against slaves. By far the best-known and best-studied exemplar of slavesploitation is *Mandingo*, a 1957 novel that was adapted into a 1961 play and a 1975 film.

61. Henry Louis Gates Jr., "An Unfathomable Place: A Conversation with Quentin Tarantino about *Django Unchained* (2012)," *Transition*, no. 112, *Django Unpacked* (2013): 51.

62. Hartman, *Scenes of Subjection*.

63. Robert von Dassanowsky, "Dr. 'King' Schultz as Ideologue and Emblem: The German Enlightenment and the Legacy of the 1848 Revolutions in *Django Unchained*," in Speck, *Quentin Tarantino's Django Unchained*, 21.

64. The Carnivalesque is a literary style. Mikhail Bakhtin, a Russian linguist and literary critic writing in the first half of the twentieth century, used this term to characterize writing that depicts the de-stabilization or reversal of power structures, albeit temporarily, as happens in traditional forms of carnival. François Rabelais, a French author from the early 1500s, is regarded by Bakhtin as an almost perfect exponent of carnivalesque writing. His most famous work, *Gargantua and Pantagruel*, is an illustration of Bakhtin's thesis. It shows a world in which transgressive social behavior thrives beneath the veneer of social order, constantly threatening to upend things. Many scholars read the carnivalesque as a cinematic mode or see it in the arts generally (film, painting, sculpture, poetry). Bakhtin's concept is often read as

a utopian antidote to repressive forms of power everywhere and a celebration of the possibility for affirmative change, however transitory in nature. *The Politics and Poetics of Transgression* (1986) by Peter Stallybrass and Allon White makes a strong case along these lines, as does Robert Stam in *Subversive Pleasures: Bakhtin, Cultural Criticism, and Film* (1989). The term originated as "carnival" in Mikhail Bakhtin's *Problems of Dostoevsky's Poetics* and was further developed in *Rabelais and His World*.

65. *Django Unchained* (Quentin Tarantino, 2012).

66. Schneider, "Finding a New *Heimat* in the Wild West," 141–59.

67. Ibid., 141.

68. Manlove, "From *Django* to *Django Unchained*.

69. I do not agree that Perry Henzell's film *The Harder They Come* is best described as a western. It does contain a significant homage to *Django*. I view it as a classic example of Third cinema in the tradition of Solonas and Getino's notion of Third cinema as outlined in their seminal essay. But I realize many colleagues in Cinema Studies view this as a western proper.

70. Some critics of *Django Unchained* found the Schultz-Django alliance unrealistic, citing it as a fault of the film. Other critics noted the historical fact that in the 1840s, German revolutionaries and progressives emigrated from Europe to the United States, where they became active in the anti-slavery movement. But the veracity of the situation is totally irrelevant because the movie is not based on actual events. It's secondary to the carnivalesque blaxploiwestern drama that Tarantino has put in motion. Pastiche aesthetics are Tarantino's first priority and modus operandi.

71. *Django Unchained* (Quentin Tarantino, 2012).

72. Amerigo Vessepi's name bears resemblance to Amerigo Vespucci (1451–1512), an Italian merchant, explorer, and navigator from the Republic of Florence, from whose name the term "America" is derived. Clearly, Tarantino is signifying on America's foundational history by associating "America" with a character who is a callous slaver. Tarantino seems to be implying that the foundation of America is predicated on, even synonymous with, human trafficking and global carceral capitalism.

73. *Django Unchained* (Quentin Tarantino, 2012).

74. The "hot box" was a method of solitary confinement used in humid and arid regions as a method of punishment. Anyone placed in one would experience extreme heat, dehydration, heat exhaustion, and even death, depending on when and how long one was kept in the box. They were often featured in women-in-prison sexploitation pictures of the 1970s featuring actresses like Pam Grier, Margaret Markov, and Teda Bracci. For example, there is one in *Black Mama, White Mama*.

75. Some critics have erroneously attributed Django's upside-down hanging to an allusion to *Mandingo*, but in fact upside-down hanging was a common visual trope in the western. There are many westerns in which this method of torture was shown before blaxploitation or slavesploitation cinema of the '70s. Even Burt Lancaster is hung upside down in *The Professionals* (Richard Brooks, 1966).

76. Bruschini et al., *Western all'Italiana*, 7.

77. Wood, *Hollywood from Vietnam to Reagan and Beyond*.

78. Jacqueline Stewart, "*Representing: Hip Hop and the Production of Black Cinema* by S. Craig Watkins," in *Film Quarterly* 54, no. 1 (2000): 57–60. Stewart reviewed Watkins's book.

79. Watkins, *Representing*.

80. Brent Lang, "Home on the Range," *Variety* 349, no. 10, September 9, 2020, 36–40.

81. Brent Lang, "Idris Elba on *Concrete Cowboy* and the Uplifting Indie's Improbable Ride to the Toronto Film Festival," *Variety*, September 9, 2020.

82. Peter Debruge, "*The Harder They Fall*," *Variety* 353, no. 14, October 13, 2021, 69.

83. Marcus Jones, *Entertainment Weekly*, Issue 1619/1620, November 2021, 112.

84. Debruge, "*Harder They Fall*."

85. Leila Latif, "*The Harder They Fall*," *Sight and Sound* 31, no. 10 (December 2021).

86. Angelique Jackson, "The New Frontier: First-Time Director Jeymes Samuel's *The Harder They Fall* Is a Bold, Music-Infused Reimagining of Old-Time Westerns," *Variety* 353, no. 14, October 13, 2021, 28–35.

87. Ibid.

Appendix. Interview with Jeff Kanew

1. On June 20, 1967, Muhammad Ali was convicted of draft evasion, sentenced to five years in prison, fined ten thousand dollars, and banned from boxing for three years. He stayed out of prison as his case was appealed and returned to the ring on October 26, 1970.

Filmography

Experimental Westerns

Harlem on the Prairie (1937)
Director: Sam Newfield
Cast: Herbert Jeffries (Jeff Kincaid); Spencer Williams (Doc Clayburn); Connie Harris (Carolina, Doc's daughter); George Randol (Sheriff); Maceo Bruce Sheffield (Wolf Cain); Mantan Moreland (Mistletoe); Flournoy E. Miller (additional dialogue); Lucius Brooks, Leon Buck, Ira Hardi, and Rudolph Hunter (as The Four Tones)

Two Gun Man from Harlem (1938)
Director: Richard C. Kahn
Cast: Herbert Jeffries (Bob Blake/The Deacon), Marguerite Whitten (Sally Thompson), Clarence Brooks (John Barker), Mantan Moreland (Bill Blake), Stymie Beard (Jimmy Thompson), Spencer Williams Jr. (Butch Carter), Mae Turner (Mrs. Ruth Steel), Jesse Lee Brooks (Sheriff), Rose Lee Lincoln (Dolores), Tom Southern (John Steel), The Cats and the Fiddle (specialty act), The Four Tones, Paul Blackman (Paul Blackman—The One Man Band)

The Bronze Buckaroo (1939)
Director: Richard C. Kahn
Cast: Herb Jeffries (Bob Blake), Artie Young (Betty Jackson), Rollie Hardin (Joe Jackson), Clarence Brooks (Buck Thorne), F. E. Miller (Slim Perkins), Lucius Brooks (Dusty), Spencer Williams (Pete), Lee Calmes (Lee), Earle Morris (bartender), The Four Tones (singing quartet)

Interracial Buddy Experiments

Sergeant Rutledge (1960)
Director: John Ford
Cast: Woody Strode (1st Sgt. Braxton Rutledge, 9th Cavalry), Jeffrey Hunter (1st Lt. Tom Cantrell, 9th Cavalry), Constance Towers (Mary Beecher), Billie Burke (Mrs.

Cordelia Fosgate), Juano Hernàndez (Sgt. Matthew Luke Skidmore, 9th Cavalry), Willis Bouchey (Lt. Col. Otis Fosgate, 9th Cavalry), Carleton Young (Capt. Shattuck, 14th Infantry, prosecutor)

Rio Conchos (1964)
Director: Gordon Douglas
Cast: Richard Boone (Major James "Jim" Lassiter), Jim Brown (Sergeant Franklyn), Stuart Whitman (Captain Haven), Tony Franciosa (Juan Luis Rodriguez/Juan Martinez), Edmond O'Brien (Colonel Theron "Gray Fox" Pardee), Wende Wagner (Sally, Apache girl), Warner Anderson (Colonel Wagner), Rodolfo Acosta (Bloodshirt the Apache chief), Barry Kelley (Croupier at Presidio), Vito Scotti (Bandit chief), Robert House Peters Jr. (Major Johnson), Kevin Hagen (Major Johnson, "Blondebeard")

Duel at Diablo (1966)
Director: Ralph Nelson
Cast: James Garner (Jess Remsberg), Sidney Poitier (Toller), Bibi Andersson (Ellen Grange), Dennis Weaver (Willard Grange), Bill Travers (Lt. Scotty McAllister), Alf Elson (Colonel Foster), John Hubbard (Major Novac, Fort Creel's C.O.), John Hoyt (Chata), William Redfield (Sergeant Ferguson), Bill Hart (Corporal Harrington), Eddie Little Sky (Alchise), John Crawford (Clay Dean), Jeff Cooper (Trooper Casey)

100 Rifles (1969)
Director: Tom Gries
Cast: Jim Brown (Sheriff Lyedecker), Raquel Welch (Sarita), Burt Reynolds (Joe "Yaqui Joe" Herrera), Fernando Lamas (General Verdugo), Dan O'Herlihy (Steven Grimes), Eric Braeden (Lt. Franz Von Klemme), Michael Forest (Humara), Aldo Sambrell (Sergeant Paletes), Soledad Miranda (Prostitute in hotel), Alberto Dalbés (Padre Francisco), Charly Bravo (Lopez), José Manuel Martín (Sarita's father)

The Learning Tree (1969)
Director: Gordon Parks
Cast: Kyle Johnson (Newt Winger), Alex Clarke (Marcus Savage), Estelle Evans (Sarah Winger), Mira Waters (Arcella Jefferson), George Mitchell (Jake Kiner), Richard Ward (Booker Savage), Malcolm Attenbury (Silas Newhall), Russell Thorson (Judge Cavanaugh), Zooey Hall (Chauncey Cavanaugh), Dana Elcar (Sheriff Kirky), Felix Nelson (Jack Winger), Joel Fluellen (Uncle Rob)

El Condor (1970)
Director: John Guillermin
Cast: Jim Brown (Luke), Lee Van Cleef (Jaroo), Patrick O'Neal (Chavez), Marianna Hill (Claudine), Iron Eyes Cody (Santana), Imogen Hassall (Dolores), Elisha Cook Jr. (old convict)

Blaxploitation vs. Black Liberation

The McMasters (1970)
Director: Alf Kjellin
Cast: Brock Peters (Benjie McMasters), Burl Ives (Mr. McMasters), David Carradine (White Feather), Nancy Kwan (Robin), Jack Palance (Kolby), Dame Clark (Spencer),

John Carradine (Preacher), L. Q. Jones (Russell), R. G. Armstrong (Watson), Alan Vint (Hank)

The Red, White, and Black (aka *Soul Soldier*) (1970)
Director: John "Bud" Cardos
Cast: Robert DoQui (Eli Brown), Isaac Fields (1st Sgt. Robertson), Barbara Hale (Mrs. Alice Grierson), Rafer Johnson (Private Armstrong), Lincoln Kilpatrick (Sergeant Hatch), Isabel Sanford (Isabel Taylor), Janee Michelle (Julie Brown), John J. Fox (The Signifier), Cesar Romero (Colonel Grierson), Byrd Holland (The Sutler), Robert Dix (Walking Horse)

Man and Boy (1971)
Director: E. W. Swackhamer
Cast: Bill Cosby (Caleb Revers), Gloria Foster (Ivy), Leif Erickson (Mossman), George Spell (Billy), Douglas Turner Ward (Christmas), John Anderson (Stretch), Henry Silva (Caine), Dub Taylor (Atkins), Yaphet Kotto (Nate), Shelley Morrison (Rosita), Richard Bull (Thornhill), Robert Lawson (Lawson), Jason Clark ("Red"), Fred Graham ("Blockers"), Jack Owens (himself)

Skin Game (1971)
Director: Paul Bogart and Gordon Douglas
Cast: James Garner (Quincy Drew/Capt. Nathaniel Mountjoy), Lou Gossett Jr. (Jason O'Rourke), Susan Clark (Ginger/Miss Abigail Blodgett), Brenda Sykes (Naomi), Edward Asner (Plunkett), Andrew Duggan (Howard Calloway), Neva Patterson (Mrs. Claggart), Parley Baer (Mr. Claggart), George Tyne (Henry P. Bonner), Royal Dano (John Brown), Pat O'Malley (William), Joel Fluellen (Uncle Abram), Napoleon Whiting (Ned), Juanita Moore (Viney)

Buck and the Preacher (1972)
Director: Sidney Poitier
Cast: Sidney Poitier (Buck), Harry Belafonte (Preacher), Ruby Dee (Ruth), Cameron Mitchell (Deshay), Julie Robinson (Sinsie), Enrique Lucero (Indian chief), Denny Miller (Floyd), Nita Talbot (Madam Esther), John Kelly (Sheriff), Tony Brubaker (Headman), James McEachin (Kingston), Clarence Muse (Cudjo), Lynn Hamilton (Sarah), Doug Johnson (Sam), Errol John (Joshua)

Black Rodeo (1972)
Director: Jeff Kanew
Cast: Muhammad Ali (himself), Woody Strode (himself/narrator), Archie Wycoff (Bud), Skeets Richardson (himself), Betsy Bramwell (herself), Rocky Watson (himself), Clarence Gonzales (Cleo), Pete Knight (Skeets), Marvel Rogers (Rocky), Rocky Watson (himself), Moses Fields (Billy the Kid), Nelson Jackson (himself), Gordon Hayes (himself), Sandy Goodman (herself), Nat Purefoy (himself), Joanne Eason (herself)

The Legend of Nigger Charley (1972)
Director: Martin Goldman
Cast: Fred Williamson ("Nigger Charley"), D'Urville Martin (Toby), Don Pedro Colley (Joshua), Thomas Anderson (Shadow), Jerry Gatlin (Sheriff Rhinehart), Alan

Gifford (Hill Carter), Will Hussung (Dr. Saunders), Gertrude Jeannette (Theo), Fred Lerner (Ollokot), Marcia McBroom (Leda), Bill Moor (Walker), Tricia O'Neil (Sarah Lyons), John Ryan (Houston), Doug Row (Dewey Lyons), Joe Santos (Reverend)

The Soul of Nigger Charley (1973)
Director: Larry Spangler
Cast: Fred Williamson (Charley), D'Urville Martin (Toby), Denise Nicholas (Elena), Pedro Armendáriz Jr. (Sandoval), Kirk Calloway (Marcellus), George Allen (Ode), Kevin Hagen (Colonel Blanchard), Michael Cameron (Sergeant Foss), Johnny Greenwood (Roy), James Garbo (Collins), Nai Bonet (Anita), Bob Minor (Fred), Fred Lerner (Woods)

Blazing Saddles (1974)
Director: Mel Brooks
Cast: Cleavon Little (Bart), Gene Wilder (Jim), Slim Pickens (Taggart), Harvey Korman (Hedley Lamarr), Madeline Kahn (Lili Von Shtüpp), Mel Brooks (Governor Lepetomane/Indian chief), Burton Gilliam (Lyle), Alex Karras (Mongo), Dom DeLuise (Buddy Bizarre), Count Basie (himself)

Boss Nigger (1975)
Director: Jack Arnold
Cast: Fred Williamson (Boss Nigger), D'Urville Martin (Amos), William Smith (Jed Clayton), Don "Red" Barry (Doctor), R. G. Armstrong (Mayor Griffin), Barbara Leigh (Miss Pruitt), Carmen Hayward (Clara Mae), Carmen Zapata (Margarita), Ben Zeller (blacksmith), Bruce Gordon (storekeeper)

Take a Hard Ride (1975)
Director: Antonio Margheriti
Cast: Jim Brown (Pike), Lee Van Cleef (Kiefer), Fred Williamson (Tyree), Catherine Spaak (Catherine), Jim Kelly (Kashtock), Dana Andrews (Morgan), Barry Sullivan (Kane), Harry Carey Jr. (Dumper), Robert Donner (Skave), Charles McGregor (Cloyd), Leonard Smith (Cangey), Ronald Howard (Halsey), Ricardo Palacios (Calvera), Robin Levitt (Chico), Buddy Joe Hooker (Angel)

Adiós Amigo (1975)
Director: Fred Williamson
Cast: Richard Pryor (Sam Spade), Fred Williamson (Big Ben), James Brown (sheriff), Mike Henry (Mary's husband), Thalmus Rasulala (Noah), Robert Phillips (notary)

Joshua (1976)
Director: Larry G. Spangler
Cast: Fred Williamson (Joshua), Cal Bartlett (Jed), Brenda Venus (Sam's wife), Isela Vega (Maria), Bud Stout (Rex), Henry Hendrick (Sam), Ralph Willingham (Weasel), Kathryn Jackson (Martha)

Revisionist Westerns: Brothas & Sistas at the O.K. Corral

Posse (1993)
Director: Mario Van Peebles

Cast: Mario Van Peebles (Jesse Lee), Stephen Baldwin (Jimmy J. "Little J" Teeters), Billy Zane (Colonel Graham), Tone Loc (Angel), Melvin Van Peebles (Papa Joe), Tom Lister Jr. (Obobo), Big Daddy Kane (Father Time), Reginald Vel Johnson (Preston), Blair Underwood (Carver), Isaac Hayes (Cable), Charles Lane (Weezie), Robert Hooks ("King David" Lee), Richard Jordan (Sheriff Bates), Pam Grier (Phoebe), Nipsey Russell (Snopes), Paul Bartel (Mayor Bigwood), Salli Richardson (Lana), Woody Strode (narrator), Aaron Neville (railroad singer), Reginald Hudlin (reporter #1), Warrington Hudlin (reporter #2), Richard Gant (Doubletree), Richard Edson (Deputy Tom), Stephen J. Cannell (Jimmy Love), Scott Bray (fire eater)

Rosewood (1997)
Director: John Singleton
Cast: Ving Rhames (Mr. Mann), Don Cheadle (Sylvester Carrier), Jon Voight (John Wright), Bruce McGill (Duke Purdy), Loren Dean (James Taylor), Esther Rolle (Aunt Sarah), Elise Neal (Beulah aka Scrappie), Bridget Coulter (Gertrude), Robert Patrick (Fanny's lover), Michael Rooker (Sheriff Walker), Catherine Kellner (Fanny Taylor), Akousa Busia (Jewel), Paul Benjamin (James Carrier), Kevin Jackson (Sam Carter), Mark Boone Junior (Poly), Muse Watson (Henry Andrews)

Buffalo Soldiers (1997, TV)
Director: Charles Haid
Cast: Danny Glover (Sgt. Washington Wyatt), Carl Lumbly (John Horse), Lamont Bentley (Corporal Sea), Tom Bower (General Pike), Timothy Busfield (Maj. Robert Carr), Glynn Turman (Sgt. Joshua "Joyu" Judges Ruth), Bob Gunton (Col. Benjamin Grierson), Keith Jefferson (Andrew Boyer), Robert Knott (Capt. Oren Draper), Clifton Powell (Soldier), Matt Ross (Captain Calhoun), Michael Warren (Cpl. Eddie Tockes), David Jean Thomas (Cpl. Roseman Lloyd), Chesley Wilson (Nana), Jeri Brunoe-Samson (Doba), Alvin William "Dutch" Lunak (Ahiga)

Wild Wild West (1999)
Director, Barry Sonnenfeld
Cast: Will Smith (James West), Kevin Kline (Artemus Gordon), Kenneth Branagh (Dr. Arliss Loveless), Salma Hayek (Rita Escobar), M. Emmet Walsh (Coleman), Ted Levine (General McGrath), Frederique Van Der Wal (Amazonia), Musetta Vander (Munitia), Sofia Eng (Miss Lippenrieder), Bai Ling (Miss East), Garcelle Beauvais (girl in water tower), Mike H. McGaughy (Big Reb), Rodney Grant (Hudson)

Realism and Neo-Blaxploitation on the Frontier

Cutting Horse (2002)
Director: Larry Clark
Cast: Albert Harris (Tyler), Cesar Flores (Sanchez), Robert Earl Crudup (Ray), Mellisa Cellura (Rosa), Susan Santiago (Anna Marie), Roberto Bethel (Doc Pete), Christopher Upham (Toby Stone), Joy Garner (Joyce Stone), Sigi Lobas (Billie Stone), Sherry Al-Mufti (Millicent Stone), Fred Barson (Slade), Robert J. Ramsey III (Mayor Mason), H. Lee Burton (Judge Hopkins), Ian Davidson (Moss), Artis Fountain (Detective Greyson), Peter Carlstrom (Detective Brown)

Gang of Roses (2003)

Director: Jean Claude La Marre

Cast: Monica Calhoun (Rachel), Lil' Kim (Chastity), Stacey Dash (Kim), Marie Matiko (Zang Li), LisaRaye McCoy (Marie), Macy Gray (black-haired woman), Louis Mandylor (Sheriff Shoeshine Michel), Bobby Brown (Left Eye Watkins), Jacinto Taras Riddick (Georgy Simone), Charity Hill (Little Suzie), Jean-Claude La Marre (Baby Face Malone), Glenn Plummer (Johnny Handsome)

Ride Sweet, Die Slow (2005)

Director: Chris W. Hill

Cast: Sarah Kozer (Annie Mae), Jesse Wells Martin (Thaddeus), Kira Madallo Sesay (Tomahawk Jane), Tracia Daye (Charlotte Walker), Julia Ling (Mei Lin), Carissa Rosario (Maggie Rainer), Jon Budinoff (Julius), Lamont Clayton (Clyde Barrister), Raphael Saadiq (Charlie Ray)

Brothers in Arms (2005)

Director: Jean-Claude La Marre

Cast: David Carradine (Driscoll), Gabriel Casseus (Linc), Raymond Cruz (Reverend), Jared Day (Wolverton's nephew), Idalis DeLeon (Sheriff Sanchez), Nancy DeMayo (saloon girl #1), David Gianopoulos (Wolverton), Peter Greene (Bert), Garry Guerrier (long-coat leader #1), Jean-Claude La Marre (Slim), Ed Lauter (Mayor Crawley), Kenya Moore (Mara), Cameron Monaghan (Timmy)

Django Unchained (2012)

Director: Quentin Tarantino

Cast: Jamie Foxx (Django Freeman), Christoph Waltz (Dr. King Schultz), Leonardo DiCaprio ("Monsieur" Calvin J. Candie), Kerry Washington (Broomhilda "Hildie" von Shaft), Samuel L. Jackson (Stephen Warren), Walton Goggins (Billy Crash), Dennis Christopher (Leonide "Leo" Moguy), James Remar (Butch Pooch/Ace Speck), David Steen (Mr. Stonecipher), Dana Gourrier (Cora), Nichole Galicia (Sheba), Laura Cayouette (Lara Lee Candie-Fitzwilly), Ato Essandoh (D'Artagnan), Sammi Rotibi (Rodney), Clay Donahue Fontenot (Luigi), Escalante Lundy (Big Fred), Miriam F. Glover (Betina), Don Johnson (Big Daddy Bennett), Franco Nero (Amerigo Vessepi)

Concrete Cowboy (2020)

Director: Ricky Staub

Cast: Caleb McLaughlin (Cole), Idris Elba (Harp), Jharrel Jerome (Smush), Byron Bowers (Rome), Lorraine Toussaint (Nessi), Clifford "Method Man" Smith (Leroy), Ivannah-Mercedes (Esha), Devenie Young (Trena), Jamil Prattis (Paris), Michael "O. G. Law" Tabon (Jalen)

The Harder They Fall (2021)

Director: Jeymes Samuel

Cast: Jonathan Majors (Nat Love), Chase Dillon (young Nat Love), Idris Elba (Rufus Buck), Zazie Beetz (Stagecoach Mary Fields), Regina King (Trudy Smith), Delroy Lindo (Bass Reeves), LaKeith Stanfield (Cherokee Bill), R. J. Cyler (Jim Beckwourth), Danielle Deadwyler (Cuffee), Edi Gathegi (Bill Pickett), Deon Cole (Wiley Escoe), Damon Wayans Jr. (Monroe Grimes), DeWanda Wise (Eleanor Love), Julio Cesar Cedillo (Jesus Cortez)

Bibliography

Aleiss, Angela. *Making the White Man's Indian: Native Americans and Hollywood Movies*. Westport, CT: Praeger Publishers, 2005.

Alexander, Michelle. *The New Jim Crow: Mass Incarceration in the Age of Colorblindness*. New York: New Press, 2012.

Allison, Deborah. "Title Sequences in the Western Genre: The Iconography of Action." *Quarterly Review of Film and Video* 25 (2008): 107–115.

Allmendinger, Blake. *The Cowboy: Representation of Labor in an American Work Culture*. New York: Oxford University Press, 1992.

———. *Imagining the African American West*. Lincoln: University of Nebraska Press, 2005.

Baldwin, James. *The Devil Finds Work*. New York: Dial Press, 1976.

———. *The Price of the Ticket: Collected Nonfiction Essays, 1948–1985*. New York: St. Martin's Press, 1985.

Barthes, Roland. *Image-Music-Text*. Translated by Stephen Heath. New York: Hill and Wang, 1977.

———. *Mythologies*. Paris: Editions du Seuil, 1957.

Basinger, Jeanine. *The World War II Combat Film: Anatomy of a Genre*. New York: Columbia University Press, 1986.

Benshoff, Harry. *Monsters in the Closet: Homosexuality and the Horror Film*. Manchester, UK: Manchester University Press, 1997.

Bergman, Carol. *Sidney Poitier*. New York: Chelsea House Publishers, 1990.

Bernardi, Daniel, ed. *The Birth of Whiteness: Race and the Emergence of U.S. Cinema*. New Brunswick, NJ: Rutgers University Press, 1996.

———, ed. *Classic Hollywood: Classic Whiteness*. Minneapolis: University of Minnesota Press, 2001.

Bernhardt, Mark. "History's Ghosts: Haunting Vince Gilligan's New Mexico: Genre, Myth, and the New Western History in *Breaking Bad*." *Journal of Popular Film and Television* 47, no. 2 (2019): 66–80.

Bhabha, Homi K. *Nation and Narration*. New York: Routledge, 1990.

Black, Doris. "Hollywood's New King of Ego." *Sepia* 22, August 1973, 37–43.

Bogle, Donald. *Toms, Coons, Mulattoes, Mammies, and Bucks: An Interpretive History of Blacks in American Films*. New York: Continuum, 1994.

Bold, Christine. "Where Did the Black Rough Riders Go?" *Canadian Review of American Studies* 39, no. 3 (2009): 273–97.

Bonilla, Yarimar. "History Unchained." *Transition*, no. 112, *Django Unpacked* (2013): 68–77.

Bourdieu, Pierre. *Distinction: A Social Critique of the Judgement of Taste*. Translated by Richard Nice. London: Routledge, 1984.

———. "The Forms of Capital." Translated by Richard Nice. In *Handbook of Theory and Research for the Sociology of Education*, edited by John G. Richardson, 241–58. New York: Greenwood, 1986.

Brod, Harry, and Michael Kaufman, eds. *Theorizing Masculinities*. Thousand Oaks, CA: Sage Publications, 1994.

Brown, Jeffrey A. *Black Superheroes, Milestone Comics, and Their Fans*. Jackson: University Press of Mississippi, 2000.

———. "Comic Book Masculinity and the New Black Superhero." *African American Review* 33, no. 1 (1999): 25–42.

Brown, Jim. *Out of Bounds*. New York: Kensington Publishing Group, 1989.

Bruschini, Antonio, Antonio Tentori, Stefano Piselli, and Riccardo Morrocchi. *Western all'Italiana: The Specialists*. Firenze: C. E. Nerbini, 1998.

Burrell, Walter Price. "*Buck and the Preacher*." *Black Stars*, February 1972, 58–60.

Burton, Art T. *Black Gun, Silver Star: The Life and Legend of Frontier Marshal Bass Reeves*. Lincoln: University of Nebraska Press, 2008.

———. *Black, Red, and Deadly: Black and Indian Gunfighters of the Indian Territory, 1870–1907*. Austin, TX: Eakin Press, 1994.

Buscombe, Edward. "Painting the Legend: Frederic Remington and the Western." *Cinema Journal* 23, no. 4 (1984): 12–27.

———, ed. *The BFI Companion to the Western*. London: British Film Institute, 1988.

———. *Stagecoach*. London: British Film Institute, 1992.

Buscombe, Edward, and Roberta Pearson, eds. *Back in the Saddle: New Essays on the Western*. London: British Film Institute, 1998.

Cameron, Ian, and Douglas Pye, eds. *The Book of Westerns*. New York: Continuum Publishing, 1996.

Campbell, Neil. "'Coming Back to Bad It Up': The Posthumous and the Post-Western." In *The Western in the Global South*, edited by Mary Higgins, Rita Keresztesi, and Dayna Oscherwitz. New York: Routledge, 2015.

———. *Post-Westerns: Cinema, Region, West*. Lincoln: University of Nebraska Press, 2013.

Cawelti, John. "Chinatown and Generic Transformation in Recent American Films." In *Film Theory and Criticism: Introductory Readings*, edited by Leo Braudy and Marshall Cohen. 7th ed. New York: Oxford University Press, 2009.

———. *The Six Gun Mystique Sequel*. Bowling Green, OH: Bowling Green State University Popular Press, 1999.

Chapman, Roger, and James Ciment, eds., *Culture Wars in America: An Encyclopedia of Issues, Viewpoints and Voices*. London: Routledge, 2014.

Chisholm, Earle. "The Legend of the Bad Nigger." *Sepia*, July 1972, 54–60.

Chisholm, Shirley. *Unbought and Unbossed*. Boston: Houghton Mifflin, 1970.

Chow, Andrew. "Old Town, New Road: How 20-Year-Old Upstart Lil Nas X Used the Internet to Beat Nashville at Its Own Game." *Time*, August 26, 2019, 54–59.

Churchill, Ward. *Fantasies of the Master Race: Literature, Cinema, and the Colonization of American Indians*. Monroe, ME: Common Courage Press, 1992.

Clark, John. *"Posse." Premiere* 6 (1993), 84.

Cleaver, Eldridge. *Soul on Ice*. New York: Dell Publishing, 1968.

Cleto, Fabio, ed. *Camp: Queer Aesthetics and the Performing Subject: A Reader*. Ann Arbor: University of Michigan Press, 1999.

Clinton, Catherine. *The Black Soldier: 1492 to the Present*. New York: Houghton Mifflin Books for Children, 2000.

Cohan, Steven. *Masked Men: Masculinity and the Movies in the Fifties*. Bloomington: Indiana University Press, 1997.

Cohan, Steven, and Ina Rae Hark. *Screening the Male: Exploring Masculinities in Hollywood Cinema*. London: Routledge, 1993.

Cornell, R. W. *Masculinities*. Cambridge, UK: Blackwell Publishers, 1995.

Countryman, Edward, and Evonne von Heussen-Countryman. *Shane*. London: British Film Institute, 1999.

Courtney, Susan. *Hollywood Fantasies of Miscegenation: Spectacular Narratives of Gender and Race, 1903–1967*. Princeton, NJ: Princeton University Press, 2005.

Crenshaw, Kimberlé. "Demarginalizing the Intersection of Race and Sex: A Black Feminist Critique of Antidiscrimination Doctrine, Feminist Theory, and Antiracist Politics." *University of Chicago Legal Forum*. Vol. 1 (1989): 139–67.

Debruge, Peter. *"The Harder They Fall." Variety* 353, no. 14, October 13, 2021, 69.

Dempsey, Michael. "John Ford: A Reassessment." *Film Quarterly* 28, no. 4, Special Book Issue (1975): 2–15.

Diawara, Manthia. "Black American Cinema: The New Realism." In *Black American Cinema*, edited by Manthia Diawara. New York: Routledge, 1993.

———. "Black Spectatorship: Problems of Identification and Resistance." *Screen* 29, no. 4 (1988): 66–79.

———. "Black Spectatorship: Problems of Identification and Resistance." In *Film Theory and Criticism: Introductory Readings*, edited by Leo Braudy and Marshall Cohen, 672–80. New York: Oxford University Press, 2016.

Dickens, Homer. *What a Drag: Men as Women and Women as Men in the Movies*. New York: Quill, 1984.

Donalson, Melvin. *Masculinity in the Interracial Buddy Film*. Jefferson, NC: McFarland, 2006.

Driessens, Olivier. "The Celebritization of Society and Culture: Understanding the Structural Dynamics of Celebrity Culture." *International Journal of Cultural Studies* (September 18, 2012): 641—57.

Drummond, Phillip. *High Noon*. London: British Film Institute, 1997.

Du Bois, W. E. B. *The Souls of Black Folk: Essays and Sketches*. Chicago: A. C. McClurg, 1903.

Duberman, Martin, ed. *Queer Representations: Reading Lives, Reading Cultures*. New York: New York University Press, 1997.

Durham, Philip, and Everett L. Jones, *The Negro Cowboys*. Lincoln: University of Nebraska Press, 1965.

Dye, R. Thomas. "Rosewood, Florida: The Destruction of an African American Community." *The Historian* 58, no. 3 (1996): 605–622.

Dyer, Richard. *White: Essays on Race and Culture*. New York: Routledge, 2017. Reprint edition. Originally published 1997.

Ellen, Holly. "Where Are the Films about Real Black Men and Women?" *New York Times*, June 2, 1974, Sec. II.

Everett, Anna. *Returning the Gaze: A Genealogy of Black Film Criticism, 1909–1949*. Durham, NC: Duke University Press, 2001.

Fanon, Frantz. *Black Skin, White Masks*. Translated by Charles Lam Markmann. New York: Grove Press, 1967. Originally published as *Peau Noire, Masques Blancs* (Paris: Editions de Seuil, 1952).

———. *A Dying Colonialism*. Translated by Haakon Chevalier. New York: Grove Press, 1965.

———. "Why We Use Violence." In *Alienation and Freedom*. London: Bloomsbury Academic, 2015.

———. *The Wretched of the Earth*. Translated by Constance Farrington. New York: Grove Press, 1963.

Field, Allyson Nadia, Jan-Christopher Horak, and Jacqueline Najuma Stewart, eds. *L.A. Rebellion: Creating a New Black Cinema*. Oakland: University of California Press, 2015.

"Football Heroes Invade Hollywood: Filmland Entices Black Grid Pros to Trade Yardage for Footage." *Ebony*, October 1969, 195.

Fowler, Arlen. *The Black Infantry in the West, 1869–1891*. Norman: University of Oklahoma Press, 1996.

Frayling, Christopher. *Sergio Leone: Something to Do with Death*. London: Faber & Faber, 2000.

Freeman, Mike. *Jim Brown: The Fierce Life of an American Hero*. New York: HarperCollins e-books. Reprint edition, 2009. Originally published 2006.

Freire, Paulo. *Pedagogy of the Oppressed*. Translated by Myra Bergman Ramos. New York: Herder and Herder, 1970.

French, Philip. *Westerns*. London: British Film Institute, 1973.

Fulwood, Neil. *The Films of Sam Peckinpah*. London: B T Batsford, 2002.

Gallagher, Tag. *John Ford: The Man and His Films*. Berkeley: University of California Press, 1986.

Garfield, Brian. *Western Films: A Complete Guide*. New York: Plenum Publishing, 1982.

Gates, Henry Louis, Jr. "An Unfathomable Place: A Conversation with Quentin Tarantino about *Django Unchained* (2012)." *Transition*, no. 112, *Django Unpacked* (2013): 51.

Gill, Waliyy. "The Western Film: Hollywood Myths and One Black Reality." *Western Journal of Black Studies* 10, no. 1 (1986): 1–5.

Gleich, Joshua. "Jim Brown: From Integration to Re-Segregation in *The Dirty Dozen* and *100 Rifles*." *Cinema Journal* 51, no. 1 (2011): 1–25.

González-Tennant, Edward. *The Rosewood Massacre: An Archaeology and History of Intersectional Violence*. Gainesville: University of Florida Press, 2018.

Goodman, George. "Durango: Poitier Meets Belafonte. Two Wary Rivals Patch Up a Fight to Make a Movie Together." *Look*, August 24, 1971, 56–61.

Grant, Lee, dir. *Sidney Poitier: One Bright Light*. American Masters. Thirteen/WNET, 2000.

Green, Douglas B. *Singing in the Saddle: The History of the Singing Cowboy*. Nashville, TN: Country Music Foundation Press, 2005.

Guerrero, Ed. *Framing Blackness: The African American Image in Film*. Philadelphia: Temple University Press, 1993.

Hall, Stuart. "Cultural Identity and Cinematic Representation." *Journal of Cinema and Media* 36 (1989): 68–81.

———. *Encoding and Decoding in the Television Discourse*. Birmingham, Eng.: Centre for Cultural Studies, University of Birmingham, 1973.

Hamalainen, Pekka. *Comanche Empire*. New Haven, CT: Yale University Press, 2008.

Harris, Cheryl I. "Whiteness as Property." *Harvard Law Review* 106, no. 8 (1993): 1707–1791.

Harris, Keith M. *Boys, Boyz, Bois: An Ethics of Black Masculinity in Film and Popular Media*. New York: Routledge, 2006.

Hartman, Saidiya. *Scenes of Subjection: Terror, Slavery, and Self-Making in Nineteenth-Century America*. New York: Oxford University Press, 1997.

Hearne, Joanna. "The Cross-Heart People: Race and Inheritance in the Silent Western." *Journal of Popular Film and Television* 30, no. 4 (2003): 181.

Henderson, Brian. "*The Searchers*: An America Dilemma." *Film Quarterly* 34, no. 2 (1980–1981): 9–23. Reprinted in *Movies and Methods: An Anthology*, Vol. 2, edited by Bill Nichols, 429–49. Berkeley: University of California Press, 1985.

Herskovits, Melville J. *The Myth of the Negro Past*. New York: Harper and Brothers, 1941.

Hicks, Heather J. "Hoodoo Economics: White Men's Work and Black Men's Magic in Contemporary American Film." *Camera Obscura* 53. Vol. 18, No. 2 (2003): 27–55.

Higgins, Mary Ellen, Rita Keresztesi, and Dayna Oscherwitz, eds. *The Western in the Global South*. New York: Routledge, 2015.

Hoberman, John. *Darwin's Athletes: How Sport Has Damaged Black America and Preserved the Myth of Race*. Boston: Houston Mifflin, 1997.

Horak, Jan-Christopher. "Tough Enough: Blaxploitation and the L.A. Rebellion." In Field et al., *L.A. Rebellion*, 119–55.

"How to Survive in Hollywood between Gigs." *Ebony* 33, no. 12 (October 1978), 34.

Howard, Sheena C., and Ronald L. Jackson II. *Black Comics: Politics of Race and Representation*. London: Bloomsbury Academic Publishing, 2013.

Impelli, Matthew. "Black Texas Cowboys on Horseback Protest George Floyd's Death in Viral Video." *Newsweek*, June 3, 2020. https://www.newsweek.com/black-texas-cowboys-horseback-protest-george-floyds-death-viral-video-1508378/.

Jackson, Angelique. "The New Frontier: First-Time Director Jeymes Samuel's *The Harder They Fall* Is a Bold, Music-Infused Reimagining of Old-Time Westerns." *Variety* 353, no. 14, October 13, 2021, 28–35.

James, Erica Moiah. "*Every Nigger Is a Star*: Reimagining Blackness from Post–Civil Rights America to the Postindependence Caribbean." *Black Camera* 8, no. 1 (2016): 55–83.

Johnson, Michael K. *Black Masculinity and the Frontier Myth in American Literature*. Norman: University of Oklahoma Press, 2002.

———. "Cowboys, Cooks, and Comics: African American Characters in Westerns of the 1930s." *Quarterly Review of Film and Video* 22, no. 3 (2005): 225–35.

———. *Hoo-Doo Cowboys and Bronze Buckaroos: Conceptions of the African American West*. Jackson: University Press of Mississippi, 2014.

Katz, William Loren. *Black Indians: A Hidden Heritage*. New York: Aladdin Paperbacks, 1997.

———. *The Black West: A Documentary and Pictorial History of the African American Role in the Westward Expansion of the United States.* New York: Harlem Moon, 2005.

Kennedy, Randall. *Nigger: The Strange Career of a Troublesome Word.* New York: Pantheon Books, 2002.

Keyser, Lester, and Andrée H. Ruszkowski. *The Cinema of Sidney Poitier: The Black Man's Changing Role on the American Screen.* San Diego: A. S. Barnes, 1980.

Kilpatrick, Jacquelyn. *Celluloid Indians: Native Americans and Film.* Lincoln: University of Nebraska Press, 1999.

Kimmel, Michael. *The Gender of Desire: Essays on Male Sexuality.* Albany: State University of New York Press, 2005.

———. "Masculinity as Homophobia: Fear, Shame, and Silence in the Construction of Gender Identity." In *Theorizing Masculinities*, edited by Harry Brod and Michael Kaufman, 119–41. Thousand Oaks, CA: Sage Publications, 1994.

Koppes, Clayton R., and Gregory D. Black. *Hollywood Goes to War: How Politics, Profits, and Propaganda Shaped World War II Movies.* Berkeley: University of California Press, 1987.

Lang, Brent. "Home on the Range." *Variety* 349, no. 10, September 9, 2020, 36–40.

———. "Idris Elba on *Concrete Cowboy* and the Uplifting Indie's Improbable Ride to the Toronto Film Festival." *Variety*, September 9, 2020.

Latif, Leila. "*The Harder They Fall.*" *Sight and Sound* 31, no. 10 (December 2021).

Lawrence, Novotny, and Gerald Butters. *Beyond Blaxploitation.* Detroit: Wayne State University Press, 2016.

Lenihan, John. *Showdown: Confronting Modern America in the Western Film.* Chicago: University of Illinois Press, 1979.

Levine, Andrea. "Sidney Poitier's Civil Rights: Rewriting the Mystique of White Womanhood in *Guess Who's Coming to Dinner* and *In the Heat of the Night.*" *American Literature* 73, no. 2 (2001): 365–86.

Leyda, Julia. "Black Audience Westerns and the Politics of Cultural Identification." *Cinema Journal* 42, no. 1 (2002): 46–70.

Liandrat-Guigues, Suzanne. *Red River.* London: British Film Institute, 2000.

Lipsitz, George. *The Possessive Investment in Whiteness: How White People Profit from Identity Politics.* Philadelphia: Temple University Press, 1998.

Loy, Phillip R. *Westerns and American Culture, 1930–1955.* Jefferson, NC: McFarland, 2001.

———. *Westerns in a Changing America, 1955–2000.* Jefferson, NC: McFarland, 2004.

Lucas, Tim. "Western Promise." *Sight and Sound* 21, no. 7 (2011).

Lupack, Barbara Tepa. *Richard E. Norman and Race Filmmaking.* Bloomington: Indiana University Press, 2014.

Lynn, Richard. "Pigmentocracy: Racial Hierarchies in the Caribbean and Latin America." *Occidental Quarterly* 8, no. 2 (2008): 25–44.

Manchel, Frank. "Losing and Finding John Ford's *Sergeant Rutledge* (1960)." *Historical Journal of Film, Radio, and Television* 17, no. 2 (1997): 245–59.

Manlove, Clifford. "From *Django* to *Django Unchained*: Love Narratives in the Global South." In *The Western in the Global South*, edited by Mary Ellen Higgins, Rita Keresztesi, and Dayna Oscherwitz, 60–78. London: Routledge, 2015.

Marable, Manning. *How Capitalism Underdeveloped Black America: Problems in Race, Political Economy, and Society.* Boston: South End Press, 1983.

Marill, Alvin H. *The Films of Sidney Poitier*. Secaucus, NJ: Citadel Press, 1978.

Martin, Michael, ed. *The Birth of a Nation: The Cinematic Past in the Present*. Bloomington: Indiana University Press, 2019.

Marubbio, Elise M. *Killing the Indian Maiden: Images of Native American Women in Film*. Lexington: University of Kentucky Press, 2006.

Mask, Mia. *Divas on Screen: Black Women in American Film*. Urbana: University of Illinois Press, 2009.

Massey, Sara R. *Black Cowboys of Texas*. College Station: Texas A & M University Press, 2000.

Maxwell, Anne. *Colonial Photography & Exhibitions*. London: Leicester University Press, 1999.

McBride, Joseph, and Michael Wilmington. "*Sergeant Rutledge*." *Velvet Light Trap: A Critical Journal of Film and Television* 2 (August 1971): 16–18.

McDaniel, Melodie. *Riding through Compton*. Seattle, WA: Minor Matters, 2018.

McGee, Patrick. *From Shane to Kill Bill: Rethinking the Western*. Malden, MA: Blackwell Publishing, 2007.

Meacham, Jon, and Tim McGraw. "Whose Country? The Distinctive American Music." *Time*, August 26, 2019, 50–53.

Metz, Christian. *Film Language: A Semiotics of Cinema*. Cambridge, UK: Oxford University Press, 1974.

Meuel, David. *The Noir Western: Darkness on the Range, 1943–1962*. Jefferson, NC: McFarland, 2015.

Miller, Cynthia J. "Tradition, Parody, and Adaptation: Jed Buell's Unconventional West." In *Hollywood's West: The American Frontier in Film*, edited by Peter C. Rollins and John E. O'Connor. Lexington: University Press of Kentucky, 2009.

Miller, Cynthia J., and A. Bowdoin Van Riper. *International Westerns: Relocating the Frontier*. Lanham, MD: Scarecrow Press, 2014.

———. *Undead in the West: Vampires, Zombies, Mummies, and Ghosts on the Cinematic Frontier*. Lanham, MD: Scarecrow Press, 2012.

Mills, Charles W. *The Racial Contract*. Ithaca, NY: Cornell University Press, 1999.

Milne, Tom. "*Take a Hard Ride*." *Monthly Film Bulletin*, January 1, 1975, 244.

Nama, Adilifu. *Super Black: American Pop Culture and Black Superheroes*. Austin: University of Texas Press, 2011.

Nankivell, John H. *Buffalo Soldier Regiment: History of the Twenty-Fifth United States Infantry, 1869–1926*. Lincoln: University of Nebraska Press, 1927.

Newton, Huey, P. "A Revolutionary Analysis of *Sweet Sweetback's Baadasssss Song*." *Black Panther Inter-Communal News Service*, June 6, 1971, A-L.

Nichols, Bill. *Representing Reality: Issues and Concepts in Documentary*. Bloomington: Indiana University Press, 1992.

Nyong'o, Tavia. "Racial Kitsch and Black Performance." *Yale Journal of Criticism: Interpretation in the Humanities* 15, no. 2 (2002): 371–91.

O'Brien, Daniel. *Black Masculinity on Film: Native Sons and White Lies*. London: Palgrave Macmillan, 2017.

Ongiri, Amy Abugo. "Death Proof: Trauma, Memory, and Black Power–Era Images in Contemporary Visual Culture." *Journal of Contemporary African Art*, no. 29 (Fall 2011): 42–49.

Parish, James Robert, and George H. Hill. *Black Action Films: Plots, Critiques, Casts, and Credits for 235 Theatrical and Made-for-Television Releases.* Jefferson, NC: McFarland, 1989.

Paul, Louis. "Fred Williamson." In *Tales from the Cult Film Trenches: Interviews with 36 Actors from Horror, Science Fiction, and Exploitation Cinema.* Jefferson, NC: McFarland, 2008.

Pearson, Sarina. "Cowboy Contradictions: Western in the Postcolonial Pacific." In *Studies in Australasian Cinema* 7, nos. 2/3 (2013): 153–64.

Pieterse, Jan Nederveen. *White on Black: Image of Africa and Blacks in Western Popular Culture.* New Haven, CT: Yale University Press, 1992.

Poitier, Sidney. *This Life.* New York: Alfred A. Knopf, 1980.

Poussaint, Alvin F. "Blaxploitation Movies: Cheap Thrills That Degrade Blacks." *Psychology Today* 7 (February 1974): 22–32.

Prather, Leon, "The Red Shirt Movement in North Carolina, 1898–1900." *Journal of Negro History* 62, no. 2 (1977): 174–84.

Pritchett, Glenda. "*Breaking Bad* and *Django Unchained*: Strange Bedfellows." In *Breaking Down* Breaking Bad*: Critical Perspectives*, edited by Matt Wanat and Leonard Engel, 139–54. Albuquerque: University of New Mexico Press, 2016.

Quigley, Martin, Jr., ed. *New Screen Techniques.* New York: Quigley Publishing, 1953.

Racho, Susan, Alberto Dominguez, and Nancy De Los Santos-Reza, dirs. *The Bronze Screen: A Hundred Years of the Latino Image in Hollywood.* Documentary. Bronze Screen Productions, Latino Entertainment Media Institute, 2002.

"The Rising Attack on Nixonomics." *Time*, February 2, 1970.

Robertson, Pamela. *Guilty Pleasures: Feminist Camp from Mae West to Madonna.* Durham, NC: Duke University Press, 1996.

Roediger, David. *The Wages of Whiteness: Race and the Making of the American Working Class.* London: Verso, 1991.

Roffman, Peter. *The Hollywood Social Problem Film: Madness, Despair, and Politics from the Depression to the Fifties.* Bloomington: Indiana University Press, 1981.

Rolli, Bryan. "'Black Panther' Proves, Yet Again, That Diversity Sells in Hollywood." *Forbes*, February 19, 2018.

Russo, Vito. *The Celluloid Closet: Homosexuality in the Movies.* New York: Harper and Row, 1981.

Samuel, Jeymes. "There's No Right Version of Wrong History." *Entertainment Weekly*, Issue 1619/1620, November 2021, 112.

Savage, William W. *Commies, Cowboys, and Jungle Queens: Comic Books and America, 1945–1954.* Hanover, NH: Wesleyan University Press, 1990.

Schaefer, Eric. *Bold, Daring, Shocking, True: A History of Exploitation Films, 1919–1959.* Durham, NC: Duke University Press, 1999.

Schlissel, Lillian. *Black Frontiers: A History of African American Heroes in the Old West.* New York: Simon and Schuster, 1995.

Schneider, Tassilo. "Finding a New Heimat in the Wild West: Karl May and the German Western of the 1960s." In *Back in the Saddle: New Essays on the Western*, edited by Edward Buscombe and Roberta Pearson, 141–59. London: British Film Institute, 1998.

Schubert, Frank N. *Voices of the Buffalo Soldier: Records, Reports, and Recollections of Military Life and Service in the West.* Albuquerque: University of New Mexico Press, 2003.

Self, Robert T. *Robert Altman's* McCabe & Mrs. Miller: *Reframing the American West.* Lawrence: University of Kansas, 2007.

Shellum, Brian G. *Black Office in a Buffalo Soldier Regiment: The Military Career of Charles Young.* Lincoln: University of Nebraska Press, 2010.

Shohat, Ella, and Robert Stam. *Unthinking Eurocentrism: Multiculturalism and the Media.* New York: Routledge, 1994.

Simmon, Scott. *The Invention of the Western Film: A Cultural History of the Genre's First Half Century.* Cambridge, UK: Cambridge University Press, 2003.

Sims, Yvonne. *Women of Blaxploitation: How the Black Action Film Heroine Changed American Popular Culture.* Jefferson, NC: McFarland, 2006.

Slotkin, Richard. *The Fatal Environment: The Myth of the Frontier in the Age of Industrialization, 1800–1890.* Norman: University of Oklahoma Press, 1985.

———. *Gunfighter Nation: The Myth of the Frontier in Twentieth-Century America.* Norman: University of Oklahoma Press, 1992.

———. *Regeneration through Violence: The Mythology of the American Frontier, 1600–1860.* Norman: University of Oklahoma Press, 2000.

Sobchack, Vivian. *The Persistence of History: Cinema, Television, and the Modern Event.* New York: Routledge, 1995.

Solanas, Fernando, and Octavio Getino. "Towards a Third Cinema." In *Movies and Methods: An Anthology*, edited by Bill Nichols, 44–64. Berkeley: University of California Press 1976.

Sollee, Kristen. "Brooklyn's Black Cowboys." *Stay Free!* no. 24, 20.

Sontag, Susan. "Notes on Camp." *Partisan Review* 31, no. 4 (1964): 515–30.

Speck, Oliver C. *Quentin Tarantino's* Django Unchained: *The Continuation of Meta-Cinema.* New York: Bloomsbury, 2014.

Stewart, Jacqueline. *Migrating to the Movies: Cinema and Black Urban Modernity.* Berkeley: University of California Press, 2005.

———. "*Representing: Hip Hop and the Production of Black Cinema* by S. Craig Watkins." *Film Quarterly* 54, no. 1 (2000): 57–60.

St. Pierre, Maurice A. "Reaganomics and Its Implications for African-American Family Life." *Journal of Black Studies* 21, no. 3 (1991): 325–40.

Strode, Woody, and Sam Young. *Goal Dust: The Warm and Candid Memoirs of a Pioneer Black Athlete and Actor.* Lanham, MD: Madison Books, 1990.

Studlar, Gaylyn, and Matthew Bernstein, *John Ford Made Westerns: Filming the Legend in the Sound Era.* Bloomington: Indiana University Press, 2001.

Tasker, Yvonne. *Spectacular Bodies: Gender, Genre, and Action Cinema.* New York: Routledge, 1993.

Taylor, Quintard. "African American Men in the American West, 1528–1990." In *In Search of the Racial Frontier: African Americans in the American West, 1528–1990*, 119–202. New York: W. W. Norton, 1998.

Thompson-Hernández, Walter. *The Compton Cowboys: The New Generation of Cowboys in America's Urban Heartland.* New York: Harper Collins, 2020.

Tolson, Arthur L., and Q. R. Hand Jr. "Reaganomics and Black Americans." *Black Scholar* 16, no. 5 (1985): 37–49.

Tulloch, Carol. *The Birth of Cool: Style Narrative of the African Diaspora.* London: Bloomsbury.

"U.S. Black Settlers of Wild West Pic Had to Be Directed by Poitier." *Variety*, March 17, 1971.

Variety Staff. "*Rio Conchos*," Variety, December 31, 1963, 82.

Vera, Hernan, and Andrew Gordon. *Screen Saviors: Hollywood Fictions of Whiteness*. Oxford, UK: Rowman and Littlefield, 2003.

Wagner, Tricia Martineau. *Black Cowboys of the Old West: True, Sensational, and Little-Known Stories from History*. Guilford, CT: Morris Book Publishing, 2011.

———. *African American Women of the Old West*. Guilford, CT: Globe Pequot Press, 2007.

Walker, Janet, ed. *Westerns: Films through History*. New York: Routledge, 2001.

Wallace, Michele. *Black Macho and the Myth of the Superwoman*. New York: Dial Press, 1978.

Wang, Jackie. *Carceral Capitalism*. South Pasadena, CA: Semiotext(e), 2018.

Watkins, S. Craig. *Representing: Hip Hop Culture and the Production of Black Cinema*. Chicago: University of Chicago Press, 1998.

Willard, Tom. *Buffalo Soldiers*. New York: Forge Books, 1997.

Winters, Jason. "Fred Williamson: The Sexy Superman." *Black Stars*, February 1978, 20–24.

Wood, Robin. *Hollywood from Vietnam to Reagan and Beyond*. New York: Columbia University Press, 2003.

———. *Rio Bravo*. London: British Film Institute, 2003.

Wyse, Chris. "Fred Williamson . . . A Special Brand of Man." *Black Stars*, December 1973, 52–61.

Zirin, Dave. *Jim Brown: Last Man Standing*. New York: Blue Rider Press, 2018.

Index

MIA MASK is a professor of film at Vassar College, where she holds the Mary Riepma Ross 1932 endowed chair of film. She has appeared on CNN's *The Movies*, the Smithsonian Channel, the Criterion Channel, and has provided commentary on National Public Radio. Her books include *Poitier Revisited: Reconsidering a Black Icon in the Obama Age* and *Divas on Screen: Black Women in American Film*.

The University of Illinois Press
is a founding member of the
Association of University Presses.

———————————————

Composed in 10.25/13 Chaparral Pro
with Clarendon LT display
by Kirsten Dennison
at the University of Illinois Press
Manufactured by Versa Press

University of Illinois Press
1325 South Oak Street
Champaign, IL 61820-6903
www.press.uillinois.edu